Other People's Houses

Other People's Houses

How Decades of Bailouts, Captive Regulators, and Toxic Bankers Made Home Mortgages a Thrilling Business

JENNIFER TAUB

Yale UNIVERSITY PRESS
NEW HAVEN AND LONDON

Published with assistance from the foundation established in memory
of James Wesley Cooper of the Class of 1865, Yale College.

Yale University Press books may be purchased in quantity for
educational, business, or
promotional use. For information, please e-mail sales.press@yale.edu
(U.S. office) or sales@yaleup.co.uk (U.K. office).

Designed by James J. Johnson.
Set in Miller type by Westchester Publishing Services.
Printed in the United States of America.

Library of Congress Cataloging-in-Publication Data
Taub, Jennifer.
Other people's houses : how decades of bailouts, captive regulators,
and toxic bankers made home mortgages a thrilling business /
Jennifer Taub.
pages cm
Includes bibliographical references and index.
ISBN 978-0-300-16898-3 (cloth : alk. paper) 1. Savings and Loan
Bailout, 1989–1995. 2. Savings and loan association failures—
Economic aspects—United States. 3. Mortgage loans—United
States. 4. Banks and banking—United States—History. 5. Financial
crises—United States—History. I. Title.
HG2151.T38 2014
332.7′20973—dc23 2013044531

A catalogue record for this book is available from the British Library.

This paper meets the requirements of ANSI/NISO Z39.48-1992
(Permanence of Paper).

10 9 8 7 6 5 4 3 2 1

For Michael

The goose that lays golden eggs has been considered a most valuable possession. But even more profitable is the privilege of taking the golden eggs laid by somebody else's goose. The investment bankers and their associates now enjoy that privilege. They control the people through the people's own money.

—Louis D. Brandeis, *Other People's Money and How the Bankers Use It* (1914)

Contents

Other People's Houses

INTRODUCTION

Lost Ground

Katherine Copeland swept out the living quarters of her family's 1,280-acre wheat and cotton farm in Chattanooga, Oklahoma. Believing a foreclosure was imminent, she apparently wanted to get things in order. She gathered refuse from drawers and cabinets, making a pile outside. When this work was completed, Katherine set the pile on fire. Then she climbed onto the burning heap and asphyxiated in the smoke. Her husband, Eugene, found her body there later that day. In the note she left on the dinner table, Katherine blamed herself for the expected loss of the land that her family had farmed since 1910 and that she had hoped to pass on to her children.[1]

Copeland's suicide gained national attention that summer of 1986 because it was not an isolated incident. Her desperate act echoed the suffering of many during the farm crisis. Due to a 1970s agricultural export boom, crop prices and thus farm incomes shot up, so farmers, encouraged by the government and private lenders, borrowed money to expand operations. Farmland prices rose. Lenders loosened underwriting standards, extending loans excessively, with the exuberant forecast that commodity prices and thus income and land values would keep rising. The banks calculated that if borrowers defaulted, the land would be good collateral to seize and sell.[2]

Then came the embargo on grain sales to the Soviet Union. When prices for grain and other commodities fell, farmland values also declined, leaving many borrowers underwater, with debt greater than their property was worth. Around the same time, to tame inflation, the Federal Reserve tightened the money supply and allowed interest rates to skyrocket. Rates peaked above 20 percent, and farmers with variable-rate loans saw their monthly payments spike, making it impossible for many to service their debt. In December 1985, the Farmers Home Administration began sending out notices of foreclosure to one-fifth of all farms in Oklahoma. But with the crash in farmland values, foreclosure was a lose-lose proposition for borrowers and lenders. Without land, farmers had little prospect of earning a living or paying back the loans, and the repossessed land's value did not cover what was owed. The wave of farm failures was followed by a wave of farm bank failures.[3]

The U.S. Congress responded in November 1986 with an amendment to the Bankruptcy Code that empowered courts to help families save their farms. They could emerge from bankruptcy with a fresh start, able to continue both commercial and family life with manageable debt. Among other things, this legislation permitted a farm debtor to reduce the outstanding principal on the farm home mortgage, as well as to get a new term length and possibly a lower interest rate. The new law gave farmers bargaining power to negotiate modifications even without bankruptcy, as their lenders were aware of the relief the court would provide if they failed to bargain. Similarly, for a time, some courts also permitted nonfarm homeowners to use another provision of the Bankruptcy Code to modify underwater mortgages for principal residences. However, in 1993, the United States Supreme Court abolished that practice.[4]

Underwater Once More

Homeowners in America are once again weighed down by mortgage debt. Like many farm families in the 1970s, homeowners were encouraged by lenders to take on more debt as property values rose. New types of mortgages with low teaser rates and low initial monthly payments enabled people to purchase homes beyond their means or borrow excessively against existing residences. Lenders promoted these confusing, often unsuitable mortgage products aggressively, along with subprime and other high-risk loans. Risky loans could be bundled—transformed assembly line–style into securities and resold to investors, earning lenders substantially more income than the safer traditional thirty-year, fixed-rate loans. Investors purchased these toxic mortgage-backed securities because they were higher yielding than other investments deemed to be triple-A quality by credit rating agencies. The value of these mortgage-linked securities depended on borrowers making monthly payments, which in turn depended on ever-increasing home prices. It was higher profitability—not consumer demand—that drove these inferior products and practices into the marketplace, and thus drove the growing real estate bubble.[5]

During the seven-year housing boom that began in 2000, home prices roughly doubled and mortgage debt increased by 80 percent. Then, in 2006, the housing bubble burst; home prices stopped rising and retreated. Mortgage defaults mushroomed. Banks that borrowed heavily to purchase toxic mortgage-linked securities for their portfolios began to collapse as did the firms that insured these instruments. The financial sector was swiftly bailed out after the chaotic Lehman Brothers bankruptcy, for fear that the collapse of other "too big to fail" firms would create cascading losses. Ordinary homeowners have not been as fortunate. Between 2006 and 2013, about five million homes were lost to foreclosure with millions more still in process. In 2013, nearly ten million homes remained underwater—approximately one-fifth of all mortgaged properties. The collective negative equity for U.S. homes still holds back our economic recovery. Thanks to the Fed holding interest rates exceptionally low and expanding the money supply, the stock market rebounded from its postcrisis trough. However, unemployment remains high and home prices low. For the broad middle class that depends on wages for survival and whose wealth is linked mainly to housing, the crisis continues.[6]

Like Katherine Copeland, many Americans internalize shame and blame. Yet this reflex ignores the more-complex machinations and long historical roots that led to the housing bubble, mortgage crisis, multitrillion dollars in direct and backdoor bank bailouts, and the Great Recession. It takes our attention from focusing on those who should be held accountable and from restoring the necessary rules to end the cycle and avoid another larger crisis.[7]

The Roots of the Mortgage Crisis

The same skyrocketing interest rates that crushed farmers in the early 1980s sank many savings and loans (S&Ls). These once-staid institutions historically channeled customer savings accounts into home loans. After interest rates spiked, they lost money paying out double-digit interest to savers while collecting, on average, single digits from the fixed-rate, long-term mortgages in their portfolios. Hundreds of S&Ls were deeply insolvent on a market-value basis. Instead of orchestrating an immediate rescue, the government decided that deregulation could help the troubled firms grow out of their problems. Responding to industry lobbying, beginning around 1980, Congress enacted liberalizing laws and the S&L federal regulator relaxed its rules. This allowed S&Ls to bring in billions of dollars in wholesale funding, which, unlike retail deposits, enabled them to grow very rapidly, but also made them more vulnerable to runs. They were freed to move beyond their home mortgage expertise to make and purchase high-yielding, risky real estate development loans and to invest in new assets, including junk bonds. States further loosened up on the S&Ls they chartered, which, like the federal thrifts, also were protected by federal deposit insurance.[8]

The S&Ls did not grow out of their problems, but instead attracted many high-flying executives who quickly piled on more losses, acted recklessly, or engaged in fraud, putting the deposit insurance fund and taxpayers at greater risk. Some vigilant officials spotted the impending catastrophe and attempted to restore sensible safety and soundness regulations, however, the reformers were greatly outnumbered and subjected to extreme pressure from industry-friendly government insiders. By 1989, hundreds of S&Ls were shut down and hundreds were rescued from failure by the government. The bailout was estimated to eventually cost between $150 billion and $500 billion.[9]

Many compare the S&L debacle to the 2008 crisis. And there are many similarities, including: (1) deregulation and desupervision, (2) "too big to fail" financial institutions, (3) poor real estate loan underwriting standards, (4) excessive leverage and heavy reliance by banks on very short-term wholesale funding, (5) use of misleading accounting practices, (6) widespread fraud, (7) naive or captured regulators sidelining the few bold regulators attempting to protect the public interest, (8) massive government bailouts, and (9) sacrifice of consumer protection to restore bank profitability. However, we should not view the S&L debacle as a mere analogy. Instead, it marked the beginning of what we alternatively call the Subprime Mortgage Crisis, the Great Recession, or the Financial Crisis of 2008. The recent meltdown was just a more severe relapse of the same underlying disease.

To show this continuity, this book traces from the 1980s to the present the middle-class homeowners and bailed out banks from *Nobelman v. American Savings Bank*. This is the 1993 Supreme Court decision that still prevents home mortgage modification through bankruptcy. Through this narrative, it becomes clear that the 2008 crisis was a continuation of the S&L debacle with the same players, some just operating under new names. In both occurrences, the same reckless banks engaging in high-risk practices failed, and the same lax regulators overlooked fraud and abuse. In 2014, these players continue on, now housed inside of new institutions with the same frailties. Many regulators are just as lax, and the top banks that still gamble with taxpayer-backed, federally insured deposits are larger than ever.[10]

A Better Harvest

A week after Katherine Copeland's suicide, about a dozen farmers gathered together to plow more than three hundred acres of the Copeland farm. Eugene, who reflected on the loss of his wife, shared with a reporter the impact that this gesture had: "At first I thought, what's the use? But the way the community is acting, I'm not going to give up now. I'm going to try." The pastor at Katherine's memorial service asked: "Is she not a plea for economic justice in the market-place?" Some measure of fairness did arrive when Congress amended the Bankruptcy Code to help farmers save their homes.

Millions of Americans today also await legal changes to help them reduce principal, save their homes, and gain a fresh start. And they, along with others who have already lost so much, deserve to discover whether the financial crisis has ended or if it is just, once again, temporarily in remission.

Part I

Highfliers

1

The Nobelmans

In late June 1984, Harriet and Leonard Nobelman borrowed $68,250 from a mortgage broker to purchase a one-bedroom condo in Dallas, Texas. The broker swiftly sold the couple's mortgage to an affiliated Texas savings and loan (S&L) association. In July, the original broker bought back their mortgage and then sold it to American Savings and Loan Association of Stockton, California, the largest S&L in the nation.[1]

Within five years, both the California and Texas institutions had failed. The federal government took them over, one in 1988, the other in 1989, and found private investors to purchase the good parts, including valuable customer deposits, bank branches, and home mortgages, at bargain prices. The government—meaning the taxpayers—helped fund these takeovers. The new owners revived the S&Ls, now stripped of their bad assets like poorly performing loans and undesirable real estate, and were able give the institutions a fresh start while making profits for themselves. The buyer of the Texas institution, through an investment partnership, was Lewis Ranieri, one of the inventors of the bank-issued (private label) mortgage-backed security, the very instrument that helped crush the S&Ls and eventually triggered the 2008 financial crisis. The buyer of the California

S&L, a shy billionaire and his group of investors, received billions of dollars in tax breaks and government guarantees for a new entity created to make the purchase, called American Savings Bank. American Savings Bank now owned the Nobelmans' mortgage.[2]

By 1990, Harriet and Leonard, who were then in their mid-fifties, had lost their jobs and were struggling with health issues. They found an attorney and filed for bankruptcy, seeking a legal discharge of some of their debt. They proposed a plan to save their condo. In addition to making up delinquent amounts, they also proposed that the remaining balance on their mortgage, $65,622, be reduced to $23,500—the unit's sunken market value. Unlike the buyers of the Texas and California S&Ls, the Nobelmans did not seek a government bailout. Instead, they wanted to use the well-established bankruptcy system as it was intended, to provide debt relief and a fresh start. Plans like theirs to modify underwater mortgages on principal residences had been approved by bankruptcy judges across the country and sanctioned by one federal circuit court at the time of their filing with three soon to follow.[3]

Yet the Nobelmans' plan was rejected—first by the bankruptcy trustee, then the bankruptcy court, then the federal court for the Northern District of Texas, and then the Federal Circuit Court of Appeals for the Fifth Circuit. Many people would have given up, but Leonard and Harriet had the support of expert lawyers who waived nearly all of their fees. And Leonard saw the bigger picture: "It's not just me," he reflected, "It's everybody in my situation." So, undeterred, the Nobelmans brought the plan to save their condo all the way up to the United States Supreme Court. The Court takes very few cases, but in December 1992 agreed to hear their appeal because there was now a division among the circuit courts on how to interpret federal bankruptcy law. This meant that people living in more than twenty states could confidently use the bankruptcy process to modify mortgages to help save their homes. However, those residing in the states covered by the Fifth Circuit—Texas, Louisiana, and Mississippi—could not. Those who urged the Supreme Court to take the case included financial firms hoping the Fifth Circuit would be affirmed and consumer advocates wishing for a reversal.[4]

And so, on Monday, April 19, 1993, the United States Supreme Court heard arguments on a dispute over a single-family condo unit worth $23,500. Clarence Thomas, then in his second season as an associate justice, was not known to ask questions of the lawyers who appeared before the Court. Though he would write the unanimous decision, he remained silent on this day, too. His chattier colleagues appeared more engaged, but the focus of their attention was limited. Their questions never strayed from the narrow path of statutory interpretation onto the more difficult terrain of social meaning.[5]

In time it would be clear that trillions of dollars were at stake.

The oral argument ran for about an hour. First up was Philip Palmer. Palmer and Rosemary Zyne were legal counsel for the petitioners, Leonard and Harriet Nobelman. Palmer got very technical, very quickly. He never mentioned his clients by name. Instead, he set out to explain why the courts below had incorrectly interpreted the Bankruptcy Code, the federal statute governing bankruptcies (this legal theory is covered in greater depth in chapter 8). In brief, while the law singled out home mortgage lenders for special protection, that protection was limited. Palmer contended that a plan like the Nobelmans' to pay back an amount equal to the value of the collateral—the condo—was permissible. From time to time, the justices interrupted the Nobelmans' lawyer to challenge him on how the proposed plan aligned with the Bankruptcy Code and with prior judicial decisions.[6]

Next to address the justices was Michael Schroeder, counsel for the respondent, American Savings Bank, which objected to the Nobelmans' bankruptcy plan. As the couple's largest creditor, it expected to be paid the full principal balance, interest, and fees. Anyone listening to the oral argument or reading the lower-court decision and later-published Supreme Court opinion would have thought that American Savings Bank was the institution that lent Leonard and Harriet the money to purchase their condo in the first place. But things were not as they seemed. Though American Savings Bank was referred to again and again as the original lender, it was not.[7]

American Savings Bank did not even exist in 1984, when the Nobelmans purchased their condo. The bank's name was similar to

American Savings and Loan Association, the California S&L that bought the Nobelmans' mortgage a month after it was originated. And, American Savings Bank did purchase American Savings and Loan with government assistance. But neither was the original lender. None of the justices inquired as to why American Savings Bank became involved; it was not within the scope of their responsibilities. The job before them was to resolve the issue of statutory interpretation, not to delve into personal and corporate histories. This is unfortunate because such excavation would have revealed a saga that included fraud, government bailouts, and prison time. This backstory was not part of the oral argument. It was not in the written opinions of the lower courts, nor did it appear in the Supreme Court's unanimous decision penned by Justice Thomas.

Also not discussed that day were the personal circumstances that brought the Nobelmans to bankruptcy.

House Hunting

In the summer of 1984, Leonard and Harriet Nobelman were in the market for a condo. They were a hardworking married couple, both employed in the insurance business. Leonard was raised in Brooklyn, New York, the child of a Holocaust survivor. Harriet was from Fort Worth, Texas, where the couple first met when Leonard worked as a mechanic at the Carswell Air Force Base. In the 1970s, when their daughter Marci was young, they possessed a spacious home with a pool. In those flush years, Leonard sold telephone answering machines to corporate customers. But when technology made the devices inexpensive and ubiquitous, there was less need for salesmen, so he shifted to selling insurance. By 1984, the couple had downsized and they were renting an apartment. Harriet wanted to own again, but something modest and low maintenance. She worried about their finances; Leonard didn't. They were far from the stereotype of the big-spending Texas family. Leonard and Harriet planned to live within their means. For their needs and income, a condominium with one bedroom and one and a half baths was ideal.[8]

They located a new development in Far North Dallas. The Parkway Lane Condominium Complex comprised about two dozen, semi-attached brick and wood-sided structures clustered around a small outdoor pool and community clubhouse. Located just off the highway, thus the "parkway" name, it would be an easy commute to Dallas and its surroundings. On June 21, they paid the Miller Condominium Corporation about $71,000 for Unit 507, on the ground floor of Building 5; included in the deal were rights to share the common areas: the pool, the clubhouse, and the grounds and walkways surrounding the buildings. Miller had financed the condo development through a loan from RepublicBank. The couple borrowed $68,250 from Murray Investment Company, a mortgage broker, to pay Miller for the condo. In the promissory note they signed, they agreed to pay back Murray a portion of principal and interest each month for thirty years, until the loan was paid off.[9]

Though it had a traditional thirty-year term, their loan had some unconventional features. The Nobelmans put down far less than the customary 20 percent of the purchase price. Also, the amounts due each month were not fixed and not completely disclosed in the promissory note. They started out with a "teaser" initial interest rate of 7.5 percent and a principal and interest payment of about $477 each month. In 1985, their rate was set to rise to 9.5 percent and they were to pay about $572 a month. In 1986, these numbers would climb to 11.5 percent and $670 per month. Then, the interest rate would be reset up or down every five years by some unspecified amount tied to the lowest of three different benchmark rates. Given these yet-to-be-determined rates, it was never made clear what interest rate they might end up paying. Also confusing was the cap on how much their monthly payment would rise or decline over the life of the loan. The language was contradictory. Ultimately, their monthly payment might be capped at around $700 or $900 per month.[10]

On the same day in June that they signed the loan documents, the couple also signed a deed of trust. This is a form used in Texas and some other states and is equivalent to a mortgage. By signing, the Nobelmans transferred legal title to their condo unit to a group of trustees—who would later include attorney Michael Schroeder, the same attorney who would contest their bankruptcy plan at the Supreme Court. Each of the trustees had the power of sale. This meant that they had, on behalf of the lender, the right to initiate a foreclosure upon the condo and to sell it if the Nobelmans defaulted. The promissory note and deed of trust together made up what we can call, for simplicity, the Nobelmans' mortgage.[11]

A few days after the condo purchase, the mortgage broker, Murray Investment Company, sold the mortgage to an affiliate, Murray Savings Association, owned by the same corporate parent. The following month it was transferred back. Then, at the end of July, a final sale landed the mortgage with a new entity, American Savings and Loan. Though this California S&L was the new owner, the Murray enterprise in Texas (through its Murray Mortgage Company operation) kept the servicing rights. This meant that Murray would collect mortgage payments and send them to American Savings and Loan each month. Leonard and Harriet simply kept paying Murray; the behind-the-scenes transfers were invisible to them.[12]

Once they settled in, the couple grew friendly with their neighbors. Harriet served as president of the board of the Parkway Lane Homeowners' Association and enjoyed spending time by the pool. Soon, Leonard bought a new car, a two-door Honda Prelude. Harriet later purchased a Honda Accord. Things went well for a while, but Leonard, who was severely diabetic, began to lose his eyesight and had to take a leave of absence from work. Meanwhile, the value of Dallas condos began to fall. About 100 of the 180 units in their complex were foreclosed upon and resold for far less than the Nobelmans had paid. Of the original owners, only twenty remained. The reduced prices had some benefits; the couple helped their daughter acquire a foreclosed two-bedroom unit for just $30,000.[13]

Then came another bad turn: Harriet had been employed by an insurance firm for a decade when it went through a merger. A few months after the new enterprise restructured, Harriet lost her job. By November 1989, five years after they moved in, both of them were jobless and they stopped making payments on their mortgage. They contacted Murray Mortgage Company to request a modification.

They knew others in the complex who had worked things out with their lenders. But Murray would not budge.[14]

There was little to sell. The cars combined were worth about $18,000 but were still subject to outstanding auto loans through the Nobelmans' credit union. They estimated that their furniture was worth $800 and clothing $1,000. Their credit union checking and savings accounts combined held less than $100. Marking down the condo to market value, their balance sheet was not healthy. In their court filing, they would later claim assets of less than $44,000 and liabilities—including the condo loan—of around $90,000, for a negative net worth of roughly $46,000. They were insolvent.[15]

Their property was posted for foreclosure. Texas is a nonjudicial foreclosure state, meaning a home can be taken without an appearance before a judge. Instead, given the deed of trust's "power of sale" language, any of the trustees could—after giving notice by mail to the Nobelmans and posting notice on the property—auction off the condo at the county courthouse steps. An auction was scheduled for Tuesday, August 7, 1990. The Nobelmans' only hope was a bankruptcy filing in federal court. Given that they were underwater, selling the condo was not a viable solution. The bankruptcy filing would stop the clock, postpone the foreclosure sale, and give Leonard and Harriet some time to figure out how they might save their home.

In six years, their condo's value had dropped from $71,000 to $23,500, a 67 percent decline. Given that historically, from 1895 to 1995, median home prices nationwide rose roughly with the pace of inflation, this was an extremely striking collapse. In the housing bubble that burst in 2006, according to the S&P/Case-Shiller index, Dallas fell only about 11 percent from a June 2007 peak to a February 2009 trough. A twenty-city composite showed a decline of around 35 percent, and in the most damaged market, Las Vegas, Nevada, home prices fell roughly 62 percent from an August 2006 peak to a March 2012 trough. For condo prices, measured by Case-Shiller in only four cities, Los Angeles was the most devastated; its prices were down 42 percent from a mid-2006 peak.[16]

So this 67 percent price drop seemed historically unmatched. Yet it was not mentioned at the Supreme Court during the oral argument or in the Court's unanimous opinion. Justice Thomas simply noted, in a phrase set off by dashes, that $23,500 was an "uncontroverted valuation," meaning the debtors alone listed the condo at that value in their bankruptcy filing. The bank and the bankruptcy trustee had been given the right to contest the valuation, but they had not. The deadline to contest the valuation and to contest the bankruptcy plan was one and the same. Both the bank and the trustee objected to the plan in plenty of time, but not to the valuation. When asked two decades later, Michael Schroeder, counsel for American Savings Bank, recalled that his client had no reason to dispute or agree to the value on the property.[17]

Why did Dallas condo prices collapse in the late 1980s? It was not due simply to a drop in oil prices that affected the local economy. The answer can be found in the history of the Empire Savings and Loan Association of Mesquite, Texas, the first thrift to be closed down due to fraud during the S&L crisis. Its illegal escapades helped artificially drive up prices in the broader Dallas condo market. Folks in Dallas still remember the man behind the fraud—a real estate developer named Danny Faulkner.[18]

2

The Condo King and His Empire

Before Danny Faulkner earned the nickname "the Condo King," he was a sixth-grade dropout from Kosciusko, Mississippi. He claimed to be the great-nephew of the novelist William Faulkner, though Danny himself said that he could neither read nor write. He followed his family to Arkansas, then to Texas, making a living painting houses. Turning forty in the early 1970s, Faulkner lined up lucrative work with the help of a mentor, including painting the suites at Texas Stadium, the former home of the Dallas Cowboys. He financed his painting business by borrowing from nearby savings and loans (S&Ls).[1]

S&Ls, located throughout the country, and savings banks, concentrated mainly in the Northeast, were the institutions that most middle-class Americans used for banking services at that time. They were commonly referred to as "thrifts," reflecting their origins as associations promoting the virtue of avoiding unnecessary consumption in order to save money for the future. Prior to 1963, the powers of Texas S&Ls were very limited. They took in deposits, mainly through passbook savings accounts and certificates of deposit (CDs), and used that money to make residential mortgage loans. That was basically it; this fulfilled their main purpose, to provide financing for individuals and families to purchase and build homes. Historically, they were not generally permitted to make commercial loans, construction loans, car loans, personal loans, or other investments. But starting in the 1960s, the restrictions on what S&Ls could do with customer deposits were gradually lifted. Without those changes, Faulkner would not have been able to borrow from an S&L. Two decades later, with federal deregulation, many of the important distinctions between thrifts and traditional banks would blur.[2]

To help keep the money flowing to his business from the S&Ls, Faulkner began investing in them. In 1979, he and some business associates gained a controlling ownership interest in Town East Savings Association of Mesquite, Texas. Town East Savings, founded in 1973, was a tiny S&L operating out of a strip mall just off Interstate 30. It had roughly two thousand depositors, whose savings it channeled into about $13 million in mortgage and car loans. After taking control, Faulkner and his group signaled their grandiose agenda by changing its name to Empire Savings and Loan Association of Mesquite.[3]

With one of his first ventures, Faulkner bought thirteen acres on a western peninsula in Lake Ray Hubbard, a large man-made lake located east of Dallas. Branding the location Faulkner Point, he planned a community of 250 attached, one- and two-bedroom lakeside condominiums. After that venture earned $3 million for him and his son, he envisioned a massive project—thousands of condo units, clustered in neighborhoods along a more than five-mile stretch of the I-30 corridor in East Dallas County, between Lake Ray Hubbard and Interstate 635. This project would take hundreds of millions of dollars. Instead of tangling with a lender that might reasonably question the merits of adding to an increasingly saturated condo market, Faulkner found a way to use his own bank. In February 1982, he tapped an experienced banker and industry lobbyist, Spencer H. Blain Jr., to replace the existing president of Empire. Then, in March, Faulkner and an associate quietly lent Blain about $850,000 to buy two-thirds of Empire's stock and thus take control. While having a single person in control was permitted for thrifts with Texas charters, it was not yet permitted for most other thrifts.[4]

The savings of two thousand mainly local depositors was not sufficient to finance Faulkner's giant condo development. At the end of 1981, Empire had just $17 million in assets, $13 million of which was from long-term residential mortgages. It had funded those mortgages using most of its $16 million in deposits. Empire's net worth, the difference between the loans it extended (assets) and its deposits (liabilities), was less than $1 million. In order to help fund hundreds of millions of dollars in loans for Faulkner's condo development scheme, Empire had to bring in more deposits—and fast. Institutions with multiple branches could gather deposits from several locations and funnel them into loans, but Empire did not have an extensive branch network. And it would take time and money to build branches. So Blain took a shortcut; he set out to attract money through brokers.[5]

Hot Money

Brokered deposits were a fast but fragile source of funding. An S&L like Empire could pay a broker—say, Merrill Lynch—to rapidly gather money in increments of $100,000 from cash-rich investors like pension funds, credit unions, commercial banks, and other institutional investors. Even individuals were good sources by pooling their savings together with the help of a deposit broker. The broker would often place many millions of dollars at one time at an S&L. These were not sticky deposits, however. Upon maturing, they could be quickly pulled out if the broker could get a higher return elsewhere.[6]

Brokered deposits were not a new phenomenon or one without risk. Problems had arisen as early as the 1950s, when it came to the attention of the central regulator for the thrift industry, the Federal Home Loan Bank Board, that there seemed to be a relationship between this hot money and unwise loans. The Bank Board had been established during President Herbert Hoover's administration in

1932, under the Federal Home Loan Bank Act to help provide liquidity to struggling thrifts during the Great Depression. This law created an entire system, with the Bank Board overseeing twelve Home Loan Banks, each of the twelve owned by the thrifts in its region of the country. The twelve district Home Loan Banks would raise money by issuing bonds to the public. This money was then used to extend loans to thrifts at below the market rate. The borrowing thrifts would pledge the mortgages in their portfolios as collateral for the loans.[7]

In 1934, Congress authorized the Bank Board to offer federal charters for thrifts. Previously, thrifts could be chartered only by the states in which they were located. The Bank Board was given the authority to regulate and supervise these federal thrifts it chartered. In addition, the Bank Board became the administrator of a deposit insurance fund for thrifts operated by the newly created Federal Savings and Loan Insurance Corporation (FSLIC). This was a government—not a private—corporation. The FSLIC insurance fund for thrifts was similar to the Federal Deposit Insurance Corporation (FDIC) fund for banks. State thrifts that decided to pay into the FSLIC insurance fund were subject to some oversight from the Bank Board, though with respect to asset powers—what they could use depositors' funds for—they followed the regulations of their home state, which were sometimes looser.[8]

In 1959, the Bank Board ruled that for thrifts that had FSLIC insurance, brokered deposits could not exceed 5 percent of total deposits. If the insurance fund were to run dry, it would be the federal government and ultimately the taxpayer who would pay. Given the fragility of brokered deposits as a source of funding, there was an attempt by Congress to forbid their use entirely. But in 1981, the Bank Board went the other way and completely removed the 5 percent cap. By 1985, testifying before a Senate subcommittee, FDIC chairman William Isaac would call brokered deposits "a clear and present threat" to the deposit insurance system.[9]

In exchange for providing cash, these big depositors received short-term certificates of deposit. When these short-term CDs matured on schedule, in a year or less, the depositor was entitled to receive back the original deposit, which, for a "jumbo" CD, was $100,000 plus interest. Empire paid the CD holders high interest, often two full percentage points above the competition. It also had to pay fees to the brokers. There was a way to make this profitable: in order to ensure a positive spread between income from loans and payouts on brokered deposits, Empire had to charge interest to its borrowers that was significantly higher than the competition charged. Yet the types of borrowers willing to pay higher-than-market rates to get a loan from Empire might have been refused by other institutions, for sensible reasons.[10]

Spencer Blain aggressively executed this strategy. When he started, brokered funds were just $1.2 million of Empire's $16 million in deposits. By the end of 1982, it had $48.4 million in brokered deposits; by mid-1983, $139 million; and by year-end 1983, this small community thrift had an astonishing $291 million in brokered deposits. Empire's assets, the vast majority of which were mortgage loans, grew correspondingly: from $17 million at the end of 1981 to $332 million just two years later.[11]

Moral Hazard

Institutions and individuals were willing to deposit $100,000 per CD in a rapidly growing, state-chartered S&L operating out of a small strip mall because of federal deposit insurance. Though chartered under Texas law, Empire had access to deposit insurance through the FSLIC administered by the Bank Board. Perversely, the most poorly managed thrifts were able to attract more deposits than the well-managed ones because they were willing to pay the highest rates to bring in money to fund their lending activities.[12]

Given the availability of insured deposits, it was in the interest of the owner of an S&L to take on as much debt or to leverage as much as the regulators would allow. With a minimum net worth requirement of 3 percent, an initial investment by owners of $3 million could be used as a basis to borrow $97 million (from depositors) and obtain $100 million in assets (through making or buying loans). With just $3 million of equity invested, owners could double their money if the S&L's assets went up in value by just 3 percent and were sold. Or, easier than that, by charging 3 points (that is, 3 percent of the principal loaned) in fees to borrowers, the S&L could bring in $3 million in fees. The owners could double their investment simply by taking these gains out of the S&L as dividends.[13]

While owners could profit by growing as fast as possible—often by making risky loans and charging high fees—this put the FSLIC fund at great risk. Money borrowed relative to assets owned is called leverage. High leverage can provide a windfall when asset prices increase, but it also magnifies losses when they decline. With a leverage ratio of 3 percent ($3 million of their own money to buy $100 million in assets), if their assets declined by more than 3 percent or a very large loan or two defaulted, then the investors' capital cushion would be wiped out. But such a loss on a loan was only shown if the borrower stopped making payments or if the loan was sold at a loss. Even if an S&L was insolvent on a market basis, on a book value (historical cost) basis, which was the permitted accounting method, a weak thrift could look strong. In this way, if the owners were able to extract big fees up front and arrange for interest payments to be paid by the borrower out of the proceeds of the loans they extended, short-term profits were assured, as were inevitable—though temporarily hidden—losses.[14]

Deregulation in Texas

Given this inherent moral hazard, the safety net of taxpayer-backed FSLIC insurance was supposed to be matched with strict regulatory supervision. And Empire had many regulators. It was examined and supervised on the state level by the Texas State Savings and Loan Department. And because it paid into the FSLIC insurance fund, it was subject to examination and supervision by the Bank Board and the district Federal Home Loan Bank. In the fall of 1983, just as Empire was growing rapidly, its federal regulator, the Home Loan Bank, moved from Little Rock, Arkansas, to the Dallas area. Only eleven of the forty-eight members of the Little Rock supervisory staff moved to the new office. In the year prior to the move, the district Home Loan Bank had examined 177 Texas S&Ls; in the year following the move, that number dropped to 100. Even with this federal oversight framework, the basic rules that governed the loans and other investments that Empire Savings and Loan could make were subject to the much less strict Texas rules.[15]

Texas had loosened up on its thrifts beginning in the 1960s. The changes that began there would later influence deregulation at the federal level of the thrift industry. Under the Texas Constitution as amended in 1904, the legislature was required to create a system of "state supervision, regulation and control" of S&Ls in order to "protect and secure" depositors and creditors. Not until 1961 did the legislature create a unique regulator with authority over the state's S&Ls, then numbering 161 with assets totaling $1.8 billion. Then, in 1963, the Texas Savings and Loan Act created a new legal regime under which the Texas Savings and Loan Department was given broad authority to expand the asset powers of the S&Ls. As a result, Texas S&Ls were the first to offer commercial loans and personal loans and to make direct investments in real estate. At first, the consumer loans were limited to a small percentage of an S&L's assets, but after 1972, Texas-chartered S&Ls had no limit. Texas also led the way with other investments; state-chartered S&Ls were allowed to use deposits to invest in corporate debt securities, including short-term commercial paper and long-term bonds. Given this freedom, the system attracted new charters, and new charters meant more fees for the state regulator, the Texas Savings and Loan Department. By 1979, there were 255 state-chartered S&Ls with $23.8 billion in assets.[16]

Whereas before the 1960s, Texas S&Ls had mainly been restricted to home mortgage loans, they were now permitted to make loans to real estate developers for acquisition, development, and construction, or "ADC" loans. At first, in 1967, these loans were capped at no more than half of an S&L's net worth. In 1983, Texas removed this limit, allowing 100 percent of deposits to be invested in nearly any venture. This was just in time for Blain and Faulkner. Even with riskier assets, the Texas thrifts paid the same amount to the FSLIC for their deposit insurance as did more restricted federally chartered thrifts and thrifts in other states with greater restrictions. In other words, they paid the same assessment rate that cautious, restricted S&Ls did for the safety net, but with their new freedoms, they were more likely to use it.[17]

In March 1980, with the Depository Institutions Deregulation and Monetary Control Act (DIDMCA), Congress had raised the full-coverage limit from $40,000 to $100,000 per FSLIC-insured account. Aware of this protection, depositors were not overly worried about the risks Blain and Faulkner would be running with their savings. Of course, if things took a turn, big depositors might flee as soon as their CDs matured just to avoid any possible payment delays during a government receivership. Meanwhile, however, the CD holders had no plans to police Empire, and the insiders had every incentive to be reckless with the depositors' funds. With insurance plus minimal government supervision, motive found opportunity.[18]

Land Flips

Shortly after he took control of Empire Savings and Loan in August 1982, Spencer Blain entered into a personal agreement to purchase a piece of property known as Chalet Ridge from a seller for about $1 million. Six months later, a friend of Danny Faulkner's paid Blain $16 million for the parcel. Where did this friend get the $16 million that he paid to Blain? He got it from Empire. In a truly arms-length transaction, Chalet Ridge would not have fetched $16 million; it would be hard to find an informed, honest buyer to pay that much for it again. Accordingly, it was unlikely that the friend would repay unless he received a new loan based on a false appraisal. This land flip had the potential to net Blain more than $14 million. Empire, owned by Blain, stood to lose the same amount if this fellow defaulted.[19]

Dozens of land flips followed. For example, in November 1982, Empire and a small network of friendly thrifts provided about $50 million in financing for a project involving sixty land parcels. Fifteen days earlier, most of that land had been purchased for about $5 million. This was an unwise risk to take with depositors' money, but this would not have disturbed the thrift because the federal insurance fund would mop up that loss if Empire ever folded. Meanwhile, Blain and Faulkner lived lavishly. Blain, who drew a $30,000 annual salary, earned more than $21 million in personal investments during his short tenure at Empire. Faulkner bought luxury cars, helicopters, and Learjets. He gave away expensive gifts like Rolex watches and F-shaped (for "Faulkner"), diamond-encrusted pins. Some participants in these land-flip deals glibly recalled that their economic purpose was to help Faulkner make enough money to buy a new Learjet. The one he had was outdated.[20]

The Condo Connection

There was a connection between Empire and the dramatic drop in condo prices. Danny Faulkner's I-30 condo project became a land-flip-based investment scam that, in the end, involved about $500 million in suspicious loans. Though Spencer Blain was nominally in charge, as a practical matter, lending at Empire was controlled by Faulkner and his associate James Toler, a former mayor of the nearby town of Garland. As recounted by journalists including Allen Pusey, Christi Harlan, and James O'Shea and documented in court decisions, Faulkner and Toler together masterminded a scheme. It can best be described in two phases.[21]

Phase 1 involved the land flip. Faulkner and friends would get together—sometimes at a place of business, other times for breakfast at the Wise Circle Grill—to pump up the price of land parcels. Wherever they gathered, their presence was signaled by the collection of Mercedes and Rolls Royce automobiles in the parking lot. On one typical occasion, a row of tables stretched down a long hallway in a Dallas office building. Investors stood in front of each table, across from Empire loan officers. At the first table on one end, the first investor would borrow money from Empire (and other friendly thrifts) to purchase a parcel of undeveloped land, typically buying it from Faulkner and Toler. When that deal closed, the loan officer would pass the paper down to the second table. The second investor would buy the same piece of land from the first for a higher price. The first investor would use the proceeds of that sale to pay off his loan and pocket the difference. The property was then sold down the row until it landed at the sixth investor, who would now pay millions more, using a loan from Empire to finance the sale. Everyone in the chain earned money on the deal, until it came to the sixth investor. This paper-passing game resulted in millions of dollars of real cash landing in the hands of the investors. It was easy to find investors for Phase 1.[22]

In the next phase, that last investor needed to unload the parcel of land, which was now pumped up twenty to thirty times its real value. Empire had an interest in getting it sold as well, since this would pay off that last big loan. The raw land would be carved into smaller parcels for a condo development scheme. Faulkner would offer people with no real estate experience a one-stop-shopping condo project. They would borrow the money to make this purchase from Empire or one of about four associated thrifts in Texas and Arkansas. For each project, these rookie would-be developers received a parcel of land; an appraisal; blueprints for a two- or three-story, multi-unit building; a construction contractor; and even marketing and sales services to help them find buyers for the condo units.[23]

Empire and its associated S&Ls did not work alone. There were appraisers on the take as well. Mortgage brokers like Paul Jensen coordinated with Empire and Faulkner and underwrote many I-30 development loans. Jensen purchased two Texas S&Ls and then used them to finance more than $100 million in loans for Faulkner and Toler's condo project. Jensen reportedly received millions of dollars in commissions and other payments. Also helping out was a man whose history of deception included a 1978 indictment in Alabama for multiple counts of fraud associated with a loan scam. This seasoned con artist would round up potential investors and help them falsify their financial statements in order to qualify for development loans.[24]

People with no real estate development or sales experience were drawn into the scheme. To make this particularly enticing—and dangerous—they put down no money of their own when they "paid" for the package. Their loans covered the entire purchase price and then some. Indeed, they were often given loans amounting to more than 100 percent of the purchase price. Some of that extra money would be set aside to make initial interest payments so that the loan would not immediately go into default and weigh on Empire's and the other thrifts' financial statements. Another piece of the excess loan was simply given to the borrower. This meant that after signing all the closing papers to finance the purchase of the turnkey condo project, the investor, instead of paying even a dime, would instead walk away with a cash "bonus" of tens of thousands of dollars.[25]

It took a lot of optimism to see how this might work out for Empire. Blain envisioned that after the condos were sold to homeowners, those homeowners would use long-term mortgages from Empire to pay off the investor-developer loans that Empire had made earlier. Empire would then sell those new residential mortgage loans to the privately owned but government-sponsored Federal National Mortgage Association (Fannie Mae). Blain hoped that the proceeds from sales of those residential loans to Fannie Mae could then be used to pay off jumbo CDs that would be coming due from all those brokered deposits. He apparently thought the whole cycle would be complete in a few years.[26]

Many of these investor-developers were pure borrowers. They invested none of their own equity and had no skin in the game. One individual participated in numerous I-30 deals, winding up with $12 million in debt and no reasonable hope of completing and selling condos. This was a problem, and not just for the borrowers, one hundred of whom would eventually be convicted for crimes related to falsifying loan documents. It was also a problem for Empire. According to experts, when Empire got involved in the condo-financing projects, the only way to pay off the jumbo CDs as they matured would have been to get the real estate development loans paid off by providing loans to buyers of at least two hundred condo units each month and turn around and sell those residential mortgages to Fannie Mae. Yet the developers were selling only four units a month. Moreover, the market could only absorb about seventy-five new units per month. The clock was ticking, waiting for the inevitable liquidity crisis when the jumbo CD holders would demand their money back.

Meanwhile, the development loans could not be sold for cash without huge losses.[27]

Where Were the Regulators?

Reviewing Empire's books in October 1982, examiners from the federal regulator of thrifts, the Federal Home Loan Bank Board, spotted Blain's initial self-dealing land flip involving a questionable appraisal and a suspicious $14 million profit facilitated by Empire. The examination also revealed unsound lending practices, excessive use of brokered deposits, and other problems. In January 1983, the examiners sent a copy of the report to the supervisors at the district Home Loan Bank in Little Rock, Arkansas. Still, these red flags did not even get the Little Rock supervisors out from behind their desks to pay a visit. Instead, they communicated their concerns to Blain in a written report sent in the mail. This was six months after that first land flip. At the end of 1982, just before the report was issued by the examiners, Empire had grown its brokered deposits to just $48 million. If regulators had moved in then, the later losses to the FSLIC deposit fund would have been minimized. Instead, Blain, Faulkner, and Toler were allowed to grow their Ponzi scheme to $305 million in insured deposits (of which about $290 million were brokered) funding more than $350 million in risky mortgages.[28]

Apparently, Blain was too busy to respond to the regulatory letter. In fact, he apparently ignored three of them until, finally, in the spring of 1983, he replied with a vague promise to improve. The Texas Savings and Loan Department, the state institution that regulated Texas-chartered thrifts, began its own examination of Empire in early 1983. Nevertheless, neither the district Home Loan Bank (then in the process of moving from Arkansas to Dallas) nor the Texas Department rushed to confront Blain or ask him to return the money. Perhaps this was because Blain was well connected. He was said to have promised his friend, the commissioner of the Texas Savings and Loan Department, that he would stop engaging in risky practices. As for federal ties, before Blain became president of Empire, he had been vice chairman of the district Home Loan Bank.

The regulators justified their inaction by pointing to Empire's healthy financial statements. Not surprisingly, independent audits would later show that those healthy financial reports were false.[29]

There were structural and historical explanations for inaction. The Federal Home Loan Bank Board was located in Washington and staffed by federal employees who were responsible for examining the thrifts. The twelve district Home Loan Banks, meanwhile, were owned by the S&Ls in their region. These owners included all of the federally chartered S&Ls and those state thrifts that chose to be members of the system or to have FSLIC coverage. The employees of the Home Loan Banks were not subject to federal restrictions on salaries. In a clear conflict of interest, they were supposed to supervise the very thrifts that owned their employer. Additionally, local supervisors received higher salaries than the federal-employee examiners and had easier jobs with less travel. The local supervisors had the power to issue directives and recommend actions, whereas the Bank Board examiners did not. Strong examiners who worked for the Bank Board could quit and move to a Home Loan Bank for significantly higher pay and more authority.[30]

Some of the forbearance was a historical practice. For a time, there was a culture of voluntary compliance. Instead of using the extreme powers they had over state-chartered thrifts, including terminating their FSLIC deposit insurance, the Home Loan Banks tried to achieve compliance informally.[31]

Given that either government takeover or ending insurance protection was an extreme measure that might lead to a run, regulators had reason to hesitate. Fortunately, Congress found a middle ground in 1966, giving the Bank Board authority to do something short of closing an insured thrift in the event of bad conduct. The Financial Institutions Supervisory Act of 1966 authorized the regulator to issue removal, cease-and-desist, and suspension orders. Regulators had asked for these powers so that, in the rare case of poor management and unsound thrifts, they could "move quickly and effectively to require adherence to the law and cessation and correction of unsafe or improper practices." Unfortunately, they did not move quickly with Empire.[32]

Throughout 1983, there were additional federal and state audits and examinations of Empire. These revealed that loan values were overstated and loan records were out of date; the auditors recommended immediate supervisory action. Investigations were also under way at the Texas State Securities Board, the Federal Bureau of Investigation, and the Internal Revenue Service. Eventually, in December 1983, the supervisors at the district Home Loan Bank in Dallas made criminal referrals to the U.S. district attorney. At that point, Empire was banned from taking in more brokered deposits. Then, in January 1984, Empire was prohibited from making any more loans and was placed under supervisory control of the Texas Savings and Loan Department.[33]

Yet Empire kept operating. The Texas Savings and Loan Department allowed Blain to keep his role as chairman until month's end and did not shut Empire down. They hoped to find a way to rescue the troubled thrift through a merger with a stronger institution. At the time, of the more than 2,000 condo units that Blain, Faulkner, and friends had financed or built, only 779 were occupied. In early 1984, Empire nearly ran out of money when it did not have the funds to pay off maturing CDs, but Faulkner personally pitched in $32 million. On the other side of the balance sheet, the bank was not able to sell many of its loans, given the high risk of default. So when borrowers defaulted, the loans had to be written down.[34]

Federal regulators did not act decisively until March 1984, when Empire was brought to the attention of Bank Board chairman Ed Gray. A former speechwriter and a Reagan loyalist who had no background in economics, law, or accounting, Gray had been appointed to the post in 1983. Despite his lack of qualifications, his nomination was supported by industry lobbyists including the Texas League, which was the trade association for S&Ls in Texas. Indeed, Gray found out that Reagan planned to nominate him for the post—not from the White House—but instead from the U.S. Savings and Loan League, which was then the national thrift lobbying organization. After hearing about problems with Empire Savings and Loan, Gray hired an appraiser to evaluate the I-30 corridor projects. On March 14, he was shown video footage filmed by that appraiser. Shot in part from a small plane, the video revealed thousands of condo units in various stages of completion. Many were just slabs of concrete foundation, referred to as "Martian landing pads." Others were partially constructed and exposed to the elements. Those that were completed were not occupied. Gray found the film physically revolting, describing it as "fiduciary pornography." He called the project "one of the most reckless and fraudulent land investment schemes this agency has ever seen." Empire was immediately shut down. Depositors were paid $273 million out of the FSLIC insurance fund—at the time, the largest payout to depositors in the fund's fifty-year history. Between 1934 and 1981, the FSLIC had lost only $630 million. By the end of 1984, the fund had only $5.6 billion to insure deposits at more than three thousand thrifts, yet the Bank Board estimated that about 434 were insolvent.[35]

While some thrifts had tapped the fund in the past, Empire was the first to be closed down for fraud. This was so remarkable at the time that Congress held hearings to uncover what went wrong. This was not just a turning point for Empire; it was a turning point for Bank Board Chairman Gray, who was determined to reregulate the thrifts. But he met tremendous resistance.[36]

Many people were prosecuted, including Faulkner, Toler, Blain, and Jensen. By 1985, more than forty-eight corporations and ninety individuals associated with Empire were tried. Empire and other thrifts involved lost more than $300 million in the I-30 condo scheme. Faulkner was convicted on forty-two counts, including racketeering, wire fraud, conspiracy, false appraisals, and accepting kickbacks. During one of his two trials, he was spotted leaning over the prosecutor's desk, reviewing his notes. When an observer said, "I thought you couldn't read," he walked away. In 1991, Faulkner was sentenced to twenty years in federal prison. During his appeal in 1993, he filed for bankruptcy. He began serving his prison sentence in January 1995 but was released in less than three years due to inoperable brain cancer. Blain, convicted on thirty-four different counts, served less than five years of his twenty-year sentence. Like Faulkner, he was released early due to brain cancer. In the end, the I-30 condo scheme cost taxpayers more than $1 billion.[37]

The Federal Home Loan Bank Board's enforcement chief during the 1980s, Rosemary Stewart, recalled that "Empire was the first big failure. It was the first real indication that things were so much worse than we knew." For Texas, the numbers are telling. At the pre-crisis peak in 1986, the 235 Texas-chartered thrifts had a total of $84 billion in assets; in 1992, the 31 remaining had just $8.3 billion. Debate ensued as to whether this was merely the case of bad management or a symptom of deregulation. Of course, this was a false dichotomy. Like common thieves, bad bank managers were attracted to areas where there were looser laws and little enforcement.[38]

Closer to Home

Faulkner and his team's condo developments were east of Dallas, and the Nobelmans' condo was located to the north, in contiguous Collin County. By the time they bought their one-bedroom unit in June 1984, many I-30 condos had been abandoned in various stages of development. Yet the market was slow to bring down condo prices when Leonard and Harriet made their purchase. It took a while for the excess capacity to be felt and acknowledged. The Parkway Lane complex was already finished, whereas the abandoned I-30 condos were not. It was not widely apparent that the entire Dallas real estate market had been overbuilt until late 1985.

The glut of condos, which would shortly be unmistakable, was part of a larger real estate financing binge. In mid-1984, owner-occupied condos in new developments were still attracting buyers. The turning point may have come that September. Six months after Bank Board chairman Gray watched the I-30 film and three months after the Nobelmans bought their condo, the Dallas County Appraisal District lowered the appraised values on 2,622 condominiums by an average of more than $30,000—a total drop in value of $90 million. The justification was that they were reclassified as apartments.[39]

By 1987, the state was in a real estate depression. As one developer put it, the music had stopped. The Texas S&Ls that were still alive had to bring real estate onto their books when they foreclosed on defaulting borrowers. When Empire failed, the foreclosed condo units that it owned fell into the hands of the U.S. government through the FSLIC, the government agency that provided deposit insurance to thrifts. The FSLIC contracted with a local firm to find renters. Real estate analysts estimated that there was a twelve-year glut of condos along the I-30 corridor in the Mesquite, Garland, and Rowlett areas. Prices did not improve. In March 1988, the FSLIC negotiated a deal to sell an equity interest in 1,941 of the I-30 condos.[40]

By 1989, a year before the Nobelmans' bankruptcy, the I-30 corridor was lined with thousands of condominiums along a spectrum of inhabitation and disrepair. Even after hundreds of units were torn down, prices did not rebound. Two-bedroom units that had sold for $50,000 to $60,000 were on the market for $20,000 to $30,000. These were located as little as twenty miles from the Parkway Complex and were also commuter locations into the Dallas business district. Leonard and Harriet, victims of fraud fueled by deregulation, had taken out their mortgage at exactly the wrong time.[41]

While the couple was indirectly affected by Empire, they had a direct connection to another institution, American Savings and Loan, the largest thrift in the country and the leading example of a century-old industry that had risen to become the biggest source of funding for home mortgages. On the very day in July 1984 that American Savings and Loan purchased the Nobelmans' mortgage, it faced a major turning point.

3

The Run on American Savings and Loan

"I need you in Stockton." This was not exactly what Bart Dzivi expected to hear from his new boss. In fact, he did not expect to hear anything from the office that day. It was the last Friday in July 1984, the morning after the grueling three-day California bar exam. Dzivi and 7,351 other prospective attorneys had endured eighteen hours of complex multiple-choice questions and essays. Fewer than half would earn passing scores. It was customary to get a little time to unwind, but instead, his boss at the Federal Home Loan Bank in San Francisco telephoned and instructed him to report to work—immediately—in Stockton, a farm town eighty miles east of San Francisco. After a little negotiating, Bart got the weekend off and agreed to report on Monday.[1]

There was a massive run on American Savings and Loan of Stockton. A subsidiary of Financial Corporation of America, American Savings and Loan was then the largest savings and loan (S&L) in the country, with $34 billion in assets. It was on the verge of collapse. Depositors, mostly institutional investors including those holding large CDs, were pulling out their money fast. About $600 million would vanish in July alone. By fall, the run would grow to $6.8 billion. The S&L simply did not have enough assets it could sell quickly to meet the depositors' withdrawals. Even though it was a California-chartered thrift, American Savings and Loan was entitled to borrow from the federal system. Moreover, should it become insolvent—if its net worth eroded—the Federal Savings and Loan Insurance Corporation (FSLIC) would be obligated to pay off the insured depositors. This was a daunting prospect since American Savings and Loan had more than $25 billion in deposits and the FSLIC fund had started the year with about $6 billion in reserves.[2]

But American Savings and Loan was not yet at that point. Though its net worth was shy of the minimum 3 percent and the thrift was required to come up with equity capital soon, ideally by issuing new stock, it was still apparently solvent according to accepted accounting standards. For now it just needed a loan to meet withdrawals. Understandably, its local federal regulator, the Federal Home Loan Bank of San Francisco, wanted to be sure that the assets on American Savings and Loan's books were sufficient collateral in case the S&L could not pay back the loan.

On Monday morning, along with paralegals from a top-tier California law firm, Bart Dzivi found himself counting collateral in the basement of American Savings and Loan's office in Stockton. This entailed going through file after file and identifying documentation of the assets—including mortgage loans—that the S&L could pledge to the Home Loan Bank in exchange for cash. The Home Loan Bank took physical possession of the mortgage notes that it selected as collateral. For emergencies like this, staff would check in at local hotels under assumed names to avoid attracting the kind of attention that might lead to more depositors withdrawing money. This stealth work was a sign of things to come for the young attorney. Rummaging through basement files in search of mortgage documentation might seem uneventful. One might expect that the greatest safety risk would be a paper cut.[3]

Two years later, in 1986, Dzivi would work on an investigation of another California institution, the Consolidated Savings Bank of Irvine. On the Friday of Memorial Day weekend, he flew down to

Orange County to orchestrate the takeover of the insolvent thrift. Because bank examiners had received physical threats in the weeks leading up to his arrival, Dzivi and his team brought armed security guards with them. After officials at Consolidated refused access to their offices, the FSLIC obtained a court order allowing the regulators to take custody of the building. Dzivi, who had been designated as a special representative of the FSLIC, brought loan documents back to his hotel to review one night. A couple of hours after ordering room service, he became violently ill and wound up in a hospital emergency room. The doctors determined that he had been poisoned, but they could not identify the substance. Later, after returning to his hotel from the hospital, he had fallen asleep when someone broke in through the door of an adjoining room in the middle of the night. Dzivi awoke and startled the intruder, who then fled. He surmised that someone associated with Consolidated had made him sick to get him to leave his hotel room "so they could grab the documents. They were concerned about potential criminal exposure, and wanted to destroy the evidence of their wrong doing." A decade later, the CEO of Consolidated would be tracked down in Hong Kong after years of dodging both a prison sentence for falsifying loan records and a separate fraud and money laundering indictment.[4]

Fortunately, the only danger involving American Savings and Loan in late July 1984 was the threat of the institution's demise, which was imminent without both liquidity and a capital infusion. The other present danger was that the FSLIC fund would be bled dry if this tottering thrift were to fall. Should it be necessary for liquidity, the S&L could turn to the Federal Reserve for a loan. However, if its net worth dwindled low enough, it would have to be shuttered or sold—both of which would require the government, really the taxpayers, to take substantial losses.[5]

Years in the Making

It is easy to blame CEO Charlie Knapp, the man at the helm of American Savings and Loan, for the massive run and its impending demise. Knapp had been in place for just one year—during which

American Savings and Loan had ballooned in size and been transformed from a staid, conservative S&L to a casino. However, this specific run and the ultimate collapse and bailout of the S&L industry was years in the making. When Knapp took over in 1983, the conditions were all in place for someone like him to blow up the thrift. These conditions were brought about by radical deregulation and desupervision. Charlie Knapp was more of an opportunist than a catalyst.[6]

The trouble at American Savings and Loan surfaced, coincidentally, during the summer of 1984, when the Nobelmans were shopping for their condo in Far North Dallas. Not a coincidence, however, was that this distress overlapped with the rise and collapse of Empire Savings Association of Mesquite, Texas. At that moment, a confluence of circumstances was attracting people like Danny Faulkner and Charlie Knapp to the once-bland industry. Until a decade or so earlier, S&Ls had been a controlled ecosystem. Then things changed.

When It Was a Wonderful Life for Thrifts

Until the 1960s, S&Ls—initially known as building and loans (B&Ls)—existed alongside other types of financial firms, including commercial banks, investment banks, and insurance companies, each with a niche, protected in part by New Deal–era regulation. S&Ls operated on a simple business model, home mortgage lending, making money on the spread—the difference between interest collected from borrowers for long-term loans and the interest paid to savers at lower, short-term rates. This spread was a sure thing as long as overhead was low, borrowers kept up their payments, savers stuck with the thrift, and interest rates remained steady.

An early and continuous thrift rival was the commercial bank. The competitive relationship between commercial banks and the S&L precursor, the B&L, is represented in Frank Capra's cinema classic *It's a Wonderful Life*, in the strained codependency between the heartless Henry Potter and earnest George Bailey. B&Ls focused on providing home mortgage loans to members, funded with members' deposited dues and with loans from commercial banks. These B&Ls operated free from federal regulation, though they were usually subject to state codes aimed at protecting depositors. It was a fairly simple business model. To survive, a B&L had to keep collecting monthly installments from savers while avoiding borrower defaults, a run by depositors, and threats from commercial banks.[7]

In *It's a Wonderful Life*, the Bailey Brothers Building and Loan borrows from Potter's commercial bank and also deposits members' dues there. They compete, however, for customers. Potter would benefit if Bailey went out of business; his bank would be able to charge higher interest on loans and pay less to attract deposits. Tactics to weaken the thrift serve as important plot points. As a shareholder and board member of the Bailey B&L, Potter urges foreclosures on delinquent borrowers and attempts to persuade the board to cease operations. He tries to take advantage of a run on the B&L and also attempts to get it shut down by the bank examiner.

Audiences watching the film in 1946 were quite familiar with B&Ls, which had been around for more than a century. These associations sprang up in response to a demand for housing following a migration of workers from rural areas to cities. One of the first was the Oxford Provident Building Association, founded in 1831 in Frankford, Philadelphia. Members of Oxford initially paid $5 to purchase a share and then a $3 fee each month. This entitled them to borrow from the association to buy homes. Initially, such savings associations were self-liquidating, dissolving after all members had borrowed and repaid their loans, but they soon evolved into more complex enterprises with perpetual existences. They promoted the idea that the centerpiece of the American Dream was the home.[8]

Commercial banks were allies and rivals of the B&Ls. Commercial banks funded their own operations by taking savings and checking deposits from customers and using them to make a variety of business loans. In those years, banks were far more tightly regulated than B&Ls at both the state and federal levels. States offered bank charters, and after 1863, a bank could also obtain a charter from the federal government to become a national bank. The national banks were supervised by the Office of the Comptroller of the Currency, a bureau of the U.S. Department of the Treasury. The passage of the Federal Reserve Act of 1913 entwined state banks with the federal system. National banks were automatically members, and state-chartered banks could join to gain access to liquidity support from the Fed.[9]

Though commercial banks competed with B&Ls for depositors in those early years, they were not a direct threat because until 1927, many (the national banks) were not permitted to make residential mortgage loans. Commercial banks were largely reliant on short-term deposits, and they focused on supplying short-term loans to farmers, shopkeepers, and other commercial enterprises. In states where they were permitted to offer home mortgages, these were typically "bullet" (now known as balloon) loans, under which only interest payments were made each month but the full balance of principal was due when the loan matured in about two years. A borrower who could not come up with the principal upon maturity would need to get a new loan from that bank or another source—such as a family member, insurance company, or mortgage company—or lose his home.[10]

In contrast to other financing arrangements, B&Ls offered mortgage loans with longer terms, up to twelve years, and also had the first amortizing mortgages, on which borrowers paid a piece of principal along with the interest each month. This meant that they would own their homes at the end of the loan term. The B&Ls could offer longer-term loans because they relied on membership fees and share sales for funding; compared to deposits, these were stable funds, as members could not demand immediate return of their money and could be required to wait thirty days to redeem.[11]

New Opportunities for Thrifts with the New Deal

The thrift industry began to thrive after the Great Depression. Beginning under Herbert Hoover and continuing during the Roosevelt administration, a new federal system to charter thrifts was established alongside the existing state system. This was created to rescue thrifts that suffered during the Great Depression and provide ongoing liquidity to the housing market. This replicated the dual banking system already established for commercial banks. As briefly described in chapter 2, at the center of the thrift financing and regulatory system was the Federal Home Loan Bank Board, which granted federal charters to thrifts. The twelve regional Federal Home Loan Banks, owned by the thrifts in their districts, were also part of the system. The new federal thrifts were to be governed like their state-chartered counterparts; they had to be mutually owned by depositors. In addition, initially, they were mainly limited to making mortgage loans on homes located within a fifty-mile (later a one-hundred-mile) radius of their home office.[12]

A second New Deal reform that nurtured the thrift industry was the Banking Act of 1933 (also known as the Glass-Steagall Act). This comprehensive statute is best known for separating commercial banking (accepting deposits and extending loans) from investment banking (underwriting and trading securities), and it is also recognized for the creation of deposit insurance for banks. But it had many other components, one of which gave thrifts a competitive advantage over banks. The Glass-Steagall Act banned commercial banks from paying interest on checking accounts (demand deposits). The law also required the Federal Reserve to make rules capping the rates that commercial banks could pay on savings accounts and on CDs (time deposits). Thrifts were not subject to the rate-cap rules and thus could attract more deposits than their bank rivals by offering higher interest.[13]

A third New Deal change that buoyed the thrifts and some of their rivals was the federal government's new role supporting mortgage lending. There were three important organizations that played that role. In 1933, the Home Owners Loan Corporation (HOLC) was created. HOLC, an agency with nearly twenty thousand employees, purchased defaulted mortgages, paying lenders less than the principal outstanding on the loans. It paid for the mortgages with U.S. government–insured bonds. HOLC then worked with the affected homeowners to refinance their mortgages to avoid foreclosure. Before it ceased lending in 1936, HOLC refinanced more than a million mortgages—about 20 percent of all mortgages in the country. While some people redefaulted, this intervention successfully helped 80 percent of owners save their homes and also provided liquidity for banks and thrifts. Fifteen years after refinancing its last mortgage, HOLC would dissolve and return a nearly $14 million surplus to the government.[14]

Then another organization was created in 1934, the Federal Housing Administration (FHA). The FHA was tasked with insuring residential mortgages that had twenty-year terms and 20-percent down payments. By offering default protection with respect to the monthly payments on the loans it insured, the FHA supported thrifts and other institutional lenders who could capture interest payments without taking on the risk that a borrower would stop paying. And, in 1938, a government agency called the Federal National Mortgage Association (Fannie Mae) was chartered to purchase qualifying mortgages from originators, including the thrifts. This secondary market in long-term, fixed-rate mortgages helped encourage home building, as local lenders who sold mortgages to Fannie could thus free up cash to make new loans. At first authorized only to purchase loans that were also insured by the FHA, a decade later Fannie Mae was granted additional authority to purchase loans guaranteed by the Veterans Administration (VA).[15]

The golden era for the thrifts came in the mid-1940s and 1950s. By then, B&Ls had been rebranded as S&Ls. In that era, the FHA loosened up and would insure loans with up to thirty-year terms and with as little as 5 percent down for new construction and 10 percent for existing homes. The legal reforms that had set in place conditions for their growth were accelerated by the GI Bill (the Servicemen's Readjustment Act), which provided low-interest, government-guaranteed loans to veterans, and a post–World War II boom (both economic and baby). In 1940, there were about 35 million housing units, of which about 44 percent or 15 million were owner occupied. By 1960, there were about 53 million housing units, of which about 62 percent or approximately 33 million were owner occupied. In this boom period between 1940 and 1960, there were nearly 20 million additional owner-occupied households. During this era, the S&Ls became the leading source of mortgage loans and also a top repository of consumer savings. With stable sources of funding—from depositors, the twelve Federal Home Loan Banks, and Fannie Mae—it appeared that the federal system established to shore up and regulate thrifts after the Great Depression was a success. However, for this success to be sustained for the thrifts, there had to be a positive spread between the income they received from mortgage loans and their funding costs.[16]

The End of the Beginning of the Golden Era

It was during the golden era in 1955 that Charlie Knapp's predecessor purchased American Savings and Loan. Under the guidance of the frugal S. Mark Taper (pronounced "tapper"), the thrift had been a bastion of safety and soundness. Taper had created American Savings and Loan of Beverly Hills by piecing together a number of thrifts into one of California's largest providers of single-family home mortgages through its more than one hundred branches. He was the sort of executive who not only brought his lunch to work in a brown paper bag but also saved and reused the bags. But in late 1983, when eighty-one-year-old Taper agreed to merge his bank with Knapp's fast-growing State Savings and Loan of Stockton, all of that changed (discussed further in chapter 6).[17]

About two decades before trouble ensued for American Savings and Loan, the thrift industry began to experience first small, then major shifts. In the late 1960s, the protective structure fostered by the New Deal began to be dismantled. In 1966, insured thrifts became subject to Reg Q; this capped the interest they could pay on their savings and CD accounts. The intent was to help lower thrifts' funding costs. Even with the new cap, though, they were permitted to pay slightly higher interest than rival commercial banks, reflecting a policy to promote housing.[18]

There were also changes to the federal government's role in the secondary mortgage market that would eventually threaten the thrifts. The first of those changes took place in 1968. Faced with the expense of the Vietnam War, President Lyndon Johnson decided to sell off Fannie Mae to investors. By 1970, Fannie was transformed into a private corporation that was owned by its stockholders with its shares listed on the New York Stock Exchange (NYSE) but overseen by the Department of Housing and Urban Development. As a private corporation, Fannie would continue to purchase mortgages from thrifts and other lenders: at first, just FHA-insured and VA-guaranteed mortgages. However, instead of using federal government funds to do so, it would now need to borrow money through the capital markets. Though a for-profit corporation, Fannie retained its public mission as a government-sponsored enterprise (GSE). As a result, Fannie benefited from an implicit guarantee: it could borrow at a lower cost than private companies with similar financial profiles because creditors believed the government would never let Fannie fail.[19]

Just as Fannie was pushed off the government books in 1970, a new entity, the Federal Home Loan Mortgage Corporation (Freddie Mac), was chartered. Unlike Fannie, Freddie was never a government agency; it was at the outset owned by the thrift industry via the twelve district Home Loan Banks. Eventually, in 1989, Freddie would go public, with its shares, like Fannie Mae's, listed on the NYSE. Freddie was designed to prevent a Fannie monopoly. It was also created to fill a gap. There was not yet a strong secondary market for "conventional" mortgages, those for which the monthly payments were not insured by government agencies like the VA and FHA. In 1971, both Freddie and Fannie began purchasing conventional mortgages on single-family homes from lenders, including S&Ls, commercial banks, and mortgage banks. These mortgages had to be "conforming," meaning they could be only of a certain size (in 1975, the limit was $55,000 for a single-family home), a certain term and payment structure, and they had to meet strict underwriting standards, including those related to the borrower's credit history and capacity to pay and the size of the loan relative to the value of the home.[20]

Unlike Fannie, which kept the loans it purchased in its portfolio, Freddie decided to sell them from the start. Instead of selling the mortgages whole, Freddie used a different technique that would later be called "securitization." Freddie did not design securitization; it copied this model from a new government agency that was created in 1968, called the Government National Mortgage Association (Ginnie Mae). Ginnie Mae was created in connection with President Johnson's spin-off of Fannie Mae and was tasked with providing guarantees for loans that qualified under the FHA, VA, and Farmers Home Administration programs. To encourage private lenders to make loans under those programs, beginning in 1970, Ginnie Mae selected mortgages it guaranteed and pooled them together. It then sold certificates to investors and used the proceeds from the certificate sales to pay the lenders for the mortgages, freeing up the lenders to make more loans. Certificate holders were paid their proportionate share of the cash flows coming from the borrowers' monthly mortgage payments. This would include regular and early payments, as well as payoffs. If there was a default, Ginnie made up the difference, so certificate holders had no credit risk. In the very first pool were $7.5 million loans. This is often described as the first publicly traded mortgage-backed security.[21]

Using this Ginnie Mae process of pooling government-insured mortgages as a model, and with the help of an investment bank, in 1971, Freddie began pooling the conventional residential mortgages it bought. The investment bank then sold bonds issued by those pools and backed by the mortgage cash flows. Bondholders received a proportionate share. The proceeds from the bond sales would be used to pay for the mortgages. Unlike "Ginnie Maes," the Freddie Mac certificates came with a private—not a government—guarantee. If the homeowner defaulted, Freddie was on the hook. Freddie charged an annual fee, known as the guarantee fee or G-fee, for this insurance. At first, the mortgages in the Freddie pools were purchased from thrifts belonging to the Federal Home Loan Banking System.[22]

While the Ginnie Mae certificates had an explicit U.S. government guarantee, Freddie's had an implicit guarantee. This meant that investors believed they were nearly as safe. At the beginning, Freddie needed Wall Street to help pool the mortgage loans, price the securities, and most important, distribute them. Yet Wall Street dealers had trouble finding buyers. Due to this factor and others, Freddie's role in the secondary market at first did not advance, and Fannie Mae would not begin securitizing mortgages for another decade.[23]

The Beginning of the End: Bypassing the S&Ls

With securitization as a model, some on Wall Street aimed to bypass the S&Ls and Freddie Mac entirely. In 1977, bankers at Salomon Brothers, led by Robert Dall, worked with peers at Bank of America to come up with a way for commercial banks to securitize their mortgages without first selling them to Freddie. This first conventional mortgage securitization was difficult to price and the sales process was not smooth. Insurance companies and other Salomon clients bought these securities, but few others did. They were sold in only about fifteen states due to state legal restrictions and to restrictions on purchases by some of the largest institutional investors—retirement funds. While it seemed like a failure, the machinery was in place.[24]

The motivation for putting the securitization machinery in full use was becoming clear. In 1975, there was nearly $900 billion in mortgage debt, up from about $90 billion in 1952. By 1980, there would be about $1.5 trillion—more than the value of the entire U.S. stock market. Wall Street wanted to earn fees securitizing and trading those mortgages. After May 1975, when fixed brokerage commissions ended, investment banks no longer had a sure source of income. New ways to make money in investment underwriting and trading were essential. Salomon's mortgage department, led by Lewis Ranieri in 1983, would help invent a new type of mortgage-backed security called the collateralized mortgage obligation (CMO) and, as a result, rake in hundreds of millions of dollars each year in the 1980s, but getting those profits would require overcoming some obstacles. Ranieri said that mortgage securitization was at first intended to "create an adjunct to the thrift industry, not a replacement for it"; however, eventually he observed that it took "away the thrifts' primary business of home lending."[25]

Surpassing the S&Ls as the central source for mortgage financing would not be easy. It was not just a business matter of having home loans extended by mortgage brokers or commercial banks and then securitized and sold by Wall Street. The laws needed to be changed so that big investors in every state could legally purchase these so-called "private-label," mortgage-backed securities that were not issued or guaranteed by Fannie or Freddie. Given that the powerful thrift lobby would oppose this change as additional competition, the investment bankers would have to convince policy makers that the S&Ls were not up to the task of supporting the mortgage market. To prove this point, there had to be a greater demand for home loans than the S&Ls could meet. This condition seemed likely, as the baby boomers were nearing the age when they would buy their own homes. Next, there had to be a funding shortfall at the S&Ls. At the moment, though, in the late 1970s, funding was protected to some degree. Reg Q still gave thrifts a slight advantage over banks in what they could pay depositors, helping attract deposits to fund home loans. Yet this rate control was not foolproof. Even with rate caps, if savings declined overall, this would hurt thrifts, and if a new type of savings vehicle came along that was not subject to Reg Q, that would spell disaster.[26]

The event that would spur two devastating changes—high interest rates and severe competition for deposits—took place one night in October 1979.

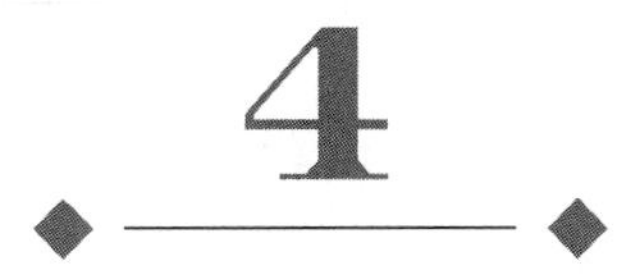

The Saturday Night Massacre

On the first Saturday in October 1979, Paul Volcker Jr. called a rare evening press conference. More than fifty reporters gathered in the Federal Reserve's ornate, two-story boardroom in Washington, D.C., to hear the Fed chairman speak. After brief introductions, Volcker wryly informed those present that, contrary to recent rumors, he had not resigned and was still alive. Then he launched into the substance of his talk: his plan to tame price inflation, which had been running at an annual rate of more than 10 percent since March. This was the nation's second experience of double-digit inflation that decade, with the first occurring in 1974. Inflation, he said, harmed business productivity and disrupted financial markets both here and abroad. Yet he barely discussed the impact of inflation on ordinary people. The talk was fairly technical. In a private meeting that morning, his words had been more dramatic when he had described his continuing fears of "the economy falling off the table."[1]

But at the public press conference, he employed bland language. He also did not detail the causes of inflation—which included Vietnam

War spending, the delinking of the dollar from gold in 1971, and two oil price spikes. He did not provide concrete examples. If he had, he might have mentioned that prices had doubled over the past decade; various consumer goods and services that cost $100 in 1969 were up to nearly $200 by 1979. And with inflation running in the double digits, they would cost $225 by 1980. At that time, energy prices were an important element of the consumer price index (CPI), the government's primary measure of inflation. Consumers felt the impact of the cost of oil at the pump and also in products and services for which oil was a raw material or a part of the embedded transportation costs. In October 1973, the Organization of Petroleum Exporting Countries (OPEC) imposed an oil embargo and raised prices in response to the U.S. support for Israel in the Yom Kippur War. Oil prices spiked again in 1979, when oil production declined after the Iranian Revolution. As a result of that recent oil shock, energy was the most significant contributor to the double-digit inflation to which Volcker referred. Energy prices would rise 45 percent, accounting for more than 75 percent of the increase in the CPI between the first quarter of 1979 and the first quarter of 1980.[2]

At the press conference, Volcker also did not discuss how inflation was good for some groups and bad for others. Yet there were winners and losers. Reining it in, and how hard, was a policy decision that would involve a large wealth transfer from one group to another.[3]

The Decision Makers

The decision to stem inflation by tightening the money supply was not made by elected officials. Under the U.S. system, such matters are controlled by majority vote of the twelve-person Federal Open Market Committee. Seven of the dozen seats on the committee are held by the seven members of the Board of Governors of the Federal Reserve, each of whom is a presidential appointee and often has an academic background in economics or law. Of the remaining five seats, one is reserved for the president of the New York Fed—a position held by Paul Volcker from August 1975 until he was appointed by President Carter in August 1979 to join the Board of Governors of the Fed as its chairman. The other four seats on the Open Market Committee are held for one-year terms on a rotating basis by the presidents of the other regional Federal Reserve banks. The twelve regional banks are owned by member banks in their regions. The presidents of the regional Fed banks are appointed by regional boards, which in turn are dominated by bankers and business leaders selected by the member banks. Given this composition and method of appointment, those who stand to lose the most with rising inflation—the banks—also have the greatest input into the decision to drastically slow it. Many of those who are helped by inflation have almost no input.[4]

Inflation's Winners and Losers

When Volcker launched his inflation-fighting plan, he did not mention that middle-class homeowners who depended on wages for their income often benefited under inflationary conditions. If they had a fixed-rate mortgage, their monthly payments would stay the same while their wages were rising. This meant that they would devote less of their growing salaries to paying back their home loans and have more money free for other choices. Manufacturers and others who borrowed to finance their enterprises could also thrive with inflation as their debt burdens became smaller, provided they could raise prices to keep up with or surpass wage increases.[5]

The more affluent typically suffered with inflation, as well as senior citizens on a fixed income or whose income largely depended on investment returns. Even if their investments grew in a given year, if inflation ran higher, they would have a net loss. Their investment income would not stretch as far and their standards of living would decline. For seniors, some of this loss could be made up if social security payments increased to keep up. Creditors also did poorly when inflation rose rapidly, as the old loans on their books would generate interest payments in less-valuable dollars. Finally, the leaders of several foreign governments, including West Germany, were concerned about inflation because the weakened dollar created losses for them, and they had met with Volcker when he was attending meetings abroad shortly before his announcement.[6]

Inflation Weakened the Savings and Loans

American Savings and Loan and other thrifts were among inflation's losers. Historically, the cornerstone of savings and loan (S&L) profitability was the spread. If you charged more interest on well-underwritten loans than you paid in interest to depositors and maintained low overhead, it was a reasonably profitable business. In the 1970s, this model was challenged. Inflation hit the S&Ls on both sides of their balance sheets. Their main assets were long-term, fixed-rate mortgages. The interest payments they received for these loans were fixed, but the value of those payments declined. Moreover, under accepted accounting standards, if an old mortgage loan was sold to generate cash for the S&L during a time when new loans would pay more interest, the old loan would bring in less than face value, generating a loss. Inflation threatened the funding side of their balance sheets as well: consumers were spending, not saving.[7]

Rising prices encouraged Americans to purchase large items on credit instead of waiting. They feared they would be priced out of the home, car, or large appliance market if they did not stretch to spend right away. Embracing debt was sensible, as one could pay back the loan with cheaper dollars. Even those who had the money to purchase a home without taking a large mortgage were encouraged to borrow more than they needed. This marked a cultural shift between those older Americans who considered it virtuous to live debt free and the baby boom generation then reaching adulthood. Between early 1975 and the Volcker press conference in October 1979, consumer credit (which included car loans and credit card balances, but did not include home mortgage loans) had grown from about $200 billion to $343 billion. Mortgage debt during that same period grew from less than $800 billion to about $1.3 trillion. Saving money seemed futile when its purchasing power was diminishing.[8]

Not only were people saving less, but they were moving what they did save into new savings vehicles that paid better: money market mutual funds, which paid more than thrifts and banks, were permitted under the Regulation Q (or Reg Q) rate caps. Prompted by pervasive advertising campaigns, consumers would send in their savings, and money market fund managers pooled it and invested it in short-term debt, such as short-term U.S.-government obligations, corporate debt, and bank CDs. In exchange, savers were given shares of the fund. These shares were priced at $1 each, and any income earned on the underlying investments was passed on to shareholders, usually in the form of monthly dividends, which could be reinvested into more shares. Money fund shares were redeemable for cash on demand, thus the need for liquid portfolio holdings.[9]

One of the first U.S. money market funds, the Reserve Fund, was launched by Bruce Bent in 1971. By 1974, there were about twenty such funds into which investors, including consumers and businesses, had poured $1 billion—in 1974 alone. At that time, money market funds paid between 10 and 11 percent. Meanwhile, due to the Reg Q restrictions, CDs paid just under 8 percent and savings accounts between 5 and 6 percent. By 1976, money market funds had gathered more than $3 billion. Besides better rates, other features made these funds attractive. Money market fund shareholders did not face any penalty for early withdrawal, unlike with a CD. One downside, though, was that unlike with a thrift or bank account, money market funds were not protected by federal deposit insurance. Yet this did not deter savers, many of whom were under the impression they could not lose their initial investment.[10]

Inflation on its own was trouble for the S&Ls, but the trouble was compounded when inflation bolstered this new competition from the money market funds. With the mortgages in their portfolios losing value and deposits dwindling, S&Ls like American Savings and Loan suffered in the 1970s. But the Volcker cure for inflation may have been worse than the disease.[11]

Volcker believed that a Fed pronouncement that it was going to slow down the growth of the money supply would send a signal to consumers that inflation was over. Upon receiving this signal, consumers would reduce borrowing and slow spending, and prices would stabilize. Not only would they stop binge buying as their expectation of inflation ended but they would also stop demanding pay increases. Stable labor costs would also help stabilize prices. This plan reflected a framework called rational expectations theory, first proposed in the late 1960s, under which one's expectation of a future event affects present actions, and thus prices. The theory held that the expectation of inflation resulted in more shopping and demands for higher wages, thus driving up prices—a self-fulfilling prophecy. Expectations of the end of inflation would drive prices down. The only problem was that one of the key drivers of high prices at the time was energy. And oil prices were not set by consumer expectations but by the OPEC cartel. Still, Volcker seemed to be testing out the theory—but he went about this test in a novel fashion.[12]

Taming Inflation

To tame inflation, the Fed would take steps to make it more costly for banks to borrow money with the expectation that the banks would then raise rates on businesses and consumers. The usual technique was to make it more expensive for banks to meet their "reserve" requirements. Under federal law, banks were required to set aside, or reserve, a fraction of the money deposited by customers in transactional accounts such as checking accounts. (Today, that amount is 10 percent of such deposits above a minimal threshold.) None of the reserve money could be used by the bank to make loans or other investments. Its purpose was to maintain a readily available source of money to meet depositors' withdrawals on transaction accounts, such as outgoing check payments. Banks were permitted to count the cash held in their vaults toward the mandated reserve amount, but the remainder was to be held at the Fed in the bank's reserve account. If a bank's reserve balance fell below the required minimum, it would need to borrow to make up the shortfall. It could borrow from its regional Federal Reserve Bank at the "discount window," or from one of its peer banks that also had a reserve account at the Fed. The interest rate for the former was the "discount rate," and the latter was the "Fed funds rate."[13]

Typically, when the Fed wished to cool off the economy, it would raise the discount rate, and the Open Market Committee would take incremental steps to cause the Fed funds rate—the short-term rate that banks charged other banks to borrow—to rise. And, indeed, one item Volcker announced at the press conference was that the Fed was raising the discount rate by one percentage point to a then record high of 12 percent. But this would not be sufficient. Causing the Fed funds rate to rise was also important, but more complicated given that the banks—not the Fed—established the rates they would charge. The purpose of elevating both rates was ultimately to affect consumer behavior. When these rates rose, the banks would need to raise rates on consumer loans. If the cost of consumer credit went up, the economy would slow.[14]

Typically, the steps to make the Fed funds rate rise began with a vote by the Open Market Committee to set an interest rate target slightly above the then prevailing Fed funds rate and then tighten the money supply until banks with excess reserves began to lend to those banks in need of reserves at the target rate. A key tool for tightening the money supply was what is called open market operations. Upon approval of the Open Market Committee, the Fed would typically sell some U.S. Treasury securities from its portfolio. These sales were performed by the trading desk at the Federal Reserve Bank of New York. When the buyer of the U.S. Treasury securities settled the transaction, the Fed would deduct the purchase amount from the buyer's bank account. Thus, the Fed's open market sales of securities would reduce the money in circulation, reduce the money available for banks to borrow to fill up their reserve accounts, and push up the Fed funds rate. When the Fed funds rate would rise, banks would have to pay more to borrow money and therefore would charge more to lend it out. Thus the prime rate, the average rate the banks reportedly charged their best corporate customers for short-term loans, would rise. Because the prime rate was a benchmark in the 1970s for many consumer loans, this process would cause consumers to pay more for new loans and to pay more on existing, variable-rate ones. If consumers had to pay more to borrow, then, the theory was that they would slow their spending and prices would stabilize.[15]

The New Volcker Cure for Inflation

At the October press conference, Volcker announced a new approach. He said the Fed would fight inflation, but without setting a specific Fed funds interest rate target. Instead, the Fed would focus on bank reserves. It would increase reserve requirements and also use open market sales of securities to reduce the money supply. Unlike in the past, when the Fed was careful to control the Fed funds rate, under the Volcker plan, it would fluctuate. Volcker warned those gathered at the press conference by saying "Let me put it this way. There could be substantial volatility on a day-to-day basis which I don't think is significant in itself, but maybe we will be surprised as banks learn to deal with this, and they're quick learners, in this area." Under the rational expectations theory, the thinking was that by draining money from the system, the national shopping spree would slow, prices would go down, and wage demands would also decline.[16]

Yet some wondered if this was just a way to raise interest rates without saying so. Fed board members also later recalled that they were really raising rates, but using this money-supply approach to make it look like they were not in control and thus not to blame for the result. Stephen Axilrod, one of Volcker's assistants and staff director for Monetary Policy, helped draft a memorandum laying out the innovative policy and also attended the Saturday evening press conference. He reflected that getting the members of the Open Market Committee to dramatically raise the Fed funds rate "relatively quickly" would not have been possible. However, he noted that "the new procedure adopted by the Volcker Fed had the advantage of getting interest rates as high as needed to restrain inflation."[17]

At first, Volcker's strategy did not work as planned. After years of double-digit inflation, people were in the habit of spending, and hearing about the plan did not significantly alter their behavior. At a House Banking Committee Hearing in the summer of 1981, Volcker told some angry members of Congress that "we see some encouraging signs that we are beginning to make progress against inflation.... The process inevitably requires time and patience." When people kept buying, prices continued to rise. Interest rates shot up and unemployment also rose. The country went through a combination of slow growth and inflation known as "stagflation."[18]

Volcker's plan had a profound effect on interest rates that businesses and consumers paid. When President Carter took office in 1977, the prime rate had been about 6.25 percent. It was 13.5 percent the week before the press conference, the so-called Saturday Night Massacre. Six months later, it hit nearly 20 percent. By summer of 1981, when Volcker was called before the House Banking Committee, it was around 20.5 percent. In between was a roller-coaster ride: rates fell as low as 11 percent in July 1980, delighting speculators, but not many others. Volcker's former assistant, Axilrod, would later recall that "it was a rockier ride than we had permitted ourselves to contemplate in advance."[19]

The soaring Fed funds rate affected average mortgage rates. To illustrate the difference before and after tightening the money supply, let's assume that a family borrowed $100,000 to buy a home in January 1977, when Carter took office. If they borrowed at the national average mortgage rate of 8.72 percent, their monthly payment would have been $785. Over the life of the loan, they would have paid just over $282,000. But if that family instead had purchased the home four years later at the same price, in October 1981, their rate would have been 18.45 percent, their monthly payment would have been $1,540, and over the life of the loan, they would have paid more than $555,000.[20]

Though interest rates skyrocketed, fell, and shot up again, restricting the money supply had not tamed inflation. It was running at an annual rate of about 12.1 percent when Volcker held his October 1979 press conference. Six months later, in April 1980, it was at 14.7 percent, and it remained in the double digits throughout the election year. Unemployment was also worse. In mid-1979, it reached a low 5.7 percent, rose to 8.5 percent by the end of 1981, and peaked at 10.8 percent by the end of 1982. Triggering a deep recession in order to halt inflation involved an uncomfortable balance of the Fed's statutory mandate to use monetary policy to "promote effectively the goals of maximum employment, stable prices, and moderate long-term interest rates."[21]

In the long run, all three came down. In 1982, around the time the Fed abandoned the reserve targeting and returned to interest rate controls, inflation was clearly back in the single digits, but it took until late 1987 for unemployment to return to the pre-Volcker levels. The prime rate would not return to around 6.25 percent, its level when Carter took office, until 1992. Still, many economists have recognized that Volcker's actions were brave and successful and set the stage for decades of prosperity. Others have asked whether less-painful measures could have produced the same results. Some observed that inflation would have stabilized when energy prices fell, with or without Volcker's shock therapy. Economist Robert Solow, later a Nobel laureate, remarked that the plan resembled "burning down the house to roast the pig."[22]

Burning Down the Savings and Loans

High interest rates also brought losers and winners. The losers included credit-sensitive industries like automobiles and housing. When the prime rate climbed to 20 percent, consumers hesitated to buy cars and homes because of the high monthly payments, or they bought cheaper cars and homes than they otherwise might. It was in December 1979 that Congress approved a bailout of Chrysler Corporation, providing $1.5 billion in loan guarantees. Other losers included President Carter, whose failure to win a second term was partly due to the damaged economy. Many borrowers with adjustable-rate loans, including farmers, also found themselves unable to make their payments.[23]

Among the casualties were the savings and loans. The industry lost almost $3 billion in 1980 and $4 billion in 1981. In 1982, 10 percent of thrifts closed or were taken over at near failure. After interest rates spiked and unemployment climbed, consumers had less money to save. Those with savings did not take them to the local S&L, but instead pulled their money out and placed it where it could work for them—in the new money market funds. Large commercial banks, meanwhile, fared far better. They were able to tap foreign sources of funding at lower than prevailing U.S. rates, and their assets were not tied up in undiversified portfolios of long-term, fixed-rate mortgages. High interest rates thus made the S&Ls weaker against both their old foes, the commercial banks, and a new contender, the money market funds.[24]

Money Market Fund Threat to the Thrifts Grows

Double-digit interest rates helped the money market funds attract even more money away from the thrifts. In March 1980, these funds were paying investors about 13.5 percent, while thrifts and banks were still paying interest on savings accounts of around 5.5 percent. For someone with $10,000 in savings, the difference was clear: he or she would earn $1,350 per year with a money market fund and just $550 with a savings account. Helped by the Fed's action and pervasive marketing campaigns, the holdings of money market funds grew from a slightly threatening $3 billion in 1976 to a game-changing $180 billion by 1983. Growth continued to $2 trillion by 2000 and would peak at $3.92 trillion in 2009. This outflow of deposits to money market funds was referred to as "disintermediation." Not only did competition from the money market funds help sink many S&Ls, but money market funds would also play an important role in the 2008 crisis.[25]

To compete with the convenience of the money market funds, thrifts wanted to let their savings account holders get their money out on demand. In the 1970s, some states began to authorize thrifts to offer checking accounts and others to offer negotiable order of withdrawal (NOW) accounts, which had the features of a checking account but paid interest like a savings account. Additionally, with the new ATMs, thrift account holders had access to their savings at any time, even at great distance. Instant access helped the S&Ls compete, but it created a different risk due to their maturity mismatch:

though mortgage assets were still long-term, deposits were increasingly short-term.[26]

Still, if the S&Ls wanted to keep their depositors and attract new ones, their biggest need was to pay greater interest on savings accounts. That would require lifting the Reg Q cap. And the only way to bring in more income on the asset side of the balance sheet to compensate for that extra interest paid out would be to charge borrowers more for mortgages and to offer new kinds of riskier loans that paid higher rates. Facing a trilogy of threats—innovation-fostered competition, inflation, and interest rates—the besieged industry went to its federal regulator, the Home Loan Bank Board, and to Congress for help. Meanwhile, Wall Street had its own requests for deregulation.

5

Deregulation Inauguration

Ronald Reagan stood on the terrace of the west front of the Capitol and squinted into the sunlight. He gazed out at the crowd gathered there and on the National Mall beyond while he waited for the welcoming applause to end. With a quick glance at his notes, he began by commending the Carter administration for cooperating in the orderly transfer of executive authority. Then the new president of the United States launched into the substance of his inaugural address. He deemed inflation an "economic affliction of great proportions" that could "shatter the lives of millions" and blamed it for idle industries and laid-off workers. He made no mention of the Federal Reserve actions that had helped bring about stagflation or of oil prices, then near their peak. Instead, he implied that it was solely an intrusive, growing federal government with its taxing and spending that had caused the downturn. "In this present crisis," he declared, "government is not the solution to our problem; government is the problem." This line received more than five seconds of applause. Then the fortieth president of the United States shared his plans: "It is my intention to curb the size and influence of the federal establishment and to demand recognition of the distinction between the powers granted to the federal government and those reserved to the states or to the people."[1]

These passages are often repeated when Reagan is remembered as a leader of deregulation. In fact, the deregulation and desupervision of the savings and loans (S&Ls) and the mortgage industry began during the Carter administration. But Reagan substantially accelerated the pace. Moreover, though he championed states' rights, when it came to consumer protection, Reagan signed legislation and his administration supported policies that stripped away the rights of states to govern themselves and their businesses and to protect their citizens.

Though he renounced "special interest groups," he brought into his administration investment bankers who guided the transformation of the thrift industry in ways that greatly profited Wall Street. For example, Reagan appointed former Merrill Lynch chairman and CEO Donald T. Regan as secretary of the Treasury. Regan was not just a Wall Street insider; many claimed that while at Merrill, he created the brokered deposits market. He would later quip that he wanted "a blood test as far as being the father of brokered deposits." There is no dispute that after his departure, his former firm was the leader in placing billions of brokered deposits at the S&Ls. And it is not contested that the Reagan administration protected brokered deposits during Regan's tenure there, a result that would benefit Wall Street and cost the taxpayers. But deregulation began before the orderly transition of executive power from Carter to Reagan.[2]

Congress and Carter Act

It was clear by 1980 that the S&Ls could not heal themselves from the troubles brought on by high interest rates and competition with money market funds for depositors. The thrift lobbying association, the U.S. League of Savings Institutions, asked for relief and Washington responded. The first phase began in March 1980—when interest rates spiked to 19 percent—when Congress passed and President Carter signed the Depository Institutions Deregulation and Monetary Control Act (DIDMCA). Congress sought to address the damage that high inflation and skyrocketing interest rates had done to thrifts and banks. It also was designed to give these institutions the ability to better compete with money market funds and began the process of blurring the distinction between thrifts and banks, treating them all as depository institutions. The law also opened up new asset powers for the thrifts, allowing them to expand well beyond just owning mortgages into riskier assets and required all depository institutions, including thrifts, to hold reserves at the Fed.[3]

In an effort to address the trouble that thrifts and banks faced with regard to bringing in and maintaining deposits, the law abolished the Reg Q interest rate cap on savings accounts. These caps would be phased out over a number of years, though the ban on paying interest on checking accounts remained. The thrifts lost their quarter-percentage-point interest rate advantage over the banks. In addition, with little debate yet great consequence, the limit on insured deposits for both banks and thrifts was raised from $40,000 to $100,000 per account.[4]

The DIDMCA also expanded the ability of federally chartered thrifts to make acquisition-development-construction (ADC) loans, the type that state-chartered Empire Savings and Loan Association of Mesquite had made. Though these loans do not necessarily involve fraud, they were considered inherently more risky than residential mortgages because many factors could affect the real estate developer's ability to pay them back. Because they presented a higher risk of default, lenders could charge higher interest rates on ADC loans. It was the promise of higher interest that made this change attractive to thrifts.[5]

Congress had first permitted federally chartered thrifts to make ADC loans just two years earlier, in 1978, and limited these loans to 5 percent of total assets. This began a dramatic shift. Whereas in 1978 more than 80 percent of S&L assets had been in residential mortgage loans, after the 1978 change and the DIDMCA, by 1986, residential mortgage loans were just 56 percent of thrifts' assets nationally. Texas had been the inspiration for allowing federally chartered thrifts to wade into real estate development loans. Indeed,

Texas was the model for all of the sweeping national deregulation of the thrift industry.[6]

The DIDMCA also addressed the S&Ls' mortgage troubles. The majority of assets that S&Ls held were thirty-year mortgages with low, fixed interest rates that were never going to pay more than single digits. This low-yielding asset problem was compounded when the Reg Q cap was lifted. Increased competition for deposits meant that thrifts would have to pay more interest to depositors, and the more they paid out, the more they would have to bring in from borrowers, but there was an obstacle—state anti-usury laws. Many states capped the amount of interest that lenders could charge to state residents. In some states, the rate caps varied based on loan type. The thrifts and banks wanted these caps to go away.

The request to sacrifice state consumer protection built on existing legal rulings. In 1978, in *Marquette National Bank of Minneapolis vs. First Omaha Service Corp.*, the United States Supreme Court addressed the question of whether the anti-usury law of the state where a borrower resides applied to loans made by a federally chartered bank (referred to as a "national bank") based in a different state. In a 9–0 decision written by Justice William Brennan, the Court held that the National Bank Act of 1863 permitted national banks to charge any rate of interest consistent with the state laws where the bank was based. In that case, the bank had issued a credit card to residents in many states but, for purposes of its national charter, maintained an address in Omaha, Nebraska. Nebraska permitted 18 percent interest on certain credit card balances, but Minnesota, for example, limited the rate to 12 percent. Brennan cited earlier precedent to describe a national bank as an "instrumentalit[y] of the Federal government, created for a public purpose, and as such necessarily subject to the paramount authority of the United States." Thus, the interest rate it charged was governed by federal, not state, law.[7]

While the *Marquette* decision was useful to institutions able to move, state-chartered thrifts with brick-and-mortar locations could not as easily move physically. The decision also disadvantaged retail stores that offered credit terms to buyers. A national bank, however, could change its charter address. Citibank saw this opportunity and persuaded South Dakota to enact favorable legislation in 1990; it moved its credit card operations to the state, eventually bringing three thousand jobs.

The new DIDMCA helped anchor thrifts by taking the right to protect consumers away from states. The statute preempted the state laws that capped the amount of interest that lenders could charge on many loans, including first mortgages on residences. On some loan types, a new federal cap was imposed; on others, there was no limit at all. States could opt out of the preemption, but only about fourteen did.[8]

Carter's Bank Board Relaxes

Under the leadership of Chairman Jay Janis, the three-member Federal Home Loan Bank Board also helped the S&Ls. In November 1980, the Bank Board abolished its 5 percent cap on brokered deposits. Brokered deposits, the hot money that Empire and many other S&Ls relied on for fast growth, had been exempt from Reg Q since 1973. With the new ruling, suddenly the S&Ls could bring in unlimited brokered deposits and pay whatever rate was necessary to attract funds. The significance of the Bank Board's action cannot be overstated. The Bank Board's move created a perverse incentive for deposit brokers like Merrill Lynch and others to direct jumbo CDs to the fastest-growing, riskiest, and most desperate S&Ls, which would pay the most. Previously, when rates were capped under Reg Q—other than for brokered deposits that could make up to 5 percent of the deposit base—weak thrifts could not pay extra interest to bring in the bulk of their deposits, so there was no incentive to funnel money there. Allowing unlimited brokered deposits created considerable risk for the Federal Savings and Loan Insurance Corporation (FSLIC) deposit insurance fund.[9]

At that time, the Bank Board also reduced the net worth requirement for insured thrifts from 5 percent to 4 percent. This meant that for every $100 in assets that an S&L owned (such as mortgage loans), it could borrow $96 instead of $95 from depositors or others. This also put the deposit insurance fund at greater risk. The risk was amplified by the fact that the loans it could hold were more likely to default.

Janis's Bank Board might have balanced these moves by protecting the FSLIC insurance fund. It could have required that a higher percentage of insurance be paid into the fund relative to the increase in loan risk types and riskier funding sources. But it did not do this. Every thrift paid a flat rate. It was as if an insurance company required homeowners in beachfront cottages in a hurricane-prone area to pay no higher rates than those well above sea level. And if the insurance provider ran short, the taxpayers—not the insurance firms—paid the claims.[10]

Reagan-Era Deregulation

By 1981, when Ronald Reagan took office, nearly every S&L in the country was insolvent on a market value basis. The average return on mortgages for insured thrifts was about 9.91 percent, but their average cost of funds was 10.92 percent. Losses mounted. By the end of 1981, their losses reached $4.66 billion. In total, the industry had a net worth on a market value basis of negative $100 billion. That year, net deposit outflows reached $25 billion. By mid-1982, the industry's negative net worth was about $150 billion. But since the accounting standards of the time did not require that loans be adjusted to their fair market value ("marked to market"), the thrifts' books did not reflect reality. The S&Ls were hemorrhaging money. Meanwhile, the FSLIC fund was dwindling.[11]

Many S&Ls should have been shut down. But this would have required using the FSLIC insurance fund to pay depositors and the fund was running low. Given the state of the industry, it was not practical to refill the fund by charging higher premiums. While the FSLIC had the statutory authority to borrow from the Treasury, the Reagan administration told the new Bank Board chairman, Richard T. Pratt, not to do so. Pratt was a finance professor at the University of Utah College of Business and was appointed chairman of the Bank Board in 1981. The administration would not give Pratt the funds to shut down the failing thrifts or to hire more examiners. Donald Regan, the Treasury secretary, would not even take Pratt's phone calls.[12]

It was essential to minimize or delay the impending costly collapse of the S&Ls. President Reagan had promised to balance the budget and cut taxes. A $100 billion charge to fund the FSLIC might have caused Congress to rethink the Economic Recovery Tax Act of 1981, under which taxes were cut by $264 billion. And a public announcement of trouble could have led to a run on the thrifts. If depositors demanded their money back, the thrifts would be forced to sell loans at considerable losses. Yet doing nothing would have made that day inevitable.[13]

Without the freedom to close down zombie thrifts, Pratt found an alternative. He would hide their problems, make it easier for the industry to explore new lines of business, and hope they would grow out of their troubles. On April 16, 1981, two days after his appointment, he announced the Bank Board's plan to simultaneously back off on restrictions on thrifts while setting them loose to explore new business opportunities. Building on his predecessor, Janis, who had permitted variable rate mortgages, Pratt further removed restrictions on these mortgages to help them flourish. This particular deregulatory change seemed sensible for the S&Ls but highly risky for consumers. For example, in the month after his arrival, when Pratt expanded the ability for federally chartered thrifts to offer adjustable-rate mortgages (ARMs), this shifted the risk of interest rate increases for new loans from S&Ls onto borrowers. These ARM loans were often structured with a low "teaser" rate, which made it easier for borrowers to qualify and thus easier for S&Ls to grow their loan portfolios. Other changes, which were seemingly cosmetic, actually imperiled the safety and soundness of the thrifts and also put the insurance fund at risk. At the same time, Pratt's Bank Board started to reduce staff and cut salaries.[14]

In January 1982, the Bank Board reduced the net worth requirement for thrifts from 4 to 3 percent. This was like being able to buy a $1 million building while putting down only $30,000 of one's own money. This Pratt move created even greater leverage for new S&Ls.

The Bank Board already allowed a thrift twenty years from when it was established to meet its net worth (capital) requirement, which the Bank Board did not eliminate until the following year.[15]

To make starting a federally chartered thrift even easier, in April 1982, Pratt's Bank Board eliminated many of the ownership rules. In the past, unlike some thrifts chartered in states like Texas, a federal thrift had to have at least 400 stockholders, of whom at least 125 had to be from the local community. Ownership concentration had been prohibited; no single person could own more than 10 percent of shares and no block of investors could own more than 25 percent. Pratt wiped those restrictions away. Now a single individual could start up or purchase a federal thrift. And instead of investing cash to meet the net worth requirement, the thrift founder could use real estate.[16]

Accounting Tricks and Tax Breaks

Pratt's Bank Board also helped the thrifts dress up their books. It let them use a liberal and misleading accounting method called Regulatory Accounting Practices (RAP) instead of Generally Accepted Accounting Principles (GAAP) for their financial statements. A congressional committee later called these "accounting gimmicks" that "masked the worsening financial condition of the industry." By using RAP, an insolvent thrift could report a positive net worth. This allowed the Bank Board to avoid selling or shuttering insolvent thrifts. There were other questionable accounting techniques. One of the most controversial was allowing S&Ls to defer their loan losses. A loan loss would occur when an S&L sold legacy mortgage loans, mortgage securities, or other similar assets. While GAAP required immediate recognition of a loan loss, RAP did not. With RAP, the thrifts were permitted to spread out their losses from these sales over a long period of time. In addition, under RAP, assets on the books that had appreciated in value (such as loans originated when interest rates had spiked and were paying more than prevailing lower rates—during the Volcker-induced rate roller coaster) could be marked to market, recorded at the higher value. Under the more transparent GAAP, unrealized gains on such assets could not be recorded until they were sold. But under RAP, assets that were not sold but had depreciated (such as legacy mortgage loans with low interest rates) could still be shown at their full historical values. Another approved technique was to permit a failing thrift to merge with a healthier one. The surviving thrift would be permitted to account for mortgage assets at their depreciated market value. But it could spread out those losses over forty years under the category of "good will," while booking income on the same assets over a much shorter period.[17]

Under the creative RAP regime, a thrift could sell legacy mortgage loans for a considerable loss but stretch out that loss over the remaining life of the loan it just sold. For example, if the thrift sold some mortgages with ten years of payments remaining for $20 million that were originally worth $30 million, it would book the $20 million in income right away. However, it could stretch out the $10 million loss over ten years, during which time the loss would be treated as an asset. As a result, the sale of those bad mortgages would initially appear profitable. This unusual accounting practice was turbocharged with a 1981 tax break. With the new tax treatment, the thrift would be allowed to use the actual $10 million loss to offset taxes paid over the previous ten years. This meant S&Ls that could show big losses on old mortgages could get money back from the Internal Revenue Service (IRS). Not surprisingly, this created the incentive for thrift managers to sell mortgages quickly to generate tax losses that would result in paper accounting gains and tax refunds.[18]

To make these sales, thrifts turned to investment banks like Salomon Brothers, which helped sell hundreds of billions of dollars in mortgages from one thrift to another. This created distorted prices; thrifts were buying the same type of mortgage for 85 cents on the dollar that they had sold for 75 cents. Of course, Wall Street mortgage desks kept the nice spread. Michael Lewis, who worked at Salomon Brothers, chronicled this practice in his book, *Liar's Poker*. Salomon's mortgage desk took advantage of the thrift presidents' inexperience with the details and rapacious culture of investment banking: "They didn't know the mentality of the people they were up against. They didn't know the value of what they were selling." When one thrift president complained that a deal was not good for his institution, the salesman at Salomon responded: "It isn't, from an economic point of view, but look at it this way, if you *don't* do it, you're out of a job." Another trader listening in on the call laughed at the thrift president's desperation.[19]

Wall Street Innovation

Selling whole mortgage loans from one thrift to another was one way to generate fees. Securitization was another. In 1977, when Bank of America, with Salomon's help, tried to securitize mortgages on its books, the effort was a failure because state laws forbade it to sell the securities widely. So, in the early 1980s, Lewis Ranieri brought in the Federal Home Loan Mortgage Corporation (Freddie Mac) to help. This was a breakthrough. Up to that time, Freddie Mac and the Federal National Mortgage Association (Fannie Mae) had helped finance new home loans that the S&Ls originated, as part of their missions to support new homeowners and new home buying, but they did not buy up old loans already on the thrifts' books. Ranieri changed this. Freddie agreed to buy up old low-interest loans and securitize them. According to Ranieri, the first time this was tried was with legacy mortgage loans held by a D.C.-based thrift with the hopeful name Perpetual Savings. Perpetual sold its mortgages to a trust that funded the purchase by selling certificates to investors as a form of debt security. Each month, the holders were paid a share of the principal and interest paid by owners of the underlying homes.

With Freddie involved, many of the obstacles that made that first Bank of America failure were not present: the securities could be sold throughout the country and to a variety of institutional investors. A mutual dependency was established. Wall Street would find the customers (often other thrifts) to buy these pass-through mortgage-backed securities, and Freddie would sit in the middle and provide the guarantee and legal exemptions. At first, these were still clunky, not tailored to purchasers who did not wish to hold long-term investments. And they were hard to price because of the uncertainty of cash flows; some borrowers might prepay, resulting in lost interest income.[20]

Further Deregulation for the S&Ls

Coordinating with the Treasury Department, Pratt helped draft legislation to further deregulate the S&Ls. Though it was named after its congressional sponsors, Republican senator Jake Garn and Democratic representative Fernand St. Germain, the law was informally called the Pratt Bill. At an industry event held a month after signing the Garn-St. Germain Depository Institutions Act of 1982 (Garn-St. Germain), President Reagan declared that he was endorsing an "Emancipation Proclamation for America's savings institutions." The law was designed to rescue the thrift industry, which was insolvent due to a combination of high-interest rates and competition from money market funds. Pratt modeled it on Texas-style deregulation. According to a former Texas state savings and loan commissioner, members of Congress copied from Texas's liberalized policies in drafting the legislation. Texas was the inspiration because between 1979 and 1981, after deregulation there, the S&Ls appeared to be more profitable than those in other states. Deregulation was assumed to be the cause of their success, and that success would, of course, be sustainable. But Congress took it a step further—removing the required 3 percent net worth requirement and leaving it to the regulators to establish a minimum level.[21]

The law lowered mortgage loan underwriting standards, abolishing the previously required loan-to-value ratios for federally chartered thrifts. This meant that borrowers could put far less money down on mortgages. Most significantly, it expanded the power of federally chartered thrifts to invest in assets well beyond residential mortgage loans. Now, 40 percent of those thrifts' assets could be nonresidential real estate loans, 30 percent consumer loans, and 10 percent commercial loans. More creative accounting came with Garn-St. Germain, as the Bank Board was given the power to allow federally insured thrifts with inadequate capital to issue "net worth" certificates. S&Ls gave these paper promises to the FSLIC in exchange for promissory notes from the FSLIC. These so-called "paper-for-paper" transactions created accounting entries that looked like equity investments by the FSLIC—thus cosmetically boosting a thrift's net worth—even though the thrift was obligated to pay back the FSLIC.[22]

Consumer Protection Further Sacrificed

Like Carter's DIDMCA, Reagan's Garn-St. Germain used Congress's powers of preemption to erode consumer protection. At the time, many states had laws in place that governed ARMs. These loans were popular with S&Ls and other lenders after October 1979 when interest rates were on the Fed-induced roller-coaster ride. The laws in some states had established caps on how much the rate could adjust upward during reset periods and for the life of the loan. Some prohibited "alternative mortgages," including those with negative amortization and balloon payments. The S&L lobby did not like these state laws because they interfered with their ability to make adjustable-rate loans. Moreover, they objected to the uneven rules—that while states placed these restrictions on their thrifts, federally chartered thrifts had more freedom in their offering of ARMs. In response, one part of Garn-St. Germain created a new law called the Alternative Mortgage Transaction Parity Act of 1982 (the Parity Act). This law allowed state-chartered thrifts to offer alternative mortgages like their federal counterparts. Industry proponents of this law contended that ARMs with teaser rates—or interest-only mortgages—that jumped up later or resulted in large balloon payments helped more borrowers achieve the American Dream of homeownership.[23]

In addition to helping S&Ls hide their growing losses, together, the DIDMCA and the Parity Act paved the way for subprime mortgages and the predatory adjustable-rate, negatively amortizing mortgages known as option ARMs (discussed further in chapter 9). Without these laws, subprime lending could not have flourished. In addition, these changes brought to life a new trade off: the government sanctioning of consumer harm to shore up insolvent banking institutions, something that would carry forward through the 2008 crisis and beyond.[24]

California, Florida, and Texas Race to the Bottom

Attracted by federal deregulation, many state-chartered S&Ls converted to federal charters. This was because while some parts of Garn-St. Germain preempted state law and thus impacted all thrifts, other parts only applied to federally chartered thrifts. This made the states nervous. The budgets of the state thrift regulators depended on industry fees. California, Florida, and Texas were particularly concerned. Together, these three chartered about half of all state thrifts with FSLIC insurance. Texas law permitted its S&Ls to have the same rights as federal thrifts (meaning they got the full benefits of Garn-St. Germain), but California law did not. To stem the loss of thrifts from the state, the California legislature passed the Nolan Act, effective January 1, 1983, and sponsored by Assemblyman Pat Nolan, who was associated with many S&L executives.[25]

The Nolan Act permitted a California thrift to channel 100 percent of deposits into any type of investment it chose. This included commercial and residential real estate and nearly anything else, including the high-yield, high-risk debt then known as "junk bonds." Michael Milken, at the investment banking firm Drexel Burnham Lambert, dominated the junk bond market. He led Drexel's underwriting of these bonds and sold them to S&Ls, pension funds, and other institutional investors. He also used junk bonds to help acquirers take over publicly traded corporations. They had high yields: the vast amount of money borrowed by acquiring firms through these bonds to take over their targets created a great risk that new owners of the acquired companies would be burdened with so much debt that they would default—thus, the higher interest. The thrifts were permitted to buy junk bonds as part of a new asset class called "direct investments." The door was wide open. In rushed people who wanted to buy old thrifts or launch new ones. Anyone with $2 million could start a thrift in California. Five years later, Pat Nolan would resign amid a rumored FBI investigation into influence peddling and political corruption. In 1994, Nolan pleaded guilty to federal racketeering charges and was sentenced to 33 months in prison.

Texas also experienced a wave of charter conversions and new applications. The staffs at the state regulators were overwhelmed and waived applicants through with little quality control. During the first year of the Nolan Act, the California Department of Savings and Loans, under Commissioner Larry Taggart, did not reject any new applicants at all.[26]

Chipping Away at Glass-Steagall

Deregulation came not just to the thrifts but to the whole financial sector. The structure from the early twentieth century, where each type of financial firm had its own niche, was eroding. The Federal Reserve started chipping away at the wall between ordinary banking (taking deposits and making loans) and investment banking (securities operations) that had been established by the Glass-Steagall Act fifty years earlier. In 1983, the Fed permitted Bank of America Corporation, the holding company for the depository institution Bank of America, to acquire Charles Schwab, a retail securities brokerage firm. The Fed decided that having a national bank affiliated with a retail securities brokerage firm did not violate Glass-Steagall. The operative language from that Depression-era law had prohibited banks from being affiliated with any entity "engaged principally in the issue, flotation, underwriting, public sale, or distribution" of securities. In addition, the Bank Holding Company Act of 1956 barred bank holding companies from acquiring nonbanking entities. However, that law empowered the Fed to permit them to own entities whose activities were "so closely related to banking . . . as to be a proper incident thereto." The Fed determined that Glass-Steagall would not be violated because Schwab would be acting merely as an agent responding to customer orders (not as a dealer selling securities for its own account). In addition, the Fed determined that the Bank Holding Company Act would not be violated because the brokerage activities that did not include investment advice were "closely related" to banking. The Court of Appeals affirmed, as did the Supreme Court.[27]

As their powers expanded and thrifts got involved in complicated classes of mortgage securitizations, junk bonds, and other asset types that their employees were not trained to select, the regulators lost power. Just as he was setting the thrifts free to experiment in new areas, Bank Board chairman Pratt reluctantly cut the examination staff at the Bank Board. Vice President George H. W. Bush, who led a task force on deregulation of the financial sector, recommended that regulators reduce the frequency of exams and the number of examiners and rely instead on computer analysis and financial statements. Pratt was threatened by the Office of Management and Budget with sanctions if he exceeded the Bank Board's spending limits.[28]

Wall Street and Washington Coordinate

Even with Freddie's help in buying and packaging legacy loans from thrifts and selling them as securities, Lewis Ranieri of Salomon Brothers was not satisfied. The securities were not refined enough to be sold broadly to investors. Many institutions were not permitted by law to buy them. Wall Street traders, meanwhile, saw a huge market from which they wanted a piece of the fees. Although it was supposed to be simply an add-on to the thrift industry, securitization began to take precedence over the function the thrifts supposedly served: to finance home loans.[29]

For mortgage securities to fit the mandates and legal restrictions of big institutional investors like multibillion-dollar pension funds, they had to be redesigned and refined. In 1983, a more sophisticated mortgage-backed security (MBS) was brought to market by Freddie Mac using a pool of First Boston mortgages. With this new version of MBS, there were multiple classes, not just one type of certificate. Instead of passing all the monthly mortgage payments through to investors equally, the payments were carved up, apportioned by class. Early on, three classes of certificates were sold. Typically, the first and safest class was first in line for payment. Holders of this first type would receive monthly principal and interest payments until the amount they invested (the principal) was paid off, in perhaps five years. The second class had a longer maturity, around twelve years, and its holders would initially earn only interest payments. Only after the first class was paid off would the holders of the second class of certificates receive payments. The third class had the longest maturity—as much as thirty years—and its holders waited the longest to get paid back. This third type was the riskiest and thus paid the most interest, as there was a possibility that the principal and interest would not get paid. Even this simple structure faced legal obstacles in the early years.[30]

With the help of Washington attorneys and a contact in the Reagan White House, Ranieri set out to remove all legal obstacles to the sale of a bank-issued version of this new mortgage security. In other words, he wanted banks to be able to pool their mortgages and sell securities backed by them without the need to work with the government-sponsored enterprise, Freddie Mac. To do this, he guided the creation of two different laws. The first, called the Secondary Mortgage Market Enhancement Act of 1984 (SMMEA), removed the legal barriers that had blocked the development of the private mortgage securities market. Until then, the Government National Mortgage Association (Ginnie Mae), Fannie Mae, and Freddie Mac had more than 95 percent of the MBS market. By early 1984, they had issued $243 billion of the outstanding MBSs and private issuers just $10 billion. The enactment of the SMMEA made privately issued MBS-permissible investments for a broad range of institutional investors, including state and national banks and S&Ls. The law even required states to treat privately issued MBSs as equivalent to U.S. government obligations, despite the MBS's greater risks. It also preempted state law so that state-chartered S&Ls, for example, could also invest, and private MBSs did not have to be registered under state securities laws.[31]

This was a tremendous achievement. Ranieri was present when President Reagan signed the SMMEA into law on October 3, 1984.

Presumptively "sophisticated" institutional investors like pension funds and insurance companies could now invest in these securities even without a guarantee from Freddie or Fannie. As a substitute for that guarantee, a privately issued MBS needed a high rating from a legally cleared credit-rating agency (referred to in various laws and rules as a Nationally Recognized Statistical Rating Organization) in order for it to be purchased by some institutional investors. While investors were granted the right to select mortgage securities to buy, they did not necessarily have the right skills. CMOs were sold with the claim that made it unnecessary for purchasers to know anything about the underlying mortgages or the creditworthiness of the borrowers.[32]

This immediately created opportunities to fleece investors. Even with the small size of the market, there had already been a notable example. In 1981, approximately twenty-five thrifts and small banks had purchased about $133 million in MBSs, for which Bank of America had acted as a trustee and escrow agent for investor funds. The underlying mortgages were on California and Texas properties with fraudulently inflated appraisals. Two convicted felons were ultimately behind the scheme. They were supposed to use the proceeds of the MBS sales to fix up apartments and convert them into condos, but they never did. Though the securities were guaranteed, the firm providing the insurance was virtually insolvent. In 1984, Bank of America agreed to buy back those nearly worthless MBSs from the thrifts and banks.[33]

Ranieri's second target for reform was the tax code. He sought to change the law to create a structure to hold the pool of mortgages for these securities that would avoid double taxation. It took longer to get the tax law changed because Ranieri faced opposition from an analyst within the Treasury Department. Undaunted, he simply hired the analyst away from the Treasury. Ranieri also tried to sideline Freddie and Fannie by proposing to limit the special tax treatment to privately issued mortgage securities, but he failed on that point. When he testified before Congress on the tax legislation, he estimated that the law would reduce homeowners' borrowing rates by about 0.75 percent. He would later explain that this estimate did not include the cost that securitization would impose on taxpayers who ultimately had to bail out the failing thrifts.[34]

All the pieces were coming together. In 1979, just after the Fed caused interest rates to skyrocket, there were more than 4,700 S&Ls and savings banks in America. By 1983, nearly one thousand had failed or had gone out of business. In an essay published a decade later, Ranieri noted that his legal changes were perfectly timed to allow securitization to accelerate the S&Ls' decline. "Securitization," he wrote, "contributed to the bankrupting of the thrift industry. The federal government started the process in the late 1970s by deregulating financial institutions. . . . Wall Street, through securitization, finished the job by taking away the thrifts' primary business of home lending." Other experts, including Larry Fink, who structured the first multi-class privately issued MBS, reflected that while securitization filled a need, it also likely made the thrift crisis worse.[35]

In 1983, Richard Pratt resigned from the Bank Board. Prior to his departure, he was said to have resolved hundreds of troubled thrifts. Some experts considered these resolutions to be merely accounting cover-ups. After leaving government service, he took a job as an executive at Merrill Lynch, selling mortgage-backed securities to S&Ls. Eventually, he became chairman of Merrill Lynch Mortgage Capital. In his new role at Merrill, he said, "We will be bringing Wall Street services to the mortgage market and to the thrift industry."[36]

American S&L's World Transformed

The residential mortgage market had significantly changed since American Savings and Loan's predecessor was established in 1922. The largest changes had come about in the 1970s, during the thrifty Mark Taper's leadership. American Savings and Loan was once a steady business: taking in deposits, making residential mortgage loans, and holding them it its portfolio. It was at one time a community-oriented enterprise, the outgrowth of a social movement focused on helping local families finance homes. Like the other S&Ls, American Savings and Loan was once operated by frugal people who were focused on earning a decent profit through conservative lending and low overhead.

Now, with wild fluctuations in interest rates, money market fund competition, the growth of the secondary market, the introduction of MBSs, the explosion of brokered deposits, and the massive deregulation and desupervision, the S&L industry had attracted new types of leaders. The change was dramatic and fast, drawing in the overconfident and the criminal. And, should the leading S&L lenders fail, waiting in the wings to take center stage were the clever bankers running the Wall Street securitization machine.

The differences were not abstract; they were very tangible for American Savings and Loan, the thrift that would purchase Leonard and Harriet Nobelman's mortgage in 1984. George Bailey would not have recognized what building and loans like his had become. Mark Taper, the one-time leader of American Savings and Loan, was the George Bailey type. In 1983, he cashed out and Charlie Knapp took over.

6

The Red Baron of Finance

Charlie Knapp entered the savings and loan (S&L) industry in California in the mid-1970s, around the same time that Danny Faulkner, enabled by Texas deregulation, took control of Empire Savings and Loan to fund his condo-building scheme. The new industry atmosphere suited Charlie Knapp. Dubbed the "Red Baron of finance," he enjoyed stunt flying vintage airplanes and was contemptuous of old-style conservative lending. After hopping from job to job at a brokerage house, investment bank, and home construction firm, Knapp finally landed a leadership position when he took over Budget Industries in 1975 from its founder, Charles Offer. It was through this transaction that Knapp eventually assumed control of American Savings and Loan, the institution that would buy the Nobelmans' mortgage in the summer of 1984.[1]

Budget was a NYSE-listed holding company incorporated in Delaware in 1968, but the underlying consumer lending business had been started up in the Los Angeles area and headquartered there since 1937. A few years before he sold to Knapp, Offer had been a victim of a foiled kidnapping. He told police that his abductors struck him with a tire iron, tied him up, stuffed him into a large canvas bag, and locked him in the trunk of his car. They drove from

Offer's Hollywood Hills home to an empty lot and when they opened the trunk, he remained still, pretending to be dead. They believed his ruse and fled. Offer also had faced angry shareholders who tried to gain seats on the Budget board of directors. Then, at age sixty-three, he had a massive heart attack that required triple bypass surgery. With these stresses, he was ready to leave. He sold his stock to Knapp, who acquired a controlling interest in Budget and replaced Offer as chairman and CEO.[2]

Historically, Budget Industries—known as Budget Finance Plan—made loans to people with limited disposable income, financing everything from home appliances to used cars and vacations. This was a developing market in 1937, as neither banks nor thrifts typically extended credit for these purchases and the first credit cards were still more than a decade in the future. For people who could not get a loan from a retail store or credit union, consumer finance companies offered a better option than a pawnshop or neighborhood loan shark. Budget expanded after World War II to locations across the country. As a sideline, in 1973, it acquired a small California S&L, State Savings and Loan Association of Stockton.[3]

Knapp saw the Budget Industries holding company as a potential financial supermarket, a legal way to provide a broad array of services to customers under one roof; Budget owned both a thrift (State Savings) and a bank (Century Bank), which in several locations shared the same lobby and customers. With the holding company structure, the profits earned by Budget's State Savings subsidiary were passed on as dividends. Budget could use this money to pay expenses, including executive salaries, and any profit was then paid out to Budget shareholders. This would take the form of either dividends or an appreciation in stock price.[4]

Because State Savings had a corporate parent, there was an additional layer of regulation. At the thrift level, State Savings was subject to regulations designed to promote its safety and soundness, protect its depositors, and protect the Federal Savings and Loan Insurance Corporation (FSLIC) deposit insurance fund. At the top level, Budget was subject to both state and federal laws to protect its shareholders. Under state corporate law, the board of directors was supposed to oversee the actions taken by senior officers—Offer, and later Knapp. And both the directors and officers owed fiduciary duties of care and loyalty to Budget's shareholders. In addition, Budget was subject to federal securities laws, as well as the regulations and oversight of the Securities and Exchange Commission (SEC). These federal securities laws and rules required, for example, quarterly and annual disclosures of Budget's financial condition—which, in turn, created potential liability for any false or misleading statements.[5]

Rapid Growth

Shortly after Charlie Knapp arrived in the early 1970s, State Savings had $433 million in assets. He tripled them by 1979. After interest rates spiked in the 1980s due to the Fed's Saturday Night Massacre, many of Knapp's competitors retreated from mortgage lending, but State Savings aggressively made more loans. These were not just residential mortgages, but the far riskier and more lucrative commercial real estate development loans known as acquisition-development-construction (ADC) loans.[6]

Like the leaders of Empire Savings and Loan, Knapp would signal his ambitions by rebranding: he changed the parent company's name from Budget Industries to the Financial Corporation of America (FCA). Then he set about beefing up State Savings. State Savings became FCA's main business operation, and the result of this aggressive lending was the tremendous growth of FCA's assets year after year. To fund the origination of these loans, someone had to go out and attract deposits. Like Spencer Blain at Empire, Knapp sought investors for short-term, jumbo CDs by paying about two percentage points above the competition. But instead of relying on outside brokers, he used two hundred highly commissioned salespeople, stationed in boiler rooms across the country, dialing for dollars. This fast growth allegedly was achieved by cutting corners; a number of Knapp's employees later claimed that they were encouraged to engage in aggressive and misleading practices to attract deposits.[7]

Many of the CDs deposited with State Savings were not fully insured by the FSLIC, making this funding even hotter and more prone to being withdrawn in large amounts at the slightest whiff of trouble. In the short term, the approach was incredibly successful. In 1982, under Knapp's direction, State Savings brought in more than $2.2 billion in new deposits. Ninety percent were short-term jumbo CDs. What came in easily could depart just as quickly, and this amount of hot money put State Savings in a precarious position. Knapp was borrowing short and lending long: State Savings was actually paying more on some deposits than it was earning on its mortgages.[8]

Knapp was gambling that interest rates would drop and he could sell the mortgages at a profit. If this did not happen, or if the hot money providers decided to leave when their CDs matured, State Savings would have difficulty providing them with their cash. The cash was tied up in long-term residential and commercial real estate development ADC loans. Even if these had been high-quality, if sold under pressure, they would result in losses. With billions in funding, State Savings originated new loans but also turned to the wholesale market to buy them. In 1981 and 1982, the thrift added more than $3 billion in loans to its balance sheet. As a result, State Savings' parent, FCA, reported assets of $6.6 billion by the end of 1982, growing from a mere $433 million in less than a decade.[9]

FCA also reported impressive profits from its American Savings and Loan operation. Even when the rest of the industry was reporting losses, in 1982, it showed a 33 percent return on equity. Many were skeptical about the veracity of this reporting and questioned the sustainability of Knapp's business plan. Knapp claimed to be making money on origination and loan-servicing fees. Yet if interest rates continued to climb, he would be in the same bind that trapped other S&Ls, losing more money on the spread between mortgage income and deposit and other funding costs. Still, investors went along for the ride. FCA's common stock price was up to $17 per share by the spring of 1981, up from 88 cents (adjusted for stock splits) since Knapp joined the corporation.[10]

Interest Rate Gamble

After the Fed's Saturday Night Massacre in October 1979, interest rates fluctuated dramatically, and Charlie Knapp decided to gamble. By bringing on loans when rates were rising, he was betting that the rates would come down and that State Savings' portfolio of new loans would then pay higher relative rates. Skeptics observed that it was not possible to make or buy up as many loans as he did without taking on a lot of bad ones. Many suspected poor underwriting, sloppy record keeping, and false appraisals of the underlying real estate.[11]

Also, it was common sense that real estate developers willing to pay extra fees to get an ADC loan at higher-than-market rates had a higher likelihood of failure. Often, such a borrower was willing to pay more only after being passed up by wiser underwriters; the additional fees and interest would be a very high-debt service. A good percentage of such projects were doomed. But Knapp must have believed that even if many borrowers became delinquent or defaulted, State Savings would make up those losses if rates fell, as he could sell off some of the loans at a profit. Some of the development loans on State Savings' books paid fixed interest of 24 percent. If rates fell to 11 percent, for example, they would be extremely salable. Even if he kept them in the portfolio, these loans would create a huge spread once the rates he had to pay to depositors fell. He was betting with taxpayer-insured deposits and apparently with little concern that borrowers might be getting into debt way over their heads.[12]

New Sources of Income

Another high-risk income generator was Knapp's origination fee and commitment fee business. Developers would pay fees in exchange for State Savings' commitment to make a loan in the future, should the developer ask for one. In addition, other S&Ls and banks paid fees for State Savings' commitment to purchase loans from them in the future. The fees it earned for these loan commitments ranged from 2 percent to 4 percent of the amount of the future loan. In other words, State Savings might charge $400,000 in exchange for the promise to make a $10 million loan when called on to do so. These fees represented as much as 25 percent of FCA's income from 1980 through 1982.[13]

This looked like free money until the day those fee payers—perhaps many at once—decided to exercise their options. At that point, real money had to be available to extend credit or buy up loans. If many demands for loans hit at the same time, State Savings would not have the money to make or buy them. Sensible accounting would have required commitment and origination fees to be recognized over the entire loan commitment period—not booked up front. And it would have been sensible for State Savings to set aside appropriate loan-loss reserves in the event that loans did not perform. But underestimating the likelihood of a future commitment or loss was a tactic. Recognizing big fees up front, and maintaining lower-than-necessary reserves would make State Savings—and its parent, FCA—look healthier and stronger than they actually were. They made Charlie Knapp and his team look smart and successful, entitled to draw big salaries and bonuses. Knapp was essentially sacrificing sustainable health for short-term gain.[14]

Knapp could never have grown so quickly or taken on so much risk without liberalized state and federal laws. After Reagan signed the Garn-St. Germain Act that radically deregulated S&Ls, California passed the Nolan Act to help keep its state-chartered thrifts. Under the Nolan Act, Knapp could use all of State Savings' insured deposits and other sources of funds to make unlimited ADC loans. Previously, these real estate development loans had been limited to a portion of assets. In addition, after State Savings' federal regulator, the Home Loan Bank Board, permitted unlimited brokered deposits in 1980, many thrifts relied heavily on hot money.[15]

This liberalized environment allowed aggressive growth, but Knapp's practices were so extreme that he drew attention to himself. As early as 1981, his enterprise was under close scrutiny by both state regulators and his local federal regulator, the district Home Loan Bank of San Francisco. On more than one occasion, State Savings earned nearly the worst possible scores, which, according to the guidelines then in place, indicated that it required close supervision and "drastic corrective action appears necessary." Threats of a cease and desist order loomed.[16]

Between 1981 and early 1983, the regulators had a series of concerns about State Savings. This included its dependence on brokered deposits, accounting treatment for loan origination and commitment fees, poor underwriting practices, low-quality loans, inflated property appraisals, low loan loss reserves, and low net worth. Other red flags included directing lucrative contracts toward businesses owned by insiders. Even the Fed was concerned. Preston Martin, vice chairman of the Fed, asked to be kept in the loop regarding Knapp's activities. Martin worried that as "lender of last resort," the Fed might one day have to step in and rescue the S&L.[17]

In late April 1983, the SEC weighed in, investigating FCA's financial statements. The SEC was concerned about the way FCA had accounted for State Savings' delinquent loans and sales of real estate it had obtained through foreclosures. Trading in FCA stock was suspended until May 2, when the company restated its earnings for the 1982 fiscal year. After the restatement, instead of showing a record profit of $36.7 million, the S&L holding company reported earnings of only $27.2 million. But things were even worse than that. The SEC required State Savings to bring back on the books the $427 million in unpaid interest, delinquent loans, and foreclosed properties that it had believed the S&L had not truly sold. According to an SEC commissioner, who later singled out State Savings in a public speech, State Savings would purport to sell bad loans and real estate by finding someone who wanted financing for a different property then lending that "buyer" enough money at below market rates to pay for both the desired property and the undesired assets. This was a classic cash-for-trash scheme.[18]

An Urge to Merge

In the midst of these troubles, in 1983, Charlie Knapp negotiated a deal with Mark Taper to merge FCA with Taper's First Charter Financial Corporation. First Charter, Taper's holding company, owned and operated American Savings and Loan Association of Beverly Hills, a thrift with a federal charter dating back to 1885. With the merger of the holding companies, their respective thrifts would also become one. Though Knapp's tactics at FCA had drawn the attention of federal and state regulators, the merger with First Charter was approved and the deal closed in August 1983. Some regulators hoped that by merging with a healthier, more conservative firm, Knapp would somehow reform his ways. It was a comfortable exit for Taper. The First Charter board of directors allowed him to walk away with nearly $300 million in cash, unlike the other owners of First Charter common stock, who were given stock in FCA.[19]

After the merger, the combined thrift, now called American Savings and Loan Association of Stockton (what we have been referring to as American Savings and Loan), had about $20 billion in assets. Charlie Knapp's holdings in FCA were worth nearly $40 million. Between the end of 1983 and mid-1984, Knapp grew American's assets from $22 billion to about $34 billion. This involved bringing in an average of $1 billion per month in deposits and using the money to originate and buy mortgages and other assets. In keeping with the times, some of those assets were mortgage bonds. At that rate of growth, American Savings and Loan could have swallowed all of Empire Savings and Loan (which peaked at around $332 million) in a week. Knapp even thought FCA could purchase and take over American Express, a New York Stock Exchange–listed company, and he began buying up shares.[20]

Knapp was still making his interest rate gamble. Jonathan Gray, a respected Wall Street analyst with Sanford C. Bernstein & Co., looked closely at FCA, and in December 1983, after the merger, issued a 150-page report recommending that investors purchase the stock only if they believed interest rates would fall. Gray was concerned about the quality of the nearly $5 billion in loans that State Savings had brought on in 1983, mostly before the merger. He was also bothered by the large number of problem loans from earlier years; the loss ratio for loans added to the State Savings portfolio in 1980 was nearly 19 percent. Gray thought losses could be even higher.[21]

Knapp's desire to buy American Express was seemingly part of a general ambition to use FCA stock as currency to take over other firms. To make this possible, the stock price had to stay high, and to keep it soaring, he needed to give the appearance of growth. In early 1984, he decided to grow by buying mortgage-backed securities (MBSs). The MBSs he bought were certificates issued by the Government National Mortgage Association (Ginnie Mae), the government agency that pooled together mortgages that were insured by the Veterans Administration (VA) or the Federal Housing Administration (FHA). Buying these MBSs would be easier for Knapp than originating or buying up mortgage loans, with all the paperwork that entailed.[22]

To fund his growth, Knapp would first bring in brokered deposits and use that money to buy Ginnie Maes. Then he engaged in a two-legged transaction known as a "repurchase agreement," or "repo." American Savings and Loan would sell the Ginnie Maes it had just purchased to a Wall Street broker in exchange for cash equal to slightly less than the value of the Ginnie Maes; and at that same moment, the thrift would agree to buy back substantially similar Ginnie Maes from the broker at a specified future date at an agreed-upon price plus interest. This repo transaction was similar to a collateralized loan, with the Wall Street broker taking the Ginnie Maes as collateral. The only difference was that if the loan was paid off, the broker might return similar—but not the same—collateral. American Savings and Loan would use the cash it received from the first leg of the repo to purchase more securities, then convert these into cash through another two-legged repo transaction. It would keep making these transactions, known as dollar-roll repurchase agreements, to grow a large portfolio of securities. Ideally, if interest rates cooperated, the thrift would make money.[23]

The regulators would later argue that these repurchase agreements should have been treated as purchases and sales and not loans. This was because the Ginnie Maes that were used as repo collateral with Wall Street counterparties were not the exact ones it bought back. On its financial statements, FCA failed to show the associated gains and losses. As documented in a federal court opinion, the Arthur Andersen accounting firm apparently approved this accounting method for about $2 billion worth of Ginnie Mae purchases. James Cirona, president of the Home Loan Bank of San Francisco, which supervised American Savings and Loan, and the SEC, which had oversight over FCA, took notice of the inaccurate accounting.[24]

Knapp used this repo technique as well as aggressive lending and acquisitions to grow. Between 1976 and 1984, Knapp grew his S&L

business from $433 million in assets to about $34 billion, or that is what FCA's financial statements claimed. In retrospect, there were plenty of reasons to doubt the accuracy of those statements, including concerns already raised about loan-loss reserves. Another practice also pumped up asset values. Apparently, American Savings and Loan also engaged in so-called "cash-for-trash" transactions, something that was done at State Savings when Knapp was in charge. This was common among corrupt S&Ls to help cover up nonperforming loans.

At American Savings and Loan, these were fraudulent loan flips that looked much like Danny Faulkner and Empire Savings and Loan's fraudulent land flips. They were pretty simple and involved unloading bad loans on new borrowers. For example, as described by William K. Black, who at that time was litigation director for the Federal Home Loan Bank Board, an S&L might have lent $60 million to a developer to construct an office building in a saturated market. There would be trouble leasing space and thus paying back the $60 million. Instead of waiting for a default and thus recording a loss, the S&L would require a new borrower who sought just $1 million (perhaps to build a restaurant) to instead borrow $80 million. As a condition of the loan, the new borrower would immediately pay $78 million to the S&L to buy the doomed $60 million office building loan. The S&L could show an $18 million gain. The new borrower would have the $1 million he sought for his building, an extra million dollars in his pocket, and the worthless office building loan that would pay him little to nothing. Thus, the new $80 million loan on the S&L's books was trash; the restaurant borrower could not pay it back. And it would default unless it could be flipped again. It was a classic Ponzi scheme.[25]

Too Big to Fail

Charlie Knapp and his wife, Brooke, were both pilots. Just months before Charlie took over American Savings and Loan, in February 1983, Brooke set a world speed record for flight around the world in a light jet, a Learjet 35A named The American Dream. Meanwhile, her husband operated a high-flying thrift in which crashing was always a risk and FSLIC deposit insurance mitigated any fear of heights. The taxpayer-backed safety net encouraged depositors to get on board his dangerous S&L. By law, the Federal Home Loan Banks could provide liquidity even to insolvent thrifts. And the Federal Reserve was also there for support.[26]

Knapp seemed to believe that he should and would remain in charge during a liquidity crisis, during which time he could borrow billions from the district Home Loan Bank. He expected that his interest rate gamble would pay off if interest rates fell in 1984. Conversely, if he bet incorrectly and losses erased American's net worth, he expected that the government would have to offer a bailout. American was both large and interconnected. Knapp knew that coming up with the money to pay off the insured depositors, while a big concern, was actually the least of the government's problems. There was not enough money in the FSLIC fund to cover all of American's deposits. Yet that was the tip of the iceberg; American owed billions of dollars not just to insured depositors but also to uninsured depositors—and to other creditors, including Wall Street brokers. If the government let American fail, its collapse would threaten the entire financial system. During a meeting with regulators in June 1984, Knapp declared: "We're too big to fail. If we go down, we'll take the whole system with us."[27]

It is often said that the phrase "too big to fail" was first used in connection with the May 1984 bailout of Continental Illinois National Bank and Trust Company. Continental was then about the sixth-largest bank in the United States. It grew rapidly between 1976 and 1981, from assets of about $21 billion to a peak of around $45 billion, by relying on wholesale funding and other hot money. Regularly, it had to borrow billions of dollars in the overnight repo market. These overnight loans would have to be paid back and then remade in the morning, or "rolled over." The refusal to roll over these overnight and short-term loans would crush the bank. In May, it faced a "run," not of the type familiar from the Great Depression with customers standing in lines on the sidewalk, but instead an institutional run.[28]

Instead of allowing the bank to collapse, the Federal Deposit Insurance Corporation (FDIC) decided to save not just the insured account holders but all depositors, even above the $100,000 limit, as well as to save general creditors. Without the FDIC's action, they might have been wiped out or received pennies on the dollar. By deeming the bank "essential," the FDIC could exercise its authority to spend unlimited amounts to rescue the institution and bail out its creditors. Though Fed chairman Paul Volcker objected, FDIC chairman William Isaac eventually won him over. Isaac believed that the banking system could not have withstood letting the uninsured depositors and general creditors lose their money. In that group were about 2,500 small banks that channeled their own deposits into Continental. Many would have collapsed if the FDIC had not protected them. Ultimately, the rescue of Continental Illinois cost FDIC more than $4.5 billion.[29]

Of course, the question arose as to whether Continental's primary regulator, the Office of the Comptroller of the Currency (OCC), should have intervened many years earlier, when Continental first showed signs of trouble. In testimony before the House Banking Committee in the fall of 1984, C. T. Connover, the head of the OCC, said that during periods of rapid growth, financial firms will show profits and thus it would have been "inappropriate" to hold them back. Separately, Charles Partee, a Fed governor said imposing "prudential restraints is meddlesome" when banks were growing because "to hold them back is just not going to be acceptable."[30]

At those hearings, held during three days in September and October 1984, "TBTF" and "too big to fail" were familiar expressions used to refer both to Continental Illinois *and* to American Savings and Loan's holding company, FCA. Congressman Stewart McKinney of Connecticut said: "With all due respect, I think seriously, we have a new kind of bank. And today there is another type created. We found it in the thrift institutions, and now we have given approval for a $1 billion brokerage deal to Financial Corporation of America. Mr. Chairman, let us not bandy words. We have a new kind of bank. It's called too big to fail. TBTF, and it's a wonderful bank."[31]

Many point to McKinney's words as the moment the phrase was coined. But Knapp apparently said "too big to fail" four months earlier, in June, and it was likely uttered behind the scenes in May, during the deliberations over whether to bail out Continental.[32]

In June 1984, when Knapp declared that American Savings and Loan was "too big to fail," he was angling for approval to borrow more than $200 million through a debenture offering and use the proceeds to buy back a quarter of FCA's stock. His threat was communicated to Bank Board chairman Ed Gray, who was already frustrated with him. In late June, when the Bank Board rejected the application, FCA canceled the debt offering. Big money managers began pulling their brokered deposits from its American Savings and Loan subsidiary. Analyst Jonathan Gray, who was threatened with litigation by FCA, was speaking out to the press about its troubles. Then, to compound the crisis, buyers of loan commitments exercised their options, demanding that loans be extended or purchased. The multibillion-dollar run on American Savings and Loan began.[33]

The Run

Bart Dzivi, the new lawyer for the San Francisco Home Loan Bank who was only partially rested after taking the bar exam in late July 1984, headed to American Savings and Loan in Stockton to count collateral. CEO Charlie Knapp headed for a yacht in the Caribbean, where he attempted to convince a *Wall Street Journal* reporter during an interview by radio telephone that the run on American Savings and Loan was not what it seemed. He claimed that some new money was coming in and that the run was voluntary; he had decided to let deposits go because interest rates were too high to pay. Meanwhile, American Savings and Loan's state regulator, Larry Taggart, commissioner of the California Department of Savings and Loan, was unreachable, apparently on a camping trip in the Sierra National Forest.[34]

The federal regulators had an eye on FCA. The SEC, with a mission to protect investors, forced FCA to restate its earnings. Knapp waited until the mid-August deadline to reveal FCA's actual numbers—which included, in the second quarter of 1984, a loss of more than $107 million instead of the previously reported $31 million profit. Knapp, fresh off the yacht with a glowing tan, tried to calm investors during an August press conference. But that day, FCA's stock closed at $5 per share, down from a recent peak of $32.75. More than $6.8 billion in deposits flowed out in the run. American was in a liquidity crisis. Without the support of the San Francisco Home Loan Bank, American would have failed.[35]

The Federal Home Loan Bank Board had no intention of keeping Knapp around while it rescued this California thrift. The lawyers at the Home Loan Bank of San Francisco found language in the Federal Home Loan Bank Act that authorized them to make loans to thrifts contingent upon any conditions the Bank Board prescribed. One mandatory condition they imposed was Charlie Knapp's departure. The board of directors at FCA (the holding company for American Savings and Loan) approved a $2 million exit payment for Knapp. Reflecting on Knapp's tenure, banking analyst Allan Bortel said, "He won the rate bet several years ago . . . this time he lost. Let's face it: he was stunt flying through the S&L industry."[36]

In August 1984, the Bank Board encouraged the FCA board to hire William Popejoy as the new CEO. Popejoy had been president of the Federal Home Loan Mortgage Corporation (Freddie Mac) before leaving in 1974 to work for Mark Taper. He left that position in 1980, bridling under Taper's controlling ways. Now he was back.[37]

In around four months, Popejoy stopped the run on American through a combination of Home Loan Bank liquidity support, smart tactics, and good luck. He brought in $2 billion in deposits and by the end of the year was able to pay down about $740 million of the nearly $4 billion in loans outstanding from the Home Loan Bank. Then interest rates went down, helping out the S&L's balance sheet. But in time, when Popejoy closely examined the enterprise, he saw that it was in worse shape than he had imagined. The Home Loan Bank of San Francisco closely supervised Popejoy. This bought everyone some time. While Popejoy worked to right the S&L, the fallout from the Knapp years continued.[38]

The Bank Board's Attempted Reregulation

Even before watching the film that showed the evidence of the Faulkner I-30 condo development scam in mid-March 1984, Bank Board chairman Ed Gray had begun to reverse the deregulation cycle and tighten up on the insured thrifts. In November 1983, just months after President Reagan appointed him, Gray showed the beginnings of a transformation. The Bank Board required that new thrifts have a minimum net worth of 7 percent, meaning they could only borrow $93 for every $100 in loans and other assets they held. This affected all federally chartered thrifts and all state-chartered thrifts that wished to have access to FSLIC insurance. It was aimed at slowing down the rapid clip at which California Savings and Loan commissioner Larry Taggart was approving new California charters.[39]

Coordinating with FDIC chairman Bill Isaac, Bank Board chairman Gray attempted to cut back on brokered deposits. The Bank Board and the FDIC jointly issued a rule that limited the amount of deposit insurance to $100,000 per broker per depository institution. But a deposit broker and a Wall Street lobbying organization successfully challenged the new rule in federal court, arguing that the agencies had exceeded their authority under the Federal Deposit Insurance Company Act. Gray was more successful a year later. In January 1985, the Bank Board limited brokered deposits to 5 percent for insured thrifts that were below their net worth requirements. It also limited the amount of direct investments, such as investing in junk bonds, for all insured thrifts. To improve oversight, Gray transferred his federal examiners to the twelve regional banks, hoping to rein in the S&L industry. Before a thrift industry audience, Gray suggested that FSLIC insurance premiums paid by S&Ls be increased relative to risk and low net worth. He then took his concerns about "go-go" thrifts and their risky lending to Congress, hoping for legislation that would restrict the thrifts to narrower asset powers.[40]

Meanwhile, the FSLIC fund had been decimated. The General Accounting Office (GAO) reported that the fund ran a $6.3 billion deficit in 1986. Gray asked Congress for permission to borrow $15 billion in the bond markets to recapitalize the fund, though experts believed it needed closer to $30 billion. Congress and the industry resisted. The U.S. League for Savings Institutions (the League), the thrift lobbying organization, wanted just $5 billion added to the fund. The more money in the fund, the more ailing thrifts would be shuttered. The largest, most insolvent thrifts lobbied hard to resist the fund's recapitalization. Though they were showing losses in income, they had an easier time attracting deposits than their healthier competitors because they paid higher interest rates. The so-called zombie thrifts, those with low to negative net worth, were thus allowed to stay open and grow. After a date to vote on the recapitalization bill was set, in late 1986, Congressman Jim Wright—who was in line to be Speaker of the House—put it on hold. Several of his large contributors and campaign fund-raisers owned S&Ls and did not like the pressure they were facing from Gray's enforcement team. In parallel, Senator Alan Cranston held the Senate version of the bill.[41]

President Reagan did not re-nominate Gray to chair the Bank Board, so, in June 1987, when his term expired, Gray departed. He was likely relieved to be gone. He later testified that: "Every single day I served as chairman of the Federal Home Loan Bank Board, the League was in control of the Congress as an institution."[42]

The man Reagan appointed to replace him, Danny Wall, diligently undermined the reregulation Gray had begun. For example, a rule to replace the loose Regulatory Accounting Practices (RAP) accounting standards with the more transparent Generally Accepted Accounting Principles (GAAP) was supposed to go into effect. Wall postponed it for nearly two years. The more truthful accounting requirement did not arrive until early January 1987, just weeks before Reagan left office. Even with the misleading practices still in place, there was no hiding the reality that the S&Ls were insolvent and a day of reckoning would arrive. However, Wall downplayed the magnitude of the crisis. In August 1987, Congress at last approved and Reagan signed the Competitive Equality Banking Act, which recapitalized the FSLIC fund, creating a new government corporation that was authorized to borrow $10.8 billion for the FSLIC. Yet only about one-third of this could be used over any twelve-month period. The legislation also kept the zombies alive with forbearance plans. Forbearance meant deliberate inaction by regulators when they were entitled to take steps against a violator. The regulators were ordered to postpone any S&L closures.[43]

Popejoy's Run

Bill Popejoy had a short honeymoon period. He conducted a close internal review of FCA's American Savings and Loan subsidiary and decided that, given the S&L's terrible condition, he could not shrink it. Instead of reducing its size and minimizing its connections to other firms in order to mitigate the "too big to fail" problem, he decided to make the opposite move. In the summer of 1986, Ed Gray verbally approved Popejoy's plan to grow FCA to $38 billion. Later that summer, at the San Francisco Home Loan Bank, Jim Cirona said no and Popejoy was then limited to growing FCA to $34 billion.[44]

Like his predecessor, Charlie Knapp, Popejoy decided to grow by loading up on mortgage-backed securities financed through volatile repurchase agreement (repo) funding. But unlike Knapp, Popejoy used a standard repo that, because it bought back the exact same collateral, could be treated as a loan. These transactions presented risk; if the value of the MBS fell—for example, if interest rates rose—American would have to post more collateral. Popejoy also became involved in complex derivative transactions to hedge interest rate risks.[45]

Losing confidence during his final month chairing the Bank Board, Ed Gray had hired Salomon Brothers to look for a buyer for American Savings and Loan. In early 1987, the Salomon team, which worked for mortgage backed security (MBS) pioneer Lewis Ranieri, took a close look at FCA's financials and spotted trouble. Accounting under the liberal RAP rules showed that American Savings and Loan had a positive net worth, but there were actually huge unrealized losses. Ranieri was informed that these losses were at least $7 billion. The team began referring to the S&L as Chernobyl. When it issued its annual report that January, FCA reported a $468-million loss for the previous year. It showed a negative net worth of $387 million. Its stock was now trading at less than $2 per share. In summer 1987, interest rates rose, and American Savings and Loan faced collateral calls from Wall Street. The billions of dollars in MBS that it had purchased under Popejoy had fallen in value and would show big losses if sold.[46]

Based on its negative net worth alone, the S&L should have been out of business. Since 1984, it had never met its regulatory capital requirements, meaning its net worth was not high enough, even under RAP. It needed about $1 billion more to be in compliance. Yet the Bank Board did not shut it down. Instead, it had issued repeated "comfort letters" to American Savings and Loan, promising to take no action against it simply due to its inadequate capital. Those comfort letters were the only things keeping Wall Street brokers from pulling repo and other wholesale funding from the S&L. And, it needed those institutional funds as it had only about $17 billion in deposits.[47]

In September 1987, FCA settled charges with the SEC that since 1980, under both Knapp and Popejoy, the holding company had inflated its earnings. FCA also sought to settle securities fraud lawsuits brought by shareholders, but it had set aside only $35 million to pay the $400 million in claims. At the end of 1987, it had a negative net worth of $163 million. By January 1988, Popejoy was rebuffed when he sought $1.5 billion in government-loan guarantees. In the spring of 1988, Bank Board chairman Danny Wall did not renew the comfort letter. So the repo lenders began to run. In an attempt to stop the run, the Bank Board took extreme action. The Bank Board decided to guarantee all depositors and general creditors. This was a repeat of what the FDIC did with Continental Illinois four years earlier. In the end, Charlie Knapp was right. American Savings and Loan was too big to fail. Even with the Bank Board's guarantee, however, creditors and depositors still continued to run with their money. The insured depositors already had a guarantee through FSLIC insurance, but they were nervous.[48]

Like his predecessor Ed Gray, Danny Wall was determined to sell American Savings and Loan. The S&L owed depositors and other creditors $30 billion, but its assets were worth several billion less. Thus, if it were liquidated, the asset sales would not raise enough cash to pay them off. He estimated that the FSLIC fund would need $3.3 billion to liquidate American Savings and Loan and pay off just the insured depositors, and now there was an even bigger guarantee. He thought he could do better for the taxpayers with a sale. However, the Federal Home Loan Bank of San Francisco was no longer patient; it had been four years since the initial run. In August 1988, it decided to cut off American Savings and Loan's life support. It would lend no more money to the troubled thrift. It also informed the Bank Board in D.C. that it would not renew a $200 million advance when it came due at the end of the month unless the FSLIC guaranteed it.[49]

The end had come. Bank Board chairman Wall could not risk a run that could deplete the FSLIC fund. On September 5, 1988, the Bank Board appointed the FSLIC as receiver for American Savings and Loan. The following day, all of its assets and liabilities were transferred into a newly chartered federal S&L also named American Savings. Bill Popejoy resigned as chairman of FCA, the S&L's holding company, and that same week FCA filed for bankruptcy protection under Chapter 11 of the Bankruptcy Code. The following year, this restructuring bankruptcy was converted to a liquidation. Eventually, bondholders and other creditors of FCA were paid only ten cents on the dollar for their claims. Now with American Savings and Loan's assets and liabilities moved into the federally chartered American Savings, the Bank Board announced that a buyer had been found—in Texas.[50]

7

The Bailout

Robert Muse Bass did not like to see his name in the newspaper. The soft-spoken forty-year-old billionaire from Fort Worth generally declined reporters' requests for interviews. As a child, Bass and his three brothers had come into a great deal of money. When their great-uncle, oil baron Sid William Richardson, died a bachelor, Robert's father, Perry Bass, maintained a piece of Richardson's businesses. Though most of Richardson's estate went to a charitable foundation, he left his nephews $2.8 million each. The brothers invested together to grow their inheritance into a collective fortune of more than $4 billion by the early 1980s. Led by the oldest brother, also named Sid, Bass Brothers Enterprises would invest in undervalued firms and help management make changes to improve the stock performance.[1]

Around 1983, Robert struck out on his own, eventually forming the Robert M. Bass Group. Stories of his business exploits regularly appeared in financial journals. This was in part due to the firm's size and notoriety—the $390 million sale of the Plaza Hotel to Donald Trump made headlines—and partly due to Bass's wealth. The Bass family was thought to be the fourth-wealthiest in America, trailing only the Mars, Newhouse, and Walton clans. Through his partnership,

Bass began buying up troubled companies and restoring them to health. American Savings was one of his purchases.[2]

With about $30 billion in assets in 1988, one million depositors, and more than 180 branches, American Savings and Loan was considered the crown jewel among the insolvent thrifts. Despite its high value, instead of engaging in competitive bidding, Federal Home Loan Bank Board chairman Danny Wall gave Bass's group several months of exclusive bargaining rights. No one else could bid.[3]

The negotiation over American Savings and Loan dragged on through the 1988 presidential election. Some believed that the Bush campaign wanted the savings and loan (S&L) industry's troubles hidden until after the vote. In the end—at a deal struck at the legendary Willard Hotel—Wall gave away the store. In exchange for about $500 million, Bass's group was promised federal government guarantees against losses and additional tax breaks to rescue American Savings and Loan. Even by the standards of other rushed arrangements, it was a very sweet deal. Bass's group paid just about 3.6 cents for each dollar of the $14 billion in deposits the group would control. For solvent thrifts, the market rate was 5 to 6 cents.[4]

The Bass Group (eventually called Keystone Holdings Partners, L.P.) would use a few private entities it created, including Keystone Holdings, Inc., for the acquisition. Before the purchase, two new federal thrifts were chartered for the Bass Group to purchase: one called American Savings Bank, the other called New West Federal Savings and Loan. American Savings Bank was the "good bank," acquiring the performing loans and other good assets from American Savings and Loan and keeping the deposits and other liabilities. New West was the "bad bank" taking the poorly performing assets. These toxic assets included billions of dollars of mortgage-backed securities that had been financed with brokered deposits and repo agreements and that were showing losses. New West's liabilities included a note, a promise to pay the "good" American Savings Bank $8 billion, which it would accomplish by selling off the bad assets. However, anticipating that the asset sales would be insufficient, the Federal Savings and Loan Insurance Corporation (FSLIC) agreed to guarantee the note. This note from New West was treated as an

$8 billion asset on American Savings Bank's books. If and when the bad assets were sold and failed to generate $8 billion, the FSLIC would make up the difference. As part of the deal, the FSLIC was given warrants entitling it to purchase up to 30 percent of the stock in Keystone, Inc., one of the parent corporations. Under complex agreements, the FSLIC agreed to treat both the $8 billion note and the warrants as equity capital for the good bank. This meant that American Savings Bank could have a lower net worth than the law now required, allowing more borrowing relative to assets than it would without this agreement.[5]

Wall arranged fourteen deals to sell thirty-four S&L deals in the final weeks of 1988. They were rushed to take advantage of an expiring tax break. Many investor rescuers put no money down at all. Two years later, House Banking Committee investigators concluded that it would have been better for the government to just pay off depositors rather than negotiate the Bass-American Savings Bank deal; the full cost to taxpayers for the deal, as of 1994, was pegged at $5.4 billion.[6]

By 1989, American Savings Bank was turning a profit. In fact, it was the most successful S&L in the country that year, earning profits of $214 million. It had gotten bad loans off its books, and because interest rates fell, it was able to sell a large chunk of its fixed-rate mortgages for a profit and replace them with variable-rate mortgages. And lower interest rates also meant it was able to pay lower rates to depositors.[7]

One of the prized assets on American Savings Bank's books was the $8 billion, ten-year, U.S. government–guaranteed note. This was provided to replace the bad loans inherited from American Savings and Loan. The note paid American Savings Bank above-market interest—beginning at 2.25 percent above the cost of deposits in California and moving to 1.75 percent above—designed to provide a guaranteed $500 million in income for Bass's group by 2000. Another source of income was the $2.2 billion in losses used to offset future income. This was worth about $200 million.[8]

This proved to be one of Robert Bass's most successful ventures. He and his partners apparently had already earned back an estimated

$244 million of their investment by 1991. Reflecting on this transaction and others that were pulled together to save southwestern thrifts, some critics have called them gifts from taxpayers to a few lucky and well-connected investors.[9]

In a streak of all-night deal-making sessions in late December 1988, under Danny Wall's direction, the Bank Board closed several deals, spending a total of nearly $40 billion for the year on hundreds of failed S&Ls. Rushing to meet the January 1 deadline, the regulators were thought to have conceded on many points and awarded sweet deals to favored investors. As bank analyst Jonathan Gray remarked: "I think you see enough evidence to say that the opportunities for profit are enormous." It is interesting that as some of those deals were hammered out, Lewis Ranieri, the father of securitized mortgages, who by then had moved on from Salomon Brothers to start an investment firm called Hyperion Partners to buy up failing S&Ls, was apparently in the room.[10]

The Bush Plan

In February 1989, less than a month after taking office, George H. W. Bush announced his plan to resolve the S&L crisis. That August, Congress passed the Financial Institutions Reform, Recovery, and Enforcement Act (FIRREA) of 1989, a 381-page law embodying most of that plan. On the day he signed the legislation, the president promised that "this legislation will safeguard and stabilize America's financial system and put in place permanent reforms so these problems will never happen again." Though advertised as a mix of rescue and reform, it was heavier on the rescue. The three major purposes of FIRREA were to recapitalize the deposit insurance fund (which was showing as much as a $56 billion deficit), to resolve (meaning to shutter or sell) the remaining five hundred failing thrifts, and to reregulate the thrift industry to avoid another similar debacle in the future. Some of the reregulation involved taking away asset powers from the federal thrifts. For example, they were required to divest all junk bond holdings within five years, and the amount of commercial mortgages they could hold was reduced. The law also required them to have 70 percent of their assets in housing-related investments and to have a minimum net worth of 3 percent. To facilitate the rescue, the law authorized $50 billion to close failed depository institutions.[11]

The law also created a new government entity, the Resolution Trust Corporation (RTC). The RTC was partially funded by a public–private partnership called Resolution Funding Corporation (REFCORP). REFCORP initially raised $30 billion of the authorized $50 billion by issuing government-guaranteed bonds to the public. Most of the remainder was funded by the U.S. Treasury, with a small contribution from the district Home Loan Banks. Eventually, Congress authorized a total of $105 billion for the RTC and another $40 billion to fund thrift resolutions in the southwest. Between 1989 and mid-1995, the RTC closed about 747 thrifts. This was in addition to the 296 thrifts the FSLIC had resolved between 1986 and 1989. As a result, between 1986 and 1995, the industry shrank by 50 percent, to about 1,600 thrifts.

When it closed down thrifts, the RTC had to dispense with its assets. After a year of operation, it decided to pool and securitize the assets—but since government guarantees were not permitted, it had to find other forms of "credit enhancements" so that the purchasers of the securities would not bear the full risk of loss. The RTC partnered with investment banks to bring these securities to market. This was a milestone, as many of the mortgages would not have been "conforming" loans and thus could not have been securitized by the Federal National Mortgage Association (Fannie Mae) and the Federal Home Loan Mortgage Corporation (Freddie Mac) and, for the most part, had not been securitized before. Among these were mortgages on commercial real estate and multifamily homes.[12]

The Keating Five

One of the failed thrifts shut down under the Bush plan was the Lincoln Savings and Loan Association of Irvine, owned by the Phoenix-based, home-construction firm American Continental Corp., the chairman of which was Charles H. Keating Jr. A few years earlier, regulators from the district Home Loan Bank in San Francisco uncovered fraud at Lincoln. It was Bart Dzivi—the young lawyer who had counted collateral in the basement of American Savings and Loan—who spotted the evidence among thousands of pages of Lincoln's documents. Keating had influenced five U.S. senators, whom he gave a total of roughly $1.3 million in gifts, donations, and contributions. They would later be known as the "Keating Five." In 1987, four of these senators met with Bank Board chairman Ed Gray, and then all five met with San Francisco Home Loan Bank Board president Jim Cirona and others. In these meetings, the Keating Five put pressure on the Bank Board to scrap a new regulation that prohibited Lincoln and other thrifts from certain direct investments—such as junk bonds—and to drop the investigation against Lincoln. After a lengthy investigation, the Senate Ethics Committee reprimanded one of the Keating Five, Alan Cranston, for "improper and repugnant" dealings with Keating, finding he had "engaged in an impermissible pattern of conduct in which fund-raising and official activities were substantially linked." Dennis DeConcini and Donald Riegle were found to have engaged in conduct that showed "poor judgment" and "gave the appearance of being improper." John Glenn and John McCain were found only to have "exercised poor judgment." John McCain would later become the Republican nominee for president of the United States.[13]

Keating also had inside help at the D.C. headquarters of the Federal Home Loan Bank System. In 1987, after Gray left and Danny Wall was appointed chairman, Wall took the investigation of Lincoln away from the San Francisco Home Loan Bank. Darrel Dochow—one of Wall's top regulators—also helped. Dochow labored from the inside to delay action against Lincoln Savings in 1987, when the local Federal Home Loan Bank in San Francisco hoped to shut it down. Two years later, in 1989, Lincoln was seized by the government and cost the U.S. taxpayers about $3 billion. Keating pleaded guilty to four counts of bankruptcy and wire fraud after his prior convictions for state securities fraud for selling high-risk bonds to elderly investors and for federal fraud, conspiracy, and racketeering were overturned.[14]

Another important Keating ally in Washington was Alan Greenspan, who was appointed chairman of the Fed by Ronald Reagan in

1987. Two years earlier, in February 1985, Greenspan was paid as a private consultant by a law firm representing Keating to write a supportive letter to regulators at the Federal Home Loan Bank of San Francisco. Greenspan's letter praised Keating and opined that Lincoln Savings and Loan had "transformed itself into a financially strong institution that presents no foreseeable risk to the [FSLIC]." Accordingly, he recommended that Lincoln be permitted to make "new and promising direct investments," such as junk bonds, beyond the then-pending limits. Greenspan later admitted to news reporters that "of course, I'm embarrassed by my failure to foresee what eventually transpired." He admitted that he was "wrong about Lincoln. I was wrong about what they would ultimately do and the problems they would ultimately create." Yet, well before he wrote his letter, Empire Savings and Loan had already failed, and American Savings and Loan had already experienced a $6 billion run. Defensively, Greenspan blamed others for relying on his letter. "How could anyone use any evaluation I would have made in early 1985 as justification more than two years later?"[15]

Modest Reform

Testifying in support of FIRREA, Treasury Secretary Nicholas Brady said, "Two watchwords guided us as we prepared a plan to solve this problem—Never Again." However, the reform offered by the law was mild. The Bank Board was dissolved, replaced by the Office of Thrift Supervision (OTS) within the Treasury and the Federal Housing Finance Board (FHFB). The OTS would charter and regulate thrifts and the FHFB would oversee thrift lending activities. The district Home Loan Banks continued. The FSLIC was also terminated, replaced by the Savings Association Insurance Fund of the Federal Deposit Insurance Corporation (FDIC). This incomplete and uneven regulation had unintended consequences. Mortgage brokers largely remained off the regulatory grid. When reregulation occurred and the regulators started closing down S&Ls, those who were allergic to regulation knew what to do. One key player was Roland Arnall, who ran Long Beach Savings. After regulations tightened on federal and state S&Ls, he decided that his S&L charter wasn't worth it. He told the examiners at the Federal Home Loan Bank in San Francisco that he no longer wanted to be a regulated thrift and literally set the certificate on fire. Arnall kept an urn on a credenza behind his desk. When employees asked what it contained, he told them it was his S&L charter. Then he continued business in the shadows, eventually building Long Beach into one of the largest subprime mortgage lenders in the country. In the first attempt to launch a big subprime mortgage business, the initial players experienced rather dramatic failures, but they would rise from the ashes.[16]

What Ever Happened to . . . ?

By 1990, every single entity that funded the Nobelmans' mortgage back in 1984 received government support and still ultimately failed. In each case, savvy investors picked up the scraps at bargain prices. The failed entities were Murray Savings and Loan, which originated the mortgage; American Savings and Loan, which bought the Nobelmans' mortgage from Murray (but had Murray Mortgage Company keep servicing it); and RepublicBank (later called First RepublicBank), which provided financing to the Miller Condo Corp., the entity that built the Parkway Lane Condominium Complex.

Murray Savings Association failed in 1989. It had $1.44 billion in assets when the FDIC (which had assumed the FSLIC's role) placed it in receivership. The chairman and former CEO of Murray's parent, Murray Financial Corporation, Jack Crozier, stepped down that summer. Several former Murray directors and officers were sued for negligence by the Resolution Trust Corporation (RTC), accused of "imprudent" lending and receiving excessive compensation. This did not stop at least one of them from purchasing a town house from the RTC at $27,000 less than its assessed value. A year later, in June 1990, Lewis Ranieri came to the rescue, buying Murray Savings from the FDIC through his investment firm, Hyperion Partners, using a thrift it owned named United Savings Association of the Southwest. With government assistance, Ranieri's United Savings purchased Murray's branches and $1.15 billion in deposits. In

October 1991, United Savings was merged into a holding company called Bank United. Bank United would become the largest thrift in Texas.[17]

American Savings and Loan, the largest S&L in the country, was supported by the Federal Home Loan Bank System from August 1984 to September 1988 and then went into FSLIC receivership. Its parent holding company, Financial Corporation of America (FCA), was liquidated through bankruptcy. The government sold the S&L's good assets to American Savings Bank. The new owner of American Savings Bank was the private holding company, Keystone, Inc., whose shares were held by Robert Bass's partnership and the U.S. government. To purchase American Savings Bank, the government provided billions of dollars in assistance to Bass's group, which itself invested only $500 million. For twenty years, until September 2008, American Savings and Loan would retain the title of the largest thrift ever to fail. RepublicBank, which had lent Miller Condo Corporation the funds to build the Parkway Lane Complex, failed in 1988 and required a $3 billion bailout.[18]

Though some of the top decision makers inside these failed institutions suffered no consequences for their actions during the S&L crisis, in many cases, bad behavior would catch up. After leaving American Savings and Loan and its holding company, FCA, Charles Knapp faced more trouble: first, in 1986, a messy divorce from Brooke and then a plane crash. And he was convicted for loan fraud, landing a six-and-a-half-year sentence—later reduced to five-and-a-quarter years—in federal prison. He served his time at Lompoc Federal Prison Camp, the same minimum-security prison where Ivan Boesky—who acted as a government informant against Michael Milken—sojourned as an inmate. This was an ironic coincidence given that Milken, the junk bond financier, had publicly referred to Knapp as a "moron." The criminal conviction related to Knapp's work after he left American Savings and Loan. He had established a partnership with Larry Taggart, the former California state S&L commissioner. Through the business they operated, they pooled mortgages and sold them to Wall Street. As it happened, just across the street from Charlie Knapp's FCA office in Irvine, California, was the headquarters of Charles Keating's Lincoln Savings and Loan. It was a dangerous neighborhood.[19]

Empire Savings and Loan, Murray Savings Association, and American Savings and Loan were not unique. More than one thousand S&L insiders received felony convictions. Even without deregulation, a taxpayer bailout of the S&L industry was inevitable. This was largely due to the sudden, skyrocketing interest rates in 1979. What was not inevitable, however, and what was very much within the control of Congress and the regulators, was the timing and the amount of the bailouts. Bill Seidman, chairman of the FDIC and the RTC, commented on the role deregulation played in the crisis: "Crooks and highfliers had found the perfect vehicle for self-enrichment. We provided them with such perverse incentives that if I were asked to defend the S&L gang in court, I'd use the defense of entrapment." This perspective was shared by many others, including journalist Martin Mayer, who in a book on the S&L debacle, singled out one particular regulator for the most blame: former Home Loan Bank Board chairman Richard Pratt. In Meyer's view, "[I]f you had to pick one individual to blame for what happened to the S&Ls and to some hundreds of billions of dollars in taxpayer money, Dick would get the honor without even campaigning."[20]

Through deregulation, an expensive problem was transformed into a much more expensive disaster. Between 1986 and 1995, about 1,500 thrifts failed. In 1996, the S&L bailouts were estimated to cost $500 billion, though other later assessments show a smaller total of $153 billion, of which taxpayers bore about 80 percent. Beyond the actual monetary costs, the costs in moral hazard—confirming that some institutions were, like the FCA, "too big to fail"—are immeasurable.[21]

Even the regulatory agencies associated with the institutions that funded the Nobelmans' mortgage failed. The Home Loan Bank Board was gone, subsumed by the OTS. The FSLIC was gone, replaced by the FDIC—Danny Wall stayed on, however, just moving over from the Federal Home Loan Bank to the OTS. Darrel Dochow, who had been so helpful to the corrupt Charles Keating, was demoted, but later—apparently carrying the same helpful attitude with him—would move up the ranks at the OTS.[22]

But the Nobelmans were still there. While American Savings and Loan was on government life support, from the summer of 1984 through December 1988, the Nobelmans kept making their mortgage payments to Murray, which was forwarding them to American Savings and Loan. Illness and job loss forced the couple to default. Then, in August 1990, they faced imminent foreclosure. American Savings Bank threatened to take away their one-bedroom condo.

8

Friends of the Court

On the first Monday in August 1990, facing imminent foreclosure, Leonard and Harriet Nobelman turned to the legal system for help. Attorney Rosemary Zyne filed for protection on their behalf in the U.S. Bankruptcy Court in Dallas. Michael Schroeder, the lawyer for American Savings Bank was scheduled to appear on the Collin County Courthouse steps the next day to auction off their one-bedroom condo. The bankruptcy filing triggered an automatic stay, a mechanism for calling a time-out and giving them some breathing room. As if by magic, the foreclosure auction was put on hold.[1]

Besides stopping the clock, the couple hoped that bankruptcy would also provide permanent relief. They had considered two paths, liquidation or reorganization. With a liquidation, filed under Chapter 7 of the Bankruptcy Code, they could erase their debts. The Nobelmans did not have the types of debt that were not dischargeable. If they chose liquidation, an appointed bankruptcy trustee would sell all of their nonprotectable assets, except those that were collateral for loans, and distribute the proceeds to their creditors. To keep their home and cars, they would have to continue to pay what they owed on the respective loans. Thus, a Chapter 7 would make sense only if Leonard and Harriet had a great deal of debt other than their car loans and mortgage. If they did, it would free them from this debt a few months after they filed. But since their main debt was the condo and their cars, this did not seem like a good choice.[2]

Another option for them was Chapter 13. With this, the Nobelmans could keep control of their assets. It was analogous to a corporation filing under Chapter 11, where the CEO and other senior managers, known as the "debtor in possession," would continue to run the business while proposing a restructuring plan and paying a portion of the outstanding debt. Chapter 13, the consumer equivalent, was designed for people with income who could afford to pay some portion of their debts in installments, over a three- to five-year period. This suited the Noblemans, who by that August were both back at work. If they paid according to the plan, they would get a fresh start, a discharge from what was left of their debt, in five years. In addition, they believed that with Chapter 13, the bankruptcy court would reduce the outstanding principal on their mortgage from $65,000 to $23,500, the actual worth of the condo.[3]

While the automatic stay provided temporary relief, the long-term outcome was uncertain. Many corporate debtors that made it through a Chapter 11 would end up filing again, and as for consumers, sometimes the promise of a fresh start was illusory. Filing was not a decision to take lightly. Despite the approximate 718,000 consumer bankruptcy filings in 1990, the Nobelmans may have felt the social stigma associated with giving up on fully paying their debts. The mark of a bankruptcy filing could remain on their credit report for up to ten years. Lenders would be able to refuse them credit or charge higher rates and exact more onerous terms.[4]

Leonard and Harriet would also be saddled with the judgments of those who thought a bankruptcy filing reflected a moral failing. Even though bankruptcy is a legally available option, plenty of people feel it is unfair to creditors and to other consumers who must continue to pay what they owe. Some who oppose bankruptcy believe it creates a "moral hazard": that the availability of debt forgiveness encourages recklessness on the part of borrowers. These concerns have a long history. From the colonial period through the mid-nineteenth century, debtors were routinely sent to prison. While the U.S. Constitution explicitly empowers Congress to create uniform bankruptcy laws, there were long battles over legislation. During those debates, debtors were often referred to in pejorative terms, and bankruptcy was seen as an aid to recklessness.[5]

The regime that the Nobelmans encountered in 1990 was fairly new, a result of the Bankruptcy Reform Act of 1978. The new code—which replaced the Bankruptcy Act that had been in effect since 1898—was designed to balance competing values. On the one hand, under principles of state contract law, borrowers usually are expected to keep their promises, but on the other hand, federal bankruptcy law provides a fresh start instead of financial ruin. The code reflects the recognition that the extension of credit is needed to fuel the economy. Yet it also embodies the practical understanding that sometimes debtors end up owing more than they can pay back. While debtors can receive a fresh start, the code also benefits creditors by providing an orderly, predictable way to divide up a debtor's assets when there is simply not enough to provide each creditor the full amount they had bargained for. The code contains mechanisms for ensuring that some creditors do not get preferential treatment and that creditors who have properly secured their loans through collateral or other means are generally given priority.[6]

But the code's creation of an orderly, streamlined system sometimes led to abuses. For example, healthy businesses have engaged in "strategic" bankruptcy filings. Firms facing large product liability claims from injured customers were able to file for protection under Chapter 11 to minimize their payments. Businesses with underfunded employee pension plans filed strategically to push off their obligations onto the government agency, the Pension Benefit Guarantee Corporation. In an influential paper, economists George Akerlof (who was awarded a Nobel Prize in Economics in 2001) and Paul Romer described the moral hazard associated with executives looting their firms through excessive pay and fraud, only to use bankruptcy to escape accountability.[7]

Leonard and Harriet were not abusers of the system. They were not dodging asbestos claims. They did not owe employee pensions.

They had not looted a business. They hadn't even maxed out their credit cards. They had only encountered cash-flow problems, like so many others who suffered an illness and a job loss. And they were victims of the fraud-induced condo glut in Dallas, which had led them to unwittingly purchase a hugely overvalued condo. In other words, they were not gaming the system; the system was designed for people like them. Nevertheless, their filing involved a strategy.[8]

Because Chapter 13 gave the court the right to modify loans in order to facilitate a restructuring, there was a possibility—but not a certainty—that they could keep their condo. They had very little debt other than the car and home loan, so it made sense to avoid Chapter 7. Unless they could keep making their payments, they would lose the condo. Chapter 13 also made sense because Leonard was working again. He had a friend who drove him to the office and an assistant was able to help with the paperwork. And Harriet had a part-time position. At least for a while, they were able to make payments.[9]

After filing, the Nobelmans were required to identify and contact all of their creditors. They had listed only two: Murray Mortgage Corporation and Community Credit Union. They later added Texas Commerce Bank. According to the claims each of these creditors filed with the court, the Nobelmans were deeply in debt. They owed Murray approximately $71,000, of which about $65,000 was identified as principal, the rest as interest and fees; they also owed $6,500 in arrearages. For the cars and another loan, they owed Community Credit Union about $21,000 and, on a credit card with the Texas Commerce Bank, nearly $1,900.[10]

In addition, they were obligated to come up with a Chapter 13 plan for using any excess monthly income—above their expected total of $2,340 a month—to pay back their debts in installments over time. They proposed to pay, with interest, about $20,000 on the cars over five years. As for the mortgage, they planned to make the exact mortgage payments required under their promissory note until $23,500, the market value of the condo, was paid. They would also pay back the arrearages with interest. They planned to complete this payment plan in five years.[11]

Why did Leonard and Harriet believe that the bankruptcy court would allow them to pay back only the market value of the condo and not the entire remaining principal on their mortgage? They came up with this proposal in consultation with their attorney, Rosemary Zyne, who was following the accepted practice for bankruptcies filed in many regions of the country. She relied on two parts of the Bankruptcy Code—Sections 1322 and 506. One part, Section 1322(b)(2), permitted the court to modify the claims made by creditors. This part of the code, however, had a qualification. It permitted the modification of the rights of secured claim holders "other than a claim secured only by a security interest in real property that is the debtor's principal residence."[12]

The Nobelmans' secured creditors included American Savings Bank, which now owned their mortgage—even though Murray Mortgage Company was still collecting payments and dealing with the bankruptcy proceedings—and the credit union that made the car loans. They were deemed "secured" because they had the right to take collateral in the event of default. The credit card lender was "unsecured" because it had extended credit without any collateral, pledge, or other security interest. The difference between secured and unsecured creditors is important in a bankruptcy. Generally speaking, secured creditors are entitled to the full value of the collateral. Unsecured creditors are generally grouped together and must divide up the value of whatever assets remain after the secured creditors have been paid.[13]

Zyne hoped that the language in Section 1322 would not be an obstacle. She would argue that the prohibition on modification of a secured claim did not apply to the Nobelmans for two reasons. First, American Savings Bank's claim was not secured "only" by a security interest in a debtor's principal residence. The deed of trust listed other collateral in addition to the residence, including a 0.67 percent interest in the common areas of the complex, escrow funds, hazard insurance proceeds, and any rent. She based this view on court decisions that supported her analysis, including one in Texas.[14]

Even if the claim was seen to be secured "only" by the principal residence, Zyne asserted, that was not fatal. Her second reason to believe the Section 1322 language would not be a problem was procedural. She believed that the Nobelmans would prevail if the court first applied another part of the Bankruptcy Code, Section 506(a), which addressed "undersecured" creditors. These were creditors whose collateral was worth less than the loan—for example, a loan with a balance of $20,000 secured by a boat worth $12,000. Under Section 506(a), the court would bifurcate the $20,000 claim. The creditor for the boat loan would then have two claims: a secured claim for $12,000 and an unsecured claim for $8,000. Using this provision, Zyne believed that $23,500 (the condo unit's market value) of American Savings Bank's claim was a secured claim, and the remainder was unsecured.[15]

Thus, she maintained, the prohibition on modification found in Section 1322 applied only to American Savings Bank's secured claim. In other words, their plan of making the regular mortgage payments to the bank for about five years, until the value of the condo was paid off, should not be considered a modification of American Savings Bank's rights as holder of the secured claim. Leonard and Harriet would pay the exact amount required each month under the 1984 promissory note until the secured claim was paid.

American Savings Bank's Objection

The Noblemans filed this plan with the bankruptcy court on October 25, 1990. Murray, as servicing agent for American Savings Bank, immediately objected. Attorney Michael Schroeder explained the thrift's position on a single page: the repayment plan violated Section 1322(b)(2). Schroeder asserted that this provision made the Nobelmans' plan invalid. Since American Savings Bank's claim for about $71,000 was secured only by the Nobelmans' residence, he argued, the court could not permit them to pay anything less. In other words, American Savings Bank wanted the entire home loan balance paid, or the full mortgage payments each month through 2014. Cutting off payments in five years was a modification of his client's rights. It was a concise objection, quickly drawn up and filed. But it was not the end of the story.[16]

Tim Truman, the standing Chapter 13 trustee, also objected, citing Section 1322(b)(2). Relying on the legislative history of the Bankruptcy Code, he argued that American Savings Bank could not be forced to accept anything less than all thirty years of payments. He believed Zyne's interpretation went against the intent of Congress, which he said was to give special treatment to residential mortgage lenders. By forbidding borrowers to use bankruptcy to modify their mortgages, Section 1322(b)(2) was specifically intended to encourage residential home ownership by allowing lenders to extend credit without fear of mortgage modification in bankruptcy. Admitting that the actual statutory language was "a bit ambiguous," Truman nevertheless encouraged the court to parse it in favor of creditors.[17]

Each side's parsing of the text served its monetary ends. Grammatically and logically, there were two valid alternatives. And, legally, the theory advanced by the Nobelmans' lawyer had been more widely endorsed, including in decisions by the Third and the Ninth Federal Circuit Courts. Soon this approach would also be adopted by the Second and Tenth Federal Circuit Courts. Even the neighboring bankruptcy court for the Eastern District of Texas supported using Section 506's bifurcation-first approach. The Nobelmans' plan would most likely have been approved if they had filed a little farther east in Texas, or in any of more than twenty other states. The theory advanced by American Savings Bank's attorney and the bankruptcy trustee, meanwhile, had found limited lower court support.[18]

JUDGMENTS

On Valentine's Day in 1991, Judge Harold C. Abramson of the U.S. Bankruptcy Court for Northern District of Texas entered his ruling against the Nobelmans. On March 12, he issued an order denying confirmation of their Chapter 13 plan, at which point, Zyne filed an appeal with the Federal District Court. Federal Judge Barefoot Sanders reviewed the case. Even though the mortgage covered rents, insurance proceeds, and the common areas, he believed the bank's loan was still secured "only" by realty. In considering the interplay between the two sections of the Bankruptcy Code, Sanders relied on the history of the law. His decision cited previous cases from other circuits and noted that Section 1322(b)(2) was "inserted on behalf of the home mortgage industry" and that "Congress intended to benefit residential real estate lenders." On June 24, 1991, he affirmed Abramson's decision to reject the plan. The Nobelmans had lost again. The next stop was the Fifth Circuit Court of Appeals, the venue for appeals from federal trial and bankruptcy courts in Texas, Louisiana, and Mississippi. On August 13, 1992, Fifth Circuit Judge Emilio Garza, writing for the three-judge panel, affirmed Sanders's decision.[19]

It was a long shot, but the Nobelmans filed a petition for writ of certiorari, requesting that the United States Supreme Court hear their appeal. The Court receives about ten thousand requests each year and agrees to take between seventy-five and eighty cases. This one, however, was calling out to be heard because the circuit courts were split over the interpretation of the code. In addition, powerful interests filed briefs urging the Court to take the case so that this pattern of favoring homeowners would end. In December 1992, the Supreme Court agreed to hear their appeal.[20]

Supreme Court

At the United States Supreme Court, the arguments and parsing of the statute got more refined. Fundamentally, however, the parties were arguing about the same thing. The Bankruptcy Code was ambiguous: two sections were at odds. Would the Court treat underwater principal residences differently from underwater boats or vacation homes? Or would lenders for first mortgages on principal homes get worse treatment in bankruptcy?

Zyne remembered thinking it was an "uphill battle" given that American Savings Bank had a lot of powerful supporters filing amicus curiae (friend of the court) briefs encouraging the Court to take the case, and then, once it did, supporting the thrift. The attorney for American Savings Bank, Michael Schroeder, recalled dozens of lawyers phoning to warn him that he was about to have his "head handed to him." Four circuit courts shared the Nobelmans' interpretation of the law, and only the Fifth Circuit supported Schroeder's.[21]

While oral argument was devoted to the language of the statute, the amicus briefs also focused on the policy implications. Those supporting the American Savings Bank side were big players in the home mortgage industry, each of whom had an interest in the outcome. They included the Mortgage Bankers Association of America, Federal Home Loan Mortgage Corporation (Freddie Mac), Federal National Mortgage Association (Fannie Mae), the National Association of Realtors, the California Association of Realtors, the American Bankers Association, the American Financial Services Association, and the Credit Union National Association, and Nationsbanc Mortgage Corporation.

The friends of American Savings Bank largely sang the same tune. The main melody was that Congress intended to promote homeownership. Thus, the Bankruptcy Code deliberately provided special treatment for residential mortgage lenders. According to the industry, they were willing to loan money to low- and moderate-income borrowers because they knew that if things went sour, they could take the borrowers' homes through foreclosure.

This might not seem logical at first, they admitted. For example, if a home was worth $100,000 and the balance owed on the mortgage was $150,000, bifurcation would require the homeowner to pay back just $100,000 over the remaining term of the loan. But in a foreclosure, the home would arguably get no more than $100,000, with some experts estimating even less. Some of the American Savings Bank supporters argued, however, that this was not the whole story. The lender could bid on the property at foreclosure, buy it, and wait for it to appreciate in value. Thus, bankruptcy would be unfair, they claimed, because the borrower would get a windfall from the house's appreciation if allowed to keep the home through Chapter 13. They argued that borrowers would rush to the bankruptcy courts whenever home prices in their area declined.[22]

In addition, they contended that credit would be tighter in the future if lenders knew that homeowners could reduce principal. In particular, American Savings Bank's supporters said they would have to turn away more borrowers, require more money down on homes, and charge higher interest rates. This would impede the public policy goal of increased homeownership.[23]

What American Savings Bank's supporters did not say was that they, the lending industry, were interested in making loans—the bigger, the better. Blocking principal reduction thus created a moral hazard. The higher the price of a property, the bigger the loan. If lenders could block borrowers from using bankruptcy to reduce principal, they had less interest in ensuring that appraisals were accurate.[24]

The Decision

The unanimous opinion, authored by Justice Thomas, was terse. Thomas found that the Noblemans' interpretation was "quite sensible as a matter of grammar" but "not compelled." He emphasized the word "rights" and insisted that there was no way, as a practical matter, to avoid modifying American Savings Bank's rights if the mortgage payments should end before the full thirty-year term. This, of course, ignored the quite reasonable interpretation that the rights that could not be modified were only with respect to the secured portion of the claim.[25]

Justice Stevens's concurrence was even shorter. He looked directly at congressional intent and policy: "At first blush it seems somewhat strange that the Bankruptcy Code should provide less protection to an individual's interest in retaining possession of his or her home than of other assets. The anomaly is, however, explained by the legislative history indicating that favorable treatment of residential [mortgage lenders] was intended to encourage the flow of capital into the home lending market."[26]

Though Stevens signed the majority opinion as well, it was his concurrence that seemed to reveal the justification for the decision. The Court was looking at two government policies that were at odds with each other: the goal of providing a fresh start to debtors in bankruptcy, and the aim of promoting homeownership. The decision favored the latter goal, but did so without reference to any empirical evidence that ending the practice of principal reduction in bankruptcy would promote homeownership, and if it did so, at what cost?[27]

Too Small to Save

The Nobelmans, it turns out, were too small to save. American Savings and Loan, with $30 billion in assets, was too big to fail. After years of operating without sufficient capital, surviving only through the government's support and its willingness not to enforce the law, the savings and loan (S&L) was sold at a bargain price to private investors whose losses were guaranteed by the taxpayers. Now, revived as American Savings Bank, it successfully used the U.S. court system to deny the Nobelmans their own fresh start. The Nobelmans' loss at the Supreme Court evokes the well-known adage by John Maynard Keynes: "Owe your banker £1,000 and you are at his mercy; owe him £1 million and the position is reversed."[28]

Sometime after filing for bankruptcy, Leonard Nobleman became housebound, blind, and in need of a kidney transplant. On January 3, 1994, overcome by diabetes, he died a few months shy of his fifty-eighth birthday. By that time, he and Harriet resided in their daughter Marci's two-bedroom unit in the Parkway Lane Complex. Marci was living in the one-bedroom condo in Building 5 that was the subject of the Supreme Court decision.[29]

The bankruptcy case dragged on, even after that day in court. The Noblemans had made up back payments, and Harriet continued paying their monthly mortgage. But in January 1995, a year after Leonard's death, Harriet was nervous about money and stopped making payments on the unit. The liquidating affiliate of American Savings Bank, New West Federal Savings and Loan Association, sold Harriet's mortgage to Alaska Seaboard Partners Limited Partnership of Baton Rouge, Louisiana. Having purchased the note and the mortgage, Alaska Seaboard now had the right to foreclose.[30]

On the first Tuesday in June 1996, Michael Schroeder stood at the steps of the Collin County Courthouse in Texas. Schroeder was the American Savings Bank lawyer whose planned auction of the condo in the summer of 1990 had been halted by the bankruptcy filing. He was also the same lawyer who appeared before the black-robed justices of the United States Supreme Court in 1993 on behalf of the billionaire Robert Bass and his partners, the owners behind American Savings Bank. Now, he stood outside a small Texas county courthouse holding the deed and auctioning off Harriet Nobelman's condo. It fetched $30,000. The buyer of the condo was Alaska Seaboard Partners Limited Partnership of Nashua, New Hampshire. In other words, Alaska Seaboard (operating through its various partnerships) as mortgage holder foreclosed on the condo and then went ahead and purchased it. This was fairly common. Often there are few or even no bidders when homes are auctioned off at the courthouse. Thus, the mortgage holder will bid.[31]

Who was Alaska Seaboard? Behind its complicated organizational structure stood a Californian named Robin Arkley Jr., the multimillionaire son of a timber magnate. Alaska Seaboard Partners quickly sold the Nobelmans' condo after the foreclosure sale; a buyer, who had postdated the papers, already had been lined up in February.[32]

In that summer of 1996, three years after the landmark Supreme Court battle, both sides had severed their ties to the case's subject matter, the one-bedroom condo. The petitioner, Leonard Nobelman, was deceased, and his wife had lost the condo to foreclosure. American Savings Bank, the respondent, had sold its rights to foreclose and never took possession of the unit. Just as control of the Nobelmans' mortgage had flipped many times, so had control of the institution that owned it. American Savings and Loan was led by Charlie Knapp from the summer of 1983 through the summer of 1984, then by Bill Popejoy until the fall of 1988, then by the government through the Federal Savings and Loan Insurance Corporation (FSLIC) until December 1988, and then by Robert Bass's Keystone group.

Each of these transitions of control happened to coincide with life-changing events for the Nobelmans. They bought their condo when American Savings and Loan began to fail in 1984; American Savings and Loan bought their mortgage on the same day that Bart Dzivi was sent to the struggling S&L in Stockton to count collateral;

and they stopped making mortgage payments in 1989, the same year that American Savings and Loan was given a fresh start through American Savings Bank. In the same coincidental pattern, a month after Harriet lost the condo through that courthouse sale, American Savings Bank had monumental transactional news of its own.

Part II

Repeat Performance

9

Friend of the Family

After an acquisition, Washington Mutual (WaMu) CEO Kerry Killinger liked to clean house. Best to send the target's managers packing and let his homegrown leaders take charge. But with the acquisition of American Savings Bank in 1996, his eighteenth bank purchase in about seven years, he broke with tradition. This deal was different from the others: it nearly doubled WaMu's size and expanded its presence well beyond the Pacific Northwest. Instantly, Killinger was in charge of the second-largest residential lender in California. And it was expensive. WaMu had issued more than 47.8 million new shares of common stock, worth about $1.7 billion, to pay for the acquisition. Most of that stock—nearly 26 million shares—went to the Bass group of investors; much of the rest, 14 million shares, went to another partial owner, the Federal Deposit Insurance Corporation (FDIC).[1]

The role of acquisitive CEO was a great advancement from Killinger's middle-class upbringing. He was raised in a two-bedroom home in Iowa that he shared with five other family members. As a young married college student, he lived with his wife and baby in a mobile home. But his circumstances never limited his sense of possibility. His mother, a full-time parent, and his father, a high school music teacher, had taught him unwavering optimism. The tendency—as a family member later recalled—was: "If you have any faults, you hide them—to a fault."[2]

By the time of the purchase, Robert Bass's group, through a holding company called Keystone Holdings, Inc., had turned American Savings Bank around. With its $8 billion government guarantee against losses from the Charlie Knapp–era assets, American Savings Bank could focus on being a thrift. It accepted deposits and originated residential and multifamily mortgages. Like most banks and thrifts, it was highly leveraged, and its funding was fragile. In this way, it differed from a homeowner with a thirty-year, fixed-rate mortgage. Unlike the homeowner, American Savings Bank could have most of its funding withdrawn at any time. In this respect, it was not unique. High leverage, fragile funding, and low liquidity are the business of banking. Because banks and thrifts took these risks using government-backed insured deposits, regulation and oversight had been imposed on them for their safety and soundness. Regulators supervised them using a rating system called CAMELS—capital adequacy, asset quality, management, earnings, liquidity, and sensitivity to market risk. Ratings ran from 1 to 5, with 1 being the best, 4 indicating unsafe and unsound practices, and 5 posing a significant risk to the deposit insurance fund and a high probability of failure through extremely unsafe and unsound practices.[3]

The Acquisition

Killinger announced the American Savings Bank acquisition, which was structured as a merger, in July 1996, just a month after Harriet Nobelman's condo was auctioned off in Texas. This was three years after American Savings Bank prevailed in the United States Supreme Court, blocking the Nobelmans and every other homeowner from using bankruptcy to modify a first mortgage on a principal residence.[4]

By extending WaMu's reach into California, with its more than thirty million residents, the American Savings Bank transaction gave WaMu scale. The deal also delivered expertise in three areas. WaMu would learn how to originate, pool, and securitize mortgages to sell to investors, the "originate to distribute" model. Killinger would receive ongoing expert mergers and acquisition advice from two new board members from the Bass group. And most significant, WaMu would adopt and nourish a residential mortgage product that American Savings Bank had perfected—the payment-option adjustable-rate mortgage, better known as the Option ARM. With this combination, Killinger had in place the building blocks of his future empire.[5]

A Call to ARMs

The Option ARM was a relatively new invention, introduced in California in the late 1970s/early 1980s, that had become American Savings Bank's flagship product by the 1990s. Initially limited to wealthy people with irregular incomes, it would not become a significant part of the home loan market until after 2002. In the 1980s, two different acts of deregulation empowered lenders to try it out. First, the Home Loan Bank Board, under Richard Pratt, gave federally chartered thrifts broader permission to offer variable-rate instead of fixed-rate residential mortgages. In doing so, he expanded on a more narrow permission granted during his predecessor, Jay Janis's leadership. Next, Congress authorized adjustable-rate mortgages, negative amortizing loans, and balloon payments—preempting state law prohibitions—through the Alternative Mortgage Transaction Parity Act of 1982 (which was part of the Garn-St. Germain Act). This law was a response to Fed chairman Paul Volcker's policy of letting interest rates fluctuate wildly, which was announced at the "Saturday Night Massacre" press conference in October 1979.[6]

When interest rates shot up, banks and thrifts that held fixed-rate loans in their portfolios were suddenly in trouble. These types of loans put all the interest rate risk on the lenders. If rates went up, a fixed-rate loan still paid the lender the lower interest; and if rates declined, borrowers could refinance (possibly with a different institution, but regardless) into a lower rate. The Bank Board and Congress solved this problem for the lender with the adjustable-rate loan, which shifted the interest rate risk to the borrower. These loans weren't perfect for the lender: when interest rates rose, monthly payments were readjusted upward, and some borrowers were unable to pay and thus had to default. But by 1983, more than 60 percent of mortgages originated by thrifts were adjustable rate. In time, lenders experimented to develop new adjustable-rate products.[7]

The Option ARM was one such product. It had two enticing features: the teaser rate, and the payment option. Borrowers started with a very low interest rate, usually around 1 percent. The rate reset upward after one to three months and was adjusted each month thereafter. But despite the reset and adjustment, the actual amount due, as shown on the monthly statement, might not change until the end of the first year. This meant a steady low payment for a full year—but it also meant that extra interest was accumulating. For example, for a $300,000 loan, the monthly teaser payment during the first year would be about $965, versus nearly $2,000 a month for the same loan with a fixed-rate mortgage (at 7 percent, roughly the prevailing rate in January 1996). If the borrower could actually afford only $965 a month, under fixed rates, he or she could borrow only about $145,000. The Option ARM allowed the borrower to buy a much more expensive home.[8]

The second attractive feature of the Option ARM involved the payment options. Even after one year, borrowers could choose how much of their mortgage payment to make each month. Typically, they could select from four choices: a traditional payment (based on a thirty-year term); a larger payment (based on a fifteen-year term); an interest-only payment; and the minimum payment, comprising just a fraction of interest.

The optional minimum payment was also about 1 percent—$965 for that $300,000 borrower. Yet the actual rate could keep rising; the unpaid interest (known as "deferred interest") would be tacked onto the loan. Instead of gradually paying off the $300,000 the homeowner originally borrowed, he or she would be piling on more debt. If the borrower had made a low down payment, as lenders encouraged, he or she would quickly be underwater. While deferred interest was bad for many borrowers, it was great for lenders like American Savings Bank and, later, WaMu. Accounting rules allowed the deferred, unpaid interest to be booked as income. The industry called this type of mortgage a "NegAm" because it created negative amortization, building up instead of chipping away at principal, eroding the borrower's equity in the home.[9]

Additionally, after five years, the Option ARM would "recast." This meant that the lender would establish a new monthly payment. The borrower had no options after that point. The new mandatory payment would be based on the principal then outstanding, including the piled-on interest. This new, larger principal would be amortized over the remaining twenty-five-year term at a new, even higher interest rate. Even before the end of the fifth year, if the borrower accumulated too much deferred interest and the principal grew too high (for WaMu, about 110 percent of the original amount), the options would be abruptly canceled and the loan would be recast into a traditional one. When the loan was recast, borrowers often experienced "payment shock," as the monthly payment suddenly doubled or tripled.[10]

When they first took out these loans, borrowers were told not to worry about the recast. If all went well, they would be making more money by that time and could make the payments. If not, they could sell their home or refinance the loan. They were not informed that, in many cases, refinancing would cost them thousands of dollars in fees or penalties. Instead, borrowers were told that home prices were climbing and they would be able to avoid those troubles. And it was essential that home prices appeared to be rising year after year. In other words, these loans only worked while the housing bubble was inflating. If prices froze or dropped, these borrowers would be stuck: they would not have enough money down to refinance, they wouldn't be able to sell, and they would likely lose their homes.[11]

The Essential Ever-Rising Prices

Home prices had to keep going up, and not just because that meant bigger loans and more fees. The entire market depended on them. One way to ensure rising prices was to push appraisers. Beginning in 2000, a group of licensed and certified real estate appraisers began circulating a petition. They were concerned about pressure on them to issue false appraisals. Though they were supposed to exercise independent judgment, they felt daily pressure to meet or exceed price targets. These were often implicit: with a sale agreement, come up with an amount equal to or greater than the sales price. For a refinance, agree with the borrower's estimate of the home's worth. Appraisers who met the targets got repeat business; those who did not were often not paid for their work and denied future business. The petition contended that lenders had been "blacklisting honest appraisers." It was eventually signed by eleven thousand appraisers and, in 2007, delivered to an agency in Washington that was created after the savings and loan (S&L) crisis to monitor appraisal standards.[12]

The lenders employing these pressure tactics allegedly included WaMu. Andrew Cuomo, then the attorney general for New York State, would later file a lawsuit against eAppraiseIT, an appraisal business used by WaMu. The lawsuit alleged that WaMu pressured the company to inflate appraisals and that the company acquiesced in order to earn fees. This was in violation of professional standards, as well as federal and state law. Between 2006 and 2007, eAppraiseIT performed more than 260,000 appraisals for WaMu, apparently earning about $50 million. In 2012, Eric Schneiderman, who replaced Cuomo as attorney general, settled the case with eAppraiseIT's new owner for $7.8 million. Upon announcing the settlement, Schneiderman noted that "coercion of appraisers to inflate home values and the erosion of appraisal independence directly contributed to the housing crisis."[13]

Another factor keeping prices high was the availability of adjustable-rate mortgages, which allowed borrowers to put in offers at higher prices. The states with the fastest-rising home values corresponded to the ones where more Option ARMs were sold. There was also a strong correlation between home price growth and the concentration of pay-option and interest-only loans. According to a 2006 report by the Harvard Joint Center for Housing Studies, in some markets, without these nontraditional loans, many borrowers could not afford houses at prevailing prices. In other markets, home prices rose because borrowers could buy higher-priced homes with teaser-rate loans.[14]

When it was first offered, the Option ARM was viewed as suitable for wealthy borrowers with uneven income streams, such as a small business owner who had extra money around the holidays. Such a borrower would benefit from the flexibility of minimum payments during the lean months but could catch up regularly. In time, however, Option ARMs were peddled to people with limited incomes who were stretching to purchase a home; they were drawn in by the short-term prospect of very low payments but were insufficiently informed or concerned about the long-term consequences. These loans were also aggressively sold to homeowners to refinance their existing mortgages; they were told they could cut their monthly mortgage payments in half and save thousands in interest payments.[15]

But they were not adequately warned of the hazards. The federal Truth in Lending Act did not mandate clear disclosure of the risks of these loans. Additionally, borrowers had no meaningful way to comparison shop because lenders usually did not offer binding quotes. And in their details and nuances, these products were often far more complex than my simplified description suggests. Their full risks could not be predicted at the outset: the borrower would need to anticipate how interest rates would move, something nobody outside the Fed could know for certain. The only certainty was that after the teaser period, their payments would go up.[16]

During the Option ARM's heyday, in 2006, experts would estimate that about 70–80 percent of borrowers paid only the monthly minimum, putting not just their own finances but the entire system at risk. At WaMu, the percentage was at times higher. From 1999 through 2006, WaMu's Option ARM borrowers selected the minimum payment 95 percent of the time. WaMu's internal marketing group produced a report showing that the less borrowers knew about Option ARMs, the easier it was to sell them. Notwithstanding the confusing details, the payment shock, and the great risk of foreclosure with these loans, WaMu and other lenders successfully fended off any legal requirement that they take into account the borrowers' ability to repay at the full recast rate.[17]

Many salespeople were uncomfortable with these Option ARM loans or even refused to sell them. But so much money was involved that the mortgage business attracted the morally flexible and converted the reluctant. Financial institutions like WaMu relied on independent brokers to originate many of their loans and paid bonuses for originating Option ARMs and other high-risk loans. Some states subjected these independent brokers to little regulation. Given the low level of scrutiny, fraud flourished. As the Financial Crisis Inquiry Commission would later note, more than 10,500 individuals with criminal records became mortgage brokers in Florida between 2000 and 2007. Of those, more than four thousand had previous convictions for crimes, including "fraud, bank robbery, racketeering, and extortion." For a broker, a $300,000 Option ARM loan at WaMu would bring a commission of as much as 3 percent of the loan, and possibly more than $9,000. At many banks, the higher the interest rate selected, or greater the upfront fees, the more money a salesperson made. This was known as the "yield-spread premium." Though many were corrupt, they were not actually renegades; this practice was condoned at the highest levels of major U.S. financial institutions.[18]

Though subprime mortgages would later command more attention, the Option ARM loan also would greatly contribute to expanding the housing bubble and creating the financial and mortgage crises.[19]

Turning Point

For Kerry Killinger, buying American Savings Bank in 1996 involved more than simply bringing in a portfolio of loans and retail branches; it meant launching a new business line. The Option ARM would become WaMu's flagship product. In 2006, around the time Options ARMs were being called "nightmare mortgages," WaMu had originated more than $42.6 billion and sold or securitized $115 billion of these risky loans. At the end of 2007, Option ARMs represented more than half of all WaMu's mortgage originations. A stunning 73 percent of these were stated-income loans, in which borrowers were not required to provide independent documentation of their income. They needed no evidence of employment such as a tax return or W-2. Whatever numbers they put on the application sufficed. The colloquial term for these mortgages was "liar loans." WaMu learned this from American Savings Bank. At the time of the WaMu takeover, 98 percent of the mortgages in American Savings Banks' portfolio were adjustable rate, mostly Option ARMs. Nearly half of these provided "low documentation" of the borrower's credit and employment history.[20]

The American Savings Bank Legacy

Killinger's mortgage group had little experience in selling Option ARMs. Before WaMu could become a leader in the promotion of risky loans, it needed an expert to show the way, and American Savings Bank offered that knowledge. It made sense to keep their expert mortgage team in place. Craig Davis, the leader of that team, was brought up from Southern California to the Seattle headquarters as an executive vice president. Once the purchase of American Savings Bank was closed in late December 1996, most of the executives that Robert Bass's group had put in place when they took over American Savings Banks eight years earlier were let go. Chairman and CEO Mario Antoci, who had joined American Savings Bank in late 1988 from Home Savings, exited on the day of closing. In addition, WaMu announced plans to lay off 220 American Savings Bank administrative employees. But Davis stayed.[21]

The purchase price for American Savings Bank (about $1.8 billion in WaMu stock) made Robert Bass (with about 8 percent of the common stock) into WaMu's largest shareholder. With this ownership position came two board seats. Two deal makers were selected: David Bonderman, co-founder of the private equity firm Texas Pacific Group, and J. Taylor Crandall, a managing partner of Oakhill Capital Management. Both had served on the board of American Savings Bank. Crandall apparently advised Killinger to keep up the acquisitions. He recalled: "I told him that, hopefully, we wouldn't stop with just American Savings. My hope was that we could grow this thing even bigger." Both would remain as directors until 2002. The U.S. government also owned part of American Savings Bank. At sale, the FDIC received fourteen million shares of stock, which it promptly sold, netting about $652 million. This was a fraction of the more than $5.4 billion the bailout of American Savings and Loan was said to have cost the government.[22]

Given the size of American Savings Bank, integrating the computer systems and employees was expected to take considerable time and patience. But despite the merger's complexity, after the deal, Kerry Killinger did not pause at all. He purchased mortgage competitor Great Western in 1997, bringing another big gain in the stock price. By the end of that year, WaMu stock was up 1,000 percent since 1990, around the time when Killinger took over. He kept going. In 1998, he bought H. F. Ahmanson, the parent company of Mario Antoci and Craig Davis's former bank, Home Savings. These purchases gave WaMu $150 billion in assets and more than two thousand branches. One year later, Killinger purchased Long Beach Mortgage, a subprime lender. In 2001, with an agreement to purchase Dime Bancorp, WaMu expanded into New York, where it planned to compete with banking giants JPMorgan Chase and Citigroup. Ads appeared on giant Times Square billboards, in Yankee Stadium, and on taxicabs. WaMu lured customers—even those with small balances—with free checking that the commercial banks did not offer. These customers could then be charged fees for ATMs, bounced checks, and other services.[23]

WaMu's rapid growth was remarkable given that the savings bank had just $7 billion in assets and fifty branches when Killinger became CEO in 1990. But by 2002, some investors suspected it was too much too soon. After the meltdown of Enron Corporation, an empire built on fraud, they wondered if WaMu was another house of cards. Jonathan Gray, the banking analyst who warned investors of Charlie Knapp's interest rate gamble at American Savings and Loan in 1983, was now concerned about the opacity at WaMu. He could not tell whether it could withstand interest rate fluctuations because WaMu would not release enough detail about the derivatives designed to hedge the hundreds of billions of dollars in mortgages it serviced. Even some board members were taken aback by the fast growth. William Gerberding, president of the University of Washington and a WaMu board member, reflected: "If someone had predicted in the 1980s that we would have bought the three largest thrifts in California, we would have thought he was smoking something. But opportunities arose, and Kerry picked them off."[24]

WaMu's rapid expansion would not have been possible without deregulation. In 1994, Killinger restructured to create a holding company, Washington Mutual, Inc., to own the various banks he would acquire. As an S&L holding company, it was regulated by the Office of Thrift Supervision, the successor to the abolished Federal Home Loan Bank Board. Right before WaMu's acquisition phase began in earnest in 1994, President Bill Clinton signed into law the Riegle-Neal Interstate Banking and Branching Efficiency Act. This made it easier for banks and state-chartered thrifts to acquire or start up branches across the country. There was rapid consolidation, as ambitious institutions bought others. To surpass the competition, Killinger began scouting out and buying up depository institutions. With the erosion and ultimate repeal in 1999 of the Glass-Steagall Act, separating commercial and investment banking, megamergers became the order of the day. Consolidation was a competitive necessity, even if the resulting firms were too big to manage.[25]

Also enabled by deregulation was the path Killinger would take after folding in these new acquisitions. He would aggressively market high-risk loans that would lead to foreclosures and homelessness of middle-class families. This was a departure from WaMu's branding as the "Friend of the Family." Ultimately, Killinger's approach would sink WaMu and wipe out its shareholders. This too was a departure from the way the savings bank had been managed before he took over. His immediate predecessor, Lou Pepper, had actually avoided the trouble other thrifts had invited. Pepper was part of the Mark Taper tradition. Taper, who led American Savings and Loan before Charlie Knapp took over in the mid 1980s, focused on the safety of customer deposits, conservative underwriting, and low overhead. Pepper took a similar approach. He seemed to carry forward the "Friend of the Family" values embedded in the WaMu culture since its founding as a building and loan one hundred years earlier. Killinger did not seem to live by these values, but did use them as a marketing tool.[26]

From the Great Fire to the Friend of the Family

In June 1889, in the basement of a Seattle building, a glue pot boiled over, setting off a massive fire. Flames swept across twenty-five city blocks, destroying much of the business district. From the ashes of that fire rose the institution that would become Washington Mutual. Organized that September as Washington National Building Loan and Investment Association, its founders included Edward O. Graves, a former assistant secretary of the U.S. Treasury Department. Graves had moved to Seattle right after the fire and established Washington National Bank. This bank had a federal charter and was forbidden by law from making loans secured by real estate, so Graves helped start the building and loan (B&L). During the next twenty years, the Washington National Building Loan and Investment Association made more than two thousand amortized loans for housing in Seattle, enough to fill roughly 250 city blocks. In 1917, the B&L was reincorporated as the Washington Mutual Savings Bank.[27]

Washington Mutual Savings Bank operated steadily until the Great Depression. Then, on Monday, February 9, 1931, news of the sudden closing of a similarly named but unrelated thrift caused a panic. WaMu's Seattle lobby was jammed with anxious depositors, and hundreds more waited outside. Only about $2 million in cash was available for some $57 million in deposits. When the savings bank closed at 4:00 p.m., many depositors were still waiting outside. That evening, WaMu's board of trustees voted to execute a plan they had discussed in the event of a run. They sent a telegram with a request, written in code, to Chase National Bank in New York. Chase agreed to help by purchasing $10 million of investment securities from WaMu's portfolio, in exchange for $10 million in cash to stop the run. As part of the arrangement, WaMu agreed to buy back the securities in the future and return the borrowed money—an early repo agreement. Chase wired the funds to a local commercial bank, which dispensed them to WaMu. Over the next three days, WaMu lost more than $5 million in deposits, but it survived.[28]

After the run, Raymond Frazier, the president of WaMu, spoke out in support of legislation to prevent the use of customer deposits to fund risky activities. Declaring that the stock market had turned into a casino, he made clear that WaMu would continue to engage in simple, safe banking. He saw it as his purpose to prudently guard the savings entrusted to the bank and made clear that he planned to limit its investments to "prime first mortgages on improved real estate and in United States government bonds and other bonds of the highest type which are both safe and readily salable for cash."[29]

Perhaps recognizing the suffering wrought by the Great Depression in 1932, Frazier decided to cut his own salary by 40 percent. He proudly told civic organizations that "after specializing in real estate loans for forty-two years, we find ourselves without a single Seattle property acquired by foreclosure." WaMu avoided foreclosures by tolerating delinquencies; as long as taxes were paid, mortgage payments could be reduced or deferred. In 1939, WaMu owned only three houses. For thirty years after the Great Depression, people came into the bank to thank the employees there for helping them keep their homes.[30]

When Franklin Roosevelt took office as president in March 1933, WaMu was in the middle of a second run. It ended when Roosevelt declared a national bank holiday. Dietrich Schmitz, who succeeded Frazier as president of the savings bank, took issue with some of FDR's New Deal reforms. He objected to the creation of deposit insurance and worried that "federal meddling" would result in the public carelessly placing deposits anywhere, believing the government would come to the rescue of bad bank management. Schmitz was not alone in this view; the banking community at large opposed federal deposit insurance, as did Senator Carter Glass and Roosevelt himself. But they finally gave in to public demand.[31]

The Bank That's More Than a Bank

In 1977, WaMu worked with the Salomon Brothers investment bank to become the first savings bank to issue its own mortgage-backed securities (MBSs). Then, like other thrifts and banks, after the 1979 interest rate hikes, WaMu struggled. It was losing deposits to the money market funds. When deregulation arrived with the Depository Institutions Deregulation and Monetary Control Act in 1980 (DIDMCA), and savings account interest rates were no longer capped, WaMu faced competition for deposits. This brought pressure to pay higher interest rates for deposits, yet higher rates meant thinner profit margins or even losses. For several months it stopped making loans entirely.[32]

To add to these problems, young depositors were more attracted to commercial banks than savings banks. Though WaMu had recently branded itself the "Friend of the Family," its depositors were growing older. The next generation was not banking there. In 1980, when interest rates were peaking, the savings bank was losing $5 million a month in net worth. At that rate, the Friend of the Family would be insolvent in a few years.[33]

Faced with these problems, Carl Eldridge, who had served as president since 1973, decided to retire. In the summer of 1981, the trustees turned to one of their own, Lou Pepper, to take over for six months until a permanent replacement could be found. Pepper knew WaMu well; he had served as outside legal counsel. After his six-month term was renewed several times, he officially took the job as CEO in 1982.[34]

From the start, Pepper revealed his thrifty managerial style. He took an approach much like Mark Taper's at American Savings and Loan. He sent a memo out to employees indicating that should they want to keep their office plants, they would have to purchase them from the company. The cost to maintain the palms and ficus, he informed them, equaled the annual salaries of six employees. This memo signaled not just that he was frugal but that he valued his employees over symbols of affluence.[35]

Under Pepper, WaMu was not going to gamble on interest rates. This was the strategy that Charlie Knapp was executing at that moment at State Savings, leading to American's troubles and the $6.8 billion run in 1984. Also, WaMu would not engage in high-risk lending such as construction loans, as many thrifts did that year. Instead, the plan was to cut costs, add fees to some previously free services, and initiate some new services. Pepper wanted to transform WaMu into "the bank that's more than a bank." Then he hoped that bank would transform its ownership structure and raise capital by selling WaMu's stock to the public.[36]

As part of the plan to expand into nonbanking services, in 1982, Pepper orchestrated the acquisition of a Spokane-based securities brokerage firm, Murphey Favre, Inc. Though this was a securities operation, recent deregulation allowed the savings bank to own it. WaMu thus became the first thrift to own a broker as well as a registered investment adviser. Murphey Favre managed more than $400 million in assets, some of which were in mutual funds.[37]

In March 1983, WaMu offered its shares to the public and converted from a mutual savings bank to a capital stock savings bank. Though it was no longer mutually owned, it still maintained its name. This marked the beginning of a period of exciting and exhausting change. The retail spaces were transformed from bank branches into "financial centers." Waiting in the lobbies were employees from the Murphey Favre Division, ready to offer customers the opportunity to invest in securities. The most attractive offer was a money market account called MEGAFUND, created for bank customers. With interest rates higher than WaMu's checking accounts, the MEGAFUND gathered customer deposits rapidly. Thrifts were permitted to compete with money market funds by offering money market accounts in 1982, under the Garn-St. Germain law. The new product delighted depositors, who poured money in, but it alarmed some competitor banks and thrifts by raising fears of an interest rate war.[38]

Killinger's Arrival

Kerry Killinger came over to WaMu in 1982 with Murphey Favre. He had joined the investment firm in 1976, where he started their first money market mutual fund. It was the right move at the right time. His money market fund was immediately successful, as it paid investors three times what banks and thrifts were paying on savings accounts. Since Killinger was Murphey Favre's largest stockholder, the sale to WaMu made him wealthy. Though he had trouble connecting with people, he was facile with finances, and Lou Pepper made him president in December 1988. When Pepper retired in 1990, Kerry was made CEO and then became chairman of the board in 1991.[39]

As CEO, Killinger first seemed to balance growth with prudence. He insisted on flying coach, ate lunch in the office, and drew a comfortable but reasonable salary. He apparently told employees that "frugal is sexy." In his first two years, he purchased a number of small banks, adding $1 billion in assets to the balance sheet. He sought out undervalued, struggling firms. In 1992, he doubled WaMu's assets to more than $16 billion, making it the second-largest depository institution in Washington State. He was also hiring—growing organically.[40]

As the firm transformed, so did Killinger. His salary escalated and he arranged for the firm to buy time-shares in several corporate jets. He filed for divorce and remarried two years later. Traveling with his new wife on the corporate jets, he spent more than a year touring the country to pep up employees at brand rallies. At these and other highly orchestrated events, rock music blared in the auditoriums and Killinger would sometimes loosen his tie and dance. This was an accomplishment for a man who, when he joined the bank, reportedly had trouble making eye contact. Though lacking in charisma, he learned from people like Craig Davis from American Savings Bank, who liked planning the next party for the sales team as much as he liked selling.[41]

In 1999, Killinger separated WaMu into three (later, four) operating divisions and appointed Craig Davis president of one of them—the Home Loans Group. This group, which went by various names over the years, was responsible for residential mortgage origination, securitization, and mortgage servicing. Davis, who had arrived only with the acquisition of American Savings Bank in 1996, came to this senior position with little knowledge of WaMu's history. Strategic decisions always had been made by a core team of executives, many of whom had been hired by the personable and frugal Lou Pepper. Together, they helped Pepper and later Killinger make balanced decisions, carefully weighing any move's effect on the entire enterprise. With the new structure, power shifted from the old executive team to the individual division presidents. Of the three, it was newcomer Craig Davis who had the most sway over Killinger and thus WaMu's overall direction. After the 1999 shake-up, former executive team member Lee Lannoye recalled: "The mortgage unit was responsible for its own bottom line. The checks and the balances were gone."[42]

10

The Factory Line

In 2001, Kerry Killinger announced his goal: Washington Mutual (WaMu) would become the nation's number one home lender. His acquisitive phase was about to end. From then on, new growth would come from pumping up loan volume. To meet this objective, Killinger put his trust in Craig Davis, his Home Loans Group president, who had a track record of success. As director of mortgage originations at American Savings Bank, Davis built up the bank's payment-option adjustable-rate mortgage (Option ARM) business. This helped turn American Savings Bank from a government bailout recipient to a hugely profitable enterprise, positioned for sale.[1]

Now Davis was motivated to fulfill his new boss's agenda. Growing mortgage originations would deliver income in three key areas. First, WaMu earned money on the spread between the interest and fees paid in by borrowers and the interest it had to pay out to attract deposits and other funding. In addition, as a servicer, WaMu earned fees for collecting payments on mortgages owned by others. Finally, WaMu brought in income, known as "gain on sale," when it sold mortgages into the secondary market, whether as whole loans or in securitized pools. This growth was funded through debt. WaMu depended on taxpayer-insured deposits, loans from the district Federal

Home Loan Bank, and other borrowing, including repo loans—short-term loans collateralized by securities in WaMu's portfolio. Like other banks, WaMu was highly leveraged. If its portfolio of loans, securities, and other assets were to decline by a small fraction, or if depositors and other lenders withdrew a fraction of funding (and it could not replace the money with fresh funding), it would be insolvent, putting the Federal Deposit Insurance Corporation (FDIC) insurance fund at risk.[2]

Craig Davis's team sought to achieve Killinger's goal through a marketing slogan, "The Power of Yes." This slogan, launched nationally in 2001, reached potential customers and employees alike. The message to borrowers was that they could turn to WaMu for hassle-free loans. It became a mantra among employees, like its rival Countrywide's "price any loan." "The Power of Yes," made pervasive through advertising, was a constant reminder that independent brokers and employees should stretch to make loans. This translated into abandoning internal underwriting guidelines and falsifying applicant data to make sure loans went through. Steven Knobel, an appraiser who worked with WaMu until 2007, said of the attitude there: "If you were alive, they would give you a loan. Actually, I think if you were dead, they would still give you a loan." This attitude was pervasive. At Countrywide an executive with a license plate that said "FUND'EM" said his bank's practice was to give anyone a loan who could fog a mirror. Carelessness and fraud were enabled from the top. As Lee Lannoye, the former vice president of corporate administration at WaMu, recalled, Craig Davis "only wanted production. It was someone else's problem to worry about credit quality."[3]

Yet no one else seemed to worry either. WaMu relied heavily on 34,000 independent brokers to originate loans, yet assigned only fourteen full-time employees to oversee their work. A Senate investigative report found that the WaMu loans generated by independent brokers and employees often involved operational and compliance deficiencies, errors, or fraudulent information. This was not unusual for an era during which some lenders were known to throw parties where managers would alter borrowers' applications to make sure they got approved.[4]

Davis and other WaMu executives also created a party atmosphere to energize the sales force. Salespeople participated in an opulent annual President's Club sales event, a many-day junket, often at exotic locales, where celebrities performed and star athletes emceed awards ceremonies. Spouses joined in the wining and dining, which included expensive gifts and activities. Some form of the President's Club had been a tradition at American Savings Bank and Home Savings before they were purchased by WaMu. Salespeople, known as loan consultants, competed to attend the annual event. They could monitor their mortgage origination numbers on the company intranet to see how close they were to garnering an invitation. Over the years, vacation spots included Cancun, the Bahamas, Maui, and Kauai. Their rival Countrywide also held elaborate incentive events.[5]

As part of the "Power of Yes" launch, the spring 2001 meeting for the 1,500 members of the East Coast, South, and Midwest sales forces was held in Atlanta. A giant convention room was styled like an evangelical revival meeting. Under a giant tent, a performer dressed in a white suit roamed through the audience, microphone in hand, stirring up the crowd with talk of WaMu's product line. Occasionally, he would stop, lift up his left arm, arch backward, and shout, "WaMu-lujah!" A gospel choir flown in from Los Angeles rhapsodized about the "Power of Yes."[6]

By the end of 2001, under Craig's leadership, the number of single-family home mortgages that were originated by WaMu climbed to $156 billion, triple the amount from 2000. In addition, WaMu had the servicing rights for hundreds of billions of dollars in mortgages. To sustain this growth, it had to make or buy even more loans. A good portion of its opportunities were refinancings. After the dot-com stock bubble burst in 2000, and the terrorist attacks on September 11, 2001, Fed chairman Alan Greenspan had guided the Federal Open Market Committee to expand the money supply and thus lower interest rates repeatedly. Lowering rates helped to bail out the stock market.[7]

As a result of Greenspan's easing, the Fed funds rate—the rate banks charge each other to borrow overnight—fell from 5.5 percent at the beginning of 2000 to 1 percent in mid-2003. Prime mortgage rates dropped from about 8 percent in early 2000 to a temporary low of 5.52 percent in mid-2003. As rates fell, mortgage lenders were in a position to make new loans and collect fees. Homeowners across the country responded to aggressive marketing to refinance their mortgages by taking out record numbers of new loans at lower rates to replace their old ones. It was a banner year. Only 2.5 million home mortgages were refinanced in 2000 for a total of about $234 billion in mortgage debt. That number grew to more than 11 million homes in 2003, representing about $2.5 trillion in mortgage debt. Refinancings made up nearly 70 percent of the total $3.8 trillion in mortgages originated that year. Due to this low-interest-rate–induced refinancing boom, by the end of 2003, homeowners were collectively saving about $4 billion per month in interest. The vast majority of these refinancings were conventional prime mortgages, a small fraction were subprime, and just under a million were government insured.[8]

Nearly half of those who refinanced their homes took cash out. For example, if a homeowner owed $270,000 but the house was worth $320,000, he or she might borrow $300,000 at a new, lower fixed rate, pay off the old loan, and pocket $30,000, leaving a $20,000 equity cushion. In 2003, homeowners cashed out $139 billion in equity. This cash could be used for anything—to pay off credit card debt, pay for college, or make home improvements. Real wages were stagnant and the costs of college, cars, and other large expenses were rising. Cash-out refinancings allowed consumption and prices to increase without wage increases.[9]

The Pivotal Year

In July 2003, as interest rates began to rise and refinancings with conventional mortgages slowed, WaMu and its competitors sought new sources for loan originations to push through the system. Killinger had recently announced that he wanted to make WaMu into a category killer: "We hope to do to this industry what Wal-Mart did to theirs, Starbucks did to theirs, Costco did to theirs and Lowe's–Home

Depot did to their industry." Further, he asserted: "I think if we've done our job, five years from now you're not going to call us a bank." This dreamy projection proved ironically accurate. In five years, WaMu would no longer be a bank. The holding company, Washington Mutual, Inc., was stripped of its banking assets by the FDIC in September 2008.[10]

While Killinger hoped WaMu would diversify into a range of lending products, the big growth happened inside the residential mortgage division. The new frontier was subprime, Option ARM, and other nonprime products able to fill the void that would be left after the drop-off in refinancings. The private-label securitization pipeline was in place, waiting for more mortgages to flow through. And the volume would be exponentially larger.[11]

Killinger was not the only one to figure this out. WaMu was up against equally ambitious competitors, including Countrywide and Ameriquest. Roland Arnall at Ameriquest was obsessed with subprime loan production. The sales staff at Ameriquest worked the phones, some pumped up on energy drinks, others on cocaine, cold-calling homeowners to persuade them to refinance from fixed-rate prime mortgages to subprime loans. Salespeople forged borrowers' signatures on disclosure forms so they would not be told how much the loan was really going to cost them or how much the broker made in fees. Closing the loan was the goal; how you got there was not important.[12]

At WaMu's Home Loans Group, a number of sales reps claimed that they were fired after refusing to sell Option ARMs. Greg Saffer, a former employee who has sued, claiming he was forced out of his job, said that WaMu overpriced its thirty-year fixed mortgages to steer borrowers into the riskier types. He also contended that his supervisors told him to inflate borrowers' incomes on loan applications. Since WaMu relied on "stated income" or "liar's loans" for the vast majority of its Option ARMs, this was an invitation to fraud. John D. Parsons, a former supervisor at a WaMu mortgage processing center who was later imprisoned for drug-related convictions, said he snorted methamphetamine daily, and other employees saw drug paraphernalia on his desk at work. This was tolerated because people saw that he "gets the job done." Parsons was creative. Once he was asked to review a loan application from a borrower claiming a six-figure income and working as a mariachi singer. Parsons had no way to verify his income, so a photo was taken of the singer standing in front of his home clad in his mariachi attire. With that photo in the file, the loan was approved.[13]

The switch from refinancings to high-risk mortgages was successful. In 2003, 64 percent of WaMu's home mortgage originations were fixed-rate. By 2004, fixed-rate mortgage originations declined to 31 percent, and by 2006, just 25 percent. Replacing the lost volume of traditional fixed-rate originations were higher-risk mortgages, including subprime, Option ARMs, and home equity loans.[14]

Fannie and Freddie Lose Market Share

With the change to riskier mortgages came another shift. While traditional lenders had historically kept the mortgages they originated in their own portfolios, now there was a push to sell these mortgages. Before legal changes during the Reagan era enabled broad sales of bank-issued (private-label) mortgage-backed securities (MBS), the Federal National Mortgage Association (Fannie Mae) and the Federal Home Loan Mortgage Corporation (Freddie Mac) had been the biggest players in the secondary market. In 1971, Freddie began securitizing the mortgages it purchased and Fannie did the same a decade later. At their peak, Fannie and Freddie had 95 percent of the MBS market. However, with the growth of private-label securitization, their market share would slip.[15]

The pivotal year was 2003—the same year that mortgage refinancings slowed and high-risk loans began to fill the pipeline. The vast majority of mortgages originated that year were sold. And whereas Fannie and Freddie had formerly dominated the pooling of these mortgages into trusts that issued securities, fully private banking entities began to take the lead—because they were willing to buy the risky loans that Fannie and Freddie refused. In 2003, Fannie and Freddie securitized nearly 57 percent of new residential mortgages.

That same year, 15 percent of the mortgages originated were securitized through private-label deals, including those created by WaMu (which had just started to securitize its own mortgages through a separate division).[16]

By 2006, Fannie and Freddie's share dropped to 37 percent of mortgages originated. Private-label securitizations that year reached $1.15 trillion—about 38 percent. Notably, that same year, WaMu was a larger issuer of MBSs than any Wall Street investment bank. It was second in line behind Countrywide, up from sixth place in 2004.[17]

Stepping into Subprime

Kerry Killinger got involved with subprime mortgages in 1999, when Washington Mutual, Inc., purchased Long Beach Mortgage. As a mortgage company, not a bank, Long Beach was fully entrenched in the originate-to-distribute model, selling its loans immediately for securitization. To get the money to fund the mortgages, it borrowed, including from Wall Street. By that time, the once specialized area of subprime lending represented about 10 percent of all new residential mortgage loans. By 2006, subprime loans would represent more than 23 percent of all mortgage originations. When Killinger discussed the acquisition with members of his executive team, many of them resisted and dragged out the deliberation. Long Beach was a subprime lender spun off from a savings and loan (S&L) founded by Roland Arnall. He had started Long Beach Savings and Loan in 1979, around the time Danny Faulkner and his real estate developer colleagues took over the S&L that they would later rename Empire Savings and Loan. When restrictions were imposed on S&Ls in 1989 after the crisis, Arnall decided to build a nonregulated mortgage broker. He was the man who burned his thrift charter in the 1990s and kept its ashes in an urn displayed in his office.[18]

Arnall was one of the first to enter the subprime lending field. Historically, borrowers who presented a greater risk of default had few choices. Standard underwriting for mortgage loans involved the three Cs—credit, capacity, and collateral. A history of paying bills on time and in full, sufficient income to pay back the loan, cash down and in the bank, and a home that was worth at least 120 percent of the amount of the loan were considered necessary for a prime mortgage loan. Borrowers might be considered high risk if their credit report showed a pattern of paying bills late or they were carrying tremendous debt, with little cash and without steady income. A subprime borrower is also often defined as someone with a Fair Isaac Corporation (FICO) credit score of 660 or less. Yet some prime borrowers with higher scores also received subprime loans. If they were denied credit from a traditional lender, they had to seek out a loan from a "hard money" lender that required more money down and charged substantially higher rates and fees.[19]

Under Arnall, Long Beach Savings began to compete with the hard money lenders by offering these borrowers lower rates. Arnall's developing business initially was enabled by federal law. The preemption of most state anti-usury laws with the enactment of the Depository Institutions Deregulation and Monetary Control Act (DIDMCA) in 1980 helped him grow subprime lending from a miniscule share of the market. Prior to that act of Congress, many states imposed interest rate ceilings that made it unprofitable for regulated lenders to take on risky loans. In the early 1990s, when he burned his charter and converted Long Beach from an S&L to a mortgage company, Arnall avoided having the Office of Thrift Supervision as his regulator. But having denied itself access to insured customer deposits, Long Beach would need a new source of funding. It had already found it on Wall Street.[20]

Long Beach had two divisions, retail (which directly made loans to borrowers) and wholesale (which bought up loans made by other originators). In 1997, Arnall spun off the wholesale piece of the business as a separate corporation and sold its shares to the public under the name Long Beach Financial Corporation. A year earlier, the retail division had paid a $3 million settlement to the Justice Department after allegedly charging higher fees to women and members of minority groups than it did to others with the same credit profiles. Arnall kept the retail division, which he renamed Ameriquest Capital Corporation.[21]

Long Beach was not just a subprime lender, it was among the worst. According to the Office of Thrift Supervision, it was among the twelve subprime lenders showing the highest credit losses in 1997 and again in 1999. The mortgages that Long Beach created were pooled to create MBSs, including classes of securities (tranches) that received the highest rating, triple-A. This rating was supposed to indicate a 1 percent to 2 percent likelihood of default. But of seventy-five tranches of Long Beach MBSs rated triple-A in 2006 by Standard & Poor's, every one either was downgraded to junk status, defaulted, or withdrawn. In the fall of 2007, shortly after Ameriquest ceased operations, WaMu shut down its subprime lending because it could no longer find investors for its mortgages. For many inside of WaMu, this disaster was foreseeable at the outset.[22]

Below the Hood at Long Beach

One executive who objected to the potential acquisition of Long Beach Mortgage in 1998, Lee Lannoye, worried that WaMu would morph into a predatory lender. Given the recent settlement with the Department of Justice due to discriminatory lending practices by the retail division at Long Beach, there was good reason to fear. Lannoye later explained: "I didn't want to have to sit in front of a regulator and explain why an African-American borrower (from Long Beach Mortgage) was paying two percentage points higher than a borrower from WaMu."[23] Lannoye resigned near the end of 1998, and once the old executive team was dismantled in the restructuring in 1999, Killinger decided to purchase Long Beach and thus enter the subprime lending market.[24]

The timing was terrible: Long Beach began to lose money almost immediately. To put the subprime subsidiary on secure footing, WaMu loosened its standards. Instead of insisting that borrowers put at least 15 percent down on a loan, for example, it allowed just 5 percent. The company began buying more stated-income loans—referred to as "liar's loans" by mortgage industry insiders. In addition, Long Beach account executives sought out hybrid ARMs. These were mortgages that started with a fixed rate for two to three years, then adjusted upward and became variable-rate loans. Like Option ARMs, these loans often caused payment shock on the reset dates.[25]

Following Killinger's directive in 2001 to grow the mortgage business, Long Beach made $11 billion in loans in 2003, up from $2.6 billion in 1998 before the acquisition. Though the executive team that approved the Long Beach purchase was told that subprime would be a small part of the business, in a few years, WaMu had become the fifth-largest subprime lender in the country. Between 2005 and 2007, it originated more than $65 billion in subprime loans. Countrywide was number one, with more than $97 billion. Long Beach under WaMu continued to rank at the top of the list of the worst subprime lenders, reaching number one in 2000 and number three in 2001.[26]

Fraudulent applications were common. Brokers invented information about applicants. As an incentive to bring in more loans, account executives were paid a higher percentage if loan volumes passed certain thresholds. To make their numbers, some salespeople and mortgage brokers reportedly bribed their managers at Long Beach to ensure that unqualified loans would make it through the system swiftly. During the summer of 2003, the top lawyer at WaMu, Fay Chapman, was contacted by a Long Beach attorney who shared his concern about the poor quality of the mortgages it was buying. WaMu was selling some of these to investors as whole loans. Others were pooled and sold as securities. But a large portion of them did not meet the guidelines that WaMu had represented to investors.[27]

Chapman assembled a team of one hundred individuals, including attorneys, appraisers, and contracting firms, to dig deeply into the loan files. She ordered securitization at Long Beach stopped during the review. After three months of effort, the results were in. Of the 4,000 mortgages sampled, only 950 met the standards for sale to investors. Missing documents and fraud were common. Killinger took Long Beach away from Craig Davis, the leader of the Home Loans Group, who had been assigned the division in 2002 when it was experiencing problems predating his leadership. In early September 2003, after the loan file review, WaMu announced an expected loss for the third quarter and a few weeks later announced that Davis was retiring. By the end of 2003, a new system of oversight was in place for the Long Beach subsidiary. The Legal Department required each mortgage be reviewed against a checklist of standards, and the board of directors received reports on "errors" at Long Beach. Securitizations started up again, as did sales of the whole loans.[28]

Then problems reappeared. In 2004, a risk officer who participated in an informal audit of the Long Beach subsidiary wrote: "The climate was very adversarial. . . . We found a total mess." A year later in early 2005, borrowers with recently originated Long Beach mortgages stopped paying. These were called "early payment defaults" (EPDs)—defaults occurring within the first three months after the loan was made—and are considered a sign of faulty underwriting. Mortgages with EPDs that had been securitized could, by contract, be pushed back by investors to WaMu. WaMu immediately investigated, reviewing three months of Long Beach loans in 2005 where the borrower had defaulted on the very first payment. According to the report, these first-payment defaults were preventable or detectable "in nearly all cases." Some of the loan files contained documents altered with correction fluid. Borrowers' signatures often varied from document to document. More than half the loans were stated-income loans. And about 92 percent of these first-payment defaults had a combined loan-to-value ratio of 100 percent, meaning that the borrower put no money down or had no equity whatsoever in the home.[29]

The audit also revealed predatory lending. A review of a sample of refinancing transactions showed that in 88 percent, policies to avoid loans that had "no net tangible benefit to the borrower" were ignored. In addition, Long Beach ignored the procedures designed to prevent loan flipping, where brokers frequently refinance borrowers, gaining fees for themselves to the detriment of the homeowner. As a result of the EPDs, Long Beach had to buy back loans with more than $800 million unpaid principal.[30]

Leaderless Home Loans Group

Kerry Killinger did not immediately replace Craig Davis. Instead, WaMu apparently spent the next two years cleaning up its home mortgage business. The Home Loans Group, including Long Beach, was overseen by at least two different executives, each of whom had other major responsibilities. There was no senior executive solely dedicated to residential mortgages. Given the unit's importance to the bottom line, as well as the risks building up, this seems like a critical mistake. Without managerial oversight at the highest levels, it would be hard to keep this group both profitable and accountable. Problems could be buried again. Once again, many loans were in default within a few months after origination. In 2005 and 2006, investors demanded that WaMu repurchase $875 million in mortgages.[31]

Still, the parties and incentives continued, including the President's Club awards. Killinger fired the Long Beach executives and finally, in July 2005, put the Home Loans Group under the direct supervision of David Schneider. Killinger was well informed of Long Beach's problems. Steve Rotella, the new president and chief operating officer hired by Killinger in 2005, communicated his impressions. In 2007, Rotella sent Killinger an e-mail via his BlackBerry under the subject line "Looking Back." He wrote: "The lesson learned here is when it smells bad, its [sic] likely rotten, so go even faster and deeper to cut it out. . . . I said the other day that [the Home Loans Group] (the original prime only) was the worst managed business I had seen in my career. (That is, until we got below the hood of Long beach.)"[32]

Signs of bad management appeared just before he arrived.

Interest Rate Hedging Debacle

In June 2004, Killinger issued a press release with terrible news related to an interest rate hedge gone wrong. He projected that WaMu's net income for all of 2004 would decline to just $2.5 billion, down from about $3.9 billion for 2003. He blamed the leaderless Home Loans Group, which had a $1.3 billion profit in 2003 but would have next to nothing in 2004. The huge profits that should have come from the mortgage servicing rights business became huge losses instead. The decline in that unit, Killinger said, was due to "expectations for a sustained increase in long-term interest rates." This was either a major mistake or a directional bet gone wrong.[33]

By 2004, WaMu had servicing rights for about $770 billion in mortgages for about five million homeowners. This involved mailing statements, collecting and cashing checks, and escrowing real estate taxes. It also involved passing along principal and interest to the mortgage holders, often trusts that issued MBSs. Thus, the cash from these mortgages would flow to the trusts and from there to the MBS holders. Even though WaMu had sold these mortgages, by keeping the servicing rights, it continued to collect a fee of some $400 per year for each mortgage. But the value of these servicing rights was affected by the rise and fall of interest rates. When rates rose, borrowers tended to hold on to their mortgages for longer than the expected average of five to seven years. This made the servicing rights more valuable. But if rates fell, borrowers would refinance earlier and thus the servicing would terminate earlier than expected.[34]

To protect against losses on the servicing rights business, WaMu had entered into complex hedging transactions using derivatives. But it was not done correctly, resulting in a $2.4 billion loss, which was only partially offset by the gains to the business unit. This and a previous hedging disaster in 2003 showed the problems of growing larger. In 2003, navigating nine different computer systems that were the legacy of rapid acquisitions, WaMu lost track of interest rate locks promised to prospective borrowers during the flood of refinancings and suffered huge losses. A Morgan Stanley analyst suggested that in mortgage banking, too big can mean too big to manage: "The mortgage business gets geometrically more complex with size."[35]

After the 2004 botched hedge, Killinger was derided in the press. Banking analyst Jonathan Gray, who had warned investors against American Savings and Loan when Knapp was making interest rate bets, had an interesting view. Back in 1997, Gray had called Killinger "the Alexander the Great of the thrift industry." In 2002, he expressed concern that WaMu might not be hedged against interest rate fluctuations. Now he wondered whether the loss was a mistake or whether Killinger was actually gambling on interest rates: "It's as if they bet that the Fed would ease and rates would fall. The Fed did everything but take out a billboard saying that it would tighten. Isn't that bizarre?" While other mortgage banks suffered when refinancing dried up, WaMu did worse. Countrywide, with a larger, hedged mortgage servicing portfolio, did not suffer the same losses.[36]

Killinger apologized for the mistake, but others paid the price. WaMu's stock had hit an all-time high of $46.55 in November 2003 but would never climb that high again. There was speculation that it would make a good takeover target or that Killinger's days as CEO were numbered. He sent a memo to the board of directors assuring them that selling WaMu was ill-advised. He promised to deliver "higher margin products," meaning riskier mortgages. And he decided to cut costs. About thirteen thousand employees lost their jobs, and branches were closed.[37]

Former CEO Lou Pepper sent Killinger a letter advising him to reduce executive pay by several million dollars: "Naturally you as CEO and COO, take the biggest hit, but if you are serious about saving the place, you will show that either it will be saved, or you will take a hit with the rest of the folks that work here, especially as the problems are not their doing." But Killinger's salary, bonus, and perks increased in 2004. The decline in earnings for 2004 appear to have motivated him to turn things around, and he saw the subprime and Option ARM loans as the key to growth. Pressure on employees to pump up volume intensified. At monthly rallies, prizes were given to the loan processors and underwriters at WaMu who funded the most loans. According to a Senate committee report, "Killinger identified residential nonprime and adjustable rate mortgages as one of the primary bank businesses driving balance sheet growth."[38]

Higher-Risk Lending Strategy

With earnings down by $1.5 billion for 2004 and talk of a takeover, Killinger increased higher-risk loans to borrowers who had not previously qualified for mortgages. In December 2004 a presentation to the board of directors about the "Higher Risk Lending Strategy" described higher-risk loans as those made when the borrower had a down payment or equity of 10 percent or less; stated-income "no documentation" loans; and those where there was "higher uncertainty about ability to pay" or "higher uncertainty about willingness to pay or collateral value." Categories included Option ARMs, home equity, and subprime.[39]

This was a transitional moment for all competitors who were originating high-risk mortgages. Around that time, one of CEO Angelo Mozilo's senior executives at Countrywide, Stan Kurland, set a similar direction. Kurland announced Countrywide's "determination to dominate the ARM market."[40]

WaMu and its peers were helped by Fed chairman Alan Greenspan. In a speech to the Credit Union National Association in early 2004, Greenspan declared that "American consumers might benefit if lenders provided greater mortgage-product alternatives." For those who were "willing to manage their own interest-rate risks, the traditional fixed-rate mortgage may be an expensive method of financing a home." More Americans were willing to manage these risks than, in fact, proved able to do so.[41]

In retrospect, it is hard to imagine how people with negatively amortizing loans were going to manage interest rate risk better than Killinger himself, whose own efforts to manage his risk resulted in a loss of more than a billion dollars. Shortly after Greenspan's speech, the Fed began again to raise interest rates from 1 percent in June up to 4.5 percent before he retired in January 2006. Mortgage rates also rose for Option ARMs and subprime borrowers with ARMs. Of course, given the delayed recasts, many borrowers would not notice for years. But the higher the rates went, the more their equity eroded and the greater their eventual payment shock. Yet for banks holding Option ARMs on their portfolios, the Fed's rate-raising guaranteed higher profits—the more deferred the interest, the greater the lenders' income.[42]

In January 2005, Killinger sought the board's approval to implement the higher-risk lending plan as an official corporate strategy. This was the strategy previously discussed with the board in December. The WaMu management team described the plan to increase volume and sell or securitize the mortgages. This presentation provided evidence that the higher-risk strategy would create problems years down the road. A PowerPoint slide shown to the board finance committee included a graph titled "Lags in Effects of Expansion," showing that losses from the new strategy would peak in mid-2007. To be sure viewers got this message, just above this high point were the words: "Peak loss rates occur several years after origination." This higher-risk lending (HRL) strategy would deliver homeowner defaults and losses to WaMu. This point was made clear in a comment running across the top of the slide: "The illustration below shows the lagged effect of losses on a Higher Risk Lending Portfolio. Our modeling indicates that credit-related losses from a newly originated HRL portfolio (one-time growth in 2005) will occur several years after origination. This was the strategy previously discussed at a December 2004 board meeting."[43]

The board approved the strategy. By showing growth now and postponing losses, Killinger would continue to collect his annual compensation. In 2006, he earned about $18 million. From 2001 to 2007, his total compensation was about $88 million. Results were delivered. Overall, the push of these high-risk loans was profound. From 2005 through 2007, WaMu originated $49 billion in subprime and $59 billion in Option ARMs. An astonishing 73 percent of the Option ARMs and 50 percent of the subprime loans on WaMu's balance sheet at the end of 2007 were stated-income (liar's) loans.[44]

In public, WaMu acted as if the nontraditional loans were offered to help homeowners, but this was not the case. The decision was about revenue. These loans, including Option ARMs and subprime, were simply more profitable. WaMu yielded higher gains on sale than the safer fixed-rate mortgages.[45]

So Much to Gain on Sale

At a presentation to the WaMu board in 2006, David Schneider, who had replaced Craig Davis as president of the Home Loans Group, revealed the value of these high-risk products. Initially, after the American Savings Bank acquisition, WaMu held onto the Option ARMs that American Savings Bank originated. Recently, however, it had begun to sell huge amounts of them. The reason to keep these in the portfolio initially was that they were a good hedge. When interest rates went up, so did the income on these loans. Even when borrowers were making the minimum payments, these were considered profitable, as the deferred interest that piled up was treated as income for the bank. But things were changing. These loans were increasingly offered to borrowers who could never afford the recast rate. They could only pay if they could refinance the loan.

Suddenly, these Option ARMs were like the old bullet loans that commercial banks offered before the Great Depression. It was a Ponzi scheme; the loans only worked for borrowers and lenders if prices kept rising. Otherwise, they would default. Selling these mortgages after they were originated was therefore essential. At the same time, originating risky loans, even knowing the borrowers would default, was still part of the plan, given the "gain on sale."

The numbers told the story. Schneider explained that if they sold the safest loans they originated—the ones that would be approved by Fannie and Freddie—they would earn 13 basis points (0.13 percent). A fixed-rate mortgage that did not qualify for government-sponsored enterprise (GSE) purchase but could be sold to Wall Street had a higher gain on sale, 19 basis points. But Option ARMs were golden: they fetched 109 basis points, or 1.09 percent. Only home equity loans and subprime were more profitable, at 1.13 and 1.5 percent, respectively. That meant a gain of more than $10–15 million per $1 billion of those high-risk loans sold compared to just $1.3 million for $1 billion of the safest. It was a no-brainer. As long as there were willing buyers and it was still legal, the practice would continue.[46]

Investor Demand and the Supply Chain

Given the higher risk of default, it is surprising that there were so many interested buyers of Option ARMs and other risky mortgages, as well as securities backed by them. Securitization, in theory, allowed investors who wanted to take the risk to do so, and others to avoid it. The trusts that owned these risky mortgages issued many groupings or tranches of securities, each catering to the risk appetites of different investors. These were like the MBSs that Lewis Ranieri helped to invent, but more complex.

Instead of three tranches, these new ones might have fifteen or more, grouped into senior, mezzanine, and equity. The senior tranches had triple-A ratings, and investors who held these triple-As were paid back first. The home mortgage cash flows were used to return what they invested, plus some interest each month, until they were paid back in a few years. The slightly more risky securities, the middle or mezzanine tranches, were paid more slowly than the triple-As. The riskiest, the equity piece, got paid last—if it got paid at all—but had the most potential return.

Selling the triple-A pieces was easy. Many so-called "sophisticated" institutional investors, including retirement funds and banks here and abroad, did not understand what they were buying or didn't bother to learn. They looked at the yield and the rating and bought. Residential MBSs paid more interest than U.S. Treasury securities and received the same ratings, so they were comfortable investing. Meanwhile, hedge funds, other asset managers, and banks often bought the equity pieces because they paid the highest interest. This piece was necessary to fund the MBSs, as some equity capital was necessary under accounting rules. The mezzanine or middle tranches were harder to sell. Some big institutional investors either could not or would not buy them, as they were not investment grade. But the middle pieces were designed to absorb the losses from defaults to protect the triple-A investors. Yet no one wanted to take that risk for so little yield.[47]

As a result, by 2005, a whole new practice had developed to get those middle pieces sold. A second pool, structured as a trust (or other type of conduit), would be set up to purchase the triple-Bs. Indeed, virtually all of the triple-B tranches that were sold were purchased by such trusts. The trusts got the money to buy the midlevel securities by issuing their own securities, called collateralized debt obligations (CDOs). This was a pool of securities instead of a pool of loans. Investors in CDOs could choose from a variety of tranches, including triple-A. The first CDO that was rated had been created by Michael Milken at Drexel Burnham Lambert in 1987 to pool junk bonds.[48]

Investment banks, including Merrill Lynch, Goldman Sachs, and Citigroup, structured many of the CDOs issued between 2004 and 2007. As underwriters, they earned sizable fees, but they took on risk because they had to hold the triple-B-rated securities until investors bought their securities. To avoid conflicts, independent CDO managers, hired by the banks, selected the MBS tranches for inclusion in the trust. Money was earned on fees and on the spread—the difference between the interest coming in from the triple-B tranches and the interest the trust had to pay out to its own CDO investors. Between 2003 and 2007, CDO managers across the industry earned about $1.5 billion in management fees. Midlevel tranches of CDOs that could not be sold to investors were often sold into a new trust called a "CDO squared."[49]

The demand by institutional investors worldwide for the triple-A tranches, and by CDO managers for triple-Bs, made it easier for lenders to fund mortgages. Sales of CDOs that depended on the cash flows from MBSs grew exponentially. In 2005, about $178 billion in such CDOs were issued; in 2006, this figure grew to $316 billion. Without this assembly line, there would not have been the high "gain on sale" percentages for the highest-risk mortgages. Wall Street's demand for MBSs coincided with Kerry Killinger's higher-risk lending strategy.[50]

Retirement funds, and other investors that could only purchase the triple-A-rated tranches, typically relied on the ratings put on these securities by the credit rating agencies. Or, they relied on credit protection they purchased separately. This credit insurance, known as "credit default swaps" and sold by firms like American International Group (AIG), would pay out if the CDOs defaulted. AIG earned fees for providing this protection. But because credit default swaps were not regulated as insurance, AIG did not have to set aside any reserves should payouts be necessary.

Meanwhile, institutional investors bought the MBSs and the triple-A-rated CDOs without deep examination. Like the homeowners at the other end of the securitization chain, they were enticed by the upside without being sufficiently informed about the risks. And like the homeowners, many of the big investors that purchased these securities, especially hedge funds, investment banks, and commercial banks, put down little of their own money. The investment banks were often highly leveraged. They borrowed more than $98 for every $100 in assets they bought. Commercial banks borrowed as much as $96 to $97—and this was only for assets they kept on the balance sheet. The accounting rules of the time let them hide a good deal of what they owed.

The higher gain on sale that Wall Street paid WaMu was based on the desire to use subprime loans and Option ARMs as raw material in the supply chain or "factory line." As former Citigroup CEO Charles Prince described it: "As more and more and more of these subprime mortgages were created as raw material for the securitization process, not surprisingly in hindsight, more and more of it was lower and lower quality . . . and that is what ended up coming out the other end of the pipeline. Wall Street obviously participated in that flow of activity."[51] The Wall Street participants in this flow included Merrill Lynch, which, after a slow start, was hugely active in mortgage CDOs. In 2003, Merrill underwrote $3.4 billion of these CDOs. But between 2004 and 2006, it became the leader in mortgage CDO underwriting, reaching $44 billion in 2006 and earning between $15 million and $20 million on every billion. Merrill's sales team sold these to pension funds, hedge funds, and other large investors. To keep this business growing, Merrill made the mistake of "eating its own cooking." It held tranches of the CDOs it underwrote on its own balance sheet. As a result, at the height of the subprime mortgage crisis in the middle of 2007, Merrill owned $41 billion in CDOs and had no willing buyers.[52]

The Rating Agencies

Why rating agencies like Moody's, Standard & Poor's (S&P), and Fitch awarded top ratings on securities backed by cash flows from mortgages that were doomed to default is an important question. Follow the money: these agencies were not paid by investors, but by the issuers of the securities. Before the era of private-label MBSs and CDOs, the ratings agencies were trained to rate government and corporate bonds. This new flood of MBSs and CDOs, as well as even more-exotic synthetic vehicles, provided more fee income for the rating agencies.[53]

When employees at S&P requested sufficient details so that they could properly assess the risk of default and thus assign a valid rating, they were verbally attacked by their supervisors. For example, an S&P employee asked for loan-level detail, meaning information about the mortgages underlying an MBS he was supposed to rate. While this would seem like a reasonable request, the employee received an e-mail response from his supervisor: "Any request for loan level tapes is TOTALLY UNREASONABLE!!! Most investors don't have it and can't provide it. We MUST produce a credit estimate. It is your responsibility to provide those credit estimates and your responsibility to devise some method for doing so."[54] And this was apparently not an anomaly. In an e-mail disclosed as part of litigation, one S&P executive wrote: "Lord help our fucking scam . . . this has to be the stupidest place I have worked at." And, a high-level analyst admitted: "As you know, I had difficulties explaining 'HOW' we got to those numbers since there is no science behind it."[55]

Fitch conducted an internal review of a sample of nonprime loan files after the nonprime securitization market stopped functioning in 2007. The reviewers found "the appearance of fraud or misrepresentation in almost every file." Most troubling, they concluded that this could have been "identified with adequate underwriting, quality control and fraud prevention tools prior to the loan funding."[56]

The Second-Worst-Managed Business

It was not just the subprime business that was mismanaged. Steve Rotella, the president and chief operating officer who joined WaMu in early 2005, noticed problems right away. He thought Long Beach was the worst-managed business he had ever seen, other than WaMu's prime mortgage operation. WaMu classified Option ARMs as part of its prime business. Rumors had been spreading within the bank for years of rampant fraud at two high-volume loan offices in Downey and Montebello, in Southern California. Loan consultant

Tom Ramirez worked at the Downey office; he had been honored as a top producer at each annual President's Club event for years. His loan of choice was the Option ARM.[57]

An internal investigation in 2005 exposed how Ramirez and his colleagues worked. Fifty-eight percent of the files at the Downey office and 83 percent of those at Montebello contained fraud, "virtually all of it," the investigators concluded, "stemming from employees in these areas circumventing policy surrounding loan verification and review." On one application, everything was invented, from the name to the social security number to the reference letters. On another, the size of the home was altered to inflate the appraised value.[58]

The report recommended that "firm action be taken to address these particular willful behaviors on the part of the employees named." The action taken with regard to these employees spoke for itself. Tom Ramirez received an invitation to the annual President's Club event held in February 2006. He was brought onstage amid much fanfare, treated like a star, and presented with a glass trophy for making 2,334 mortgages in 2005, amounting to $697 million in loans. Some of these he made directly; others were originated by junior loan consultants under his supervision. Senior management called Ramirez a "true visionary." "No one in history," one executive gushed, "has put more people into their first home." Minutes later, Earvin "Magic" Johnson came onstage to praise the President's Club members. The investigative report alleging that Ramirez's mortgages were laced with fraud was apparently forgotten.[59]

The fraud at the Downey and Montebello offices was not unique for WaMu. Fraud was the inevitable and well-known by-product of pressure on employees to get loans funded. The incentive structure ensured that loan officers were paid more per loan if they reached volume targets. Even risk-management personnel were evaluated based on their support of revenue growth. Troubles in the prime loan group were ignored.[60]

WaMu's senior management delayed considering the unpleasant reality that their highest-volume salesmen were contributing to the bottom line by either overlooking or committing fraud. Yet they also ignored something larger. Rising single-family home prices, fed by their lending practices, had led to a record level of new home construction. Whereas home construction had historically comprised about 4 percent of the gross domestic product (GDP), by 2005 it was up to 6 percent. Then vacancies began to rise. In late 2005, the vacancy rate passed its historic peak and kept rising. With more supply than demand, prices could only head in the other direction. Senior management, who for years had avoided dealing with fraud, also closed their eyes to the other elephant in the room, the rapidly inflating multitrillion-dollar housing bubble. Now, that bubble was collapsing.[61]

11

The Bubble

Everybody saw it coming. It was not a question of whether American home prices were inflated beyond sustainable levels. The only mystery was precisely when the bubble would burst, what the precipitating event would be, how big the losses would be, and who would bear them. At 10:03 a.m. on March 10, 2005, Kerry Killinger sent an e-mail message to James Vanasek, his chief enterprise risk officer.[1]

Killinger was responding to a compliance update that Vanasek had sent earlier that morning. He started with a few words of encouragement. "Thanks Jim. Overall, it appears we are making some good progress. Hopefully, the Regulators will agree that we are making some progress." Then he included a cautionary note, rather like a stop sign for a car that has already driven over a cliff:

> I suspect the toughest thing for us will be to navigate through a period of high home prices, increased competitive conditions for reduced underwriting standards, and our need to grow the balance sheet. I have never seen such a high-risk housing market as market after market thinks they are unique and for whatever reason are not likely to experience price declines. This typically signifies a bubble.[2]

That afternoon, Vanasek responded: "I could not agree more. All the classic signs are there and the likely outcome is probably not great. We would all like to think the air can come out of the balloon slowly but history would not lean you in that direction."[3]

This was not the first exchange at Washington Mutual (WaMu) about the housing bubble. According to an e-mail from Vanasek to the appraisal and underwriting staff in fall 2004, Killinger and other senior executives were worried about the bubble. Similar concerns surfaced at Countrywide, where risk managers internally warned of the negative impact of risky lending.[4]

Nevertheless, in January 2005, WaMu management presented the higher-risk lending strategy for the board of directors' approval. This strategy was certain to cause both homeowner defaults and losses for WaMu. Although the March 2005 e-mail exchange with Vanasek may not have been his first words about the bubble, it is still notable for other reasons. It revealed the trade-off Killinger likely perceived between growth and consumer protection and showed how competitive pressures produced a race to the bottom in lending standards. If WaMu didn't make the loan or buy it from an independent broker or wholesaler, someone else would.[5]

Killinger's e-mail confession to Vanasek demonstrates that any hope for a large business to self-regulate at the expense of profit is likely not tenable on a playing field with competitors waiting to take one's place. And especially not when a CEO and other top executives are compensated for driving up short-term profits and thus the stock price, even when losses are certain to follow. The 2008 board-committee-approved formula for calculating cash bonuses for top WaMu executives excluded mortgage losses and foreclosure expenses.[6]

Vanasek did try to persuade Killinger to forgo short-term profits and market share to protect the business in the long run. In 2004, he personally implored Killinger to take a stand to stop the worst high-risk lending. Vanasek suggested that WaMu place a full-page advertisement in the *Wall Street Journal* "disavowing many of the then-current industry underwriting practices, such as 100 percent loan-to-value subprime loans, and thereby adopt what I termed responsible lending practices." He understood that this would involve relinquishing "a degree of market share and [they would] lose some of the originators to competition," but felt it was important for WaMu to "take an industry-leading position against deteriorating underwriting standards and products that were not in the best interests of the industry, the bank or the consumers." Vanasek received no response to that appeal. He was by then accustomed to being ignored by senior management. Killinger had decided to stay on the field rather than work to change the rules of the game.[7]

In December 2005, several months after the "bubble" exchange, Vanasek retired. Once he left, many of the risk management policies he had implemented as the chief enterprise risk officer were overlooked or discarded. Around this time, former CEO Lou Pepper stopped working as an adviser to WaMu. By then, he recalled that "it had turned into a different place. . . . It wasn't as friendly, it wasn't as nice." Killinger's voices of reason were gone.[8]

Expert Bubble Talk

Outside the firm, warnings were sounded that a housing bubble was growing and that predatory lending would harm not only individuals but the entire financial system. Among the first to speak out was economist Dean Baker of the Center for Economic and Policy Research. In August 2002, he published a briefing paper entitled "The Run-Up in Home Prices: Is It Real or Is It Another Bubble?" In the paper, Baker noted that since 1995, home prices had risen out of step with overall inflation. He also saw a widening divergence between the cost to rent and the cost to own. This suggested that something beyond the fundamental value of a place to live was driving up prices.[9]

Baker noted that the housing bubble had created an additional $2.7 trillion in household wealth by 2002. In the short term, this had a positive impact on the economy. Home construction boomed, and the demand for goods and services rose as homeowners saved less and spent more—both because they saw their homes as a store of savings and because they were cashing out equity and spending it on goods and services. Baker warned that when the bubble burst, both families and the overall economy would suffer. Homeowners would lose their home equity and the economy would lose a critical source of demand once housing construction fell. Meanwhile, the benefits the bubble delivered persuaded some to pretend it wasn't there and keep it growing. As data would later show, between 2003 and 2008, fees associated with home sales and mortgage originations generated about $2 trillion.[10]

In the summer of 2005, Robert Shiller, an economist at Yale (who was awarded the Nobel Prize in Economics in 2013), and Karl Case, an economist at Wellesley, charted the dramatic rise in home prices. Shiller began speaking out about the biggest housing boom in our nation's history, suggesting that the same irrational exuberance that drove up stock prices between 1995 and 2000 was now affecting housing prices. "This is the biggest boom we've ever had." He had predicted the end of the dot-com bubble in his book *Irrational Exuberance*, published just as the bubble burst in 2000.[11]

There was talk of a bubble later, in summer of 2005, at an annual gathering of economists in Jackson Hole, Wyoming, sponsored by the Federal Reserve Bank of Kansas City. Susan Wachter, a professor of real estate and finance at Wharton, discussed a paper in which she suggested that the United States might soon suffer a crisis comparable to the one that affected Asia in the 1990s. She later recalled that her presentation was "universally panned" and that an economist with the Mortgage Bankers Association called her supposition "absurd." Paul McCulley, a managing director at the giant investment management firm Pacific Investment Management Company, LLC (PIMCO), saw "serious signs of bubbles" in 2005. He sent credit analysts from PIMCO to twenty different cities where they saw "the outright degradation of underwriting standards." The firm cut back on its exposure to risky residential mortgage-linked securities.[12]

The way homes were financed helped create the bubble. Millions of people were willing to pay higher and higher prices for homes, even though they could not actually make their mortgage payments unless they refinanced. Banks, thrifts, hedge funds, and other financial firms invested in assets dependent on borrowers' making their payments. These assets included residential mortgages, residential mortgage-backed securities (MBSs), collateralized debt obligations (CDOs) built from those securities, synthetic versions of these CDOs, and derivatives linked to them. Like homeowners, these financial institutions that invested in these securities often were highly leveraged; should home values decline, they would need to de-leverage and sell off their mortgage-linked assets into a falling market. They, like homeowners, depended on rising home prices. If one domino fell, many would follow.

Ponzi Financing

The situation resembled what the late Hyman Minsky called "Ponzi finance," in a theory he articulated in 1986. Minsky was a professor at Washington University and later a distinguished scholar at the Levy Economics Institute of Bard College. Since the recent crisis, his Financial Instability Hypothesis has attracted broader attention. Building on John Maynard Keynes, Minsky hypothesized that the main causes of instability in financial markets were not external factors but internal, "endogenous" ones. He identified three distinct debt structures: hedge, speculative, and Ponzi finance. An entity with a hedge financing structure is able to meet all of its contractual obligations using incoming cash flows. The second type of entity, one with a speculative financing structure, can make interest payments on debt but does not have enough cash coming in to pay principal balances when due and thus needs to refinance or "roll over" that debt. The third type, an entity with a Ponzi financing structure, does not have sufficient cash flow from operations to pay either interest or principal on outstanding debt. To survive, it must either continue to borrow money or sell assets.[13]

Minksy suggested that an economy with more entities with hedge financing was more stable than one dominated by speculative and Ponzi finance. Over time, he wrote, capitalist economies move from financing regimes that foster stability to ones that create instability. In other words, they move toward riskier financing structures. If speculative and Ponzi finance dominate during periods of asset inflation, then when the monetary supply is tightened and interest rates rise, those entities without adequate cash flows will be forced to sell assets in a hurry, collapsing asset prices.[14]

Martin Wolfson, a professor of economics at Notre Dame, also studied the relationship between leverage, bubbles, and crises. In his book, *Financial Crises: Understanding the Postwar U.S. Experience*, he surveyed the historical theories of financial crises and found that all of them involved the accumulation of debt. John Geanakoplos, a professor of economics at Yale, described a related process—excess borrowing drives up asset prices: "In the absence of intervention, leverage becomes too high in boom times, and too low in bad times. As a result, in boom times asset prices are too high, and in crisis times they are too low. This is the leverage cycle."[15]

Booms and busts, though enabled by debt and other forms of leverage, are not inevitable. For financial firms, honest accounting and countercyclical safety and soundness ("prudential") supervision can help prevent massive bubbles from inflating. These measures must be widely enforced, however, or else money will move to the place of least scrutiny. Prudential supervision is the role of the banking regulators, including our central bank, the Federal Reserve. This is what former Fed chairman William McChesney Martin famously described in 1955 to an audience of investment bankers. He said that the central banker "is in the position of the chaperone who has ordered the punch bowl removed just when the party was really warming up." But early intervention to prevent Ponzi financing requires a willing Fed chairman.[16]

THE GREENSPAN PUT

When Fed chairman Alan Greenspan finally began speaking about the overheated housing market, he suggested it was a localized phenomenon, not a national one and that it had not quite reached the bubble phase. In a September 2005 satellite address to the American Bankers Association convention in Palm Desert, California, he said: "In the United States, signs of froth have clearly emerged in some local markets where home prices seem to have risen to unsustainable levels." He commented on the "long list of novel mortgage products, not only interest-only mortgages but also . . . option ARMs, which allow for a limited amount of negative amortization." These loans could hurt homeowners because "they expose borrowers to more interest-rate and house-price risk than the standard thirty-year, fixed-rate mortgage and because they are seen as vehicles that enable marginally qualified, highly leveraged borrowers to purchase homes at inflated prices."[17]

Greenspan warned that "to the extent that some households may be employing [the more exotic mortgages] to purchase a home that would otherwise be unaffordable, their use is adding to the pressures in the marketplace." At the time, about 70 percent of homeowners with Option ARMs who made minimum payments were doing just that—information to which the Fed chairman surely had access. He also drew a connection between these loans and the deflation of a bubble: "In the event of widespread cooling in house prices, these borrowers, and the institutions that service them, could be exposed to significant losses."[18]

Around this time, Utah attorney Sheila Canavan attended a meeting of the Fed Consumer Advisory Council. This council was created in 1976 and comprised up to thirty members appointed by the Fed's Board of Governors. It was tasked with meeting at least annually and consulting with the Fed on consumer-related matters. Canavan worried about the large percentage of interest-only mortgages in California. She later testified to the Financial Crisis Inquiry Commission (FCIC) that she told the Fed governors at the meeting, "we're facing something down the road that we haven't faced before and we are going to be looking at a safety and soundness crisis." After that meeting, a staff member of the Fed Division of Banking Supervision and Regulation asked the largest banks what types of exotic loans they were making and brought those results back to the Fed governors. He described the results as "alarming." Not only was there a high percentage of nontraditional loans, but two-thirds of those loans were stated income or "liar's loans." According to former Fed governor Susan Bies, the report was ignored because some of the governors and the regional Fed directors "wanted to come to a different answer."[19]

By that point in late 2005, the supply of housing had outstripped demand. Vacancy rates were passing their historic peak. Raising interest rates would likely deflate the bubble but cause a crisis. A better move would have been to require sound underwriting standards years earlier, forbidding lenders to get homeowners into loans they could not afford to pay on the reset or recast dates. This would have helped avoid the run-up in home prices. Greenspan's ideological opposition to government regulation is one reason it did not happen.[20]

As he would explain after the crash in October 2008, Greenspan's entire framework rested on a faulty foundation. That "intellectual edifice" collapsed along with housing prices and the financial system. Before he came to that realization, however, Greenspan thought banks would never sacrifice long-term shareholder value for short-term gain. Such a view overlooked the competitive pressures and incentives that CEOs faced.[21]

As for bubbles, Greenspan believed it was better to let them expand and burst, and then mop up. The cleaning up involved expanding the money supply, causing interest rates to decline, and thus stimulating the economy. On several occasions, Greenspan made it clear that through the Federal Open Market Committee, he would ease the money supply to help rescue the banks from their own decision to leverage up for profit. In a speech delivered in 2000, he recognized the relationship between low capital (high leverage) and banks externalizing their losses, requiring the Fed, as lender-of-last resort, to bail them out:

> [W]e have chosen capital standards that by any stretch of the imagination cannot protect against all potential adverse loss outcomes. There is implicit in this exercise the admission that, in certain episodes, problems at commercial banks and other financial institutions, when their risk-management systems prove inadequate, will be handled by central banks. At the same time, society on the whole should require that we set this bar very high. Hundred-year floods come only once every hundred years. Financial institutions should expect to look to the central bank only in extremely rare situations.[22]

This implicit promise to lower interest rates to help the banks if necessary was known as the "Greenspan Put." The holder of a put option has the right to sell an asset to a buyer at a specific price before a future deadline. For example, the owner of stock currently trading at $50 per share who believes it might decline in value could purchase a put option, granting the right, but not the obligation, to sell those shares to a counterparty for $50 each. This has the advantage of allowing the shareholder to obtain gains if the stock actually goes up in price, while also protecting against losses. Thus, the Greenspan Put referred to a kind of insurance, or floor on losses. Greenspan had succeeded with this mop-up technique before. He guided the Fed to lower interest rates after the stock market crash of 1987 and after the dot-com stock bubble burst in 2000. These moves each helped boost the stock market, as investors sought higher returns than the very low interest on debt securities. By announcing that he intended to intervene in the future to stabilize the market, Greenspan created a moral hazard. Banks and other financial firms would not take precautions but would profit through high leverage and risky assets, because Greenspan had reduced their risk.[23]

Though Greenspan cautioned that the Fed would intervene only once a century, in fact, easing and other government support of failed financial firms was already happening more frequently. Since his tenure began in 1987, in addition to mopping up after the stock market crash, the savings and loan (S&L) bailouts had occurred, the implosion of the giant hedge fund Long-Term Capital Management had required a private rescue organized by the New York Fed, and the Fed had mopped up after the dot-com bubble. In January 2004, Greenspan would again advocate a bailout after collapse. Addressing the American Economic Association in San Diego, he said that it was his plan "to mitigate the fallout when it occurs and, hopefully, ease the transition to the next expansion." Once again, he implied that the Fed would do for any asset bubble what it had done since his tenure began: allow it to inflate and burst, and clean up the mess. The economy had always recovered after his past interventions, though the most recent recovery, after the dot-com bubble, was not attributable to monetary policy as much as to a new bubble—housing.

The wealth effect and cash-out refinancings from that bubble stimulated the construction industry and consumer spending.[24]

Moreover, unlike previous bubbles under his watch, which related only to securities, the housing bubble affected securities, banking, and many people's greatest—sometimes only—store of savings. And it was more than just an asset, it was a home.

The Bullet

Greenspan had authority beyond just monetary policy. The Fed also had responsibility for consumer protection. Under the Home Ownership and Equity Protection Act of 1994 (HOEPA), to prevent the Ponzi financing that was taking over the economy, Greenspan's Fed could make rules that applied to all mortgage originators, not just banks. He and other members of the Fed Board of Governors were urged to do so. But year after year, the Fed ignored this advice. Greenspan retired in early 2006, less than six months before housing prices would reverse. His replacement as chairman, Ben Bernanke, would have to mop up after him. Greenspan never did use his authority under HOEPA. If he had done so, the time to act would have been well before originators like WaMu began building their entire strategic plans on high-risk loans.[25]

Other federal regulators suggested early intervention. In 2001, Sheila Bair was in Washington, pushing for restrictions on high-risk lending. Bair came to Washington from Kansas in the 1980s to work for Senator Bob Dole and served as Assistant Secretary for Financial Institutions in the George W. Bush Treasury Department from 2001 to 2002. In that role, she tried to curtail the worst abuses but was thwarted. After a brief period in academia, she returned to Washington as chairman of the Federal Deposit Insurance Corporation (FDIC) in the summer of 2006. After purchasing a database that provided detail on outstanding mortgages, Bair was surprised to learn that abusive practices that had been on the fringes in 2002 were now mainstream. She later shared with the Financial Crisis Inquiry Commission (FCIC) her view of the "one bullet" that would have prevented the crisis:

> I absolutely would have been over at the Fed writing rules, prescribing mortgage lending standards across the board for

> everybody, bank and nonbank, that you cannot make a mortgage unless you have documented income that the borrower can repay the loan.[26]

In the summer of 2006, when Bair became chairman of the FDIC, WaMu was a leader in making mortgages without documented income. Kerry Killinger's strategic plan depended on it. At the end of September 2006, the federal banking regulators jointly published voluntary guidance regarding nontraditional mortgages. Even though it was not mandatory, industry lobbyists had fought to prevent and delay these guidelines. Fed governor Susan Bies recalled: "The members of Congress pushed back. Some of our internal people at the Fed pushed back." In contrast, the lobbying association for mortgage insurance companies supported cutting back on risky loans.[27]

One provision of the nonbinding guidance was especially important for WaMu's flagship Option ARM product:

> An institution's analysis of a borrower's repayment capacity should include an evaluation of their ability to repay the debt by final maturity at the fully indexed rate . . . . In addition, for products that permit negative amortization, the repayment analysis should be based upon the initial loan amount plus any balance increase that may accrue from the negative amortization provision.[28]

The guidance also said that regulators would deem loans "unsafe and unsound" if repayment depended solely on the borrower's selling the home in order to pay it back. In other words, this guidance tried to end one form of Ponzi financing.[29]

Much of the guidance was common sense, except that lenders were not using common sense. For example, the guidance recommended that lenders "more diligently verify and document a borrowers income" when making a high-risk loan. It also suggested that sales materials present "clear and balanced" information about the benefits and risks of Option ARMs.[30]

When the voluntary guidance was issued, big players decided to ignore it, including WaMu. This was a considered judgment: analysts inside WaMu ran the numbers. If WaMu followed the guidance, its loan volume would drop 33 percent. This was because since 2004, when WaMu originated Option ARMs, it did not use the full indexed rate in deciding whether to approve these loans. In response to the internal analysis in March 2007, Ron Cathcart, the chief enterprise risk officer, sent an e-mail to Home Loans Group president, Dave Schneider, indicating that these facts suggested "holding off on implementation [of the guidelines] until required to act for public relations . . . or regulatory reasons."[31]

In retrospect, this should not be too surprising. The big subprime and nontraditional originators' business models were built around precisely the bad practices the banking agencies hoped they would avoid. This guidance was not much more than a continuation of the Greenspan era, where the expectation was that voluntary self-regulation or "private ordering" would effectively regulate the market.[32]

But nobody was behaving the way Alan Greenspan's ideology said they would. The years of forbearance, of refusal to create regulations that would have banned the high-risk loans, were based on expectations of what motivates private market actors. Before a congressional committee in 2008, after the meltdown, Greenspan explained:

> Those of us who have looked to the self-interest of lending institutions to protect shareholder's equity (myself especially) are in a state of shocked disbelief. Such counterparty surveillance is a central pillar of our financial markets' state of balance. If it fails, as occurred this year, market stability is undermined.[33]

In fact, nobody was looking out for long-term shareholder equity. Thus, voluntary guidance was no restraint on abusive lending practices. For example, Kerry Killinger did not stop originating toxic loans, though doing so hurt his shareholders in the long run. Counterparties lending money to WaMu, as well as Wall Street firms that transformed WaMu's MBSs into CDOs and those who purchased them, did not show restraint while there were fees to be made, though this hurt their shareholders as well.

Greenspan also thought "sophisticated investors" would police the markets better than regulators. Yet he and others espousing a hands-off approach later realized that institutional investors did not have the necessary information or skills; they relied on triple-A ratings from the credit rating agencies. These rating agencies that were supposed to act as private gatekeepers did not restrain fraud and abuse; they earned fees and ignored the loan-level data. Until these high-risk lending practices were made illegal, they would continue to inflate the bubble and set up the country for a major reversal, and homeowners for foreclosure.[34]

Greenspan appeared not to expect that in the face of the giant bubble, with no regulator or firm willing to stop the music, Wall Street would do what it could do. And what it could do was trade. If the whole system was going to collapse, the smart money set up deals so they could get paid when disaster struck. They used credit default swaps to place their bets. In the simplest sense, these savvy traders at the wisest investment banks and hedge funds would get paid if borrowers with loans from originators—including WaMu and its Long Beach subsidiary—defaulted. These were among the mortgages handpicked by hedge funds with help from Wall Street bankers, as they were likely to default.

I'm Short Your House

By February 2006, just after Greenspan retired, it was widely known that mortgages originated by WaMu's Long Beach subsidiary were defaulting at higher rates than others. As a result, MBSs dependent on the cash flows from those borrowers were troubled. Greg Lippmann, a CDO trader at Deutsche Bank, shared his views in an e-mail. In reference to a subprime residential MBS issued by Long Beach, Lippmann wrote: "This bond blows."[35]

Lippmann was drumming up business, arranging the sale of credit default swaps. These were the insurance-like contracts that paid the buyer if the referenced security, such as an MBS or CDO tranche, defaulted. His strategy was like encouraging investors to take out insurance on homes they did not own because the structures were likely to be destroyed by fire. Instead of protection from potential home fires, though, he was brokering protection from potential home mortgage defaults. He was helping investors bet against or "short" other people's houses, anticipating a big payday if families in America lost their homes. Lippmann looked at the data and saw which residential MBSs were the worst. Such determinations could be based on geographic concentration of the dwellings or the reputation of the lender. He advised others, including hedge funds, what they should bet against. Among the "bad names" he identified were mortgages securitized by WaMu, including those from Long Beach. For example, during the fall of 2006, Lippmann sent this message to a client:

> LBMLT-06-5 M9-375. Long Beach is one of the weakest names in the market. We shorted this bond to a CDO in the mid-300s on October 13. Deal was done before S&P changed their criteria on July 1. . . . Less than half the loans have full documentation . . . . This is a real pig.[36]

Lippmann described the way investment banks underwrote CDOs as a "CDO system" and as a "Ponzi scheme." He complimented one client who seemed to be a quick study: "u have picked some crap right away so u have figured it out." In addition to such praise, Lippmann also gave his clients T-shirts on which the words "I'm short your house" were printed.[37]

Staying the Course

By early 2005, there were two common ways to deal with the multitrillion-dollar bubble in the room. One was the strategy of some prescient hedge funds and investment banks: to place big bets that would pay off when the crash came. Kerry Killinger took the second path; aware of the impending crash, he stayed the course. He kept originating toxic, high-risk mortgages and pushing them through the assembly line as MBSs. His competitors did the same, including Angelo Mozilo, CEO of Countrywide.

Between 2004 and 2007 after the refinancing business dried up, Mozilo had reluctantly moved from traditional mortgages into Option ARMs and interest-only structures. In September 2006, he revealed his worries in an e-mail message: "We have no way, with any reasonable certainty, to assess the real risk of holding these loans on our balance sheet." Still bothered the next day, Mozilo urged his team to sell off the Option ARMs in the Countrywide portfolio. He hoped to take advantage of a pricing anomaly before it was too late. Yet, like Killinger, Mozilo kept originating Option ARMs. And he was handsomely rewarded: beginning in November 2006, he sold his Countrywide stock holdings for approximately $140 million.[38]

Kerry Killinger, with his board's approval, continued his high-risk, higher-margin lending strategy. At a Senate investigative hearing in 2010, he said that he regularly warned others about the bubble and also that he put the high-risk strategy "on hold." Corporate records do not fully support his claim. In a June 2006 memo, he informed the board that the Home Loans Group planned to "curtail low margin Government and conventional fixed rate originations and servicing, and to significantly increase our origination and servicing of high margin home equity, Alt A., sub prime and option ARMS." The pace continued; Killinger wanted the Home Loans Group to "grow its market share" of these products "to over 10%." Even in 2007, he shared a similar strategic plan for the coming year: "We will continue to emphasize higher-risk adjusted return products."[39]

Killinger stayed the course because there were still buyers for these mortgages, as well as for the MBSs that WaMu securitized. Those buyers included Wall Street banks as well as the Federal National Mortgage Association (Fannie Mae) and the Federal Home Loan Mortgage Corporation (Freddie Mac), the government-sponsored enterprises (GSEs). But the GSEs initially made these purchases reluctantly.

Pressure at Fannie and Freddie

Killinger likely felt pressure to make or buy loans of increasingly poor quality to keep up with competitors like Countrywide, Ameriquest, IndyMac, and New Century Financial. Once WaMu's Long Beach subsidiary and other subprime lenders owned loans, they turned around and sold them. The major banks and investment banks, eager purchasers, competed to gain market share in the securitization of the riskiest loans into residential MBSs. Some purchased or developed their own subprime or high-risk lenders to create the raw materials they needed. For example, Bear Stearns, Citigroup, JPMorgan Chase, Merrill Lynch, Lehman, Wachovia, and Wells Fargo each owned or operated their own subprime lending units. Even General Electric and H&R Block had subprime lenders.[40]

Of course, Fannie and Freddie (the GSEs) never originated any home loans, subprime or other. And, unlike the eager banks on Wall Street, they were reluctant purchasers of nonconforming loans, such as subprime, stated income, and Option ARMs. Historically, the GSEs had only purchased traditional, thirty-year fixed loans that were underwritten very conservatively with high down payments. Only when loans met these standards were they deemed "conforming" and thus good to purchase.[41]

In 2005, shortly after being elevated from COO to CEO of Fannie Mae, Daniel Mudd sat down with Angelo Mozilo in California. Fannie was already a key customer: About one quarter of the loans Fannie purchased came from Countrywide. Mozilo wanted that volume to increase and to include a greater amount of high-risk loans. Mozilo told Mudd that Fannie was "becoming irrelevant." Fannie and Freddie had already begun to lose overall market share. Mozilo laid on the pressure, telling Mudd: "You need us more than we need you . . . and if you don't take these loans, you'll find you can lose much more." The hard sell may have been unnecessary. In 2004, before Mudd became CEO, internal memos at Fannie showed a desire to "deepen [the Countrywide] relationship at all levels." Mudd personally received a discounted $3 million loan from Countrywide to refinance his existing mortgage. The discount was so great that Countrywide apparently took a loss on the loan.[42]

At the time that Mozilo threatened to pull away from Fannie, Fannie was also struggling to keep loan volume from WaMu. In 2003, the big year for refinancings, WaMu sold $174 billion in loans to Fannie and just $2.2 billion to Freddie. Together, this represented 40 percent of its total originations. In 2005, WaMu ended its near-exclusive relationship with Fannie because Freddie became willing to buy WaMu's Option ARMs in large quantities. On the table during their discussions was whether Freddie would accept "lower documentation standards." Year after year, Fannie purchased less and less volume from WaMu while Freddie gained. Overall WaMu's sales to both GSEs declined from 40 percent of its originations in 2003 to a range of 10 to 23 percent through 2006.[43]

Fannie Mae, like Freddie Mac, was torn between two distinct missions, one public and one private. On one hand, it was a creature of federal statute and had a public mission to provide liquidity, affordability, and stability to the U.S. housing market. Like Freddie, it sought to fulfill this mission by buying conservatively underwritten mortgages, pooling them into a trust, and selling securities issued by those trusts. Purchasers of the securities issued by the trusts Fannie set up paid a fee, known as a G-fee, in exchange for a guarantee that Fannie would make principal and interest payments should the borrowers fail to do so. In 2004, the fee was about 20 basis points or 0.2 percent. This made these securities extremely safe. Only if Fannie was in trouble financially would it fail to honor the guarantee. And because it was a creature of Congress, every investor believed that the government would bail out Fannie and Freddie should they stumble—the implicit government guarantee. The GSEs made money if the G-fees collected exceeded their credit losses. Thus, the key risk to this guarantee business was credit risk. To manage that risk, they used complex computer models. The more risky a loan was perceived to be, the higher the G-fee charged to investors who purchased securities backed by such mortgages.[44]

The second way Fannie and Freddie served their housing mission was by purchasing for their portfolios mortgages originated by others. They also purchased privately issued MBSs but did not purchase CDOs. Their portfolios were large: Fannie began 2004 with more than $1 trillion in assets and Freddie with $800 billion. For this portfolio business, they made money the way traditional banks did, on the spread between the cost of funding and the income brought in by the mortgages and the MBSs they bought. But unlike traditional banks, Fannie and Freddie had lower funding costs because of the implicit government guarantee.[45]

The risks to the portfolio side of the business include that the borrowers of the underlying mortgages would default (credit risk), and that they might pay back their loans early and thus pay less interest (prepayment risk). There was also interest rate risk, the same risk that the GSEs and the S&Ls faced back in the 1980s: the value of the MBSs would decline if rates rose. Thus, to manage the portfolio business, Fannie and Freddie had to enter into hedges that were designed to offset losses created when interest rates shifted.[46]

In addition to their housing missions, Fannie and Freddie were also private corporations. When deciding to guarantee riskier loans and purchase riskier MBSs, Fannie's CEO, Daniel Mudd, owed a duty to provide sustainable returns to Fannie's shareholders. As such, he and Freddie's CEO sought ways to grow the business and return increasing profits. Some big investors were not shy about reminding the GSEs of this duty. One hedge fund manager called to complain that Fannie was not taking enough risk: "Are you stupid or blind? Your job is to make me money!"[47]

When Mudd made the decision to take on more risk, it had a massive impact. Between 2005 and 2008, Fannie would purchase or guarantee $270 billion in risky loans. It was too much, too fast. Fannie's systems were not built to handle the complexity. Marc Gott, the former head of Fannie's Loan Servicing Department, recalled: "We didn't really know what we were buying. . . . This system was designed for plain vanilla loans, and we were trying to push chocolate sundaes through the gears."[48]

Loans like Option ARMs, which were negative amortizing, as well as stated-income ("liar's") loans were new to the GSEs. It was hard for their computer systems to predict the risk of default. Thus, when Fannie or Freddie set its guarantee fees, they were not sufficient. Fannie's chief risk officer, hired in 2006, recommended to Mudd that given the increased risk of default, Fannie should charge a higher G-fee. He also warned Mudd that a housing bubble had formed but said he was ignored. In addition, buying up complex MBSs for the portfolio side involved even more risk. Though Mudd did not recall pressuring employees to hew to the new strategy, that is how some remembered it. At least two individuals present at a meeting with Mudd recall him ordering them to "get aggressive on risk-taking, or get out of the company." In that same era, Freddie Mac also ramped up its purchase of high-risk loans.[49]

Undermining the Risk Department

Killinger was also increasing risk, even as WaMu's risk and compliance employees were undermined. The job of a Compliance Department includes helping a business set up and follow policies and procedures to ensure that the company and its employees comply with laws, regulations, and terms of settlements. Compliance employees can be lawyers and often work closely with the Legal Department. A CEO not interested in complying with the law might undermine the compliance personnel. Several banks and other financial institutions leading up to the 2008 crisis seemed to have such CEOs. At WaMu, a 2007 report written by Susie Clark, an Office of Thrift Supervision (OTS) examiner, noted that between 2000 and 2007, Killinger had gone through nine different compliance leaders. As a result, she contended, the WaMu "compliance management program has suffered from a lack of steady consistent leadership." In case this did not capture her readers' attention, she added:

> This amount of turnover is very unusual for an institution of this size and is a cause for concern. The Board of Directors should commission an evaluation of why smart, successful, effective managers can't succeed in this position. If you would like my opinion, just ask. (HINT: It has to do with top management not buying into the importance of compliance and turf warfare and Kerry not liking bad news.)[50]

The Bubble Deflates

As always, Kerry Killinger was optimistic, even in the face of the downturn. By the middle of 2006, overbuilding during the mortgage-debt-fueled housing construction boom was putting downward pressure on prices, and the median price of homes in the United States started to decline for the first time in more than a decade. Home sales also dropped off by 15 percent from the peak. With prices also dropping, borrowers who could not make subprime mortgage payments on reset or Option ARM payments on recast could neither refinance nor sell because, at best, they had no equity. At worst, they had negative equity. By the end of 2006, more than eighty thousand subprime borrowers were behind on their monthly payments. Many of these mortgages were originated at WaMu, including Long Beach.[51]

The Federal Open Market Committee (FOMC) gathered on June 28 and 29, 2006, for its monthly meeting. The transcripts of that meeting, released in 2012, include not just what was said but also note, in brackets, when there was laughter. There was quite a bit of nervous laughter over those two days. At one point, George Guynn, president of the Federal Reserve Bank of Atlanta, provided an update of the economic conditions in his region, the Sixth District, which included Alabama, Florida, Georgia, and parts of Tennessee, Louisiana, and Mississippi. The transcript reads:

> Housing prices are not falling quite as much as the decline in sales and the rise in unsold inventories might suggest. We are getting reports that builders are now making concessions and providing upgrades, such as marble countertops and other extras, and in one case even throwing in a free Mini Cooper to sweeten the deal [laughter] rather than reducing prices. So real house prices may be declining more than the data suggest.[52]

These sweeteners affected appraisals. If someone paid $20,000 extra for a home because it came with a car, the sale price shown on the deed would be padded by that amount, and the padded amount would be recorded at the registry of deeds and used as data in appraisals of similar homes. Moreover, without the sweeteners, vacancy levels would be even higher. At that same meeting, it was observed that the various exotic mortgages, including ones that reset or recast, would not do so en masse until after 2007.[53]

In September 2006, the Bush administration was greatly concerned about the subprime crisis and its impact on the banking industry. The head of the Office of Federal Housing Enterprise Oversight (OFHEO), the agency that supervised Fannie and Freddie, authorized them to purchase up to $50 billion in subprime loans. At the September 20, 2006, meeting of the FOMC, Janet Yellen, who was then president of the Federal Reserve Bank of San Francisco, described what was happening in the Twelfth District, which included Alaska, Arizona, California, Hawaii, Idaho, Nevada, Oregon, Utah, and Washington. She recounted that during a discussion with a builder, he informed her that:

> home inventory has gone through the roof, so to speak. [Laughter] He literally said that. With the share of unsold homes topping 80 percent in some of the new subdivisions around Phoenix and Las Vegas, he has labeled these the new ghost towns of the West. . . . He had toured some new subdivisions on the outskirts of Boise and discovered that the houses, most of which are unoccupied, are now being dressed up to look occupied—with curtains, things in the driveway, and so forth—so as not to discourage potential buyers . . . builders now routinely offer huge incentives, and price cuts appear inevitable. . . . We need to keep a very close eye on the incoming data and watch whether the housing slowdown is turning into a slump.[54]

Alan Greenspan, who had left the Fed in February, had his own idea: burn down the houses. It was reminiscent of economist Robert Solow's comment about the Fed's plan in 1979 to let interest rates rise in order to tame inflation, which Solow compared to "burning down the house to roast the pig." When news of the statement came out, after much criticism, Greenspan explained himself. He told reporters that while he knew it was not "viable politically," he believed when he made the statement that it was the low-cost option. "Of all of the alternatives that were available," he suggested, "had the United States Government taken all of those units off the market and really prevented prices from falling as sharply as they did, the net effect would have been far less onerous than what we have run into."[55]

Soon, another indicator of trouble appeared. On February 27, 2007, Freddie Mac announced that it would stop buying certain risky mortgages and related securities. It would buy adjustable-rate mortgages only if the underwriters had determined that the borrowers were capable of paying not just the initial teaser rate but also the fully adjusted rate on reset or recast.[56]

Kerry's Optimism

Amid the decline, Kerry Killinger was thinking about an acquisition. Toward the end of 2006, Roland Arnall had put Ameriquest up for sale. Ameriquest had recently settled a suit with forty-nine states and the District of Columbia for $325 million. The complaint related to overcharging borrowers for mortgages and pressuring appraisers to submit inflated home values. Ameriquest employees also had promised borrowers no prepayment penalties but then changed the documents after they were signed. Arnall had settled with the Department of Justice in the 1990s, based on similar accusations. In 2005, while the newer settlement was pending, Arnall, a large campaign contributor, was nominated by President George W. Bush to be the U.S. ambassador to the Netherlands. At his Senate confirmation hearing, Arnall said that "Mistakes have been made" and when that happens, "We fix the problems." He served as ambassador from early 2006 until just weeks before his death in 2008.[57]

Kerry Killinger thought Ameriquest might be a bargain, given how nervous everyone was about stocks related to housing. The deal did not go forward. Meanwhile, mortgage originators, including WaMu, rushed to package up subprime mortgages and get them out the door, to put the risk of default in somebody else's hands. In the game of musical chairs, everyone sensed the music was about to stop. There was risk all along the assembly line.[58]

After subprime borrowers, the next group to default were those with Option ARMs. WaMu's portfolio was loaded with these mortgages. Kerry needed his team to sell as many of these loans as they could. The sense was that they were overpriced. After encouragement from Killinger to think seriously about selling the Option ARMs in WaMu's portfolio, Cheryl Feltgen, the chief risk officer for the Home Loans Group, sent an e-mail to her team on February 20, 2007, with the word "URGENT" in the subject line: "Gain on sale is attractive and this could be a way to address California concentration, rising delinquencies, falling house prices in California with a favorable arbitrage given that the market seems not yet to be discounting a lot for those factors." So employees combed through the files, examining loan-level details. Shortly thereafter, WaMu had selected 1,900 delinquency-prone Option ARMs worth approximately $1 billion, pooled them into the WMALT 2007-OA3 trust, and sold securities issued by that trust to investors in March 2007. About 87 percent of these securities received triple-A ratings. Since then, all of these investment-grade securities from that trust have been downgraded to junk status. More than half of the Option ARMs were delinquent within three years, and a quarter of the borrowers were in foreclosure.[59]

Contained

In March 2007, after the median price of existing homes had fallen by 3 percent in the previous year, Fed chairman Ben Bernanke testified before the Joint Economic Committee of Congress. Bernanke described home prices as "flattening" and noted that deliquencies on adjustable-rate loans to subprime borrowers were on the rise. He assured lawmakers that "the impact on the broader economy and financial markets of the problems in the subprime market seems likely to be contained." Yet it was clear that the downturn was spreading. In early April, the giant subprime lender New Century filed for bankruptcy. Later that month, the credit-rating agency Standard & Poor's put out a special report expressing concern about the rising home mortgage delinquencies for "recent vintage" subprime loans. The rating agency intimated that for at least two years, lax underwriting standards had been a "topic of speculation."[60]

Also that spring, FDIC chairman Bair was alarmed at the level of foreclosures among borrowers with high-risk loans. She met with bankers, encouraging them to restructure loans for borrowers who were about to experience payment shock to help them save their homes. Huge numbers of Option ARMs were about to recast, and many of subprimes would reset. Reports spread that the types of loans WaMu and Long Beach originated were starting to default in record numbers. Foreclosures began to grow: about $750 million of WaMu's mortgages were in foreclosure by June and more than $1.7 billion of its subprime loans were delinquent. Nevertheless, at the June 2006 board meeting, Kerry Killinger said he planned to continue on the higher-risk lending path. As one executive present remembered, only one board member questioned his strategy.[61]

By summer, many of the high-risk mortgages WaMu had originated over the years were toxic. The cash flows from these mortgages were paid through to MBS holders. Some of the holders of these securities were trusts set up for the purpose of buying them. These trusts, in turn, issued CDOs. So a portion of the mortgage payments made each month by borrowers with loans originated by WaMu ended up in trusts and were paid out to holders of the CDO securities. Some of these securities were held by hedge funds. The investment bank Bear Stearns managed two hedge funds that were heavily invested in CDOs whose values depended on toxic mortgages originated by WaMu and its competitors.[62]

These two celebrated hedge funds managed by Bear Stearns began posting losses for the first time in spring 2007. The more borrowers with WaMu or other mortgages became delinquent or defaulted, the more the funds lost value. For example, the two hedge funds purchased $300 million in securities from a CDO structure called Timberwolf, which was assembled and rushed to market in March 2007 by Goldman Sachs. The value of the Timberwolf tranches the Bear Stearns funds purchased was linked to the value of WaMu Option ARMs. In an internal e-mail made public by Senator Carl Levin during a 2010 hearing, Tom Montag, a Goldman senior executive, described Timberwolf as "one shitty deal." Yet even after that e-mail, Goldman kept selling Timberwolf securities to clients, listing it as a top sales priority.[63]

Back in January 2005, the WaMu finance committee of the board of directors was shown a PowerPoint slide entitled "Lags in Effects of Expansion." It showed that losses resulting from the new high-risk loan strategy would peak in mid-2007. WaMu had spent 2005 in furious competition to churn out subprime and other toxic mortgages. Now the moment marked on the PowerPoint slide had arrived: many of those high-risk mortgages were defaulting at the same time. Losses were appearing right on schedule.[64]

WaMu's losses were passed along the securitization chain, where some eventually landed at the funds managed by Bear Stearns. Almost immediately, Goldman began marking down the Timberwolf tranches and in June 2007, the Bear hedge funds sold them back to Goldman at a sizable loss. Later the securities would become worthless. Passing along WaMu losses was as planned. In 2005, a staff member at the FDIC wrote that "management believes . . . that the impact [of a reversal in housing prices] on [Washington Mutual Bank] . . . would be manageable, since the riskiest segments of production are sold to investors, and that these investors will bear the brunt of a bursting housing bubble."[65]

It was these very risks that landed at the Bear Stearns hedge funds in the summer of 2007. The resulting troubles would begin the transformation of the subprime mortgage meltdown into a global financial crisis. Whether Fed chairman Ben Bernanke thought so or not, the problems were no longer contained.

12

First to Fall

Bear Stearns CEO Jimmy Cayne did not carry a cell phone or BlackBerry. For ten days in July 2007, he was at a bridge tournament in Nashville, Tennessee. Bridge was his passion; after dropping out of college and then joining the army, he came to New York from Chicago in 1964, hoping to play professionally. To support himself, he took a variety of jobs, including driving a cab and selling adding machines and municipal bonds. When he interviewed for a job at the Bear Stearns investment bank in 1969, he boasted about his card-playing skills to Ace Greenberg. At the time, Bear was a partnership and Greenberg one of the partners. "Mr. Greenberg," Cayne said, "if you study bridge the rest of your life, if you play with the best partners and you achieve your potential, you will never play bridge like I play bridge." He got the job. By 1993, he was CEO, and by 2001, chairman of the board. Under his leadership, Bear grew its securitization business, and the stock price rose.[1]

In Nashville, Cayne checked in with executives in the morning and played bridge throughout the afternoon. This event was a welcome escape for him, as were the Fridays he took off in the summer to play golf in New Jersey. He did not talk business on the course, nor did he carry a cell phone or e-mail device; some said this would have violated club rules. During the bridge tournament, Cayne's firm was at the eye of the storm. There was trouble at two hedge funds that Bear Stearns managed. Just days before the bridge tournament, Bear informed investors that their holdings were nearly worthless.[2]

A hedge fund is like a mutual fund, but it is exempt from many Securities and Exchange Commission (SEC) regulations because its securities may only be sold to "accredited" investors as measured by wealth, not skill. Managers of hedge funds thus have much more freedom than mutual fund managers. Unlike mutual funds, hedge funds are permitted to employ unlimited amounts of leverage and have historically not been subject to regulations that prohibit conflicts of interest between the manager and the fund. In addition, unlike mutual funds, hedge fund holdings, asset valuation, and strategies are obscure even to their own investors, and hedge fund managers can charge much higher fees, including fees based on asset appreciation.[3]

Young Funds

The first of the two Bear Stearns–managed hedge funds was launched in 2003 and the second in 2006. Though Bear had a small stake of house money in the funds, most of the estimated $1.6 billion in equity came from outside investors. In addition to equity, however, the funds brought in many more billions of dollars of debt. They borrowed from investment banks, including Goldman Sachs, JPMorgan, and Merrill Lynch, through the overnight and short-term repo market. Under these repurchase agreements, lenders would provide cash to the hedge funds and the funds would put up collateral. The agreements obligated the funds to return the cash plus interest on maturity, often the next morning, at which point the cash lenders would return the collateral. If the hedge fund could not pay back the cash, the lender could sell the collateral.[4]

The two hedge funds heavily invested in subprime and other nontraditional mortgage-linked securities, including collateralized debt obligations (CDOs), many of which depended on cash flows from—or were linked to—the values of mortgages originated by high-risk lenders like Washington Mutual (WaMu). If homeowners didn't make their monthly mortgage payments in full and on time, the mortgage-backed securities (MBSs) and CDOs would lose value. These securities served as collateral for the repo loans. Thus, if a repo lender decided not to roll over the funding on a given morning, the hedge funds would either have to find someone else to furnish a new loan or sell off some of the securities or other assets.[5]

The first Bear hedge fund thrived, as did its managers Ralph Cioffi and Matthew Tannin. Cioffi apparently earned more than $10 million a year in compensation and purchased two Ferraris and several homes, including a Manhattan apartment and a Southampton Long Island mansion. This success led to the 2006 startup of the second fund. After forty months of dazzling performance, in early 2007, the two hedge funds began to show losses in asset value. An April 2007 internal report on the CDO market anticipated that even the triple-A tranches held by Bear's hedge funds were at risk of declining in value. Reacting to that report, Tannin sent an e-mail to Cioffi declaring that the "subprime market looks pretty damn ugly" and if the report was accurate, then they should shut down the hedge funds because the "entire subprime market is toast." But a few days later they assured investors during a conference call that all was well.[6]

In May, investors learned of the losses and began redeeming their equity positions for cash. With the hedge funds' asset values continuing to slide, Bear Stearns suspended redemptions explaining that there were not "sufficient liquid assets to pay investors." Creditors also were anxious. Merrill Lynch threatened to pull repo funding from the hedge funds. To provide confidence, Bear Stearns announced that it was prepared to spend $3.2 billion to rescue the funds, if necessary. But by the third week in June, Merrill had already walked away with $850 million in collateral. However, when Merrill tried to sell the CDOs it seized, due to the poor prices offered, the auctions were canceled. Watching this, other lenders did not want the toxic collateral and thus settled for cash. The funds were collapsing.[7]

Before Cayne left for his bridge tournament in July, the rating agencies had downgraded hundreds of residential MBSs and CDOs. Among this group were those backed by cash flows from mortgages originated by WaMu, including Long Beach. Though Long Beach loans represented about 6 percent of the subprime mortgages securitized in 2006, they received 14 percent of the subprime downgrades.[8]

Also at the Nashville tournament was Warren Spector. Spector was the co-president of Bear Stearns, possibly next in line for CEO, and also headed up the firm's asset management business, the division that ran the two hedge funds. When Cayne returned from Nashville, he asked Spector to resign. Cayne was apparently annoyed that Spector had been out of town at such a critical moment. Bear Stearns announced Spector's resignation a few days later. His co-president, Alan Schwartz, would be president and chief operating officer, next in line for Cayne's role. Cayne decided to let one of the hedge funds fail but lent more than a $1.6 billion to the other. Still, the assets the surviving fund owned, mortgaged-linked securities, kept losing value. Bear eventually lost $1.2 billion of the money it lent the fund. In September, the stress overwhelmed Jimmy Cayne. He was rushed to the hospital, close to death with a serious infection. But he survived and, for a while, held on to his position as CEO.[9]

AIG Discovers the Fraud-Laced Files

By 2007, two years after WaMu's internal investigation team found massive fraud at the Montebello and Downey loan offices, where Option ARMs were the signature products, WaMu's senior management still had not taken firm action. Instead, they kept inviting the top producers at those offices to the annual, lavish President's Club Award events in tropical locales. Ron Cathcart, the new WaMu enterprise risk manager, who joined the firm in December 2005, was not informed of the fraud. It is likely that no action would have been taken were it not for American International Group (AIG).[10]

That June of 2007, AIG employees examined the loan-level detail on WaMu mortgages and were disturbed by what they discovered. As one line of its business, AIG sold private mortgage insurance. These policies are often required by lenders when borrowers put less than 20 percent down on a home. If a homeowner defaulted or was foreclosed upon, AIG would have to pay the mortgage holder. Spotting the fraud in Downey and Montebello loan files, AIG reported

WaMu to California regulators, who then alerted the Office of Thrift Supervision. At the request of the OTS, WaMu began a second internal investigation. This one would take ten months to complete.[11]

Glass Houses

AIG had its own troubles that summer. Seemingly out of the blue, the investment banking firm Goldman Sachs was demanding billions of dollars from an AIG business unit located in London. This group, called AIG Financial Products (AIGFP), sold credit default swaps (CDSs). AIG's dominance in the CDS market traced its roots back to Michael Milken at Drexel Burnham Lambert, which had sunk in February 1990 just before Milken pleaded guilty to several felonies. Milken had developed the below investment grade ("junk bond") market to help fund corporate takeovers. Several savings and loans (S&Ls) were some of his largest clients. For example, Milken helped Charles Keating finance his takeover of Lincoln Savings and Loan, after which Lincoln was a regular customer for Milken's junk bonds. The investigation of Milken began about 1987, and in the resulting diaspora, some former Drexel employees landed at AIG in London. The London unit focused at first on interest rate swaps, but around 1998, it entered the fledgling CDS market.[12]

Credit default swaps were invented in 1991 by employees of Bankers Trust but in 1994 were further advanced and popularized by a team of investment bankers at JPMorgan. These CDS instruments, designed to help solve the problem of credit risk, worked like insurance. The early buyers of CDSs were often banks concerned about a corporate borrower's potential default. A simple solution would be to sell the loan, but sometimes this was difficult or undesirable, as it might result in a loss or could offend the corporation, which might also be an important client. To offload some of that risk and avoid showing a loss, the bank could buy protection through a CDS. The seller of protection would collect premiums from the bank; in exchange, the seller promised that if the corporate borrower defaulted, it would buy the loan from the bank at the original value. Settlement could also be in cash, where the buyer, instead of delivering the now troubled loan, would just receive the difference between the loan's pre-default value and current value. Besides a default on the specific corporate loan a bank owned, the bank might also define "credit events" to include, for example, any other default by the corporation or a decline in the corporation's credit rating. AIG's London office became a large seller of CDS protection.[13]

Early on, the loans and bonds on which AIG sold credit protection were fairly transparent. But when they began to sell CDSs for residential MBSs and CDOs based on them, the clarity vanished. The names and credit histories of the underlying homeowners were not shared with investors in these mortgage-linked securities. While there had not been a nationwide downturn in housing prices since World War II, some investors were still nervous. Whereas the MBS issued by Freddie and Fannie came with an implicit government guarantee, the private label variety issued by Wall Street, WaMu, Countrywide, and others did not. Potential investors were worried that there was not sufficient data available to see whether, for example, defaults on mortgage loans might not occur independently but could be correlated across geographic regions. If so, a geographically diverse pool of mortgages would not reduce risk. As a result of these types of concerns, even for those securities with triple-A ratings, investors sought credit protection from firms like AIG.[14]

AIG wrote its first CDS in 1998 with JPMorgan. In its early years selling credit protection, AIG earned only 2 cents (2 basis points) for every hundred dollars of risk it insured. This gave it as little as $20,000 per year in premiums for $100 million in loans. Joseph Cassano, who worked under Milken at Drexel, joined the unit when it was founded, and in 2002 became its head, considered the premiums from CDS contracts easy money given the triple-A rating on the bonds the firm was insuring. In the 1990s, there were very few players in the CDS market. But the market expanded from less than $1 trillion outstanding in 2000 to nearly $60 trillion by 2007.[15]

After 2003, when Kerry Killinger began to emphasize higher-risk loans, the market also changed. The same shift took place at Countrywide. Whereas in 2003, 95 percent of Countrywide's mortgages were plain vanilla, fixed-rate loans, by 2006, it was originating

21 percent of its loans as Option ARMs and 11 percent as subprime. Even CEO Angelo Mozilo confessed in an e-mail that it was not possible to know "how these loans will perform in a stressed environment of higher unemployment, reduced values and slowing home sales." And somehow, AIG's Financial Products unit neither anticipated the shift nor perceived it when it was occurring.[16]

Because CDSs were not legally considered insurance, AIG did not have to set aside reserves to cover future losses—and it didn't. In addition, its Financial Products (FP) Division was not regulated like a bank and thus was not subject to capital or reserve requirements. Though AIG's regulator at the parent level was the Office of Thrift Supervision (OTS), no one had strong oversight over the FP unit. Counterparties buying protection felt confident that AIG would be able to cover their losses. AIGFP's parent company, American International Group, Inc., had a triple-A rating and the CDS contracts were unconditionally guaranteed at the parent level. Neither counterparties, employees, senior management, nor the board saw any potential losses—even when AIG's rating was lowered to AA by summer of 2005. Self-regulation failed.[17]

While AIG missed the true risk in the mortgage markets, others who did see it ended up buying credit protection from AIG. Some purchasers owned the MBSs or the CDOs they sought to insure. By transferring some of this risk, a bank or thrift would reduce its required regulatory capital. Purchasing credit protection also allowed holders of lower-rated residential MBSs and CDOs to treat them like triple-A. Banks could use customer deposits to buy risky tranches of mortgage securities, but treat them as the equivalent of risk-free U.S. government securities. Banks and thrifts told regulators there was "no risk" of their losing money because the provider of credit protection, often AIG, was obligated to pay.[18]

However, many buyers of CDSs from AIG did not actually own the CDOs for which they were purchasing protection. It was as if they were buying insurance on an entire neighborhood of homes as a massive fire approached. They had no insurable interest in the homes. Their only investment was the premiums. If the fire abated, they would have paid the premiums for nothing. But if it arrived and wiped out the neighborhood, they would be entitled to the full value of the buildings. Ultimately, AIG ended up on the other side of about $78 billion of those bets. This included exposure to tranches of securities, the values of which were linked to high-risk home loans originated by WaMu.[19]

Collateral Calls at AIG

In the summer of 2007, while AIG employees were digging into loan files at WaMu in California, all hell was breaking loose in London. Faced with the subprime crisis, Joe Cassano steadfastly defended the risk the London unit had swallowed. During an August conference call with investors, Cassano and his staff explained that they had stress-tested their exposure and that it held up to a "continuous recessionary cycle." Cassano explained:

> [T]he combination of the diversity, the combination of the underlying credit quality, and then the stresses that we put it through to make sure that we can hit these marks, it is hard for us without being flippant, to even see a scenario within any kind of realm of reason that would see us losing $1 in any of those transactions.[20]

One reason Cassano's remark inspired confidence was the data. In sixty years, since the late 1940s, real estate prices had never fallen all at once on a nationwide basis. Yet things were clearly different now. The securitization machine, spurred on by the ability to buy credit protection from firms like AIG, helped drive up housing prices. Moreover, the loans that dominated the housing market until around 2004 were soundly underwritten, standard thirty-year, fixed-rate mortgages. Growth of higher-risk mortgages would create massive defaults, and this was what AIG was selling protection for. Of course, another motivator for blind acceptance of stale data was money. Cassano would earn $300 million during his time at AIG. Martin Sullivan, CEO of AIG, echoed Cassano's assurance, adding, "That's why I am sleeping a little bit easier at night."[21]

What neither mentioned to investors was that AIG was required to pay money to some CDS buyers like Goldman Sachs, even if the referenced loans or securities did not default. In other words, by analogy, there were certain conditions short of a fire burning down the house that would require the insurance firm to give the homeowner cash. These conditions might be a very long dry spell in a fire-prone area or a lowering of the insurer's own credit rating. AIG had sold protection on the safest CDO tranches, the ones that were purportedly the least vulnerable to the failure of homeowners to make their mortgage payments. Even if the referenced MBS tranches were still paying investors, if the prices of the tranches fell, Goldman could demand cash payments from AIG. This risk was already apparent by the time of that August investor call, because in July, the rating agencies had downgraded tens of billions of dollars of CDOs (including triple-A tranches). As a result, Goldman Sachs sent a collateral call to AIG requesting $1.8 billion in cash. By mid-August, before Cassano departed for a vacation bicycling through Germany and Austria, he agreed to pay Goldman $450 million. But the dispute continued. In September, Goldman requested another $1.5 billion, a figure that kept rising as mortgage defaults rose and MBS prices deteriorated.[22]

The amounts actually owed under contract for these collateral calls were unclear and subject to negotiation. The contracts allowed for AIG and the protection buyer (such as Goldman Sachs) to seek market pricing. But given the lack of buyers for MBSs and CDOs that were subject to credit protection, the fair market price was impossible to determine, and AIG and Goldman argued strenuously about credible values. Joe Cassano apparently said at a board meeting that fall: "Just because Goldman says this is the right valuation, you shouldn't assume it's correct because Goldman said it. My brother works at Goldman and he's an idiot." By the summer of 2008, AIG would pay out more than $16.5 billion in cash to back its credit default swaps.[23]

Not the Only Game in Town

AIG was not the only provider of credit protection on risky mortgage-linked securities. There was another way to bet against the American homeowner. The invention had a different name at first but later morphed into the synthetic CDO. When an investor, such as a European bank, bought securities issued by a synthetic, its money went into the CDO trust (or other conduit type) and was used to purchase some safe instruments intended to hold their value. The trust then "sold" credit protection on selected mid-level, such as triple-B, tranches of residential MBSs. The buyer of the protection might be a hedge fund, which would then make regular premium payments to the trust. The cash flow from these premium payments went into the trust and would be paid out to the CDO investors. In exchange for its premiums, the hedge fund would receive protection on the selected tranches. The protection buyers did not usually own any of those MBS tranches, but simply wanted to bet against them. If the triple-B tranches were downgraded or defaulted, for example, then the CDO trust would be obligated to pay the hedge fund. Again, it was like fire insurance, but the hedge fund didn't actually own the homes: it was betting on a fire, and if one came, the trust would have to pay. If there was not enough money in the trust, then the triple-A securities issued by the trust would decline in value, and the CDO investors holding the triple-As would lose some or all of their investment. This could happen very quickly, as these synthetic CDOs were highly leveraged. Very little money was invested at the start relative to the amount of coverage the trust promised to provide.[24]

In addition to needing investors to buy the debt tranches someone needed to invest in the small, equity piece. Often the same hedge fund that bought the credit protection was also the equity holder. Having a prominent hedge fund as the equity investor was an important part of the sales pitch. For example, when John Paulson, a well-known hedge fund manager, approached Goldman Sachs toward the end of 2006 and asked the investment bank to help him bet against the housing market, Paulson had his fund become an equity investor. Goldman then found institutional investors for the debt tranches: in spring 2007, the German bank IKB invested $150 million and the Dutch bank ABN Amro (ABN) invested $900 million in debt securities issued by a synthetic CDO called ABACUS. These and other investors were told that triple-B residential MBSs for which the CDO would sell protection would be selected by an independent asset manager, ACA. They were not told that ACA was working with John Paulson to select risky triple-B tranches. IKB and ABN were never told that the credit protection being sold was covering tranches that were being handpicked for failure. And Goldman never told them or CDO manager ACA that Paulson planned to bet against them by buying the credit protection on the deal. IKB lost almost all of its $150 million investment, and RBS, which had bought ABN's position, paid Goldman $840 million to unwind it. Paulson made $1 billion on his "bet."[25]

These synthetic deals, which were very popular, layered more risk onto subprime and nontraditional mortgages. The Bear Stearns hedge funds that collapsed in June 2007 had purchased some of these synthetic CDOs. This included securities sold by Goldman Sachs through the Timberwolf deal. The value of the Timberwolf tranches purchased depended upon the performance not just of the WaMu Option ARMs, but also of ABACUS CDO tranches.[26]

In the fall of 2007, many experts, including the Fed chairman Ben Bernanke, believed the crisis would be contained. But they did not take into account the money at risk on side bets. For the transaction with Paulson and ACA, Goldman Sachs paid a record $550 million to settle civil fraud charges by the SEC. It was not the only bank sponsoring these synthetic structures, some of which involved mortgages originated by WaMu's Long Beach subsidiary.[27]

A family's failure to make its payments on a loan originated by lenders like WaMu, once a very local economic event, could now spread across the globe to investors who either depended on the cash flows from those mortgages or were involved in the new synthetic game, whereby they were selling credit protection to savvier investors who would get paid billions when far-off people faced losing their homes.

Fall Foreclosures

In the fall of 2007, a survey of mortgage servicers showed that only a miniscule amount of the resetting or recasting home mortgages had been restructured. Meanwhile, borrowers—not just those with subprime loans—were defaulting and foreclosures were soaring. Federal Deposit Insurance Corporation (FDIC) chairman Sheila Bair wrote an op-ed suggesting that mortgage servicers should refinance all mortgages that were resetting. She challenged the assertion that refinancing would encourage moral hazard, arguing instead that "avoiding foreclosure would protect neighboring properties and hasten the recovery." She was later branded as difficult and "not a team player."[28]

That fall, WaMu wrote down the value of the high-risk mortgages it owned. By the end of 2007, it also wrote down the value of its Home Loans Group by $1.6 billion. At that time about 47 percent of the loans on WaMu's balance sheet were Option ARMs—loans where borrowers could make a minimum payment of as low as 1 to 2 percent until a recast date a few years later, when the fully indexed, new higher monthly payment on the often larger principal balance would be due. Of these, 73 percent were stated income ("liar's") loans. Of the total value of these WaMu Option ARMs, 84 percent was negatively amortizing, with principal balances growing. These borrowers were falling underwater not just from the decline in housing prices in California and Florida, where the loans were concentrated, but also from the toxic loans themselves. But Killinger was still hopeful. During an investor conference call he said he was "pleased with how we've managed the company during this period of stress." With trouble in sight and loan losses piling up, his treasurer repeatedly urged him to cut the dividend paid to shareholders. His treasurer wanted him to preserve a greater equity cushion to absorb losses. Killinger finally agreed. More trouble was brewing. WaMu's stock price had dropped by 65 percent, causing shareholder unrest and legal challenges contending that it was imprudent to keep a portion of the employee retirement fund in WaMu stock.[29]

Echoes of the Past

While the smaller Washington Mutual savings bank had avoided the S&L crisis under Lou Pepper's prudent management in the 1980s, under Kerry Killinger, WaMu resembled Empire Savings and Loan, American Savings and Loan, and Continental Illinois all rolled into one. After years of rapid growth, aggressive loan making during an asset bubble, and reliance on insured deposits and hot money, the crash was inevitable. Killinger's last good year was 2006, when WaMu showed a $3.5 billion profit. This was its second straight year of great success, and WaMu ended that year with $346 billion in assets. Its deposits and other liabilities totaled about $320 billion. A huge portion of WaMu's funding was wholesale and thus prone to runs: about $44 billion was brokered deposits, of which half was institutional, and $12 billion came from overnight or short-term repo loans.[30]

After the eventful summer of 2007, with its massive ratings downgrades, things turned negative for WaMu. No one at the top should have been surprised. This was the exact point on the chart that had been presented to the board of directors in early 2005 as the period when the impact of the high-risk lending policy would deliver losses. As a result of the collapse of the housing bubble, which Killinger had helped to inflate, WaMu reported a $67 million loss for 2007.[31]

The bank ended 2007 with $328 billion in assets, with deposits and other liabilities totaling $303 billion. Of this, only $20 billion was brokered, but only $2 billion of that was from institutions—down 89 percent, and repo cash was down to $4 billion. The wholesale and institutional money had already started to run. Filling the gap from the private sector lender's departures was $64 billion in advances from the Federal Home Loan Bank of San Francisco, up from $44 billion the previous year. Though the Federal Home Loan Bank Board had been abolished in 1989 and replaced with the Office of Thrift Supervision, the district Home Loan Banks continued on as lenders. Like its predecessor American Savings and Loan, WaMu had turned to the district bank when it faced trouble, this time for an extra $20 billion.[32]

Kerry Killinger was now presiding over the very type of bank that a former WaMu president had scorned about seventy-five years earlier. After the Great Crash in 1933, Dietrich Schmitz had spoken out against the creation of federal deposit insurance. He worried that the new federal safety net would weaken market discipline and allow poorly managed banks to survive and flourish. Now Killinger was dependent on billions in taxpayer-backed FDIC-insured deposits and billions of dollars in overnight or short-term funding that could dry up quickly.[33]

If Lou Pepper had been around, he might have said it was high time to take responsibility. But Killinger was no longer the aggressive young executive who took commercial flights and ate lunch at his desk. The married college student living in a mobile home with his young bride and baby was a stranger. Now he was used to corporate jets and multiple residences, including a $6.4 million home in Palm Desert, purchased in 2007. His mentor, Lou Pepper, was no longer providing informal advice. He was not there to tell Killinger to take some losses. But others would make that demand in much louder tones.[34]

A New Year

At the beginning of 2008, Treasury Secretary Henry Paulson was worried about the banking system generally, and certain firms in particular. The Federal National Mortgage Association (Fannie Mae) and the Federal Home Loan Mortgage Corporation (Freddie Mac) were of great concern. Paulson sent Robert Steel, the Under Secretary for Domestic Finance, to visit Fannie and Freddie to encourage them to raise equity capital to create a buffer from losses. While Fannie raised $7.4 billion, Freddie raised nothing.[35]

In February 2008, the Office of Thrift Supervision decided to downgrade WaMu. Though it had held a score of 2, with 1 being the best and 5 the worst, given the apparent loan problems, the regulator planned to give WaMu a 3. After his risk officer, Ron Cathcart, came personally to deliver this information, Killinger told him, "I don't like to hear bad news," and walked out of the room before Cathcart could respond.[36]

There was more bad news to come. At the annual meeting of WaMu shareholders in April 2008, when Killinger's board-approved bonus was described, the audience booed. The bonus was calculated without accounting for mortgage loan losses, which were considerable.

A majority of shareholders also voted to split the roles of chairman and CEO. Though merely advisory, Killinger soon did relinquish his position as chairman of the board of directors but kept his CEO title. After the annual meeting, Killinger expressed dismay to the press. However, he should have expected the reaction. Years earlier, after the 2004 interest rate hedge miscalculation, Lou Pepper had sent him a letter suggesting he should take a pay cut. Such a move would have sent a powerful signal to shareholders that he also had skin in the game. Now things were far worse. There was fear everywhere. In January, Countrywide had nearly failed and was being sold to Bank of America. Also in January, Standard & Poor's (S&P) was back at it, downgrading or placing on credit watch more than eight thousand residential MBSs and CDOs.[37]

And that was outside the firm. Inside, WaMu had its own troubles, but Killinger seemed to avoid facing them. Raised in a family where optimism was expected and faults were to be hidden, he seemed to do the same with voices revealing problems at WaMu. Ronald Cathcart was one such voice. Cathcart, who had replaced Jim Vanasek as chief enterprise risk officer in 2005, was deeply concerned about the volume of high-risk mortgages WaMu originated and packaged for sale. When he spoke out, however, he said he was admonished. He said that other members of senior management presented outdated projections in order to make loan losses appear lower than they really were. In early 2007, Cathcart provided honest data to the board and questioned the outdated figures presented by the other executives. After that, he said he was no longer invited to board meetings. A year later in January 2008, before the annual meeting of shareholders, he was "fully isolated." Concerned that the regulators might have stale information, he called Darrel Dochow at the Office of Thrift Supervision to provide the regulator with updated loan loss figures. Cathcart was fired that April.[38]

Killinger's team was not just hiding fresh data. They also tried to withhold the results of the ten-month review of the problem in its prime loans, initiated after AIG refused to insure mortgages coming from the Downey and Montebello offices. That internal report, produced by the audit and legal group, was complete in April 2008, but

WaMu initially kept it from the Office of Thrift Supervision, claiming attorney-client privilege.[39]

Millions of people depended on Killinger's management skills. They included insiders like management and rank-and-file employees, as well as common stock holders of Washington Mutual, Inc., bond holders, and other lenders. Depositors who had savings accounts at WaMu also depended on Killinger's stewardship. Other dependents included those who invested in the residential MBSs that paid off based on the cash flows of WaMu-originated mortgages. At a farther remove, there were investors who held CDOs, securities that paid based on cash flows from tranches of WaMu-sponsored MBSs. Killinger was not the only target of shareholders' frustration. They also focused on the board of directors, though not everything was known at the time. They probably did not know, for example, that the Board Finance Committee received a presentation in 2005 showing losses would arrive by mid-2007. And at the 2007 annual board strategy meeting, even when the risks associated with the types of mortgage loans were more obvious, apparently only one board member objected to Killinger's intention to stay the course.[40]

Bear Run

After stepping down as CEO of Bear Stearns early in 2008, Jimmy Cayne stayed on as chairman of the board. That February, he spent $27 million to purchase two adjacent apartments in New York's Plaza Hotel with a view of Central Park. Now it was March, time for another bridge tournament: the North American Bridge Championship in Detroit. Cayne was doing well in a pairs event on March 13. His firm was not. On that single day, Bear Stearns lost $10 billion in cash. It had only $2 billion left. This institutional run was an echo of the collapse of the Bear-managed hedge funds the previous summer. But this time the run was on the firm itself. Though no longer an executive, Cayne, like the other board members, owed fiduciary duties, including care of and loyalty to Bear Stearns and its shareholders.[41]

On Thursday, March 13, at Cayne's tournament, bridge was played from 1:00 to 5:00 p.m., and later from 7:30 to 11 p.m.—a long day.

The stakes were much higher back in New York. Alan Schwartz, who had become CEO in January, held a series of conference calls with the board of directors in an effort to save the company. They were trying to arrange a line of credit from JPMorgan Chase and the Fed. Cayne later said he was not informed of the firm's troubles until that night, though he apparently did participate in some of these discussions. He did not leave Detroit until Saturday afternoon, as he was waiting for a private plane home.[42]

Instead of letting Bear Stearns file for bankruptcy, a rescue package was brokered by Treasury Secretary Paulson and Timothy Geithner, then president of the New York Fed. On Sunday, March 16, the Bear Stearns board of directors agreed to sell the firm to JPMorgan Chase for $2 a share, though the price would later be raised to $10. A year earlier, Bear Stearns stock had traded at $171 a share. As part of the deal, JPMorgan Chase CEO Jamie Dimon arranged for the Fed to provide a $30 billion loan at a below-market interest rate; the collateral he would provide for the loan was $30 billion in mortgage securities from Bear Stearns. If the sale of those assets failed to yield the $30 billion, JPMorgan Chase would pay the first $1 billion in losses; the Fed would assume the next $29 billion. This was a sugar-coated deal, reminiscent of the type arranged in late 1988 to rescue the S&Ls. Just like the bailout of American Savings and Loan, the bailout of Bear Stearns involved shedding the sinking firm of its toxic assets with a government guarantee. As Secretary Paulson later recalled, Jamie Dimon was not eager at first because he had his eye on another struggling institution—Washington Mutual. However, the deal was attractive; Bear owed JPMorgan Chase about $9.7 billion. Additionally, Dimon's bank was rumored to be an even larger derivatives exposure to Bear. Thus he had an interest in avoiding bankruptcy.[43]

The decision by the Federal Reserve to give JPMorgan Chase $30 billion to prop up Bear Stearns was monumental. By comparison, it made the Continental Illinois bailout that established the "Too Big to Fail" banking precedent look quaint. The Fed was supposed to use its emergency lending powers to support traditional banks—in other words, depository institutions like commercial banks and thrifts that paid into the federal insurance system and were subject to reserve requirements and prudential supervision. But Bear was an investment bank. To facilitate the transaction, the New York Fed created a new entity, Maiden Lane LLC, into which JPMorgan Chase transferred the $30 billion in troubled mortgaged-linked securities from the Bear Stearns portfolio. Maiden Lane was to have ten years to sell these assets. And JPMorgan Chase was supposed to take the first $1 billion in losses.[44]

Years later, after losing a court battle initiated by Bloomberg L.P., the Fed reluctantly revealed the holdings of the Maiden Lane portfolio: it included securities backed by mortgages originated by Washington Mutual and its rival Countrywide. In one such $281 million holding, called WAMU 06-A13 2XPPP, about 94 percent of the mortgages were made with little or no documentation of the borrower's income. By 2010, nearly 10 percent of the borrowers, whose payments served as the cash flow for that security, had been foreclosed on. Of those who remained, almost 25 percent were more than two months late on their payments.[45]

The Senate Banking Committee held hearings on the taxpayer-backed Bear rescue in April 2008. The obvious concern was moral hazard. If the government was willing to bail out this investment bank by guaranteeing $29 billion in Jamie Dimon's losses, wouldn't others, in similar fragile positions, expect the same rescue? Would they forgo opportunities to solve their own problems and instead push them off on the government? Dimon defended the purchase, contending he was not getting a sweet deal because "buying a house is not the same as buying a house on fire." Geithner justified the New York Fed's $30 billion in support, claiming without it there would be "a greater probability of widespread insolvencies, severe and protracted damage to the financial system and, ultimately, to the economy as a whole." Fed chairman Bernanke also defended the sale, telling the Senate committee, "Bear Stearns didn't fare very well in this operation. . . . Shareholders took losses. I don't think it's a situation that any firm would willingly choose to endure." He further asserted that "The benefit of our action is not Bear Stearns, or even Wall Street, it's Main Street."[46]

Cayne apologized both to employees and to the public. He had earned around $424 million in compensation over the years—an estimated $34 million in 2006 alone. Though he took some losses after Bear's decline, his net worth was still around $600 million. As part of the deal, Cayne received 4.6 million shares of JPMorgan Chase stock. Though he at times blamed a conspiracy of hedge funds and investment banks for Bear's fall, he admitted in August 2008: "I didn't stop it. I didn't rein in the leverage."[47]

What brought Bear to its end was excessive debt used to fund hard-to-sell assets. Like other investment banks, a great deal of that debt was very short term, often overnight. Bear Stearns faced a sudden run because of its dependency on overnight repo funding. Before its demise, it borrowed $50 billion every day, renewing it each evening, subject to the lender's discretion. It used this money to finance more than 70 percent of the mortgage-linked securities on its balance sheet. The moral hazard concern was justified. After the Bear bailout, investment banks like Lehman Brothers passed over many opportunities for equity investments. Instead, they ramped up the repo lending but hid it through questionable, though apparently legal, accounting techniques. Others did seek out private assistance but also hoped for a government backstop. All of this stemmed from the unprecedented bailout of Bear Stearns.[48]

Years later, FDIC chairman Bair told *New York Times* reporter Joe Nocera that "they should have let Bear Stearns fail." She elaborated:

> I'm a traditionalist. Banks and bank-holding companies are in the safety net. That's why they have deposit insurance. Investment banks take higher risks, and they are supposed to be outside the safety net. If they make enough mistakes, they are supposed to fail. So, yes, I was amazed when they saved it. I couldn't believe it. When they told me about it, I said: "Guess what: Investment banks fail."[49]

While the rescue of Bear was quite public, less attention was paid to a much larger sum of money being spent to support the system. In March, the Fed expanded its liquidity program, the Term Securities Lending Facility (TSLF), to provide banks with $200 billion in U.S.

Treasury securities for twenty-eight days, instead of overnight, in exchange for assets including their troubled private label mortgage-related securities. Throughout the crisis and bailout, the Fed created other mechanisms and programs to provide trillions of dollars in support and continued to expand the liquidity program by accepting a wider range of assets from a variety of counterparties, and for longer terms.[50]

Help from the Friends of the Friend of the Family

Desperate for capital in early 2008, Killinger turned to TPG Capital (previously known as Texas Pacific Group), a private equity firm co-founded by former WaMu board member David Bonderman. Bonderman had been associated with Robert Bass in the 1988 takeover of American Savings and Loan through American Savings Bank. After Washington Mutual, Inc., purchased American Savings Bank, Bonderman served as a WaMu director until 2002. In April 2008, Bonderman's TPG joined with additional unnamed investors and provided a $7 billion cash infusion in exchange for 176 million new shares of common stock at $8.75 a share, as well as $5.5 billion in convertible preferred stock and warrants. This deal substantially diluted the value of existing shares. Killinger had just passed up an offer from JPMorgan Chase to buy the whole company for $8 a share—in the eyes of many angry shareholders, a far better deal, given that by mid-June their stock was trading at $6.67.[51]

The new equity capital bought a little time for WaMu. But its CEO was still in denial. As his bank struggled, Kerry Killinger resembled Spencer Blain at Empire Savings and Loan and Charlie Knapp and Bill Popejoy at American Savings and Loan. As Empire's CEO, Blain had worked with Danny Faulkner to finance a land-flipping condo scheme that depended on false appraisals and passing along an asset from investor to investor, until the last one, namely the government, provided a bailout. Similarly, as WaMu's CEO, Killinger had worked with thousands of mortgage brokers and real estate agents, depending on false appraisals, flipping mortgages from one investor to another, until the government provided a bailout.[52]

Charlie Knapp, a CEO fueled by his personal ambitions to take over firms and turn them profitable, had grown American Savings and Loan using brokered deposits and repo funding, and by taking huge interest rate gambles. He was ultimately pushed out by the government and replaced by Bill Popejoy. Though he planned to shrink the bank, Popejoy realized that he needed to keep growing to stay afloat, so he repeated Knapp's interest rate gamble, investing in MBSs using fragile repo funding. Like them, Killinger was obsessed with growth and got tangled in an interest rate hedging debacle. In June, his own board of directors stripped him of his title as chairman. Though he had staved off a collapse, he appeared to be headed down the escalator, not up.

Like Blain, Faulkner, Knapp, and Popejoy, Killinger was enabled by deregulation and desupervision. There were responsible regulators and legislators who attempted to fix these problems to avoid the S&L crisis. Similarly, in the run-up to the 2007–2008 mortgage crisis, two regulators in particular tried to stop the predatory practices at places like WaMu and speculation at AIG and beyond. These two women, Sheila Bair and Brooksley Born, tried to head off these practices before they moved from the margins to the center. But their efforts were obstructed, and they were personally attacked by their more powerful Washington colleagues.

13

Surf and Turf

John Reich (pronounced "rich") made it clear to Sheila Bair by e-mail that he did not want to be disturbed—by her. It was August 6, 2008, and he was on a cruise ship vacation. Bair was chairman of the Federal Deposit Insurance Corporation (FDIC), and Reich was director of the Office of Thrift Supervision (OTS). The OTS had been created in 1989 to replace the abolished Federal Home Loan Bank Board. It had already had a rough year; several of the largest thrifts under Reich's jurisdiction had failed or were on the verge of collapse.[1]

The casualties included Washington Mutual's chief rival, Countrywide Financial Corporation, co-founded and led by Angelo Mozilo. Countrywide was the nation's largest subprime lender, with about $200 billion in assets and nearly that much in liabilities. It was near bankruptcy when Bank of America CEO Ken Lewis came to the rescue in January 2008, agreeing to buy the giant for $4 billion. This was equivalent to about $7.16 per share, which was down from roughly $45 per share a year earlier.[2]

In July, IndyMac, another subprime lending thrift, was closed by the OTS and the FDIC was named conservator. IndyMac was the fifth depository institution to fail that year, and it was expected to cost the deposit insurance fund nearly $9 billion. As a result, the FDIC was required by law to replenish the fund, which had to contain at least 1.15 percent of all insured deposits. Bair hoped to do so by raising the annual assessment fee paid into the fund by banks that engaged in riskier activities. Before that could happen, however, a sudden waive of failures could wipe it out or necessitate reaching into taxpayers' pockets.[3]

For Reich, Countrywide and IndyMac were just the beginning. Also on the verge of failure was American International Group (AIG), one of the world's largest insurers, with $1 trillion in assets. The entire AIG enterprise, including its noninsurance subsidiaries, was under OTS jurisdiction. Of particular relevance was that this oversight included the London-operated AIG Financial Products unit, where Joe Cassano and his team wrote credit default swaps (CDSs) on $80 billion of the purportedly safest tranches of collateralized debt obligations. Of these bonds, $64 billion were backed by subprime mortgages. AIG, which once boasted a triple-A credit rating, was near its demise. Since the continuing collateral calls from Goldman Sachs had begun a year earlier, AIG had paid out more than $16.5 billion on its CDSs. Cassano, who had said he could not see "within any realm of reason" paying out even one dollar on AIG-insured CDSs, had miscalculated.[4]

AIG had also taken big risks with funds that should have been invested safely. It took in customer premiums from the life insurance policies it sold and invested them in "safe," thus low-yielding, securities. This was the money it would need to pay future claims to beneficiaries. Investing these premiums in safe instruments was a legal requirement, but not very profitable. To boost the return, AIG lent $90 billion of the safe securities to other investors for a fee, requiring them to provide AIG with cash collateral equal to their value. But instead of just holding the cash or investing it in other low-risk, highly liquid securities, such as short-term U.S. Treasury bonds, AIG used some of it to purchase $45 billion in longer-duration, higher-yielding, residential mortgage-backed securities (MBSs). The problem was that in the fall of 2008, the initial borrowers of the safe securities would ask for their cash back, forcing AIG to sell the MBSs at a time when buyers were scarce and not willing to pay anything near full price. By fall of 2008, AIG's securities lending counterparties had demanded $24 billion in cash.[5]

The OTS, a thrift regulator, was a curious choice for AIG, primarily an insurance firm. This choice was a result of two legal changes. First was the enactment in 1999 of the Gramm-Leach-Bliley Act, which repealed much of the remaining Glass-Steagall provisions that had separated traditional banking (deposit-taking) from investment banking (securities operations). After the law passed and with OTS approval, AIG started a tiny federal thrift. That made it a savings and loan (S&L) holding company with OTS as its regulator. In that capacity, OTS mainly focused on the impact the holding company had on the small S&L. Then, after 2004, AIG, like other financial institutions with operations in Europe, was subject to a European Union (EU) directive requiring it to have a "consolidated supervisor" in its home country. There was no U.S. federal insurance regulator, so AIG decided its consolidated supervisor was the OTS, and the OTS persuaded the EU it was qualified to do so. This meant that the state insurance regulators, mainly New York and Pennsylvania, were the functional regulators for the core insurance business, while the OTS, as consolidated supervisor, was responsible for the other business divisions and for coordinating supervision of the entire enterprise. As a practical matter, what this meant for the AIGFP unit in London is that it avoided the scrutiny of the United Kingdom's more exacting regulator.[6]

Looking back, John Reich's deputy, Scott Polakoff, admitted that the OTS was not equal to the task. In 2009, he told members of the Senate Banking Committee that "[w]e in 2004 should have taken an entirely different approach than what we wound up taking regarding the credit default swaps." Of course, it was difficult to have a sound approach given that Reich himself later told the Financial Crisis Inquiry Commission (FCIC) that the FP unit was like a "gnat on an elephant" and that he had "no clue—no idea—what [AIG's] CDS liability was."[7]

On that day in August 2008, aside from AIG, Washington Mutual (WaMu) also needed Reich's most immediate attention. After the run at IndyMac, where customers camped out overnight in tents, there had been a bank run at WaMu. Some $9 billion net was withdrawn in the month of July, and this did not even include brokered deposits and other institutional funding. After that, however, money slowly came back in. The FDIC had calculated in July that WaMu needed to raise an additional $5 billion in capital, but the OTS disagreed. Also, the FDIC wanted to downgrade WaMu from a CAMELS—capital adequacy, asset quality, management, earnings, liquidity, and sensitivity to market risk—rating of 3 to 4, thinking the bank might be near its end. That was why Sheila Bair had interrupted John Reich's vacation with an e-mail on Wednesday. A conference call among federal banking regulators was scheduled for that Friday, and she wanted to give Reich a heads-up that she intended to propose a contingency plan for WaMu should its condition deteriorate. She wanted to suggest that she discreetly line up bidders in advance of insolvency, and that, after selecting the highest bidder, the regulators be prepared to close WaMu and sell it. Bair mentioned in her e-mail that she had support from the Fed.[8]

Bair was trying to engage Reich on this topic because WaMu was subject to oversight by both his OTS and her FDIC. The FDIC had the authority to resolve (meaning to take over and shut down or sell) WaMu should it become critically undercapitalized or unable to meet deposit outflows during a run. "Critically undercapitalized" meant holding tangible equity capital of 2 percent or less (in other words, owing $98 for every $100 in assets it held) without a plan to restore it. In those circumstances, under the prompt corrective action provisions of the Federal Deposit Insurance Corporation Improvement Act of 1991 (FDICIA), action was not optional. It was required. This law was designed to end the "too big to fail" problem that first surfaced in 1984 with the government bailouts of Continental Illinois and American Savings and Loan. Under FDICIA, WaMu would have to be dismantled at least cost to the FDIC deposit insurance fund unless the "systemic risk" exception was invoked. This would require two-thirds of the members of the boards of both the Fed and the FDIC to determine that shutting down WaMu would have a serious adverse impact on the economy or financial stability. Additionally, the treasury secretary, in consultation with the president, would need to approve. If the regulators invoked this "systemic risk" exception—which had never been used since the law was enacted—then the FDIC could use the deposit insurance fund to keep WaMu open. Otherwise, the OTS, as the primary regulator, would have to shut down WaMu within 90 days and appoint the FDIC as receiver or conservator.[9]

In her e-mail, Bair suggested that they might be able to sell the "whole bank" and thus minimize the risk to the deposit insurance fund. Clearly, this would work best if, at the time of sale, the value of the assets exceeded the value of the liabilities. If they waited too long, the FDIC might face a big loss. Given that the much smaller IndyMac cost the deposit insurance fund nearly $9 billion, Bair had reason to want a different outcome for WaMu.[10]

From a historical perspective, delaying the shutdown of WaMu under the "systemic risk" exception could involve making the same mistake twice: it might repeat the drawn-out bailout and subsequent failure of American Savings and Loan. This is not an analogy; these were the same players under new names. Washington Mutual Bank literally *was* American Savings and Loan. The FDIC certificate number, 32633, used by Robert Bass's American Savings Bank (which bought American Savings and Loan deposits and good assets in late December 1988), was the same number that Washington Mutual Bank was using in 2008.[11]

The holding company Washington Mutual, Inc. (WMI), was created in 1994, and the original Washington Mutual Savings Bank (certificate number 9576) that had been founded back in 1889 was made a subsidiary of WMI. In December 1996, WMI bought American Savings Bank. Thus, the original thrift (9576) and American Savings Bank (32633) were subsidiaries of the same parent corporation. With the acquisition by WMI, American Savings Bank's name was changed to Washington Mutual, F.A. After that, Kerry Killinger used this renamed American Savings Bank (32633) to acquire Great Western, Home Savings, Bank United, Dime Savings, and many other thrifts. Then, the renamed American Savings Bank (32633) acquired the original Washington Mutual Savings Bank (9576) on January 1, 2005. After that, the surviving thrift, number 32633, was renamed Washington Mutual Bank. Thus, technically, that old American Savings

Bank entity, the successor to American that was founded by Robert Bass, now called Washington Mutual Bank, was the survivor. Beyond the legal DNA, WaMu also inherited from American Savings Bank its culture and California presence, having doubled its size with the acquisition and taken on its flagship Option ARM product and originate-to-distribute model.[12]

Thus, the impending trouble in August 2008 was the second potential failure of American Savings and Loan, now operating under the name Washington Mutual. And it was the second potential failure of the same federal regulator. The Office of Thrift Supervision was also operating under a new name: it had been the Federal Home Loan Bank Board—the agency that from the run on American Savings and Loan in the summer of 1984 until late 1988 had kept the critically undercapitalized zombie thrift alive on government support. This forbearance cost the taxpayers $5.4 billion.[13]

While it is common to say that the OTS was "abolished," its own employees saw it as only a cosmetic change. According to Chana Joffe-Walt, a National Public Radio reporter, former Federal Home Loan Bank Board employees recalled a day in 1989 when

> they left the office . . . and they walked across the street to a hotel. They turned on the TV, and they sat and watched the first President Bush stand up at a podium and declare, "Never again will America allow any insured institution [to] operate without enough money." And then the agency employees watched as the President trashed their agency. The press conference ended, they turned off the TV, left the hotel, crossed the street, and went back to work. Pretty soon someone came by and changed the sign: The Office of Thrift Supervision.[14]

Along with new names, the stakes were much higher this time around. Washington Mutual was far bigger. American Savings and Loan, with more than $30 billion in assets when it was finally shut down by the government and sold in 1988, had been the largest thrift failure until IndyMac. WaMu, however, had more than $300 billion in assets, supported by liabilities that included more than $180 billion in deposits, of which $140 billion were FDIC insured. With that much at risk, Bair was highly motivated to come up with a plan.[15]

In his reply to Bair later that day, Reich showed his frustration. He wrote, in part:

> Dear Sheila,
>
> You really know how to stir up a colleague's vacation.
>
> I do not under any circumstances want to discuss this on Friday's conference call, in which I may or may not be able to participate, depending on cell phone service availability on the cruise ship location. . . . This is an OTS regulated institution, not an FDIC regulated institution. We make any decision on solvency, not the FDIC, and I have staff equally as competent as staff at the FDIC, whom I know well. . . . The government should not be in the business of arranging mergers—particularly before they are necessary, and we are not at that point in WaMu's situation.[16]

This hostility was not new. The relationship between the two agencies had soured a couple of years earlier. In 2004, WaMu had changed primary federal regulators from the FDIC to the OTS. Between then and 2006, there was a cooperative relationship: OTS staff had included FDIC staff in important matters, including on-site examinations, and had given the FDIC access to necessary data. But that changed in 2006, shortly after Reich arrived. The OTS blocked FDIC staff from physical access to the WaMu offices and electronic access to computer databases. According to an FDIC assistant regional director, one of the individuals who executed this policy was Darrel Dochow.[17]

Dochow became the OTS regional director of the West Region in September 2007, supervising seventy thrift institutions and their holding companies. Together, these institutions, which included Countrywide, IndyMac, and WaMu, held half of all the thrift assets nationwide. The 2007 OTS *Annual Report*, which featured Dochow's photo, described the West Region as containing "the largest lending institutions in the country that are at the forefront of innovation in nationwide home mortgage lending." The report also boasted that:

> Some thrifts in the OTS West Region have been offering nontraditional mortgage products for decades, including adjustable-rate mortgages and interest-only mortgages. OTS examiners are well-versed on how institutions can manage and mitigate the risks associated with these products to keep their

> operations safe and sound, and provide consumers with adequate disclosure and protection.[18]

Yet the West Region had only 165 employees in 2007, and this included the 53 new hires in 2006 and 2007. WaMu, the largest institution that the OTS supervised, had 49,403 employees. Strength of purpose in holding thrifts accountable could have outweighed strength in numbers, but apparently there was little of that either. The *Annual Report* described a cozy relationship: "In the West Region, our constant themes are innovation, diversity and positive, constructive relationships with the thrift institutions we supervise and with our other constituents." And Dochow did not have a history of toughness.[19]

During the S&L crisis, Darrel Dochow was employed by the Federal Home Loan Bank system working for Bank Board director Danny Wall. In that capacity, he helped delay shutting down the reckless thrift Lincoln Savings and Loan, run by Charles Keating, who later pleaded guilty to fraud charges. The failure of Lincoln cost taxpayers approximately $3 billion. Now he was regulating the most reckless subprime, Option ARM, and nontraditional lenders. As banking analyst Mike Mayo would later comment, "It was like putting a pyromaniac in charge of the forestry service." In that capacity, he received several e-mails from both FDIC and OTS staff that revealed the extensive efforts made to keep the FDIC from seeing what was going on at WaMu.[20]

In January 2006, for example, Michael Finn sent an e-mail revealing a new OTS policy. At the time, John Reich was OTS director, but Bair had not yet arrived at the FDIC. Finn, Dochow's predecessor as West Regional director of OTS, sent the e-mail to his subordinates, including Dochow:

> The message was crystal clear today. Absolutely no FDIC participation on any OTS 1 and 2 rated exams. We should only be copying FDIC on 3, 4 and 5 ROE transmittals—no cc or bcc on ROEs of 1s and 2s. We should also deny FDIC requests to participate on HC or affiliate exams. I'll fill you in when I return. Permission for FDIC to join us on WaMu and Downey will stand for now, but they should not be indirect [*sic*] contact with thrift management or be requesting info directly from the thrift.[21]

In other words, for institutions with top CAMELS ratings (the best rating was a 1), the FDIC was to be shut out. This included WaMu. By that time, WaMu's high-risk lending strategy was well under way. The stonewalling continued, even as FDIC staff sent repeated e-mails requesting access. In 2007, the FDIC wanted to examine files to determine whether WaMu was in compliance with the new voluntary interagency guidance on nontraditional loans. The OTS said no. The disputes went up to OTS deputy director Scott Polakoff. In July 2008—during the $9 billion run on WaMu—Polakoff sent an e-mail to Dochow, who by then was the West Regional director:

> I have read the attached letter from the FDIC regarding supervision of WaMu and am once again disappointed that the FDIC has confused its role as insurer with the role of the Primary Federal Regulator. Its letter is both inappropriate and disingenuous. I would like to see our response to the FDIC, which I assume will remind it that we, as the PFR will continue to effectively supervise the entity and will continue to consider FDIC's views.[22]

Blocking the FDIC from monitoring and supervising WaMu was helpful to Kerry Killinger. The FDIC consistently gave WaMu worse ratings on CAMELS reviews than the OTS did. Also, the FDIC had the power to shut down WaMu. Some suspect that money motivated both the lax standards and the OTS's hostile attitude toward the FDIC. Like the other banking regulators, the OTS was funded by assessments on the institutions it regulated. The more thrifts it supervised, the larger its budget. But a thrift could leave the OTS, for example, by changing charters and becoming a commercial bank. If it chose a national bank charter, the Office of the Comptroller of the Currency (OCC) would be its primary regulator, with the Fed supervising its holding company. If the thrift chose a state bank charter but with a membership in the Federal Reserve System, then, in addition to the state banking regulator, it would be regulated by the Fed. And if it selected a state bank charter without Fed membership, its primary federal regulator would be the FDIC.[23]

It was well known that John Reich did not want to lose Washington Mutual. This enterprise alone supplied more than 12 percent of the OTS budget in 2008. In May 2007, Reich sent an e-mail to a colleague canceling their lunch plans. He was having lunch instead, he wrote, with Kerry Killinger, "my largest constituent asset-wise." This closeness extended to the regulatory relationship. In July 2008, in an apologetic e-mail, Reich informed Killinger that he was going to issue a memo of understanding (MOU) focused on improvements that were needed at WaMu. An MOU was a serious, though private, supervisory action. Failure to comply could lead to a public cease and desist order. In his e-mail to Killinger, Reich wrote that he was already remiss in failing to issue an MOU in February, when WaMu was downgraded from a 2 to a 3. He apologized twice in the e-mail and suggested that the MOU was needed for appearances: "If someone were looking over our shoulders, they would probably be surprised we don't already have one in place." It took three months, until late August 2008, to negotiate the terms of the MOU, which was not signed until September.[24]

Reich worked just as hard to retain the other institutions that the OTS regulated. Shortly after he became director, in the summer of 2005, the OTS began courting Countrywide. While the Fed supervised the parent company, Countrywide Financial Corporation, its national bank subsidiary Countrywide Bank, N.A., had the OCC as its federal regulator. If the subsidiary became a thrift, then both it and the parent would have the OTS as its primary regulator. In 2006, Darrel Dochow met with Countrywide executives to pitch OTS as the friendlier choice. In August 2006, Angelo Mozilo explained to Countrywide executives why he favored the OTS over the Fed as a regulator: "It appears that the Fed is now troubled by pay options while the OTS is not. Since pay options are a major component of both our volumes and profitability the Fed may force us into a decision faster than we would like." Countrywide's chief risk officer agreed: "[b]ased on my meetings with the FRB [Federal Reserve Bank] and OTS, the OTS appears to be both more familiar and more comfortable with Option ARMs." The application to switch to the OTS was approved in March 2007. Countrywide may have come to regret this decision in August 2007, when it sought emergency funding from the Federal Reserve and was denied.[25]

The practice of shopping around for regulators created a race to the bottom in appraisals, lending standards, and loan-loss reserves. Yet, it is not clear that reducing the number of regulators and consolidating their functions would make supervision and enforcement more effective. To address the fragmentation of the various banking and financial market regulators, in March of 2008, Secretary Paulson issued a "blueprint" for reform. This model envisioned just three regulators focused on distinct areas. The Fed would focus on market stability across the entire system. The OTS would be folded into the OCC, which would then focus on safety and soundness of depository institutions. And the Securities and Exchange Commission (SEC) would merge with the Commodity Futures Trading Commission (CFTC), with the resulting regulator focused on protecting consumers and investors. Also in 2008, in an effort led by former Fed chairman Volcker, the Group of Thirty (a private organization whose members include financial industry leaders, academics, and former regulators), recommended similar streamlining. Supporters of consolidation and centralization often contend that reducing the complexity will result in higher standards and facilitate coordination with international regulators. However, some who favor the status quo worry that reducing the number of financial institution regulators would only make it easier for the industry to capture the remaining agencies.[26]

Other supporters of the status quo, including Fed chairman Alan Greenspan, seemed to prefer the multiple agencies fighting for turf. In March 1994, Greenspan told the Senate Banking Committee: "The current structure provides banks with a method . . . of shifting their regulator, an effective test that provides a limit on the arbitrary position or excessively rigid posture of any one regulator. The pressure of a potential loss of institutions has inhibited excessive regulation and acted as a countervailing force to the bias of a regulatory agency to overregulate." It was a curious statement. Greenspan said this in 1994, just five years after the taxpayers committed hundreds of billions of dollars to rescue the S&Ls after they burned out because of deregulation, lax supervision, and government-enabled accounting cover-ups. As the Fed chairman since 1987, he had a front row seat for that debacle.[27]

Agency DNA

John Reich was not unique in his acquiescent attitude. His immediate predecessor, James Gilleran, was just as friendly. In 2003, when he was the OTS director, Gilleran posed with three banking lobbyists behind a stack of paper wrapped in red tape, meant to represent federal regulations. Behind them was a backdrop that read "Cutting Red Tape." Also in the picture was Reich, then a vice chairman of the FDIC, holding up gardening shears; Director Gilleran brandished a chain saw. The photo appeared in the FDIC Annual Report for 2003, when Sheila Bair's predecessor, Donald Powell, was chairman. In the report, Powell highlighted Reich's efforts to eliminate "outdated, unnecessary or unduly burdensome" regulations. In 2004, Gilleran championed the growth of the Option ARM, asserting in a speech that "our goal is to allow thrifts to operate with a wide breadth of freedom from regulatory intrusion." When Reich became OTS director, he also praised Option ARMs, even after the federal banking regulators came out with the joint guidance on nontraditional mortgages. This guidance suggested that if lenders offered negatively amortizing loans, they should consider the borrower's ability to make the full index payments, not just the initial teaser payments. This was the guidance that WaMu and many others ignored.[28]

Before Bair arrived in the summer of 2006, the FDIC seemed more accommodating to bank management. In 2005, in an e-mail entitled "Potential Impact of a Possible Housing Bubble on Washington Mutual Bank," an FDIC examiner wrote:

> Management acknowledges the risks posed by current market conditions and recognizes that a potential decline in housing prices is a distinct possibility. Management believes, however that the impact on [Washington Mutual Bank] would be manageable, since the riskiest segments of production are sold to investors, and that these investors will bear the brunt of a bursting housing bubble.

The FDIC at that time seemed comfortable with an impending mortgage crisis as long as the risk was borne by someone other than the banks it was set up to insure. Bair, however, believed in "market discipline," whereby the shareholders and creditors of the banks should take losses ahead of the taxpayers. Her arrival, and mission to protect depositors and taxpayers, was perhaps resented by those who saw the banks as their constituency. She said things like, "our job is to protect customers, not banks."[29]

Turf wars alone did not bring either WaMu or the broader financial system to the brink of collapse. By summer's end in 2008, the problems were nearing their peak. Losses were mounting and trouble lay ahead, but Americans were distracted by the very dramatic and lengthy U.S. presidential primary campaigns and paying little attention to these details. Throughout that summer, the news cycle fixated first on the high-stakes Democratic nomination battle and then, in early September, on John McCain's vice presidential running mate, Alaska governor Sarah Palin. Meanwhile, major economic problems were percolating. Seemingly out of nowhere in mid-September, what we would soon call "the greatest downturn since the Great Depression" was suddenly upon us. But in the words of the Financial Crisis Inquiry Commission, "the vulnerabilities that created the potential for crisis were years in the making."[30]

14

Legal Enablers of the Toxic Chain

For Kerry Killinger, the vulnerabilities that created the potential for crisis were also years in the making. The very conditions that drove up Washington Mutual's (WaMu's) stock price and made him an extremely wealthy man contained the seeds of the company's and his own destruction. On September 4, 2008, those seeds began to bear fruit. Two members of the WaMu board of directors came to Seattle headquarters when there was no board meeting scheduled. They entered Killinger's office and shut the door. After they departed, Killinger beckoned his assistant. When he told her he had been fired, she expressed sympathy. He answered, "It's just so embarrassing." This was not an expression of regret about the many people harmed by his actions, but instead a concern about his bruised ego.[1]

A terrible summer had led up to that moment. Despite the $7 billion lifeline from David Bonderman's Texas Pacific Group, WaMu continued to struggle. In early June, after a banking analyst announced his expectation that WaMu would lose nearly $22 billion through 2011, the stock price fell by more than 14 percent. With the bank run, in mid-July the stock tumbled to $3.23, a steep drop from where it traded above $45 the previous year. To combat waning confidence in the bank, Killinger began speaking publicly of the new plan to emphasize the retail division—except when he went off script. Before a Rotary Club that summer, he joked about the securitization supply chain: "I think you guys could have gone out and securitized your coats and pants and shirts—somebody might have bought it."[2]

Though Kerry Killinger's long-term strategic plans and day-to-day decisions were guided by competitive pressures and a desire to grow earnings, there was another force at play. He grew WaMu into a reckless lender not just because of competitive pressures, because the board of directors failed to rein him in, or because of turf-battling regulators. He did it because he could. After twenty years of deregulation, most of it was legal. And what wasn't legal was ignored, due to years of government desupervision.[3]

Killinger was both a leader and a follower. He led his company off the cliff, but he did so because lawmakers and regulators took down the guardrails and eliminated the speed limits. It took the government about two decades to get rid of the most important financial safety rules. These rules, embodied in a system enacted during the New Deal, had for about fifty years prevented people like Danny Faulkner, Charlie Knapp, and Kerry Killinger from running their companies off the road and taking the taxpayers with them. Blain, Faulkner, and their associates had their fraudulent land flips, Knapp had his cash-for-trash loan deals, and Killinger had the toxic mortgage supply chain. Though deregulation and desupervision enabled the S&L crisis, the subsequent legal reforms did not eliminate risk to borrowers, lenders, taxpayers, or to the entire system. Instead, risk grew, but through sophisticated financial innovation, it was strategically directed away from Wall Street to homeowners and taxpayers.[4]

Decades of Deregulation and Desupervision

Each link of the toxic mortgage supply chain was made possible by at least one specific act or omission during these decades. The acts included federal court decisions, acts of Congress and state legislatures, and agency rulemakings and guidance. The omissions included regulatory forbearance by the Fed, other banking regulators and the SEC, and inaction by Congress. The acts were equivalent to removing stop signs, traffic lights, and speed limits at dangerous intersections. The omissions were like failing to put up new signs, lights, and speed limits on newly built roads. These financial safety protections were removed out of a false sense of security. The fifty years from the New Deal reforms of the 1930s to the S&L crisis of the 1980s had been a time of stability, without major panics or boom-and-bust cycles. Influential economists and policy makers argued that the safety measures were no longer needed and that the market could regulate itself. This thinking led to the dismantling of the New Deal regulatory framework and the failure to impose safety standards on new players operating in the shadows and on new financial instruments.[5]

But even as it undermined the aspects of the New Deal regime that reined in risk taking at banks, the government kept in place and even expanded those pieces of the regime that provided private banks with a safety net backed by the federal government. The range of firms with access to the safety net grew along with its size. Each of the five links of the toxic mortgage supply chain was enabled by specific legal acts and omissions. Without these legal enablers, we would not have had the boom, the bust, the bank collapses, and the huge numbers of underwater homeowners.[6]

The First Link

The first link of the chain was the origination of high-risk residential mortgages. WaMu was an active originator of subprime, Option ARM and other high-risk loans, both directly through its prime business and its Long Beach subsidiary, including purchasing loans made by independent brokers and wholesalers. This activity became possible on a nationwide basis in the 1980s, with the enactments of the Depository Institutions Deregulation and Monetary Control Act of 1980 (DIDMCA) and the Alternative Mortgage Transaction Parity Act of 1982 (the Parity Act). Without these laws, neither subprime nor high-risk Option ARM and other negative-amortizing lending could have flourished. The DIDMCA, passed at the end of the Carter administration with strong lobbying support from the U.S. League of Savings Institutions, prevented most states from enforcing usury laws that would have capped the amount of interest on first mortgages. Its timing in 1980 responded to Paul Volcker's Fed allowing interest rates to skyrocket well above the states' usury caps. The law benefited the thrifts and banks but created greater risk for consumers and taxpayers. Senator Alan Cranston, later one of the "Keating Five," was reportedly part of the backroom deal in which the bill was quietly amended to raise deposit insurance coverage, and thus taxpayer risk, from $45,000 to $100,000 per account.[7]

The Parity Act was part of the 1982 Garn-St. Germain Act, which President Reagan called the thrift industry's "emancipation proclamation." It permitted adjustable-rate mortgages (ARMs) as well as those that were negatively amortizing or had balloon payments. This law expanded upon action by the savings and loan (S&L) regulator, the Federal Home Loan Bank Board, which recently had granted federally chartered thrifts the right to offer variable-rate mortgages. The Parity Act preempted state law, thus extending this right to state-chartered thrifts and also authorizing all thrifts to offer a slew of even riskier home loan types. Garn-St. Germain was guided through the Congress by Bank Board chairman Richard Pratt. After he left government service, Pratt took a position at Merrill Lynch selling mortgage bonds to S&Ls. He eventually became chairman of Merrill Lynch Mortgage Capital.[8]

This first link, the origination of high-risk mortgages, was also enabled by the federal courts. The 1993 decision in *Nobelman v. American Savings Bank* gave lenders false comfort that even if borrowers found themselves underwater, the lenders would get paid. Borrowers would have to keep making the same payments on the same terms in order to keep their homes. Previously, federal circuit courts covering more than twenty states had permitted bankruptcy courts to reduce the amount outstanding on a mortgage loan to the home's depressed market value. When the Supreme Court in *Nobelman* blocked this relief, lenders had added incentive to place people in homes they could not afford, to pump up appraisals, and to sell negatively amortizing loans.[9]

The Federal Home Loan Mortgage Corporation (Freddie Mac) and the Federal National Mortgage Association (Fannie Mae), the government-sponsored enterprises (GSEs), also enabled this first link by lowering underwriting standards for the mortgages they purchased. Until the mid-1990s, the GSEs typically required 10–20 percent down payments and other conservative standards. In 1993, a few months after the *Nobelman* decision, they piloted the "Alternative Qualifying" program, under which lending standards were loosened for home loans that qualified as "conforming" and thus purchasable by the GSEs. Yet, the greatest harm occurred more than a decade later. By 2004, the GSEs purchased 40 percent of all private label subprime MBSs, up from about 10 percent in 2001. Around that time, to satisfy originators like Countrywide, to gain market share and to earn profits for their shareholders, Fannie and Freddie also began to buy loans for which there was no documentation of borrowers' income (liar's loans, though a small fraction of the total volume). This was exactly when WaMu was implementing its "Higher Risk Lending Strategy." Though Fannie and Freddie were never originators, they supported risky practices by purchasing and guaranteeing high-risk mortgages. In early 2007, when Freddie Mac announced it would stop buying liar's loans, the damage was already done.[10]

The first link was also significantly enabled by the failure of Alan Greenspan's Federal Reserve to adopt rules forbidding reckless mortgage lending. Indeed, the Fed was the only regulatory agency that had the power to curb abusive, confusing, and predatory lending by each and every type of mortgage originator. Had Greenspan acted, the entire mortgage crisis could have been averted. The Fed was given authority to prohibit reckless lending under the Home Ownership and Equity Protection Act of 1994 (HOEPA). This law gave the Fed very broad "discretionary authority" to "by regulation or order . . . prohibit acts or practices" related to both mortgage loans that the Fed found "unfair" or "deceptive" and "refinancing of mortgage loans" that the Fed found to be "associated with abusive lending practices, or that are otherwise not in the interest of the borrower." Though the Fed adopted a rule in 2001, it related to another part of HOEPA that regulated "high cost" loans and was so narrowly drawn that it affected just 1 percent of subprime loans.[11]

The Fed was well aware of its broad homeowner protection authority. Speaking in Cleveland in March 2001, Fed governor Edward Gramlich made it clear that under HOEPA, the Fed could combat the worst practices. He continued to express his concerns in 2002 about the "increasing reports of abusive, unethical and in some cases, illegal, lending practices." Though Greenspan said in 2003 that the disclosure on a Countrywide mortgage application would be difficult for a PhD to understand, he still did not implement HOEPA. One consumer advocate recalled suggesting to Fed governors during a 2004 meeting of the Fed Consumer Advisory Council that given mounting bad loans based on false appraisals, firms like Lehman and Bear Stearns were in jeopardy. She recalled that the Fed officials generally dismissed her stories as "anecdotal" and assured her that their models did not predict such trouble.[12]

The Fed's authority was extremely broad and applied to all mortgage originators, not just banks and thrifts, but also independent brokers. It could have created a level playing field and combated the very problem Kerry Killinger wrote about in his March 2005 e-mail—the increasing competitive pressure to lower underwriting standards. Given the Fed's failure to act, Congress could have filled the gap and either clearly prohibited negatively amortizing loans, prohibited offering a loan when there were no documented financial resources to pay it back at the fully amortized rate, or mandated a rulemaking. As the Financial Crisis Inquiry Commission (FCIC) concluded in its final report: "In an environment of minimal government restrictions, the number of nontraditional loans surged and lending standards declined."[13]

The Office of Thrift Supervision (OTS) further weakened consumer protections in 1996, when it adopted a rule permitting federal thrifts to ignore state consumer protection laws. Around 1999, when states began to enact statutes—known as "mini-HOEPA" laws—forbidding predatory lending, federal thrifts were exempt. Even when community organizers approached the OTS in 2000, asking for an end to predatory loans that harmed consumers and put lenders at risk, the OTS did not stop the practices. In addition, the OTS relaxed its interpretation of the Parity Act allowing for thrifts to offer adjustable rate loans with prepayment penalties.[14]

Finally, the creation of high-risk mortgages was enabled by the primary federal regulator for national banks, the Office of the Comptroller of the Currency (OCC). Led by John Hawke and later John Dugan, the OCC actively prevented state lawmakers, regulators, and law enforcers from protecting consumers. One way the OCC did this was to stop state attorneys general from pursuing predatory lending cases. For example, according to former Minnesota prosecutor Prentiss Cox, in 2001, Julie Williams, the chief counsel of the OCC, warned the state attorneys general in a meeting in Washington that the OCC would "quash" any efforts to interfere with national banks' consumer practices.[15]

Another example of the OCC's thwarting state efforts was litigation. Wachovia Bank, N.A., a national bank, operated its mortgage lending business through a subsidiary Wachovia Mortgage Corporation, which was chartered under North Carolina law. This subsidiary offered home mortgage loans in several states, including Michigan. Under Michigan law, mortgage companies had to register with its Office of Financial and Insurance Regulation and become subject to its supervision. In 2003, Wachovia informed the state that it would not register, and when Michigan said it was required to do so, Wachovia sued. The case went to the United States Supreme Court. In April 2007, in *Watters v. Wachovia Bank*, the Court ruled 5–3 for Wachovia (Justice Thomas recused himself because his son and daughter-in-law worked for Wachovia). The opinion, written by Justice Ruth Bader Ginsburg, stated that the National Bank Act and the related OCC regulations trumped Michigan law. During the proceedings, the OCC joined with the American Bankers Association and the Mortgage Bankers Association in support of Wachovia, whereas forty-nine states plus Puerto Rico and the District of Columbia sided with Michigan. As a result, the OCC became the sole regulator of mortgage companies with national bank parents and effectively blocked the states' ability to impose consumer protection laws on them.[16]

The Second Link

The second link of the toxic mortgage supply chain was securitization: the pooling of high-risk mortgages into trusts or other conduits, which issued residential mortgage-backed securities (MBSs), purchased by investors. WaMu was an active part of the securitization link. It sold some of its mortgage loans whole to Wall Street banks, which securitized them, and it also securitized many on its own. The money that investors put into MBSs was used to pay WaMu for the mortgages it placed in the trust. In turn, WaMu used the money to help families finance home purchases or refinancings and to pay the independent brokers and employees who actually met with the borrowers.

This link, the ability of lenders and Wall Street to pool mortgages and sell MBSs without the assistance of Fannie and Freddie, depended on the Secondary Mortgage Market Enhancement Act of 1984 (SMMEA). This law removed the legal barriers that had blocked the development of the private mortgage securities market. Before 1984, Fannie, Freddie, and the Government National Mortgage Association (Ginnie Mae) had more than 95 percent of the MBS market. This law was a major turning point. It made private-label MBSs permissible holdings for a broad range of institutional investors, including national banks and pension funds. But because the residential mortgages sold into these pools did not meet the high GSE standards and there was no GSE guarantee, the law mandated a substitute. Under SMMEA, these "nonagency" MBSs required a top rating from at least one Nationally Recognized Statistical Rating Organization (credit-rating agency). In addition, SMMEA required states to treat private-label MBSs as equivalent to U.S. government obligations for purposes of state laws that would have otherwise prohibited banks and S&Ls from buying. It also preempted state securities laws, so that the private-label MBSs did not have to be registered with them, which would have entailed state-by-state review, disclosures, and sales restrictions.[17]

Also enabling this securitization link was the Tax Reform Act of 1986, which allowed MBSs to avoid double taxation. The law created the Real Estate Mortgage Investment Conduit (REMIC), another name to describe the trusts and other entities used to pool the mortgages. This allowed for innovation: private-label versions of the vehicles that government agency Ginnie Mae had first used in 1970 for the mortgages it pooled. The Ginnie Mae structure had allowed only for the pass through of mortgage cash flows, divided up proportionately to the certificate holders. With REMICs, cash flows from pooled mortgages could be split up into classes, known as tranches. This allowed one tranche to be prioritized over another, so as to (in theory) concentrate the risk of default with those classes that paid higher interest to investors. It also allowed for new structures that could distribute the cash flows in a variety of ways, such as selling tranches of securities that only received interest payments from the underlying mortgages. Without the tax law change to approve this REMIC structure, there would have been double taxation—at the trust level and to the investors. Thus, the SMMEA allowed banks that originated mortgage loans that the GSEs would not purchase to get them off their balance sheets.[18]

These laws created a viable secondary market for mortgages that were either too big or too risky for Fannie or Freddie to purchase. They also expanded the ability of mortgage brokers to originate huge numbers of loans outside the banking system without the need to gather deposits to do so. Instead, brokers relied on lenders, who themselves often relied on Wall Street's ability to gather investor cash through the sale of these MBSs. Lenders would fund the loans made by brokers, knowing they could off-load them to Wall Street, or in the case of WaMu, turn them into securities directly. Lenders thus had little to no incentive to monitor the work at the front lines. Without market discipline over independent brokers, and without limits on the types of loans they could make, predatory and fraudulent lending flourished. While the contracts that accompanied the mortgage bonds bought by investors made representations about the quality of the underlying mortgages, these standards were often ignored.[19]

The person who, with the Reagan administration's support, shepherded both the Secondary Mortgage Market Enhancement Act and the tax law change through Congress was Lewis Ranieri, now known as the father of mortgage finance. A bond trader who became a vice chairman at Salomon Brothers, Ranieri began an investment partnership in the late 1980s to buy up distressed S&Ls from the government. In 2004, he was described by *Businessweek* as one of the "greatest innovators of the past 75 years." After the mortgage crisis arrived, he denounced the misuse by lenders and Wall Street of the securitization structures he helped create: "This isn't checkers . . . . These are real people losing their homes." Ranieri saw that the system of financing American homeownership had morphed into a means of speculation: "I do feel guilty. I wasn't out to invent the biggest floating craps game of all time, but that's what happened."[20]

Also enabling this securitization link was the erosion and repeal of the Glass-Steagall Act's separation of securities operations (underwriting the issuance of debt and equity securities) from traditional banking (taking deposits and making loans). Glass-Steagall was enacted in 1933, after the mixture of commercial banking with securities operations in the 1920s resulted in massive speculation in securities, fostered a boom and bust, and ruined many unsophisticated investors. The law required that these distinct businesses be housed in separate entities. With the creation of deposit insurance, commercial banks had access to the federal deposit insurance fund, as well as liquidity support from the Federal Reserve. They were no longer permitted to speculate or take other excessive risks because the losses would be borne by taxpayers.[21]

The wall began to erode in the 1980s, when the Fed, led by Alan Greenspan, began to allow commercial banks to use special subsidiaries to underwrite equity and debt securities. By 1999, three of the forty-five commercial banks with such special subsidiaries—Citigroup, Chase Manhattan Bank, and Bank of America—were among the top ten underwriters of U.S. securities. In 1994, when geographic expansion was permitted, megamergers followed. In response to commercial banks taking market share from them, investment banks decided to enter into traditional banking. They began to acquire thrifts and industrial loan companies in order to use those deposits to fund their purchases of securities and other assets.[22]

Eventually, both commercial and investment banks wanted to knock down the walls completely. The near-final blow occurred in 1998, when the Fed allowed Citibank to merge with Travelers. Shortly thereafter, Congress repealed what little was left of Glass-Steagall by enacting the Financial Services Modernization Act of 1999 (the

"Gramm-Leach-Bliley Act"). This law created the financial holding company, through which universal banks could engage in traditional banking, investment banking, and insurance underwriting. Universal banks like Citigroup, Bank of America, and JPMorgan Chase could now operate many links of the mortgage securitization chain under one roof—from origination to securitization to the creation of collateralized debt obligations (CDOs). And they could do all that while still enjoying federal deposit insurance and liquidity support from the Fed.[23]

This securitization link was also enabled by the U.S. banking regulators' decision to follow guidance from the international body, the Basel Committee on Banking Supervision. Historically, depository institutions (banks and thrifts) were subject to capital standards. For commercial banks, these included a minimum leverage ratio of about 3 percent, which meant borrowing no more than $97 for every $100 in total assets. Banks were also subject to "risk-weighted" capital standards. This imposed a minimum of 8 percent capital to risk-weighted assets. For example, an asset with a 0 percent risk weighting would need no capital backing, and one with a 100 percent risk weighting would need 8 percent, meaning borrowing just $92 to finance every $100 of such assets.[24]

In a November 2001 rulemaking, the Fed, OCC, OTS, and FDIC lowered the amount of capital required for banks and thrifts that held private-label MBSs. Whereas these mortgage bonds previously had been given a 50 percent risk weighting, after that date, they were given a 20 percent weighting. This meant that instead of being required to have 4 percent capital, they needed only 1.6 percent, and thus could borrow $9.84 billion to purchase $10 billion in private-label MBSs, if they had triple-A or double-A ratings. This applied whether the underlying mortgages were high-down-payment, thirty-year fixed, high-risk Option ARMs, liar's loans, or subprime loans with a low down payment. A whole mortgage loan held in the bank's portfolio, meanwhile, still had a 50 percent risk weighting. This new interagency rule encouraged banks and thrifts to securitize mortgages; they could borrow more to hold them than whole loans. And borrowing more meant greater profits, at least while prices of these assets were rising. In 2002, investment banks began to work closely with the rating agencies to create credit enhancements and other means to transform pools of high-risk mortgages into mortgage bonds, most of which had triple-A or double-A ratings.[25]

The Third Link

The third link in the toxic mortgage chain was the sale of the midlevel and riskiest tranches of private-label residential MBSs to a second trust that then issued CDOs and sold them to investors. Tranches of WaMu securities were sold into these trusts, even though WaMu never created its own CDOs. The securities issued by the CDOs were then purchased by large institutional investors, including investment banks and hedge funds in the United States and abroad. If real buyers could not be found, purchasers of CDO tranches could also be a third trust that would then issue its own CDOs, known as "CDOsquareds." The cash flows from the mortgages that WaMu originated flowed from the first to the second link, into this third link, into the CDOs and CDOsquareds.[26]

The creation of CDOs was enabled by the Securities and Exchange Commission (SEC). In 1992, the SEC adopted Rule 3a-7 under the Investment Company Act of 1940. This rule expanded the ability of an asset-backed conduit that issued CDOs to avoid being classified as an "investment company." Almost every pool of investments is captured by this definition and thus the law, unless there is a statutory or regulatory exemption. Escaping this classification was meaningful: designation as an investment company brought limitations that CDO managers hoped to avoid. Pools of whole mortgage loans already had a statutory exemption from the law as did pools of auto loans, boat loans, and credit card receivables. But CDO structures that pooled mortgage bonds had to rely on a different exemption in the statute, Section 3(c)(1). This was the section that private pools of capital (now known as hedge funds and private equity funds) depended upon to avoid the strict controls of the investment company designation. But this private fund exemption was not ideal for CDOs, as at the time, it limited the number of owners to one hundred. Relief came with the new 3a-7 exemptive rule as CDO conduits that contained pools of mortgage bonds, could operate free of the 1940 act and its accompanying regulations. This SEC action also cleared the way for synthetic CDOs, the sales of which would expand when credit default swaps (CDSs) flourished.[27]

The exemptive rule was issued after the SEC Division of Investment Management published a report concluding that given high credit ratings, asset-backed securities were "relatively safe." The SEC staff was also comforted by the fact that the purchasers of these securities were supposedly sophisticated "institutional investors, including banks, savings and loans, pension funds, insurance companies and money managers," who had the knowledge and skills to understand these products. The staff believed that these institutions conducted "their own due diligence review before investing."[28]

The proliferation of CDOs was also enabled by changed accounting standards. While the SEC has authority to establish accounting standards, it instead relied on private-sector bodies such as the Financial Accounting Standards Board (FASB) to do so. In the 1970s, when the FASB was created, a financing transaction had to be reported on a corporation's (including a bank's) balance sheet. This meant that the amount borrowed by the bank showed up as a liability on the right side, and the value of the asset—such as commercial loans made by the bank to business enterprises, or residential mortgages made to consumers—appeared on the left. Eventually, however, off-balance-sheet financing was developed—the types of structures that Enron Corporation used to hide its debt. After the 2001 Enron meltdown, the FASB tried to impose standards that made balance sheets more honest, but by December 2003, industry pressure had largely reduced these efforts to minor changes. Between 1992 and 2007, off-balance-sheet assets of financial institutions increased by some 1,500 percent, whereas on-balance-sheet assets grew by only 200 percent.[29]

The CDO structure was one such off-balance-sheet entity. The structure used to issue CDOs was what accountants called a "variable-interest entity." A sponsoring bank would set up a new trust or conduit that gathered money from investors (mainly debt holders, with a small percentage of equity holders), which was then paid to the sponsoring bank to buy MBSs from its portfolio. This made the bank's balance sheet look better. It could use the cash to pay down some of its own debts, and the MBS would disappear. As banking analyst Christopher Whalen of Institutional Risk Analytics observed, "They are supposed to be separate from the bank, but the economic reality is that they are the same."[30]

These off-balance-sheet entities could be abused if the sponsoring bank retained some obligation to compensate the buyer if the mortgage bonds went bad. If so, then what the financial statements called cash received for the sale of MBSs should really have been recorded as a cash loan received in exchange for MBS as collateral. And, an investor looking at the bank's balance sheet might be misled to believe that the bank had less debt and thus less risk than it truly had. The leverage would be understated. This was analogous to the accounting manipulation that brought down Enron.[31]

As for the third link, lax accounting rules allowed banks to use CDO structures to hide debt off their balance sheets. The misuse of CDOs helped bring about the financial crisis. Citigroup, the universal bank created through the erosion of Glass-Steagall, was an example. Citi set up off-balance-sheet entities and sold them MBSs and other assets. For funding, these conduits issued triple-A short-term debt securities (commercial paper) to investors. To help attract money, Citi's traders gave investors a "liquidity put." This was a contractual guarantee that required Citi to buy back the short-term debt securities from investors at face value if they became illiquid. In 2007, Citi bought back $25 billion worth of the commercial paper at face value when it was trading well below that. This cost the bank $14 billion. The hidden debt was back on the bank's balance sheet and likely should have been at the outset. The OCC's examiners were aware of these puts but apparently viewed them as outside their concerns because they were inside the investment bank part of Citi, not the depository institution.[32]

The Fourth Link

The fourth link in the toxic mortgage chain was the sale of credit default swaps (CDSs) to owners of residential MBSs and CDOs to help protect them from the risk of default and help them leverage more. Private-label MBSs did not come with a Fannie Mae or Freddie Mac guarantee, so the role of the CDS was to replicate that protection. A triple-A rating was not always enough for nervous investors. They still wanted to lay off the risk of default on high-risk mortgages originated by lenders like WaMu. American International Group (AIG) sold many billions of dollars in CDSs, including some on CDO tranches whose cash flows came from WaMu mortgages.

Buyers of credit protection hoped to reduce the regulatory limits on how much they could borrow (leverage) against high-risk mortgage securities in their portfolios. Buying a CDS convinced the regulators that the risk of loss had been transferred to a third party. Thus, CDS contracts used with residential MBSs and CDOs helped banks leverage but concentrated a great deal of risk at firms like AIG.

Other buyers of protection did not even own the underlying securities. They used CDSs to place bets that selected mortgage bonds would default. Paying premiums was like buying a lottery ticket, but given the ability to select MBSs that were likely to fail, the odds of a jackpot were significantly greater. The CDS gave rise to the synthetic CDO. Investors who held highly rated tranches of synthetic CDOs did not depend on actual cash flows from homeowners. Instead, their cash flows came from premiums paid on CDS contracts sold by the trust that issued CDOs to them. The investors would lose money if mortgages referenced in the CDS contracts defaulted. Many of these synthetic CDO investors did not realize that mortgages most likely to default were deliberately chosen for credit protection. Mortgages thought to be prudently underwritten were excluded. Mortgages originated by WaMu, including its Long Beach subsidiary, were ideal choices, as they were, referred to by a top CDO trader as, "one of the weakest names in the market." Notably, WaMu Option ARMs were referenced for the infamous Timberwolf CDOs sold by Goldman Sachs to Bear Stearns.[33]

This fourth link, the development of the CDS market including synthetic CDOs, was enabled by a number of legal changes. The most significant was the Commodity Futures Modernization Act of 2000 (CFMA). The CFMA deregulated derivatives and transformed CDSs from contracts that minimized risk to ones that were used for speculation. With this law, a bank or other investor was allowed to buy protection to cover an event of default on a whole loan, bond, or other debt security it did not own. In addition, as a result of the CFMA, a secondary market developed for CDS contracts, allowing protection obligations under a single contract to be sold many times. Finally, the CFMA allowed the sale of credit protection on very obscure securities. When CDSs were invented by Bankers Trust and popularized by JPMorgan in the early 1990s, they were limited to corporate bonds where the issuer was a known enterprise with recognizable products and services and publicly available financial statements. But after "modernization" CDSs were sold for bonds issued by conduits (or trusts) that had little transparency.[34]

The passage of the CFMA enabled the growth of the CDS market and thus the origination of high-risk private-label MBSs, CDOs, and synthetic CDOs. The law explicitly stated that "it shall supersede and preempt the application of any State or local law that prohibits or regulates gaming or the operation of bucket shops." The need for this language reflected the knowledge that CDSs were a type of gambling. They permitted parties to bet on a security's financial performance without investing in it.[35]

The CFMA also helped solidify the rights of CDS buyers and sellers. As legal scholar Lynn Stout has explained, the new law actually deregulated derivatives. It removed "in one fell swoop, a legal constraint on derivatives speculation that dated back not just decades, but centuries." In the nineteenth century, derivatives were known as "difference contracts" and were typically bets on the future prices of commodities or some other "underlying" reference. If a party to such an agreement went to court to enforce it, a judge might refuse. Under the common law "rule against difference contracts," a judge would enforce the arrangement only if at least one party had an economic interest in the underlying asset or security. This common law rule was first abolished in the United Kingdom, then in the United States with the CFMA. Stout predicted in 1999 that the unregulated derivatives market would create a financial crisis.[36]

Other enablers of the use of credit protection to support the toxic supply chain were Fed chairman Alan Greenspan, Treasury secretary Robert Rubin, and deputy Treasury secretary Lawrence Summers.

In 1999, when experts like Professor Stout were warning of the perils of unregulated derivatives, these gentlemen sought to enact the CFMA. They did this to head off efforts by Brooksley Born—chair of the Commodity Futures Trading Commission (CFTC)—to regulate CDSs and the rest of the murky credit derivatives market. Derivatives were very lucrative for Wall Street banks. The total worldwide value of these contracts in 1998 was $70 trillion in face value and about $2.5 trillion in market value. Born was concerned that this lightly regulated market could cause great harm. Speculation with derivatives had caused the meltdown of the giant Long Term Capital Management hedge fund in 1998 and the sudden bankruptcy of Orange County in 1994. But President Clinton's economic advisers convinced him that these instruments were benign and should be exempt from regulation.[37]

Through the CFTC, Born was planning to issue a concept release inviting comments on the question of whether certain derivatives, including "credit swaps," should be better regulated. Larry Summers and others pressured her not to do so. At one point, Summers phoned Born with a threat. As one of her lieutenants, Michael Greenberger later recalled, Summers told Born: "I have 13 bankers in my office and they say if you go forward with this you will cause the worst financial crisis since World War II." She ignored Summers and issued the concept release in May. To block her from moving forward, Congress passed legislation in October 1998, placing a moratorium on any regulations concerning customized derivatives.[38]

In November 1999, Greenspan and Summers signed a report on derivatives as members of the President's Working Group on Financial Markets, an advisory body established by President Reagan by executive order in 1988. The Working Group report recommended that Congress deregulate, and asked for "legal certainty for swaps." They argued that swap agreements did not "warrant regulation" under the Commodity Exchange Act (CEA) for three reasons. First, "the sophisticated counterparties that use [over-the-counter] derivatives simply do not require the same protections under the CEA as those required by retail investors." Second, there was already enough regulation of most swap counterparties. Third, most swaps were "not susceptible to manipulation." Brooksley Born did not sign the report. She had already resigned. Ten years later, in mid-2008, the face value of derivatives outstanding worldwide was $673 trillion with a total market value of $20 trillion.[39]

In addition to the CFMA, Robert Rubin, a former chairman of Goldman Sachs, was also a driving force behind the repeal of Glass-Steagall. In 1999, just before the repeal passed, Treasury secretary Rubin left government service to become chairman of the executive committee at Citigroup, an institution that benefited from the repeal. At Citigroup, Rubin allegedly received numerous warnings about corruption in the mortgage supply chain. Richard Bowen, who had just been promoted at Citi, had discovered that 60 percent of the mortgages Citi was buying to securitize were defective. After numerous e-mails and meetings with his superiors, he was not getting any response. So he sent Rubin and three other officials a memo with the subject line including the words: "URGENT—READ IMMEDIATELY." Bowen said his concerns were not addressed; instead, he was demoted and marginalized. He told the Financial Crisis Inquiry Commission that he went from supervising about two hundred people to two, and that he received a poor review and a reduced bonus. In contrast, Rubin, who later said he did not know about the liquidity puts that resulted in Citi losing $14 billion, and who apparently did not respond to Bowen's concerns, earned more than $115 million—plus stock options—before he left Citi in 2009.[40]

The Fifth Link

The fifth link, leverage along every segment of the toxic mortgage supply chain—in particular, high leverage on Main Street, at mortgage lenders, on Wall Street, and among hedge funds—was also enabled by legal acts and omissions. It was the imprudent use of debt that allowed banks and thrifts to purchase so many mortgage-linked securities, including CDOs. Excessive leverage, including dependence on overnight and short-term repurchase agreements, was enabled by several acts and omissions. The first was the 2001 interagency rulemaking by the Fed, OCC, OTS, and FDIC (discussed above) that allowed banks and thrifts to borrow more against subprime and other high-risk mortgage-backed securities than they could against the same type of whole mortgage loans.

Another enabler of excessive leverage was a 2004 SEC rulemaking that both established the "consolidated supervised entity" program for the top five investment banks and amended the net capital rule for their broker-dealer subsidiaries. Until 2004, borrowing levels of the investment bank holding companies had not been regulated at all, but their U.S. broker-dealer subsidiaries had been subject to SEC regulation since 1934. Most of the investment banks ran their securities operations through these subsidiaries. In 1975, the SEC imposed capital requirements on broker-dealers with the net capital rule. This rule set out methods to calculate a broker-dealer's net worth. The purpose was to ensure that if a broker-dealer failed, it would have sufficient assets available to pay off most creditors, including retail customers. Net capital was calculated by totaling the market value of all tradable assets in the broker-dealer's portfolio and discounting or applying a "haircut" to those assets based on how difficult they might be to sell at full value. The rule established an early-warning limit on debt to net capital of 12 to 1—in other words, about 8 percent net capital, and set a cap of 15 to 1. While small broker-dealers used these ratios, the largest ones had, since the 1970s, used a different guideline. The top firms followed the alternative requirement to have net capital equal to 2 percent of the cash held in customer accounts (other than margin borrowed by the customer). Between the time that the rule was enacted in 1975 and 2004, it had been a success. There were few broker-dealer liquidations and almost no customers or counterparties lost money during a broker-dealer insolvency.[41]

This changed in 2004 when, as part of a bargain, the SEC amended the net capital rule for the five largest broker-dealers. They were subsidiaries of Bear Stearns, Goldman Sachs, Lehman Brothers, Merrill Lynch, and Morgan Stanley. At that time, these holding companies were faced with a new European Union directive: because they had operations in Europe, they were required to designate a consolidated supervisor in their home country. This was the same requirement that AIG had faced, and it ended up selecting the OTS. The large investment banks selected the SEC and were deemed "consolidated supervised entities," giving the SEC oversight over investment banks at the parent level for the first time.[42]

Under the 2004 rule change, the SEC allowed the broker-dealer subsidiaries of these five investment banks to use an "alternative method of computing net capital" that was dependent on their own internal mathematical models. Upon proposing the rule change, the SEC estimated that "broker-dealers taking advantage of the alternative capital computation would realize an average reduction in capital deductions of approximately 40%." Afterward, leverage ratios at investment banks increased, some up to about 33 to 1. This meant equity of just 3 percent, or borrowing up to $97 for every $100 in total assets.

The actual impact of the 2004 rule change is hotly debated. Some experts, including Erik Sirri—the former director of the SEC Division of Trading and Markets—contend the rule is unfairly maligned. He and others note that leverage levels at the investment banks were just as high in the late 1990s before they later dipped. And they often note that while leverage did ramp up again after the rule change, that causation has not been established between the change and the increase.[43]

Other experts, including Lee Pickard, also a former director of the SEC Division of Trading and Markets who helped draft the net capital rule in 1975, contend the changes either "substantially" or partially contributed to increased leverage. Pickard observed that "The losses incurred by Bear Stearns and other large broker–dealers were not caused by 'rumors' or a 'crisis of confidence,' but rather by inadequate net capital and the lack of constraints on the incurring of debt." It is indisputable, however, that using the "alternative" calculation method allowed for the appearance of the same net capital figure while taking on more debt. According to Robert Pozen, the former chairman of MFS Management, "[u]nder this alternative method, the ratio of average assets to net capital" at the five banks "more than doubled."[44]

That debate aside, it is clear that the 2004 designation of the SEC as an enterprise-wide regulator for complex universal banks was a disaster. The SEC admittedly exercised very little supervision at the parent level. According to a later SEC chair, Mary Schapiro, when the five investment banks took on consolidated supervised entity (CSE) status, the "SEC did not have the staff, the resources . . . or the mindset to be the prudential regulator of the largest financial institutions in the world." Under her predecessor, Christopher Cox, the SEC assigned only twenty-four people to monitor those five banks. Cox later described the CSE program as "fundamentally flawed from the beginning." On the SEC's watch, excess leverage undermined the financial health of the top five investment banks and brought the financial system to the brink of crisis. Three of the five—Bear, Lehman, and Merrill—failed between March and September 2008. The other two, Goldman and Morgan Stanley, would apply to convert to bank holding companies in September to stave off failure.[45]

This fifth link also involved borrowing through the short-term, often overnight, repurchase agreement ("repo") market. This fragile wholesale funding was a problem in the S&L crisis and amplified in 2008. Repo lenders were often cash-rich institutions, such as money market mutual funds and investment banks. Washington Mutual relied on repo funding, as did the Wall Street banks, including Bear Stearns and other purchasers of securities backed by cash flows from WaMu's mortgages. This reliance helped build up bank balance sheets when assets were rising but put the entire system in great peril when asset prices declined. Bear Stearns, the first to collapse, was felled by a "run on repo."[46]

Though obscure, the repo market was enormous. Some of the top investment banks funded hundreds of billions of dollars of their securities portfolios in the repo market. Before it failed, Bear borrowed about $50 billion overnight, every day. Estimates on the total size of the U.S. repo market vary. According to the New York Fed, at its peak in March 2008, the "tri-party" repo market—the largest and most transparent segment of this shadow banking system—reached $2.8 trillion, and the total market possibly $4.5 trillion. The tri-party name refers to those repo agreements that rely upon a clearing bank—either BNY Mellon or JPMorgan Chase—to handle the cash and collateral exchanges. It was the run on this shadow banking system—beginning that month with Bear and continuing with Lehman in September—that transformed the high-risk mortgage securities meltdown into a global financial crisis.[47]

This happened because repo was a central hub for interconnection. Repo borrowers largely depended for cash on money market funds and other lenders. If they got nervous and pulled their cash, the whole system would fall. At the beginning of September, it looked like the money market funds might not have a choice. This would be quite a catastrophe given that money funds supplied between one-third to one-quarter of cash in the tri-party repo market—between about $700 to $900 billion at the peak, most of which was provided overnight. This was because money market funds relied on short-term funding from their own investors (who had the right to redeem with one day's notice) and thus the funds were themselves vulnerable to runs. These money fund investors included corporations that each evening swept cash from their bank accounts into the funds.[48]

If these corporations panicked and redeemed their money market shares, it could mean the sudden withdrawal of hundreds of billions of dollars of liquidity from the money funds and then, in turn, from the repo borrowers—a credit crunch. In addition, the money funds are big cash suppliers to banks and businesses that borrowed through the short-term commercial paper markets. If the funds could not roll over commercial paper, and if businesses did not have the money to pay back the funds, the businesses would face a sudden liquidity problem. They would need to find cash somewhere and might draw down their lines of credit at their banks. The banks that must meet such demands for funding, the very same conglomerates that were involved in toxic mortgage securities, would then be short on liquidity. It was like a tinderbox.[49]

A legal change that enabled this reliance by banks on excessive debt through the short-term repo market was the Bankruptcy Abuse Prevention and Consumer Protection Act of 2005 (BAPCPA). With this law, Congress amended the Bankruptcy Code to expand the special treatment that repo cash lenders were given in a borrower's bankruptcy. The treatment had previously been extended only to repos backed by safe collateral such as U.S. government obligations.

The new law expanded this treatment to private-label MBSs and CDOs. As a result, investment banks like Lehman Brothers were able to grow their balance sheets and load up on assets far riskier than government securities. Repo lenders might not have been as willing to supply liquidity for these toxic mortgage securities if they believed they would be treated like ordinary creditors in bankruptcy.[50]

On filing for bankruptcy, a debtor usually has the benefit of an automatic stay—a moratorium on making payments to creditors. Once the automatic stay is in effect, the creditors must wait to see how much they will receive out of the estate. In addition, they are subject to the court's avoidance powers and claw back rights. The former permit the court to cancel contracts and the latter to claw preferential payments made by a debtor to any creditors during a short window of time before the bankruptcy filing. Unlike other creditors, lenders of cash against specially protected types of repo collateral are not subject to the stay, avoidance powers, or the power to claw back preferential payments.

This meant that a repo cash lender that had U.S. Treasuries as collateral, for example, would not need permission to use its contractual rights to close out the agreement and liquidate the collateral. In addition, the interest paid would not be clawed back as a preference. However, before 2005, it was not clear what would happen to repo agreements backed by mortgage-linked securities. Uncertainty ended in 2005 with BAPCPA, when Congress expanded the safe harbor to protect additional collateral types, including "mortgage related securities . . . mortgage loans, interests in mortgage related securities or mortgage loans."[51]

In addition to encouraging lending against higher-risk collateral like toxic mortgage securities, the special protection for repo lenders fostered runs on weak firms. Legal scholar Stephen Lubben has explained that this special treatment "contribute[s] to the failure of an already weakened firm, by fostering a run on the firm, [and] has consequent effects on the markets generally, as parties rush to sell trades with the debtor and buy corresponding positions with new counterparties." Thomas Hoenig, former president of the Federal Reserve Bank of Kansas City, currently vice chairman of the FDIC, stated that the "threat of runs by repo lenders will be significantly reduced" if Congress removes the special protection for repurchase agreements in bankruptcy.[52]

Flipping the Risk of Default

The toxic mortgage supply chain resembled Danny Faulkner's tables lined up in Dallas office buildings. Investors he had rounded up flipped land using false appraisals, with each successive buyer earning a gain on sale, until the last one was left holding an overvalued parcel financed by a loan from Empire Savings and Loan, the thrift that Faulkner controlled. Empire got its funding from brokered deposits, gathered by firms like Merrill Lynch. When the brokered deposits ran in 1984, Empire failed and required $273 from the deposit insurance fund to pay off its depositors. Just three years earlier, Empire had only $17 million in deposits. Had the regulators not ignored the red flags and shut down or sold Empire at the first sign of fraud, the losses would have been contained.[53]

Similarly, had the Fed and other banking regulators stopped the risky practices early on, and if Congress had not created laws to support and condone high-risk lending and fraud, the massive bubble would not have inflated and individuals would not find their down payments gone, their homes underwater. The toxic mortgage supply chain scheme was similar to Empire's, but instead of flipping land, they were flipping mortgages. With the toxic mortgage supply chain, the asset being sold was the right to the monthly mortgage payment cash flows. The two parties in the position to lose everything were the first borrower and the last investors holding the risk associated with those cash flows. This mortgage-flipping scheme also relied on hot money. These were repurchase agreements (repos), very short-term and often overnight loans. Investment banks, money market mutual funds, and others supplied short-term cash to help originators and also other investment banks finance the loans and securities they had purchased before they were packaged up and sold off as MBSs or CDOs.

On September 10, 2008, a month after John Reich returned to the Office of Thrift Supervision from his vacation, FDIC chair Sheila

Bair informed him that she planned to downgrade Washington Mutual to a CAMELS rating of 4. The previous day, Bair had contacted Kerry Killinger's replacement, Alan Fishman, to inform him that the FDIC and the OTS had a disagreement about the rating. After a curt reply to Bair, Reich sent an e-mail to his deputy, Scott Polakoff: "I cannot believe the continuing audacity of this woman."[54]

15

THE GREAT BETRAYAL

On September 16, 2008, Barack Obama, the Democratic nominee for president of the United States, addressed a cheering crowd of 2,000 at the Colorado School of Mines in Golden, Colorado. Sarah Palin, the Republican vice-presidential candidate, had visited Golden the previous day. Meanwhile, Republican presidential nominee John McCain was in Jacksonville, Florida, assuring the public that despite the "turmoil in our financial markets and Wall Street . . . the fundamentals of our economy are strong."[1]

But the financial system was falling apart, bringing the broader economy down with it. The burst of the housing bubble had set in motion a series of failures that tracked the toxic mortgage supply chain. First to go were the homeowners facing foreclosure, then the irresponsible lenders, and now the mortgage securitizers, credit protection providers, and short-term repo lenders were starting to fail.

The day before Obama's rally, on September 15, 2008, Lehman Brothers Holdings, Inc., had filed for bankruptcy. Lehman, one of the oldest investment houses in the country, was founded in 1850 as the Lehman Brothers Partnership, an Alabama cotton brokerage that later expanded into other commodities, then securities. Beginning in 1906, with its early ally Goldman Sachs, Lehman underwrote the stock offerings of American corporations like Sears, Roebuck & Co. It had survived the Civil War and the 9/11 terrorist attacks on the World Trade Center, but Lehman could not survive the toxic mortgage supply chain or its own overdependence on the short-term repo market. It had $200 billion in overnight repo loans a week before it crashed. Lehman was large and very interconnected; it had $639 billion in assets supported by $613 billion in debt and more than 100,000 creditors. Its bankruptcy filing was the largest in American history. That same day, Bank of America Corporation announced the purchase of Merrill Lynch & Co., rescuing the investment bank from the brink of collapse. With Bear Stearns having failed the previous spring, only two of the five giant independent investment banks remained: Goldman Sachs Group, Inc., and Morgan Stanley. Within a week, in order to get liquidity support from the Fed, they would end their status as investment banks and convert to bank holding companies. An era had ended.[2]

The Lehman bankruptcy spread panic throughout the banking and shadow banking system. The day after the filing, the day of Barack Obama's Colorado rally, the Reserve Primary Fund was in serious trouble. Reserve Primary, one of the country's oldest money market funds, historically had invested in short-term U.S. government securities. But in an effort to boost yield in 2007, Bruce Bent Sr. and his son Bruce Bent II, who lead the advisory firm that managed the fund, changed its objectives to allow for a broader class of investments, including $785 million in short-term repo loans and other debt issued by Lehman Brothers. This was about 1.2 percent of the total $62 billion portfolio. As a result of the extra risk the Bents piled on, Reserve Primary had an eye-popping 4.04 percent average monthly yield, when the industry averaged 2.75 percent. By 8:37 a.m. on September 15, investors concerned about the Lehman exposure had redeemed $5.2 billion from Reserve Primary. To meet these cash redemptions, a rush to sell the fund's holdings delivered more losses. The next day total redemptions reached $40 billion and the Bents sought a lifeline from the Fed. They were turned down. After the market closed, Reserve Primary announced it "broke the buck," meaning its net asset value—the value of the securities in its portfolio divided by shares outstanding—had dropped from $1 per share to below $0.9950. Bent Sr. was on vacation in Italy.[3]

When Reserve Primary broke the buck, it inspired a sudden, massive run on other money market funds. Up until then, many considered money market funds to be a higher-yielding, but equally safe, alternative to a bank account. Not anymore. Nervous institutional investors pulled out $300 billion in cash that week of September 15. To come up with cash, many of the money market funds had to rapidly liquidate their short-term investments. This meant that they did not renew or "roll over" hundreds of billions of dollars in repo and other short-term financing to banks and industrial firms. Businesses like General Electric Capital Corporation, the largest user of commercial paper—with about $74 billion outstanding—depended on rollovers to keep the lights on. With the short-term credit markets frozen, many businesses and local governments had to search for other sources of funding. Some were proactive: American Electric Power had no immediate needs, but wanted a "cushion of cash," so drew down $2 billion from a $3.9 billion credit line it held with twenty-seven banks, arranged by JPMorgan Chase and Barclays, tapping into these banks' diminishing liquidity. The run on the shadow banking system had spread to the commercial sector and beyond.[4]

To stop the run on money market funds and help restore liquidity to the commercial sector, the Treasury Department announced that it would temporarily guarantee the $1 net asset value for more than $3 trillion in money market fund shares, for losses up to $50 billion. In addition, the Fed agreed to use its emergency powers to lend money at low rates to commercial banks so that they could buy up the assets of the money market funds that were forced to liquidate. These two moves stopped the run, but they were unprecedented: the taxpayers were now standing behind the performance of an investment product, not a bank. In addition, a month later, the Fed would bail out businesses and banks when it agreed to directly purchase up to $1.8 trillion in commercial paper.[5]

Also on the day of Obama's Colorado rally, a $16.7 billion run on Washington Mutual (WaMu) was underway. It was six weeks after John Reich, the director of the Office of Thrift Supervision (OTS), bristled when FDIC chairman Sheila Bair interrupted his cruise vacation with concerns about the sinking thrift. The run on WaMu ended on September 25 when, by order of the OTS, the FDIC was appointed receiver of Washington Mutual Bank and sold it—including $176 billion in home mortgages—to JPMorgan Chase for $1.9 billion. At last Jamie Dimon, who had had his eye on WaMu since March, got what he desired. The parent company, Washington Mutual, Inc., filed for bankruptcy protection the next day, making Washington Mutual Bank the largest U.S. depository institution in history to fail. In its earlier life as American Savings and Loan, it was the largest thrift to fail.[6]

That same day—September 16—after an attempt at private rescue failed, the Federal Reserve used its emergency authority under Section 13(3) of the Federal Reserve Act to provide $85 billion to American International Group (AIG), $62 billion of which the giant insurer immediately used to pay off its credit default swap (CDS) counterparties, including Goldman Sachs, at 100 cents on the dollar. This was the beginning of a $182 billion government bailout of AIG. Before providing the lifeline, New York Fed president, Timothy Geithner was told that AIG's failure could be "more systemic" than Lehman's. In exchange, the U.S. Treasury received preferred stock and warrants that if exchanged would give the government a nearly 80 percent ownership stake in AIG. These events occurred just a week after the government seized control of the Federal National Mortgage Association (Fannie Mae) and the Federal Home Loan Mortgage Corporation (Freddie Mac), extending $187 billion in Treasury support. It had all unraveled very fast.[7]

On Saturday, September 20, to avoid another panic like the one caused by the Lehman bankruptcy, President George W. Bush asked the Congress to bail out the entire sinking financial system. The Fed had already supported the banks' and shadow banks' liquidity with low-cost loans and other credit facilities and would eventually provide trillions of dollars in support. Treasury had already rescued the money market funds and the GSEs. Now the president was turning to Congress for more. Before leaving office, Bush would admit: "I've abandoned free-market principles to save the free-market system." This was not entirely true. Certainly, the middlemen in the chain—

the securitizers, credit protection providers, and short-term and overnight lenders—were spared the rough justice of market discipline. But homeowners at the beginning of the chain were expected to bear their full losses.[8]

Washington Loophole

This disparity between the middlemen and the homeowners must have been on Barack Obama's mind that Tuesday morning at the Colorado rally. After acknowledging the severe financial crisis, Obama proclaimed: "We can't have a situation like the old [savings and loan] scandal where it's heads the investors win, and tails taxpayers lose." Then he endorsed using bankruptcy proceedings to help underwater homeowners reduce the principal on their loans. "Unlike Senator McCain," he promised, "I will change our bankruptcy laws to make it easier for families to stay in their homes." He said that "if you're a family that owns one house, bankruptcy judges are actually barred from helping you keep a roof over your head by writing down the value of your mortgage." He denounced the anomalous treatment of mortgages on a principal residence, compared to vacation homes and other debt, as "the kind of out-of-touch Washington loophole that makes no sense." With this speech, he was echoing consumer and housing advocates, including those at the Center for Responsible Lending, who already believed it was necessary to write down mortgage principal and that the best way to do so was through the bankruptcy courts. But because the *Nobelman* decision stood in the way, an amendment to the statute was necessary.[9]

A week later, on Tuesday, September 23, Treasury secretary Paulson and Fed chairman Ben Bernanke made nationally televised appearances before Congress, making the case for the bailout. Paulson wanted $700 billion, about what the entire Iraq War had cost up to that point, and more than $2,000 for each person in the nation. Paulson, a former CEO of Goldman Sachs, admitted: "I share the outrage that people have. It's embarrassing to look at this, and I think it's embarrassing to the United States of America."[10]

Defending the bailout figure, President Bush said: "This is a big package, because this was a big problem." While the numbers were big, the details were small. Paulson's proposal was three pages long; he wanted nearly unlimited control to use the $700 billion to buy up and sell mortgage-related assets. Members of Congress from both sides of the aisle hesitated to give Paulson so much discretion with so little oversight. Deeming this a "blank check," many insisted that any bailout would require appropriate restraints on authority and more detail. Legal scholar Jonathan Macey described Paulson's proposal as requesting the largest transfer of power from Congress to the executive branch that he had ever witnessed. One line in Paulson's proposal said that "[d]ecisions by the Secretary pursuant to the authority of this Act are non-reviewable and committed to agency discretion, and may not be reviewed by any court of law or any administrative agency."[11]

Dropping Bankruptcy Reform

While these and other concerns were being hotly debated in Congress and across the country, Barack Obama changed his position on mortgage principal reduction. First, he spoke privately with House Speaker Nancy Pelosi and Senate majority leader Harry Reid. Then he shared his new position at a press briefing in Clearwater, Florida, on Wednesday, September 24. After describing how he had called John McCain to suggest they work together in a bipartisan way to help the country through the crisis, Obama added:

> [E]arlier this week, I had said to the speaker of the House, as well as Harry Reid, that issues like bankruptcy reform, which are very important to Democrats, is probably something that we shouldn't try to do in this piece of legislation. . . . And my hope is that Senator McCain is going to be talking to Republicans, and sending them the same message, that there are some issues that they may be concerned about or things that are priorities for them.[12]

Bankruptcy law reform would have given millions of sunken homeowners the ability to bargain in the shadow of bankruptcy. Nominee Obama had just given away their chance at leverage.

But McCain did not offer anything in return. Instead, minutes after Obama got off the phone with him, he went on television to announce he was suspending his campaign and might cancel the debate with Obama scheduled for that Friday. Instead, he was going to rush down to Washington to help out. Taken by surprise, Obama held a press conference to say that he would join his competitor at a meeting with President Bush on Thursday to discuss the bailout legislation. The following day, the two candidates together called for bipartisan support to rescue the economy. Obama said that the rescue plan should assist the "millions of families facing foreclosure" and not just the banks. Yet, in the closed-door Washington meetings that followed, he made it clear that he had dropped bankruptcy reform, at least for the time being. Advocates like Julia Gordon, then senior policy counsel with the Center for Responsible Lending, remember the moment well. Obama insisted that it didn't belong in the Bush legislation, though he promised to get it done if he were elected. Then, after the election, housing advocates including Gordon met regularly with the Obama transition team to discuss bankruptcy reform.[13]

Even then there was growing momentum for principal reduction, though many expected that banks, if cajoled, would voluntarily write down mortgage principal for underwater homeowners. Supporters of principal reduction included Henry Paulson, Ben Bernanke, Sheila Bair, and many economists and legal scholars. There were some unexpected advocates as well. Lewis Ranieri, the father of mortgage finance, recognized the problems that securitization presented when a borrower was in trouble and would benefit from having his loan restructured. He spoke first in 2007, then a year later in May 2008, telling an audience at a financial conference:

> You are almost always better off restructuring a loan in a crisis with a borrower than going to a foreclosure. In the past that was never at issue because the loan was always in the hands of someone acting as a fiduciary. The bank, or someone like a bank owned them, and they always exercised their best judgment and their interest. The problem now with the size of securitization and so many loans are . . . in a security where structurally nobody is acting as the fiduciary . . . [Y]ou are going to . . . have

> to cut the Gordian knot of the securitization of these loans because otherwise if we keep letting these things go into foreclosure it's a feedback loop where it will ultimately crush the consumer economy.[14]

The primary solution to the problem, Ranieri suggested, was "financial innovation." What was needed, however, was not financial and it was not an innovation. It was a legal tradition—bankruptcy.

The Broken Bargain

President Bush signed the bailout legislation—the Emergency Economic Stabilization Act—on October 3, 2008. Of the $700 billion Troubled Asset Relief Program (TARP) commitment in the bailout, $50 billion was supposed to be used to help homeowners. That is why many Democrats voted for it. This money has barely been used, and the programs implemented by Treasury were largely ineffective. Yet it was at the heart of the bargain with Congress and the taxpayers.[15]

To sell the public on the bailouts, politicians and economists evoked the specter of the Great Depression. Without immediate government intervention, we would face a similar downturn. This brought to mind 1932, when Franklin D. Roosevelt first campaigned for office, three years after the Great Crash. The country was mired in unemployment and despair. Half of the home mortgages were in default. For those with jobs, wages had collapsed to below poverty levels. There were bread lines around the corners of city blocks. People swarmed through garbage dumps, desperately grabbing at rancid meat.[16]

It was these conditions that were discussed in the media and at dinner tables in the fall of 2008, when President Bush encouraged the country and the Congress to support a massive bailout of the banks to avoid another Great Depression. As it was initially sold, the purpose of the $700 billion was to have the Treasury purchase toxic mortgage assets from the banks. Quickly, however, Secretary Paulson decided to use his broad authority under the law to simply provide the banks with fresh capital. The reason this was needed, instead of just having the Fed provide loans to them, was that at least one of the largest firms—Citibank—was nearly insolvent. As Sheila Bair later explained, "The fact remained that with the exception of Citi, the commercial banks' capital levels seemed to be adequate." Moreover, if the toxic mortgage assets were purchased at their actual market value, this would not help the banks at all, but if they were purchased at their inflated values, the taxpayers would be rightly angry.[17]

Ben Bernanke, the chairman of the Fed, was a noted expert on the Great Depression and believed it could have been avoided had the Federal Reserve provided sufficient liquidity to the system. This was not done after the Great Crash: Herbert Hoover took the advice of his Treasury secretary, Andrew Mellon, who recommended no stimulus but instead to "liquidate labor, liquidate stocks, liquidate the farmers, liquidate real estate." Bernanke instead followed the prescription of the British economist Walter Bagehot, who, in his 1873 classic *Lombard Street: A Description of the Money Market*, promoted the concept of the central bank as "lender of last resort": "A panic . . . is a species of neuralgia, and according to the rules of science you must not starve it. The holders of the cash reserve must . . . advance it most freely . . . to others. They must lend to merchants, to minor bankers, to 'this man and that man,' whenever the security is good. In wild periods of alarm, one failure makes many." The Fed provided trillions of dollars through various programs to support the commercial paper market and money market funds. In addition, there was money from the FDIC to provide liquidity and loan guarantees.[18]

Bernanke later defended the bailouts, drawing upon both fear and promise. He explained at a public forum:

> [I]t wasn't to help the big firms that we intervened. It was to stabilize the financial system and protect the entire global economy. Now, you might ask . . . . Why are we doing that? It's a terrible problem. It's a problem called a too-big-to-fail problem. These companies have turned out to be too big to allow to collapse because . . . when the elephant falls down, all the grass gets crushed as well.[19]

The public, however, did not see it that way. They saw the moral hazard associated with bailing out the banks while allowing the same bankers to stay on and receive bonuses. Moreover, Bagehot did not simply recommend lending freely, but doing so at a "penalty rate."

The rates charged for the capital infusions and for liquidity from the Fed were not penalty rates. In addition, Bagehot conditioned that such lending should be against good collateral.[20]

Whereas the old Washington Mutual bank in the era before securitization did not foreclose on homeowners during the Great Depression, in 2008, there was no longer a personal and local tie between the borrower and lender. It was not even clear who owned any given mortgage anymore and who could restructure it when the borrower faced foreclosure. Moreover, consumers and the entire system were much more leveraged. So flooding the system with cheap money from the Fed via the banks would not necessarily cause it to trickle down to consumers. They were beyond maxed out—underwater not just on their homes but often their entire balance sheets. Two things were needed. One was a large stimulus to create jobs so people had money, thus creating demand for goods and services to make up for the sudden loss of demand when the housing bubble deflated. The other, more pressing need was to allow homeowners to deleverage.[21]

El Momento de la Verdad: The Moment of Truth

A few minutes past 11:00 a.m. on April 30, 2009, Illinois senator Richard Durbin lifted a large poster off the carpeted Senate floor, placed it on a wooden easel, and began speaking. The poster showed a giant photograph of two neighboring houses. On the left was a boarded-up property; on the right, a well-maintained home. Durbin explained that the value of the occupied residence was threatened by the foreclosed, vandalized space next door. This was not an isolated phenomenon; the scene was replicated in cities and towns across the country. Foreclosed and abandoned dwellings littered urban and suburban neighborhoods, further driving down already depressed home values. And many of the former occupants of the now-empty spaces were being pushed into poverty. Durbin addressed the few colleagues assembled in the Senate chamber that morning and the cable news cameras, arguing for a change in the law to respond to the collapse of home prices and the related foreclosure crisis.[22]

When Durbin spoke, millions of underwater homeowners owed more on their mortgages than their houses were worth. Millions more faced foreclosure. In an attempt to prevent defaults and foreclosures, Durbin hoped to give bankruptcy court judges the power to reduce the balance owed on a residential mortgage to the home's market value. The House of Representatives had already passed a bill to that effect; Durbin hoped the Senate would do the same. But the bill then moving through the Senate, called the Helping Families Save Their Homes Act, did not yet contain language pertaining to mortgage modification through bankruptcy. Thus, he proposed his amendment.[23]

The purpose of the House bill and the Durbin amendment was to solve the problem created by the *Nobelman v. American Savings Bank* decision—to restore mortgage modification rights for homeowners. The Durbin amendment included a shared-appreciation provision; while homeowners could reduce principal to current deflated market values, they would also have to share the gain in value with the lender upon later sale. The Congressional Budget Office (CBO) determined that more than a million homeowners would benefit from the legislation and that the bankruptcy reform measure would cost the taxpayers nothing. This was not the first time Durbin sought this reform; a year earlier, after the mortgage crisis was well under way, he introduced a similar bill. After Durbin and others finished speaking, the Senate would be voting.[24]

The Opposition

In the months leading up to the day of the Senate vote, other than Citibank, the largest banks fought the proposal. Sixty different financial service, insurance, and real estate firms spent $42 million on lobbyists in the first quarter of 2009 to help block this and other reforms. The biggest spender by far, at $5.7 million, was the National Association of Realtors, whose chief economist had, near the peak of the bubble, published a book entitled, *Why the Real Estate Boom Will Not Bust—And How You Can Profit from It.* The book's cover featured a family standing inside of a picket-fenced lawn, gazing up at a small home levitating in the air.[25]

Industry opponents loudly predicted the perils that would follow should principal reduction through bankruptcy be allowed again. They gave this process the pejorative name "cram-down." While supporters used more legally accurate terms like principal reduction, lien stripping, or bifurcation, cram-down caught on and influenced the debate. Those who opposed the amendment contended that restoring this right to homeowners would increase the cost of home loans for everyone and make credit unavailable to some borrowers; it would flood bankruptcy courts with filings by borrowers at whim whenever home prices dipped; it would undermine the sanctity of contracts; it would promote "moral hazard" by encouraging borrowers to take out loans they cannot pay back; and it would be unfair to other homeowners and lenders.

None of these arguments is persuasive. First, regarding the impact on the cost and availability of credit, there was, and still is, scarce empirical data on the effect of principal reduction in consumer bankruptcies. Recent research by scholars Adam J. Levitin and Joshua Goodman shows that there would be either no or very slight impact on the cost of credit and its availability. Where the cost of credit might increase, it would do so only for high-risk borrowers. This finding undermines the argument that all borrowers would absorb any risk premium associated with making mortgage modification available. Even if lending became slightly more expensive, this would be better than paying for the alternative—the full cost of easy credit, when it results in trillions of dollars in lost wealth and a deep recession.[26]

Making a larger down payment, being prevented from cashing out any equity, or paying slightly more each month is less costly than buying a home at an inflated value that later declines. For many of us, this would be reasonable "insurance" against the contagious impact of poor underwriting and of foreclosures and the devastating circumstances of losing our homes during a national economic downturn due to debt burdens. Moreover, if toxic loan types like the Option ARM became more scarce, this would be a positive outcome for borrowers, lenders, and neighborhood communities.

Similarly, when the Bankruptcy Code was amended in 1986 to create a new Chapter 12 to help farm families save their homes, opponents argued that it would make farm credit prohibitively expensive or even completely unavailable. A 1989 report by the GAO (then referred to as the General Accounting Office) showed that some farm lenders raised their interest rates by half a percentage point at most; many made no increase at all. And, to the extent that costs would increase in the future, even critics suggested that rates would only go up by between 0.25 percent and 1 percent, and it would be the weaker borrowers that would have to pay more for credit, not everyone.[27]

Second, the claim that bankruptcy courts would be flooded is not supported by available evidence. The limited data suggest that filings would not increase or overwhelm the courts; instead, the prospect of bankruptcy would encourage out-of-court settlements by creating an incentive for loan servicers to bargain. The CBO estimated an additional 350,000 bankruptcy filings over a ten-year period, only a 3.5 percent increase. This CBO forecast is in line with the experience of farm family bankruptcies after the enactment of Chapter 12. The GAO reported that 30,000 filings had been expected the first year the law was in effect, but instead there were only 8,500 cases in the law's first two years, and fewer as time went on. This was a small number relative to the approximate 450,000 consumer and 81,000 commercial bankruptcy filings in 1986 alone. Trying to account for the low number of bankruptcy filings, economists at the Federal Reserve Bank of Cleveland recently speculated that Chapter 12 "worked without working." Creditors, understanding they could fare worse in court, allowed many farm debtors to negotiate modifications without filing. This phenomenon is known in the commercial sector as bargaining "in the shadow" of bankruptcy. Creditors frequently work out deals with delinquent businesses to avoid a worse outcome in bankruptcy court; debtors, in turn, are willing to give a little to avoid the stigma of bankruptcy.[28]

Though consumer filings would not substantially increase, the Durbin Amendment could "work without working" by encouraging lenders to adjust borrowers' principal before bankruptcy became an issue or with the threat of bankruptcy looming. In contrast, the status quo of voluntary restructurings involves inefficiencies, fraud, and a very large backlog. With no incentive to come to the table to modify mortgages, servicers may delay and stonewall and be unwilling to coordinate any necessary approvals from myriad investors in securities that are affected by a particular borrower's request for restructuring.

Third, regarding the sanctity of contracts, bankruptcy law already provides tools that allow for the rejection and modification of contracts. Even in consumer bankruptcy, other classes of secured loans are stripped down. Moreover, contract law doctrine has long recognized that not all promises are enforceable. It is simply not true that all contracts are sacred. The question should be whether it is good policy that the law singles out first liens on primary residences for different treatment. Additionally, bankruptcy courts are particularly suited for dealing with one of the key obstacles in voluntary mortgage modifications—the unwillingness of mortgage servicers to take on the risk of lawsuits from mortgage securities holders for breach of contract. Bankruptcy courts already handle similar situations to help restructure corporate debt when bondholders do not consent. This promotes a certain level of risk taking in allowing businesses to get a fresh start.[29]

Fourth, the concern about moral hazard is misplaced. The term *moral hazard* is used by economists to describe the outcome when one party has the power to take risks but does not bear the associated losses. Opponents claim that bankruptcy reform would empower borrowers to intentionally take on more debt than they can afford. This observation should not be the end of the analysis. To be a problem, one must also presume that lenders cannot take precautions. Borrowers already have an incentive to take on more debt than they can pay back, and it is the very nature of conservative underwriting by loan originators that hedges against such risk.

What history shows is not that originators and lenders lack the ability to properly underwrite, but that they face a moral hazard themselves: if they can earn big fees passing along risk to others, they will ignore borrower-default risk. In the recent housing bubble, lenders had the ability to refuse to fund poorly underwritten loans and chose not to. Instead, they strenuously fought attempts by both federal and state regulators to require prudent underwriting. Consider the huge numbers of loans that were made without requiring borrowers to provide documentation of their income (so-called stated-income loans, or what the industry openly referred to as "liar loans"); where the lender helped fix the appraisal above market value; and where employees and independent brokers were paid higher fees to push borrowers to take out higher-rate—and thus higher-risk—loans than they were qualified for.

Contrary to the opponents' concern about borrower moral hazard, the evidence suggests that the moral hazard actually rests with lenders who originate and distribute residential mortgages and other loans, and who are backed by the safety net of federal deposit insurance or low-cost loans from the Fed. These lenders have the incentive to prey on borrowers and otherwise make unwise loans because they pass along the risk to someone else. What actually caused borrowers to fall underwater largely were actions outside of homeowners' control. Meanwhile, those who profited from unwise and predatory loans had every incentive to continue making them. While regulations have now tightened on underwriting, historical patterns and the power of the financial lobby suggest that once memories fade, they will be loosened if not wiped away. Bankruptcy reform would help prevent the moral hazard of irresponsible lending.[30]

Fifth, some voiced concerns based on unfairness to those who have toiled and sacrificed to pay their debts on time, who are also underwater but do not qualify for or want to enter bankruptcy, or those who have paid off their homes. The response is that helping others save their homes helps these people too, since abandoned homes and housing foreclosures drive down prices. It is hard to sell one's home with boarded-up houses nearby. Moreover, bankruptcy always allows delinquent borrowers to get relief while others keep paying their debts on time; thus, it is unfair to single out those with a single residence.[31]

Others think that it is unfair for borrowers to stiff mortgage holders, believing that lenders extended credit in good faith or that even if some lenders were predatory or abusive, so were some borrowers. These people contend that evidence that a particular borrower was a victim of sharp or fraudulent tactics is not relevant. This argument ignores the evidence of widespread fraud and abuse, including the thousands of former felons who entered the mortgage brokerage business. It also fails to consider that these practices, including fraudulent appraisals and widespread lending without any documentation of income, helped inflate the bubble, affecting all borrowers. Even if there were some deceptive borrowers, this does not justify denying all borrowers assistance while allowing institutions and individuals that reaped huge profits from these practices to receive trillions of dollars in support. To have banks and bankers face limited consequences from their knowing participation in inflating the housing bubble continues the moral hazard we truly needed to worry about.

The Vote

At 2:47 p.m. on April 30, 2009, the Senate voted on the Durbin Amendment. The measure failed. Only forty-five senators, all members of the Democratic caucus, voted for principal reduction through bankruptcy. The fifty-one who voted against were a bipartisan mix. Shortly afterward, Durbin informed an Illinois radio show host that on Capitol Hill, the banks "frankly own the place." But that was not always the case. There was a brief window of time in September 2008 when the banks came begging for help. That was when the government had stronger bargaining power. Years later, when asked how bankruptcy reform was lost, Massachusetts congressman Barney Frank bluntly remarked: "Obama gave it away on the way to the White House."[32]

In 2010, when the Republicans gained a House majority, upon being designated chairman of the House Financial Services Committee, Alabama Republican Spencer Bachus told a local newspaper: "In Washington, the view is that the banks are to be regulated, my view is that Washington and the regulators are there to serve the banks." Bachus was one of the representatives who had voted in March against the House bill to empower bankruptcy judges to prevent foreclosures.[33]

Though Barack Obama had assured consumer advocates that he would get bankruptcy reform done if he was elected, when the heat was on, his Treasury Department did not push to get the law changed.

Yet, throughout 2009, the Democrats controlled the Congress, notably with a filibuster-proof majority in the Senate. In 2013, Michael Barr, former assistant secretary of the Treasury for Financial Institutions, concurred. At a gathering of legal academics in New Orleans, he said that while the Obama administration "did not oppose" bankruptcy reform, it "did not push" it. He explained that the priorities at the time were passing the stimulus and the Affordable Care Act. Whatever pressure could be placed on senators would have been at a cost to those other pieces of legislation and unlikely to yield enough votes to pass. Barr also said that the version that finally was presented to the Senate had been weakened and would not have helped enough homeowners.[34]

The Failed Programs

What ultimately passed both chambers in May 2009 and was signed by the president was called the Helping Families Save Their Homes Act. It was a misnomer. The act instituted a voluntary program that encouraged—but did not require—lenders to modify loan terms. This affected a small number of borrowers and did not reduce principal for any of them. Meanwhile, the same law conferred many benefits on the banks. Instead of mortgage modification through bankruptcy, Washington created other programs. The central one was the Treasury Department's Home Affordable Modification Program (HAMP) heralded as a program that would assist between three to four million borrowers. By July 2011, it was clearly not working as promised. Roughly 700,000 mortgages had been modified under HAMP, but millions of homes were foreclosed upon, with millions more in the pipeline. By then, HAMP had used only $3 billion of the $50 billion authorized.[35]

HAMP didn't work because the banks didn't want it to. Homeowners were being dual-tracked; strung along on their modification applications while the foreclosure process proceeded. In sworn statements filed in federal court, several Bank of America employees claimed that they frequently lied to homeowners and were paid bonuses if they sent them into foreclosure. One recalled the "blitz" when they would deny mortgage applications en masse that were more than sixty days old—sometimes 600 to 1,500 all at once.[36]

The special inspector general for the TARP, Neil Barofsky, saw problems with the HAMP program early on. He learned at a briefing that the Treasury Department was putting banks, the mortgage servicers, in charge of it. This presented a huge conflict of interest. While the investors in mortgage-linked securities might benefit if a loan were restructured so that borrowers could stay in their homes, the servicer would lose out. When a borrower falls behind on payments, servicers earn late fees and incur other expenses. In a foreclosure, the servicer's fees and expenses are paid off ahead of the mortgage owner—often a securitization trust. Under their servicing contracts, they are not reimbursed for costs of renegotiating mortgages. Banks like JPMorgan Chase, which had inherited a giant mortgage-servicing portfolio from WaMu, had an incentive to block modification so that the home would go into foreclosure, whereas the investors in those mortgage-backed securities would often do better if the loan were restructured. According to Barofsky, it was the "Treasury's failure to adequately address this inherent conflict of interest [that] would eventually help cripple its mortgage modification program."[37]

Another problem Barofsky identified was that the Treasury was moving the goalposts. A Treasury Department official, Herb Allison, claimed in 2010 that the HAMP's purpose was not to help people stay in their homes, but simply to have mortgage servicers make offers to borrowers for trial modifications. In 2009, even after the HAMP was implemented, foreclosure filings increased to 2.8 million, up from 2.3 million in 2008. Bank repossessions also rose, to nearly 1 million in 2009. The true measure of the program's success would be permanent modifications. By the end of 2009, there had been only seventy thousand permanent modifications, and these did not usually involve any principal reduction. When asked by Elizabeth Warren, then the head of the Congressional Oversight Panel, to explain why, Treasury Secretary Timothy Geithner said that it would have been "dramatically more expensive for the American taxpayer, harder to justify," and it would "create much greater risk of unfairness." Other efforts were equally weak. For example, there was a separate Department of

Housing and Urban Development (HUD) program that was originally projected to reach 1.5 million households. By the end of 2011, only 646 homeowners had been helped by HUD.[38]

When the HAMP was announced in February 2009, there was immediate backlash. CNBC on-air editor Rick Santelli appeared on the floor of the Chicago Mercantile Exchange and began to rage. Santelli, a former derivatives trader, shouted that "the government is promoting bad behavior" and there should be a public vote on whether "we want to subsidize the losers' mortgages." He shouted: "This is America? How many of you people want to pay for your neighbor's mortgage that has an extra bathroom and can't pay their bills? Raise their hands!" This sentiment helped doom the bankruptcy reform legislation that would have cost taxpayers nothing. Santelli added: "We're thinking of having a Chicago Tea Party in July. All you capitalists that want to show up to Lake Michigan, I'm going to start organizing."[39]

Santelli's rant—which was rebroadcast widely—played into to our worst emotions. And, it became a rallying cry for the Tea Party movement. It was filled with misplaced blame and steeped in envy. It lacked reason and historical context. It was okay to short someone's house through credit derivatives, commit trillions of dollars to rescue the banking system, and fail to prosecute the top bankers who facilitated the fraud, but not to help save other people's houses. Yet, if foreclosures were stemmed, the value of our own homes would be protected, our neighborhoods made safer, and public services and private sector jobs maintained.[40]

Looking back in the summer of 2012, former Senator Ted Kaufman of Delaware shared his views about the 2009 vote on principal reduction: "If we'd passed cram-down, we'd be better off now." In the lead-up to the April 30 vote, Kaufman met with lobbyists from the many banks in his state who were "up in arms." He said he asked them, "Give me one reason why a home should be treated differently under bankruptcy." If they could provide an answer, he would not vote for the reform. But they couldn't. Asked why the Treasury program had failed, Kaufman explained: "Safety and soundness [of the banks] was their priority. They did not put their heart and soul into" helping homeowners.

This was certainly an echo. Secretary Geithner did not use the power he was given. Barofsky described this as “a choice” by the Treasury not to “live up to its side of the legislative bargain to use TARP to preserve homeownership.” This recalls Alan Greenspan not using the Fed’s HOEPA authority to prevent predatory lending, and thus the entire crisis. On some issues, Greenspan had a change of perspective. He realized he had found “a flaw” in his whole way of thinking about markets. Whether he also regrets not helping homeowners is another question.[41]

Part III

Myth Confronts Reality

16

Dispelling Myths about the Crisis

The news cameras kept recording after the power failed. Complete darkness. Then a heavy red curtain was swept aside, allowing a bit of sunlight to stream into the wood-paneled hearing room. This natural illumination had a strange effect on Alan Greenspan, the day's first witness. He was seated before the Financial Crisis Inquiry Commission (FCIC), a ten-member panel of private citizens appointed by Congress to examine the causes of the financial and economic crisis. By that day, in April 2010, the FCIC had already conducted several hearings and public meetings. Greenspan had spent much of the morning before the power outage in a defensive mode, denying that, as chairman of the Fed for nearly two decades, he had the tools to predict or prevent the subprime mortgage meltdown and the connected global financial crisis.[1]

Yet he had admitted to the panel: "I was right 70 percent of the time, but I was wrong 30 percent of the time. And there are an awful lot of mistakes" over the years. Now, in the semidarkness, Greenspan retreated a bit. He responded to a question about whether he believed there still was excessive debt in the banking system with a nod, a gesture not captured on the official record. The commissioner who posed the question remarked that he saw Greenspan nod. An audience member said he had not nodded. Greenspan sat silently, not offering to clarify. Minutes later, the hearing adjourned and the witness departed.[2]

That was classic Greenspan: bright moments of clarity followed by obfuscation and retreat. Eighteen months earlier in October 2008, in his most candid moment, he told a congressional subcommittee that he had found "a flaw" in his entire system of thought. He had adhered for decades to a particular view of how markets operated, only to discover several decades later he'd been very wrong. Yet the question for the panel that April morning was whether the crisis could have been avoided.[3]

At the hearing, Greenspan explained that the origination of subprime mortgages had posed no problems between 1990 and 2002. In that early era, he said, it was a contained market, but then things changed. It was the expansive sale of adjustable rate subprime mortgages, followed by the securitization of these mortgages, and the transformation of those securities into collateralized debt obligations (CDOs) that caused problems. There was a huge demand from Europe for CDOs backed by such mortgages, thus fueling increasingly higher-risk originations. Greenspan also made it clear that without "adequate capital and liquidity," the "system will fail to function." He called for additional equity capital (less borrowing relative to assets held). He said he now realized that our banking system had been undercapitalized for forty to fifty years. But in 2011, when it came time to require banks to have greater equity capital, he publicly denounced "an excess of buffers" in an op-ed in the *Financial Times.* Seeming to forget the savings and loan (S&L) crisis of just twenty years earlier, he asked: "How much of its ongoing output should a society wish to devote to fending off once-in-50 or 100-year crises?" This was Greenspan, light and dark.[4]

While he admitted in the abstract to being wrong 30 percent of the time, the FCIC found it impossible to pin him down on particular acts or omissions. Instead, he pointed toward many others who contributed to the problem. His view was supported by the evidence but was nevertheless incomplete. He asserted that effective markets depended on enforcement against fraud and misrepresentation. When asked by FCIC chairman Phil Angelides what the Fed had done to combat fraud, Greenspan admitted that between 2000 and 2006, it had made only two criminal referrals to the Justice Department. In contrast, in 2005, the Federal Bureau of Investigation (FBI) had 22,000 cases of mortgage fraud under investigation. Greenspan dismissed this figure, contending that out of 55 million outstanding residential mortgages, 22,000 did not indicate a systemic problem. Angelides then asked him to explain why the Fed had made only two referrals. Greenspan explained that in all other cases of concern, they had been able to achieve compliance without the need for criminal enforcement. He said, "[a] goodly part of supervision and regulation is to get things solved so that if somebody is in violation of something and you can get them to adjust so that the regulators are satisfied, it never gets to the point where it's a referral for enforcement in some form or another." This non-enforcement policy created an incentive for misbehavior. Cracking down both through criminal and civil enforcement is not just about compliance, but also a vital part of deterrence.[5]

Brooksley Born, Again

One of the appointees to the FCIC was Brooksley Born, who had resigned from her position as commissioner of the Commodity Futures Trading Commission (CFTC) in 1999. It was appropriate for her to at last face Alan Greenspan, who with others in the Clinton administration had deregulated derivatives and helped create the conditions for the meltdown.

While Angelides questioned Greenspan about his record on combating fraud, perhaps on Born's mind was a lunchtime conversation she'd had with him in 1996. She had just become chairman of the CFTC but was not new to Washington. She had been a partner at the Arnold & Porter law firm for many years and, before her appointment to lead the agency, had briefly served as a commissioner. In her new leadership role, Born was already concerned about risks associated with derivatives, a key area of the CFTC's jurisdiction.[6]

Over lunch, Greenspan had shared with Born his view of market fraud. As she later recalled: "He explained there wasn't a need for a law against fraud because if a floor broker was committing fraud, the customer would figure it out and stop doing business with him." Born challenged him on this view, contending that as an attorney, she believed that prohibitions on fraud were essential. At Arnold & Porter, for instance, she had represented clients entangled in the Hunt brothers' conspiracy to manipulate the price of silver and defraud investors. After hearing her out, Greenspan replied: "Well, Brooksley, I guess you and I will never agree about fraud." The exchange was so unsettling that she shared the conversation with her top aides, Michael Greenberger and Daniel Waldman, who confirmed her account of the discussion. This encounter was particularly disturbing given Greenspan's influence, not just over the economy but over President Clinton and the other banking regulators. This conversation would not be the last or the most contentious of their encounters.[7]

Today, she asked him this question: "In your view, did credit default swaps, which are a type of over-the-counter derivatives contract, play any role in causing or exacerbating the financial crisis?" Greenspan did not answer directly, although he knew what she was getting at. He said that to his knowledge, they had not been discussed at the President's Working Group; they were "not on the agenda" at the time. That may have been his recollection, but the report that he signed in 1999 did include "credit swaps." Born reminded him that in 1996, the Fed had issued supervisory guidance on them.[8]

Next, Born asked him about his libertarian views and whether he thought the Fed was to blame for the crisis. Specifically she asked whether the Fed had

> fail[ed] to carry out its mandates, . . . [in that] . . . the Fed and the banking regulators failed to prevent the housing bubble; they failed to prevent the predatory lending scandal; they failed to prevent our biggest banks and bank holding companies from engaging in activities that would bring them to the verge of

> collapse without massive taxpayer bailouts; they failed to recognize the systemic risk posed by an unregulated over-the-counter derivatives market; and they permitted the financial system and the economy to reach the brink of disaster.[9]

Greenspan never answered that question. But he did deny that his "views on regulation" interfered with his performance: "I took an oath of office to support the laws of the land," he said, and he insisted that he had enforced the laws, including those he "would not have constructed in the way they were constructed," as "that was my job." Born had a limited amount of time to ask her questions and Greenspan to answer. It was the next commissioner's turn. Greenspan concluded by informing her: "So I know my time has run out, but I really fundamentally disagree with your point of view."[10]

After the long day, as after many others at the FCIC, it was difficult to fully understand the truth about the crisis. When a single witness can equivocate over a period of hours and then over a period of years, it is easy to think there is no there, there.[11]

Truth about the Financial Crisis

After the crisis, many expected that the blameworthy would be punished or at the least be required to return their ill-gotten gains—but they weren't, and they didn't. Many thought that those who were injured would be made whole, but most weren't. And many hoped that there would be a restoration of the financial safety rules to ensure that industry leaders could no longer gamble the equity of their firms to the point of ruin. This didn't happen, but it's not too late. It is useful, then, to identify the persistent myths about the causes of the financial crisis and the resulting Dodd-Frank reform legislation and related implementation.[12]

Myth 1

There has been no official bipartisan consensus on the causes of the financial crisis: An official government report was produced in April 2011 by the Senate Permanent Subcommittee on Investigations, led by Chairman Carl Levin (D-MI) and Ranking Member Tom Coburn (R-OK), titled *Wall Street and the Financial Crisis: Anatomy of a Financial Collapse.* The "Levin-Coburn Report," a 639-page document, including 2,849 footnotes unanimously and unambiguously concluded that "the [2008] crisis was not a natural disaster, but the result of high risk, complex financial products; undisclosed conflicts of interest; and the failure of regulators, the credit rating agencies, and the market itself to rein in the excesses of Wall Street."[13]

This myth got traction in January 2011, when after conducting over five hundred interviews and holding twelve days of hearings, the Financial Crisis Inquiry Commission (FCIC) failed to produce a unified report. The 545-page book the panel did publish, titled *The Financial Crisis Inquiry Report: Final Report of the National Commission on the Causes of the Financial and Economic Crisis in the United States*, had three sections. The first part was a lengthy majority report endorsed by the six Democratic appointees. This was followed by two much shorter dissents. Reading the three parts together, it is clear that all ten commissioners agreed that the collapse of the U.S. housing bubble was the proximate cause of the crisis.[14]

In addition, there was substantial consensus among nine of the commissioners. For these nine—including three of the four Republican appointees—the centerpiece of the consensus was that poor risk management at U.S. financial institutions was a chief contributor to the crisis. For example, all nine agreed that risk management failures at financial institutions led to insufficient capital and a reliance on short-term borrowing.[15]

Myth 2

The financial crisis was an accident without human causes: The Levin-Coburn Report clearly concludes that the crisis was not a natural disaster. In the FCIC Report, the Majority, Primary Dissent, and Solo Dissent also agree on this point. Without question, the crisis was caused by people. The Primary Dissent identifies a list of "ten essential causes" that point to human decisions and actions, yet it suggests that the outcome could *not* have been prevented. The Majority is clear in its contention that the disaster, at least in the magnitude we experienced, was preventable: "The crisis was the result of human action and inaction, not of Mother Nature or computer models gone haywire." The Solo Dissent also points to human causes: "To avoid the next financial crisis, we must understand what caused the one from which we are now slowly emerging, and take action to avoid the same mistakes in the future." In addition to these official reports, experts have renounced this false narrative.[16]

Myth 3

The financial crisis was brought about because the Community Reinvestment Act of 1977 forced banks to lend to people with low incomes who could not afford to pay back their mortgages: The FCIC Majority and Primary Dissent roundly reject this myth, leaving the Solo Dissent as the lone proponent of this shaky story. The Community Reinvestment Act (CRA) was enacted to prevent banks from refusing to extend loans to creditworthy borrowers in particular neighborhoods, a practice known as "redlining." The FCIC Majority notes that "the CRA requires banks and savings and loans to lend, invest, and provide services to the communities from which they take deposits, consistent with bank safety and soundness." Further, it states that

> the CRA was not a significant factor in subprime lending or the crisis. Many subprime lenders were not subject to the CRA. Research indicates only 6% of high-cost loans—a proxy for subprime loans—had any connection to the law. Loans made by CRA-regulated lenders in the neighborhoods in which they were required to lend were half as likely to default as similar loans made in the same neighborhoods by independent mortgage originators not subject to the law.[17]

Similarly, the Primary Dissent explicitly states that the Community Reinvestment Act was not a "significant cause." Many government officials and scholars have also rejected this myth. In contrast, the Solo Dissent singles out U.S. government housing policy, including the CRA, as the sine qua non of the financial crisis.[18]

Myth 4

The giant government-sponsored enterprises (GSEs), Fannie Mae and Freddie Mac, caused the financial crisis because the government pushed them to guarantee mortgage loans to people with low incomes as part of their public housing mission: Not exactly—both the FCIC Majority Report and the Primary Dissent agree that Fannie and Freddie on their own did not cause the financial crisis. They focus blame largely on the private-label mortgage market. Fannie and Freddie did not originate any loans; the "exotic" and high-risk loans were designed by and extended to borrowers through the private-label pipeline. While the Majority and the Primary Dissent concur that Fannie and Freddie's business model was flawed, they also agree that affordable housing goals neither drove Fannie and Freddie to ruin nor caused them to create the overwhelming demand for predatory, high-risk, mortgages.[19]

The Majority Report stated that the affordable housing goals that the Department of Housing and Urban Development (HUD) gave to the GSEs "did contribute marginally" to their purchase of risky mortgages. But it was the desire to gain market share and increase executive compensation that drove the management teams at Fannie and Freddie to fill their portfolios with high-risk private-label mortgage-backed securities. It was the growth of their portfolio business for profit coupled with a 75–1 leverage ratio—not their public housing mission—that caused them to fail. Fannie and Freddie "had a deeply flawed business model as publicly traded corporations with the implicit backing of and subsidies from the federal government and with a public mission."[20]

Similarly, the Primary Dissent concluded that "Fannie Mae and Freddie Mac did not by themselves cause the crisis, but they contributed significantly in a number of ways." It noted that U.S. housing policy does not itself explain the housing bubble. The Primary Dissent echoed the Majority in contending that "Fannie Mae and Freddie Mac's failures were the result of policymakers using the power of government to blend public purpose with private gains and then socializing the losses." In his Solo Dissent, Peter Wallison blamed housing policy and the GSEs for the crisis.[21]

Myth 5

Mistakes were made, but there was not widespread fraud and abuse throughout the financial system: There is evidence of widespread fraud and abuse throughout the private mortgage market. Examples exist across the mortgage supply chain, beginning with fraud in mortgage documentation and ending with the peddling of worthless synthetic mortgage-related bonds to guileless institutional investors. From borrowers, to brokers, to lenders, to bank securitizers, to credit-rating agencies, to investment bankers, the Majority Report found evidence of either fraud or corrupt and abusive behavior across each link. It describes FBI agents warning of mortgage fraud in 2004 and 2005 and housing advocates early and consistently trying to get the attention of regulators to crack down on predatory lending. As for abuse, the bipartisan Levin-Coburn Report and the FCIC Majority provided many instances of lenders making loans they clearly knew borrowers could not afford.[22]

The Primary Dissent agreed that the industry's conduct went well beyond mistakes and errors: "Securitizers lowered credit quality standards and Mortgage originators took advantage of this to create junk mortgages." Although Wallison's Solo Dissent rejected the notion that fraud was an "essential cause" of the crisis, he agreed that it was a "contributing factor and a deplorable effect of the bubble." He acknowledged that "mortgage fraud increased substantially" beginning in the 1990s "during the housing bubble" and that "this fraud did tremendous harm." But unlike the Majority and Primary Dissent, Wallison blamed "predatory borrowers" as the ones who "engaged in mortgage fraud."[23]

Myth 6

The financial crisis was caused by too much government regulation: Deregulation and regulatory forbearance—too little regulation, rather than too much—contributed to the crisis. The entire toxic-mortgage supply chain was enabled by decades of deregulation and desupervision. The Levin-Coburn Report included more than eighty pages focused exclusively on the regulatory failure at one agency, the Office of Thrift Supervision (OTS). It also made recommendations for further reform beyond Dodd-Frank's changes. The FCIC Majority stated that more than three decades of:

> deregulation and reliance on self-regulation by financial institutions, championed by former Federal Reserve chairman Alan Greenspan and others, supported by successive administrations and Congresses, and actively pushed by the powerful financial industry at every turn, had stripped away key safeguards, which could have helped avoid catastrophe. This approach had opened up gaps in oversight of critical areas with trillions of dollars at risk, such as the shadow banking system and over-the-counter derivatives markets. In addition, the government permitted financial firms to pick their preferred regulators in what became a race to the weakest supervisor.[24]

Similarly, the Primary Dissent identified "ineffective regulatory regimes" for nonbank mortgage lenders as an important "causal factor." It faulted "lenient regulatory oversight on mortgage origination" at the federally regulated bank and thrift lenders Wachovia, Washington Mutual, and Countrywide.[25]

In the Solo Dissent, Wallison claimed the Majority had "completely ignored" solid evidence that there were not thirty years of deregulation. He pointed to the FDIC Improvement Act of 1991 (FDICIA), a law that he said "was celebrated at the time of its enactment as finally giving the regulators the power to put an end to bank crises."[26]

Contrary to his assertion, the Majority did discuss FDICIA; it has nothing to do with the deregulation that enabled high-risk mortgage lending and securitizing. This law requires the FDIC to shut down or sell a failing bank or thrift. The law did not apply to independent investment banks like Bear Stearns and Lehman Brothers; for them the choice was bailout or bankruptcy. And, there were loopholes in FDICIA. If the regulators determined that the firm posed a "systemic risk" to the financial system, the FDIC did not have to pursue a resolution of "least cost" to the deposit insurance fund. Also, the Fed was permitted to make emergency loans to failing banks. Given these loopholes, the Majority explained that FDICIA sent a "mixed message: you are not too big to fail—until and unless you are too big to fail. So the possibility of bailouts for the biggest, most centrally placed institutions—in the commercial and shadow banking industries—remained an open question until the next crisis, 16 years later." Indeed, the "systemic risk" exception would be invoked several times during the bailouts.[27]

Myth 7

Nobody saw it coming: Plenty of people saw it coming, and said so. The problem wasn't seeing, it was listening. As both the Levin-Coburn Report and the FCIC Majority showed, financial sector insiders, consumer advocates, regulators, economists, and other experts saw the warning signs. They spoke out frequently about the housing bubble and the mortgage underwriting practices that fueled it. Yet most whistleblowers were ignored or ridiculed at best, and fired and blacklisted at worst.[28]

The Primary Dissent emphasized that some players in the market saw what was ahead: "Managers of many large and midsize financial institutions in the United States and Europe amassed enormous concentrations of highly correlated housing risk on their balance sheets. In doing so they turned a building housing crisis into a subsequent crisis of failing financial institutions. Some did this knowingly; others, unknowingly."[29]

The Solo Dissent stated that the housing bubble was clearly growing but also claimed that the "number of defaults and delinquencies among these mortgages far exceeded anything that even the most sophisticated market participants expected."[30]

Myth 8

The financial crisis was unavoidable. And financial crises of this magnitude are inevitable: The Majority Report unequivocally stated that "this financial crisis was avoidable. . . . The captains of finance and the public stewards of our financial system ignored warnings and failed to question, understand, and manage evolving risks within a system essential to the well-being of the American public." The Solo Dissent contended that. "No financial system . . . could have survived the failure of large numbers of high risk mortgages once the bubble began to deflate." However, it blamed housing policy, not bankers, for the creation of the high-risk mortgages.[31]

This myth that we cannot avoid large-scale financial crises is particularly corrosive, as those who are in its thrall reason that since crashes are inevitable, regulation is fruitless. But this is not the necessary conclusion. There were no major financial crises between the New Deal and the S&L crisis, a span of fifty years when each type of firm was protected in its own niche and limited in their activities. Deregulation delivered the S&L debacle and the related 2008 financial crisis. This inevitability myth also distorts the view of Hyman Minsky, the economist who advanced the theory in 1986 that markets are prone to instability. The sensible reaction to this recognition is not to let the system keep running up risk and collapsing, but instead to create countercyclical buffers. This could involve doubling equity capital requirements in good times when it appears an asset bubble is inflating, so as to slow down its growth and create a better cushion on the downturn. It might also require higher capital to finance those assets the prices of which tend to rise and fall with the business cycle.[32]

Myth 9

The Dodd-Frank Act has ended "too big to fail": In 2009 Federal Reserve chairman Ben Bernanke defended the multi-trillion-dollar bailouts, explaining that "it wasn't to help the big firms that we intervened. . . . [W]hen the elephant falls down, all the grass gets crushed as well." Today, the elephants are larger than ever, and the grass is still crushed. The conditions that brought the financial system to the brink of failure in 2008 persist. The top banks are bigger, and they still borrow trillions of dollars in the short-term and overnight repo markets, leaving them vulnerable to runs.[33]

Because they are perceived as "too big to fail," the largest banks borrow money more cheaply, receiving an $83 billion annual subsidy according to a *Bloomberg News* study, which also suggests that the profits earned by these top banks are "almost entirely a gift from

U.S. taxpayers." Regulatory proposals have been made to modestly raise equity capital for giant banks, but the permitted leverage ratio is still just 3 percent (equity to total assets). This means borrowing $97 for every $100 in assets, or a 33-1 leverage ratio. This level of leverage was a key factor in the 2008 crisis.[34]

The law pins most of its hopes on new powers granted to the FDIC to dismantle failing bank holding companies and "systemically important" nonbank financial institutions. This is an alternative to the terrible choice between the chaos of a Lehman-like bankruptcy and taxpayer-funded bailouts. Many question whether regulators will have the courage to pull the plug on a dying financial firm and others worry that this won't work in cross-border insolvencies. However, the FDIC is confident that its experience resolving large banks and thrifts will translate well. During the contentious legislative process, the requirement that banks finance an orderly resolution fund to be used by the FDIC during the resolution process was taken out. Politicians, including House Minority Leader John Boehner, actually contended that bank pre-funding would be a taxpayer-funded bailout. This Orwellian argument carried the day, so under Dodd-Frank, upon the takeover of a failing firm, taxpayers will front the money the FDIC needs via a line of credit from the Treasury. If the proceeds from selling pieces of the failed institution are not sufficient to pay back the Treasury, the surviving banks will be assessed.[35]

There are strong tools in Dodd-Frank, and time may tell if they are used effectively. The law called for nearly four hundred rulemakings by regulators already struggling with insufficient funding. Fewer than half of the rules have been issued, and more than a hundred deadlines have been missed. Among the delays is the implementation of Section 619 of Dodd-Frank, often referred to as the "Volcker Rule." This provision bans banking entities (that have access to FDIC insurance and loans from the Fed) from engaging in proprietary trading—buying and selling securities for profit. The Volcker Rule also limits how much such banking entities can invest in hedge funds and private equity funds. It was meant to be a modern day Glass-Steagall, creating a separation between firms that have access to the public safety net from those that make high-risk bets. The provision was drafted and shepherded through the legislative process by Senator Jeff Merkley and Senator Carl Levin. However, it was named for former Fed chairman Paul Volcker, who initially recommended these restrictions to President Obama.[36]

Myth 10

The bankers are the victims of greedy homeowners who borrowed money and did not pay it back: Some homeowners participated in fraud, and others were simply unrealistic or were speculating that housing prices would continue to rise. But a much larger number were victims either of abusive lending practices or of the housing bubble and burst that diminished their home values and retirement savings.

Even the hopeful and the speculators were no different from some apparently naive bank executives like JPMorgan CEO Jamie Dimon, who told the FCIC: "In mortgage underwriting, somehow we just missed, you know, that home prices don't go up forever and that it's not sufficient to have stated income." Even if we accept this at face value, it does not follow that bankers are victims of homeowners. Many homeowners made the same error. The difference is that the banks got trillions of dollars in bailouts and backstops, and their employees kept their billions in bonuses. Meanwhile, since the burst of the housing bubble, there have been about five million home foreclosures, with millions more underway. Ten million homes are underwater—approximately one-fifth of all mortgaged properties. Unemployment remains high and home prices low. The gains of the post-crisis recovery have been uneven. The net worth for the top 7 percent of Americans increased by 28 percent while the net worth for the bottom 93 percent declined by approximately 4 percent.[37]

In addition, blaming subprime borrowers doesn't hold up mathematically. According to former Goldman Sachs executive Nomi Prins, even if every single subprime mortgage defaulted, the total money lost would have been $1.4 trillion. Yet much more was committed by the Fed, Treasury, and FDIC in the financial crisis. It is not credible to blame subprime mortgage borrowers alone for the crisis.

It was additionally the desire of banks to make profitable trades and the desire of hedge funds to speculate on mortgage-backed securities that brought down the system. It was the billions upon billions of side bets that put far more at risk than the total value of all the subprime mortgages.[38]

As for banks being the victims, this myth is typically not propagated by bankers but by service providers, those who stand to gain from maintaining friendly relationships with banks. For example, Steve Eckhaus, an attorney who negotiates executive compensation packages, is one such denier. Over his career, Eckhaus claims to have helped bankers secure more than $5 billion in pay. Among his clients were executives from Lehman Brothers, Merrill Lynch, and Morgan Stanley. Defending his clients and the financial sector in general, Eckhaus has said: "To blame Wall Street for the financial meltdown is absurd."[39]

Notwithstanding this pay negotiator's assertion that Wall Street was not to blame, when put under oath, bankers do not concur. Bank of America CEO Brian Moynihan told the FCIC: "Over the course of the crisis, we, as an industry, caused a lot of damage. Never has it been clearer how poor business judgments we have made have affected Main Street." At an FCIC hearing in January 2010, JPMorgan Chase CEO Jamie Dimon told the Commission, "I blame the management teams 100% . . . and no one else."[40]

EPILOGUE

Cast Again

We all were sea-swallow'd, though some cast again,
And by that destiny to perform an act
Whereof what's past is prologue; what to come
In yours and my discharge.

—William Shakespeare, *The Tempest*

The Whale

In May 2012, describing an estimated $2 billion trading loss, JPMorgan Chase's telegenic CEO Jamie Dimon flatly stated: "We made a terrible, egregious mistake. There's almost no excuse for it." It was nearly an apology, and certainly a reversal for Dimon. Until that moment, politicians, the press, and the public had seen him as a shrewd risk manager, the only Wall Street banker to emerge unscathed from the financial crisis. Now he appeared to be toppling off his pedestal.[1]

A month earlier, Dimon had brushed aside rumors about trouble at JPMorgan Chase's London-based Chief Investment Office (CIO), a business unit that managed the bank's excess cash. The portfolio in question was big because the bank had about $1.1 trillion in customer deposits, channeled into $750 billion in loans. The London office handled the roughly $350 billion difference. This giant London portfolio was a part of JPMorgan Chase's $2.3 trillion in total assets, which were funded by about $2.1 trillion in debt—leaving a net worth (or equity capital) of $190 billion. Much of what the giant banking firm owed to others could be withdrawn in the very short term—between one day and three months. This included not just customer deposits but also more than $250 billion in short-term wholesale funding, largely through repo agreements.[2]

That spring, former JPMorgan Chase executives revealed that the bank's CIO in London was investing federally insured customer deposits in highly risky assets. Of the bank's $1.1 trillion in deposits, approximately $400 billion was backed by federal deposit insurance. Until recently, JPMorgan Chase apparently had used its excess insured deposits to invest in hedges, to protect the bank from interest rate risks and minimize losses in the event of a credit crisis. Recently, however, it began using the cash to speculate. For a couple of years, JPMorgan Chase's big bets had paid off; in 2010, the CIO generated a $5 billion profit—delivering one-quarter of the bank's net income for that year. But, in April 2012, a rumor surfaced that Bruno Iksil, an employee in the London office had amassed so large a position in credit derivatives that other traders referred to him as the "London Whale." It appeared that the bank's CIO had been transformed into a high-risk proprietary trading desk, profiting from the very activities that Section 619 of the Dodd-Frank Act, known as the "Volcker Rule," was designed to prevent. But, although the law was signed in 2010, Section 619 would not go into effect until that summer, and due to industry pressure and disagreements among the five agencies tasked with the rulemaking, the final rule to fully implement it was nowhere near done.[3]

When news accounts in April suggested a large trading loss at JPMorgan Chase, Jamie Dimon had dismissed the affair as "a complete tempest in a teapot." He had added, "Every bank has a major portfolio and in those portfolios you make investments that you think are wise, that offset your exposures." The bank's chief financial officer, Doug Braunstein told investors that "[w]e are very comfortable with our positions as they are held today, and I would add that all of those positions are fully transparent to the regulators." But after a more robust internal investigation, Dimon acknowledged in

May that he expected a $2 billion loss related to the CIO's synthetic credit portfolio. Then, in June, he revealed that the losses were actually closer to $5.8 billion. In early 2013, the bank reported that the loss had reached $6.2 billion. As facts trickled out, the London Whale, trader Bruno Iksil, was fired and the head of the CIO, Ina Drew, resigned and agreed to forfeit two years' compensation.[4]

Jamie Dimon's near apology in 2012 echoed the one made by Washington Mutual (WaMu) CEO Kerry Killinger after a complex series of hedging transactions using derivatives blew up in 2004. Like Killinger, Dimon had expanded his bank very quickly—and during this growth, the CIO portfolio had grown from $76 billion to $350 billion in just five years. Once again, this was not an analogy but a continuation. According to bank executives, the London Whale's strategy was designed to offset some of the risk that JPMorgan Chase took on after it bought the failed WaMu Bank. In other words, this $6.2 billion loss stemmed in part from assets brought into the bank during the Kerry Killinger era.[5]

The London Whale loss was not the only WaMu legacy. Buying WaMu moved JPMorgan Chase from third place in total deposits to first in the United States and made it the third-largest mortgage servicer. But WaMu also came with a portfolio of problem loans and litigation. For example, in 2011, the bank was defending a lawsuit by Greg Saffer, the employee who claimed he was pushed out of his job because he refused to sell Option ARMs. Lawyers for JPMorgan Chase said that WaMu's loans were not predatory and "complied with all disclosure laws and regulations." By mid-2010, nearly $75 billion of the WaMu home loans were nonperforming. Yet in 2008, when JPMorgan Chase bought WaMu, it apparently set aside just $30 billion against bad loans.[6]

More problems from WaMu-era mortgages plagued the bank. In early 2011, the Federal Housing Finance Agency (FHFA) as conservator of Fannie Mae and Freddie Mac sued JPMorgan Chase and sixteen other financial institutions. The suit accused JPMorgan Chase of common law fraud and violating the federal securities laws when it peddled private-label residential mortgage-backed securities (MBS) to Fannie and Freddie. This included toxic MBSs sold by

Bear Stearns and WaMu (including its Long Beach division). There was no escaping it: with the benefits of these acquisitions came also the associated liabilities. This was not a surprise to Dimon; before his bank bought Bear Stearns and WaMu, he did consider the legal liabilities. "We weren't completely stupid," he acknowledged.[7]

Appearing on the list of individual defendants named in this FHFA lawsuit was Craig S. Davis, the executive whom Kerry Killinger retained to head up the Home Loans Group after WaMu purchased American Savings Bank in 1996. The complaint alleged Davis and others had signed registration statements in 2003 for MBSs that were sold to Fannie and Freddie. According to the complaint, the registration statements contained "materially false or misleading statements or omissions" and the defendants "falsely represented that the underlying mortgage loans complied with certain underwriting guidelines and standards, including representations that significantly overstated the ability of the borrowers to repay their mortgage loans."[8]

Included on the list of bad MBSs Fannie and Freddie purchased were tranches of the WMALT 2007-OA3 trust. This trust was rushed together by employees who were encouraged to rid California mortgages from WaMu's portfolio. A risk officer called this a "favorable arbitrage" opportunity, as prices on California homes were declining, but "the market seems not yet to be discounting a lot for those factors." This trust contained a hand-picked selection of 1,900 delinquency-prone Option ARMs worth approximately $1 billion. While 87 percent of these securities received triple-A ratings, all of the securities issued by the trust were downgraded to junk status. Within a few years, more than half of the Option ARMs were delinquent and a quarter of the borrowers were in foreclosure.[9]

The Nobelmans

On June 12, 2011, seventeen years after her husband succumbed to diabetes, Harriet Nobelman passed away at home in the Parkway Lane complex in Far North Dallas, in the two-bedroom condo she and Leonard had helped their daughter Marci purchase, which she later gave back to Harriet. Today, the gated complex faces new challenges. With crime rising, the homeowners association now employs security guards to patrol the common areas.[10]

The Condo Flippers

Danny Faulkner was released from prison in 1998, having served fewer than three years of his twenty-year sentence. He had been diagnosed with inoperable brain cancer and was thought to have six months to live. But once out of prison, he survived for nearly fifteen more years. He died at age seventy-nine, from complications of pneumonia, at a Texas hospice in May 2012. His family attributed his survival to his love of people. In the end, his real estate fraud cost the government $1 billion. His partner in crime, former Garland mayor James Toler, predeceased him by a few months, at age seventy-six. Toler had been released from prison after serving a little more than five and a half years of his twenty-year sentence.[11]

The Misfortune Hunter

In 2010, the Louisiana Office of Financial Institutions closed Statewide Bank in Covington and appointed the Federal Deposit Insurance Corporation (FDIC) receiver. It was the first financial institution failure in Louisiana since 2003, and it cost the deposit insurance fund an estimated $38 million. Statewide was owned by Robin Arkley Jr., the man behind Alaska Seaboard Partners, which had purchased the Nobelmans' mortgage from American Savings Bank's affiliate, New West, in early 1996 and foreclosed on the one-bedroom condo that summer. Sometime before it failed, Statewide apparently had issued a mortgage for a parcel of land in connection with a larger riverfront condo project that went sour—but the lot did not exist. By 2010, Arkley had become well known in Humboldt County, California, as both a generous philanthropist and a "foreclosure magnate" who made a business of purchasing distressed mortgages and foreclosing on the homeowners. That year, Bank of America sued Arkley for $50 million in connection with the financing of a pool of commercial and residential mortgage loans.[12]

The Neighbors

In late June 2012, Stockton, California, the former home of American Savings and Loan, struggled to negotiate a private restructuring of its debt. When that state-mandated mediation failed, Stockton, with 300,000 residents, became the largest city in America to file for bankruptcy, an honor it would relinquish when Detroit filed a year later. After having witnessed the collapse of American Savings and Loan, a thrift that grew too fast on too much debt in the 1980s, the town of Stockton followed a similar path. The real estate boom beginning in 2000 had delivered a high-rise hotel and many new neighborhoods. By 2012, Stockton had the second-highest foreclosure rate and second-highest crime rate in the United States. Its creditors filed objections to the bankruptcy, arguing that the city was not an eligible Chapter 9 debtor because it did not negotiate in good faith.[13]

In April 2013, after a three-day trial, the U.S. Bankruptcy Court for the Eastern District of California ruled that the Stockton was eligible for bankruptcy. In the June opinion that followed, Judge Christopher Klein wrote: "Stockton was ground zero for the subprime mortgage crisis." He appeared to refer only to the victims there—including foreclosed-upon homeowners and unemployed workers. But, of course, as former home to Charlie Knapp's American Savings and Loan, it was also ground zero for rogue banking.[14]

The Bankers

The FDIC sued WaMu CEO Kerry Killinger, COO Stephen Rotella, and the head of the Home Loans Group, David Schneider. In its complaint, the FDIC contended that the trio had "widely and indiscriminately" used sales techniques to steer borrowers into Option ARMs they could not afford. The case was settled for $64.7 million, but none of the executives admitted wrongdoing. Insurance policies taken out by the company on behalf of these executives covered almost the entire settlement. The three executives contributed only $425,000. Killinger paid $275,000 in cash. Between 2001 and 2007, he had received more than $88 million in compensation. The full proceeds of the settlement went to the creditors of holding company

Washington Mutual, Inc. The Justice Department had already dropped its criminal investigation of WaMu; officials stated that "the evidence does not meet the exacting standards for criminal charges in connection with the bank's failure."[15]

In August 2013, a nine-person jury found Fabrice Tourre, the former Goldman Sachs vice president, liable on six counts of securities fraud for misleading investors in 2007 about the role hedge fund manager John Paulson played in structuring and betting against the synthetic mortgage-linked CDO structure known as ABACUS. Investors lost $1 billion on the deal. In e-mails to his girlfriend, Tourre had joked that he sold the toxic securities to "widows and orphans." While appealing the verdict, he is pursuing a doctorate in economics. Goldman Sachs had already settled this matter with the SEC for $550 million in 2010 without admitting wrongdoing.[16]

In October 2013, in a civil case brought by federal prosecutors, a unanimous jury found Countrywide, Bank of America, and bank executive Rebecca Mairone liable for fraud for selling defective mortgages to Fannie Mae and Freddie Mac. The sales at issue resulted in $1 billion in losses to the GSEs and many foreclosures. Celebrating the victory, Manhattan U.S. Attorney Preet Bharara said defendants had "adopted a program that they called 'the Hustle,' which treated quality control and underwriting as a joke. In a rush to feed at the trough of easy mortgage money on the eve of the financial crisis, Bank of America purchased Countrywide, thinking it had gobbled up a cash cow. That profit, however, was built on fraud." Bharara was seeking an $848 million fine. Bank of America promised to appeal on behalf of itself and the former executive asserting that Mairone "never engaged in any fraud because there wasn't any fraud." At the time of the verdict, she was working for JPMorgan Chase.[17]

The Government Regulators

Bart Dzivi, the young lawyer who sat in the basement of American Savings and Loan counting collateral during the 1984 run, worked as a staff member on the Financial Crisis Inquiry Commission (FCIC) in 2009 through 2010. FDIC chairman Sheila Bair left government service and headed to the Pew Charitable Trusts. She has set up the Systemic Risk Council, a private-sector, volunteer organization to help monitor and accelerate the slow pace of financial regulatory reform from the outside. Paul Volcker, who helped strengthen the Dodd-Frank Act, is a senor advisor.[18]

In December 2008, the Office of Thrift Supervision (OTS) suspended West Regional director Darrel Dochow. An investigation alleged that Dochow assisted giant subprime mortgage originator IndyMac in cooking its books. He was accused of helping IndyMac, before it failed, to appear healthier than it was by backdating capital infusions. When it collapsed, IndyMac cost the FDIC deposit insurance fund nearly $9 billion. The press release issued by the Treasury Department's Office of the Inspector General said this was "not an isolated incident." During the S&L crisis, Dochow had helped Lincoln Savings and Loan delay being closed down. And during the 2008 crisis, he supervised WaMu, Countrywide, and IndyMac. Dochow retired from government service in 2009 with a full pension. The OTS was merged into the Office of the Controller of the Currency (OCC), pursuant to the Dodd-Frank Act, and ceased to exist in 2011.[19]

The Treasury Secretaries and the Fed Chairman

During his final days in office in January 2013, Treasury Secretary Timothy Geithner was asked by investment manager and Pulitzer Prize–winning author Liaquat Ahamed whether "bankers have too much political muscle in this country." Geithner responded: "Not anymore. There's always some risk of regulatory capture in the Congress or of regulators that would undermine reform. . . . It is true that there is an ongoing political effort to legislate a weakening Dodd-Frank or block appointees. But that effort does not have much political force now." Yet, since Dodd-Frank was enacted in 2010, the financial services lobby devoted considerable resources to delay implementation of the strongest parts and was still engaged in that process. By July 2013, since his departure from the Obama administration, former secretary Geithner had reportedly received $400,000 in speaking fees for just three appearances, including $200,000 for a speech at a Deutsche Bank conference.[20]

In May 2013, Geithner's replacement, Secretary Jack Lew, appeared before the Senate Banking Committee. He was there in his capacity as chair of the new Financial Stability Oversight Council, a position reserved for the Treasury secretary. During his prepared remarks, Lew said that we were making "significant progress" in establishing a "more resilient and stable financial system" and were closer to the end of that process than the beginning. Lew insisted that the problem of "too big to fail" could end even without making the top banks any smaller. Senator Elizabeth Warren, a new member of the Banking Committee challenged Lew on this point:

> We all said back in 2008/2009 the problem that caused the financial crash in part was concentration in the banking industry. And what do we see now? We see more concentration. One of the tools considered for Dodd-Frank was a way to end that concentration. So let me try the question a different way. How big do the biggest banks have to get before we consider breaking them up? They're 30 percent bigger now than they were five years ago.

Secretary Lew did not directly respond: "Size is one factor, but it's not the only factor" in reducing systemic risk. He also noted that "part of the reason that some of those institutions grew [between 2008 and now] is that there were other institutions that failed that had to be reorganized and it was an unusual period of time where we were ironically seeing a shrinking of the number of players because of the failure of institutions." Yet, this method of resolving institutions by having failed ones bought by the stronger survivors was not so unusual; it had been the practice since the S&L crisis and it was the mode enshrined in the Dodd-Frank Act. By July, Lew had a greater sense of urgency. At an investor conference in New York, he said that by 2014, the "core elements of Dodd-Frank will be substantially in place" and by that point, if "we cannot, with an honest, straight face, say that we have ended too big to fail, we are going to have to look at other options."[21]

In October 2013, former Fed chairman Alan Greenspan made the radio and television talk show rounds discussing his new book

The Map and the Territory. Greenspan said the way to prevent a future crisis is to substantially increase equity capital requirements for banks. He explained, "you'd need government regulation to set up the capital standards because most banks, as I've seen, will fight endlessly trying to get as little capital requirements as possible." When pushed by one television host, Greenspan recommended an equity capital requirement of 22 percent. He did not indicate whether that would a pure leverage ratio (of equity divided by total assets), or would have risk-weighted assets in the denominator.[22]

The Shadow Banking System

Ralph Cioffi and Matthew Tannin—managers of the two Bear Stearns hedge funds, the failures of which in 2007 signaled the transformation of the nonprime mortgage crisis into a full-blown financial crisis—were prosecuted in 2009 for federal crimes including conspiracy, wire fraud, and securities fraud. A jury acquitted them. An expert witness for the defense argued that they were not to blame; it was the drying up of liquidity that caused their funds to collapse, not the subprime CDOs they held. This is like defending Charles Ponzi by saying everything was fine until investors stopped giving him money.[23]

In 2009, the Securities and Exchange Commission (SEC) sued Bruce Bent Sr. and his son for securities fraud. The Bents managed Reserve Primary, the money market fund that had $785 billion in repo loans and other investments in Lehman Brothers' short-term debt. When the fund "broke the buck" and failed on September 16, 2008, a $300 billion run by mainly institutional investors on money market funds that week alone spread into the commercial sector. The SEC contended that the duo and their management firm "engaged in a systematic campaign to deceive the investing public into believing that the Primary Fund—their flagship money market fund—was safe and secure despite its substantial Lehman holdings." The complaint alleged they knowingly disseminated "false information to the Primary Fund's Board of Trustees, investors, and rating agencies." In November 2012, after a four-week trial, a jury found the Bents not liable for fraud but did find the son negligent. One of the jurors explained: "There wasn't quite enough evidence for recklessness." Experts called this a setback for the SEC; however, the fund's investment adviser and the affiliated broker-dealer that sold the fund shares were found liable for fraud.[24]

Underwater Homeowners

In July 2012, the Treasury program that would call for principal reduction for mortgages owned by Fannie Mae and Freddie Mac was rejected by Ed DeMarco, the head of the Federal Housing Finance Agency (FHFA). Though the FHFA's own study showed that taxpayers would likely gain $1 billion and the FHFA would gain $3.7 billion from principal reduction, DeMarco refused to offer it. He was a holdover from the George W. Bush administration who became acting director of the FHFA after Bush's appointee resigned. President Obama did not replace him because the Senate Republicans blocked attempts to appoint a permanent director. In spring 2013, President Obama nominated Mel Watt to serve as the permanent director of the FHFA. The nomination pleased housing advocates as they expected Watt, a Democratic congressman from North Carolina, to push the principal reduction policy. The Senate Banking committee approved him; however, as of October 2013, Watt's confirmation was stalled in the full Senate.[25]

In July 2013, the Special Inspector for the Troubled Asset Relief Program issued a report documenting continued shortcomings of the Treasury Department's Home Affordable Modification Program (HAMP). When rolled out in 2009, the Obama administration said HAMP would help between three to four million families save their homes. Yet, only 865,000 homeowners had saved their homes from foreclosure through permanent modifications of their mortgages. Principal reduction is rare under the program. About 87 percent of homeowners with permanent modifications saw their principal stay the same or increase. Those who had principal reduced were about half as likely to redefault.[26]

Meanwhile, creative efforts to help homeowners on the local level abounded. In July 2013, the city council of Richmond, California, announced plans to purchase from investors, at current market values, 624 underwater home mortgages with principal balances averaging $370,000. The city would then restructure the loans, making payments more affordable. The city informed investors that if they failed to sell, the city would seize the mortgages under its power of eminent domain. In August, Wells Fargo (a trustee for pools of mortgages including those on homes in Richmond) and other banks acting for a group of investors, sued in federal court seeking to block the plan, contending that the use of eminent domain would be unconstitutional. In September the federal judge dismissed Wells Fargo's case, calling it premature: "The court is not offering an opinion about whether it would or would not" approve the use of eminent domain. "But this is not ripe for determination." Richmond is allied with Mortgage Resolution Partners, a private firm that would help fund the purchases and possibly profit from the process.[27]

Cities including Springfield, Massachusetts, have passed ordinances requiring lenders who foreclosed on homes to put up a bond of at least $10,000 to the city, so that in the likely event the bank-owned property was neglected, the city could pay to maintain it. In October 2013, upon announcing plans to begin enforcing the law, Springfield mayor Domenic Sarno held a press conference and said, "When Wall Street received a bailout, Main Street was left to fend for ourselves. The implementation of this ordinance gives the city a significant tool to hold absentee landlords and irresponsible institutions accountable for the distress that has been wrought throughout the city." The Massachusetts Bankers Association challenged the ordinance in court, but it was upheld by a federal judge in 2012.[28]

Port in the Storm

In efforts to stave off criticism and roll back financial reform, in January 2013, at the World Economic Forum in Davos, Switzerland, Jamie Dimon said that banks like JPMorgan Chase were "ports in the storm." He had characterized the crisis similarly in 2012 at a Council of Foreign Relations meeting, suggesting that he did the government a favor when JPMorgan Chase purchased Bear Stearns in March 2008. The $30 billion in guarantees from the Federal Reserve appeared to be left out of the story. Also overlooked was the fact that his bank benefited from that acquisition. By that time, in early 2013, Dimon may have needed shelter from judgment raining down on him from the board, shareholders, and regulators.[29]

In January 2013, the JPMorgan Chase board cut Dimon's pay in half, setting it at $11.5 million, down from $23.1 million. That same month, the Fed and the Office of the Comptroller of the Currency (OCC) issued enforcement actions against the bank related to risk-management system failures requiring that the bank fix its internal control problems and improve oversight of its trading. In addition, the bank received a cease and desist order related to failure to comply with anti-money laundering laws. Yet, there were no monetary penalties.[30]

By March 2013, the *New York Times* reported that at least eight different federal agencies were investigating JPMorgan Chase. Some areas of inquiry included whether executives had mislead regulators about the extent of the trading losses. Federal prosecutors and the Federal Bureau of Investigation (FBI) were also examining the bank. The regulatory probes went beyond the London Whale trades to other areas of potential noncompliance, including harm to thousands of foreclosed-upon homeowners. Also of interest to investigators was potential criminal liability, stemming from the bank's twenty-year relationship with Bernard Madoff, who was convicted in 2008 after pleading guilty to eleven felonies—including securities fraud, investment adviser fraud, mail fraud, wire fraud, false statements, and perjury related to a more than $50 billion Ponzi scheme. Indeed, the $6.2 billion trading loss might have been the tip of the iceberg. It was overshadowed by the mounting settlement costs and soaring legal bills.[31]

In his annual letter to shareholders sent out in April, Dimon admitted that "[t]he London Whale was the stupidest and most embarrassing situation I have ever been a part of," and said, "I deeply apologize to you, our shareholders, and to others, including our regulators, who were affected by this mistake." He said that the bank had fixed the problem and was ready to move on: "We are the safest and soundest bank on the planet. . . . I make this promise: We will be a port of safety in the next storm."[32]

The Whale Report

The next month, on May 15, 2013, a Senate subcommittee led by Senator Carl Levin and Senator John McCain released a 307-page report on the London Whale trades in conjunction with a hearing with government and bank witnesses. Dimon was not called to appear, though he had been a witness at both the Senate Banking Committee and House Financial Services Committee the previous summer. The Whale Report revealed that a more than $6 billion trading loss had been predicted in early March 2012 through the bank's own comprehensive internal risk measure, but that the bank's market risk executive, Peter Weiland, dismissed this warning as "garbage." This dismissive and permissive behavior continued, as the CIO breached risk limit after risk limit.[33]

According to Ina Drew, who testified at the hearing, Jamie Dimon was aware of the risk-limit breaches. And, according to the hearing testimony and report, executives yelled at government bank examiners from the OCC and called them "stupid" if they did not agree with the examiner's recommendations. Dimon apparently directed employees to withhold CIO profit and loss reports from the regulators. When CFO Doug Braunstein revealed that he had resumed providing the reports, Dimon raised his voice and told Braunstein that it was up to him—Dimon—to decide if the OCC should get the reports. Moreover, as the Whale Report revealed, the CIO changed its pricing practices to make losses on its portfolio positions look smaller. This practice continued even after the story of the Whale trades broke, and even after it was clear that the investment bank division of JPMorgan Chase was pricing similar positions the way the CIO had done in the past.[34]

In the report and hearing, the OCC did not come out unscathed. As the bank's primary regulator, the OCC was the same body that in 2001 blocked the states from enforcing their own anti-predatory lending laws to protect borrowers. It was the same regulator that, pursuant to the Dodd-Frank Act, took over the responsibilities of the dissolved Office of Thrift Supervision (which did not rein in WaMu), which itself was the renamed Federal Home Loan Bank Board (which helped grow the reckless American Savings and Loan and then sold it for a song to American Savings Bank). Now the OCC had a third chance with JPMorgan Chase. But, according to lead OCC examiner Scott Waterhouse, the agency did not find out about the London Whale trades, nor did it ask to see the CIO portfolio until the *Wall Street Journal* broke the story in April 2012.[35]

High and Dry

Also in May 2013, Dimon faced a shareholder resolution requesting that the company split the roles of CEO and chairman of the Board of Directors, so that no single individual could hold both titles. The previous year, a similar resolution that was also nonbinding had received the support of more than 40 percent of shares voted. Taking the threat seriously in 2013, Dimon engaged in a high-profile campaign—meeting with large investors to beg to keep his job as chairman of the board. It was part courtship, part threat. Just two weeks before the annual meeting on May 21, by which time voting would be cut off, Dimon addressed a private gathering that included representatives from Fidelity Investments, Goldman Sachs, and TIAA-CREF. As was leaked to the press, when asked what he would do if the shareholders voted him out and the board honored that vote, Dimon said he might leave the bank entirely. The proposal failed, with only 32 percent support.[36]

Even after reporting record annual profits of $21.3 billion and surviving the shareholder vote, the WaMu transaction was still a drag on Dimon. In a cable news interview in July, when the bank's mortgage business was compared to its more successful competitor Wells Fargo, Dimon explained that JPMorgan Chase was lagging due to integrating both Bear Stearns and WaMu. During that same interview, Dimon said that he would not have quit even if the shareholders voted to strip him of the chairman role: "I was very clear, I would never have left my company high and dry."[37]

At the end of summer 2013, the bank had revealed it was under civil and criminal investigation by the U.S. Attorney for the Eastern District of California for WaMu's securitization of high-risk mortgages between 2005 and 2007. Then, on August 14, two JPMorgan Chase employees—Javier Martin-Artajo and Julien Grout—were indicted for their roles allegedly covering up the London Whale losses. Artajo was trader Bruno Iksil's boss and Grout was Iksil's subordinate. At the press conference announcing the indictments, U.S. Attorney Preet Bharara said, "under pressure from above," Artajo and Grout "began to cook the books . . . [T]his was not a tempest in a teapot. . . . capitalism works best when its captains do not lie and cheat [and when they] play by the same rules as everyone else. . . . Companies themselves need to pay closer attention to the cultures they create." It came out that in a March 2012 conversation, Grout told Iksil, "It will be a big fiasco and it will be a big drama when in fact, everybody should have, should have seen it coming a long time ago."[38]

Jamie Dimon's winning streak was ending. In September, to end the London Whale probes, JPMorgan Chase paid the SEC, OCC, Fed, and the U.K. financial regulator $920 million in civil penalties. The bank was also required to admit to violating the securities laws, something rarely included in a civil settlement agreement with the government. Then, in October, after ten years of steady profits, JPMorgan Chase reported a quarterly loss of $380 million. This was due to more than $9 billion dollars in litigation expenses associated with the London Whale fiasco as well as the mortgage securities litigation—including the case brought by the FHFA in 2011 regarding the toxic loans JPMorgan, Bear Stearns, and WaMu sold to Fannie and Freddie. Dimon told investors, "while we expect our litigation costs should abate and normalize over time, they may continue to be volatile over the next several quarters."[39]

Stories leaked in late October that JPMorgan Chase might agree to pay $13 billion to settle several outstanding claims with the government—the largest amount paid to the government by a single corporation. This included the FHFA case related to sales of bad mortgage securities to Fannie and Freddie, a case brought by the New York attorney general Eric Schneiderman, and pending civil charges by the Department of Justice. The number seemed big, but it was only 60 percent of the prior year's profit, and a good portion of it could be tax deductible.[40]

Of the $13 billion proposed settlement, $4 billion was to be used to help struggling homeowners. It also included a $2 billion to $3 billion penalty for those mortgage securities JPMorgan Chase itself sold. But, there was something missing; there was no release from criminal liability. Dimon had sought a nonprosecution agreement to end the federal criminal investigation in California. But in late October, Attorney General Eric Holder was still holding firm in his refusal to drop the pending criminal cases. He wanted JPMorgan Chase to enter a guilty plea.[41]

Big Dumb Banks

After the London Whale news broke, commentators quickly rushed in—some to attack and others to defend Dimon and JPMorgan Chase and to read meaning into the billions of dollars of losses. Defenders claimed that the amount was small change compared to the entire bank's more than $2.3 trillion in assets, and that in any case, the firm would weather this storm. Calls to break up the banks continued, and not just from regulators and consumer advocates. Reformers argued that this was exactly the type of proprietary trading that was prohibited by Section 619 of the Dodd-Frank Act, also known as the "Volcker Rule." It was still unclear whether the London Whale's trades would be a permissible hedge or a forbidden bet.

Analysts noted that JPMorgan Chase and the five other giant bank holding companies—Bank of America, Citigroup, Wells Fargo, Goldman Sachs, and Morgan Stanley—were worth more broken up. Sandy Weill, the former Citigroup CEO and architect of the repeal of Glass-Steagall, publicly called for breaking up the banks. Regulators including Richard Fisher, president of the Dallas Fed; Tom Hoenig, former president of the Kansas City Fed and now an FDIC board member; and former FDIC chairman Sheila Bair also joined the chorus, along with many others. These banks not only continued to create systemic risk but were also putting shareholders at risk. And, in July

2013, Senators Warren and McCain introduced a bill they called a "21st Century Glass-Steagall," aimed at once again separating commercial banking (deposit taking and loan making) from investment banking (securities operations), but without as many exceptions.[42]

Looking back on the June 2012 Senate Banking Committee hearing on the London Whale trades, where Jamie Dimon had appeared as a witness, the question of just how to dismantle a failing bank surfaced. Senator Jerry Moran of Kansas asked Dimon about JPMorgan Chase's "living will." The living will was a document that the Dodd-Frank Act required giant banking enterprises to create so that if they failed, they could be dissolved by the FDIC without a taxpayer-funded bailout. Before the passage of Dodd-Frank, the FDIC's power to act as a receiver for a failed bank was limited to depository institutions. So, for example, although it took over the WaMu Bank, the holding company, Washington Mutual, Inc., had to file for bankruptcy. And since Lehman Brothers Holdings, Inc., was an investment bank and not a depository institution, it had to go through bankruptcy. Broader resolution powers were given to the FDIC in order to avoid another bad choice between a Lehman-style chaotic bankruptcy and a bailout for systemically important financial firms.

Dimon told Senator Moran he agreed that "we have to allow our big institutions to fail. . . . You want to be sure they can fail and not damage the American economy and the American public." He said he preferred to call this resolution process "bankruptcy for big dumb banks." With bankruptcy, he'd "fire the management, fire the board" and "wipe out the equity." Unsecured creditors would receive only what they would have gotten in bankruptcy.

Jamie Dimon was right. Bankruptcy is needed to discipline businesses that borrow excessively. In addition, as he implied, it is also important to discipline the lenders. Secured creditors are also important. But when it comes to consumer bankruptcy, specifically with regard to first liens on principal residences, mortgage lenders get special treatment. This is a mistake. Without the prospect that a homeowner will be able to file for bankruptcy, receive a reasonable discharge of debt, gain a fresh start, and keep his or her home, mortgage lenders will act irresponsibly.

Dimon also told Senator Moran that he had confidence in the FDIC's ability to smoothly shut down "big dumb banks," noting that the FDIC had "taken down a lot of large banks without damaging the American public." He called for "Old Testament" justice, whereby the failed bank is dismantled and has its name "buried in disgrace." For example, he suggested, "you may remember American Savings Bank."[43]

Notes

Introduction

1. Donald E. Green, *A History of the Oklahoma State University Division of Agriculture* (Stillwater: Oklahoma State University Press, 1990), 362; "Woman's Suicide Renews Farm Community's Bonds," *Inquirer Wire Services*, July 20, 1986; Keith Schneider, "Rash of Suicides in Oklahoma Shows That the Crisis on the Farm Goes On," *New York Times*, August 17, 1987.

2. Green, *History*, 359–360; T. Jason Soderstrum, "Farm Crisis of 1982," in *The American Economy: A Historical Encyclopedia*, ed. Cynthia C. Northrup (Santa Barbara, CA: ABC-CLIO, 2011), 106.

3. Green, *History*, 359–362; Thomas J. Fitzpatrick IV and James B. Thomson, "Stripdowns and Bankruptcy: Lessons from Agricultural Bankruptcy Reform, Economic Commentary," Federal Reserve Bank of Cleveland, August 3, 2010; Charles W. Calomiris, R. Glenn Hubbard, and James H. Stock, "Growing in Debt: The 'Farm Crisis' and Public Policy," National Bureau of Economic Research Working Paper No. 2085, November 1986; Don Kendall, "Some Want USDA's Embargo Report Tossed in the Shredder," Associated Press, December 21, 1986: farm group disputed the USDA study finding that embargoes of the late 1970s and early 1980s did not cause crisis.

4. Bankruptcy Judges, U.S. Trustees, and Family Farmer Bankruptcy Act of 1986, Pub. L. No. 99-554, 100 Stat. 3088: which passed in October, but became effective in November of 1980; Katherine Porter, "Phantom Farmers: Chapter 12 of the Bankruptcy Code," *American Bankruptcy Law Journal* 79 (2005): 727, 731–732; U.S. General Accounting Office, "Farm Finance: Participants' Views on Issues Surrounding Chapter 12 Bankruptcy," Briefing Report to Congressional Requesters, GAO/RCED-89-142BR, May 1989, available at http://archive.gao.gov/d25t7/138655.pdf; Fitzpatrick and Thomson, "Stripdowns and Bankruptcy."

5. Financial Crisis Inquiry Commission, *The Financial Crisis Inquiry Report: Final Report of the National Commission on the Causes of the Financial*

and Economic Crisis in the United States, authorized ed. (New York: Public Affairs, 2011); U.S. Senate, Permanent Subcommittee on Investigations, Committee on Homeland Security and Governmental Affairs, Majority and Minority Staff Report, *Wall Street and the Financial Crisis: Anatomy of a Financial Collapse*, April 13, 2011.

6. Martin S. Feldstein, "How to Stop the Drop in Home Values," *New York Times*, October 12, 2011; John D. Geanakoplos and Susan P. Koniak, "Matters of Principal," *New York Times*, op-ed, March 4, 2009: "we proposed that Washington pass legislation that would remove the right to modify loans or decide on foreclosure from the servicers and give it to community banks hired by the government"; Congressional Oversight Panel, *March 2011 Oversight Report: The Final Report of the Congressional Oversight Panel*, March 16, 2011, 6, available at http://cybercemetery.unt.edu/archive/cop/20110401232213/http://cop.senate.gov/documents/cop-031611-report.pdf; Dean Baker, *False Profits: Recovering from the Bubble Economy* (Sausalito, CA: PoliPoint Press, 2010), 30–32; RealtyTrac Staff, "1.8 Million U.S. Properties with Foreclosure Filings in 2012," January 4, 2013: "In January 2013, 10.9 million homeowners nationwide—representing 26 percent of all outstanding homes with a mortgage—were seriously underwater." RealtyTrac Staff, "Judicial Foreclosure Actions Hit 30-Month High in April, Overall U.S. Foreclosure Activity Drops to 6-Year Low," May 7, 2013: "11.3 million mortgages nationwide were seriously underwater"; Kathleen M. Howley, "Subprime Borrowers with Best Credit Score Denied Help," *Bloomberg*, July 16, 2013: "nearly 10 million still underwater"; Jeffrey P. Cohen, Cletus C. Coughlin, and David A. Lopez, "The Boom and Bust of U.S. Housing Prices from Various Geographic Perspectives," *Federal Reserve Bank of St. Louis Review* 95 (September/October 2012): 341; Richard Fry and Paul Taylor, "An Uneven Recovery, 2009–2011: A Rise in Wealth for the Wealthy; Declines for the Lower 93%," Pew Research Center Report, April 23, 2013, 1: net worth for top 7% increased by 28% while the net worth for bottom 93% declined by approximately 4%.

7. Stephanie Armour, "Foreclosures Take an Emotional Toll on Many Homeowners," *USA Today*, May 16, 2008.

8. David L. Mason, *From Buildings and Loans to Bail-Outs: A History of the American Savings and Loan Industry, 1831–1995* (Cambridge: Cambridge University Press, 2004), 213–240; Martin Mayer, *The Greatest-Ever Bank Robbery: The Collapse of the Savings and Loan Industry* (New York: Charles Scribner's Sons, 1990), 1–5, 22, 61; William K. Black, *The Best Way to Rob a Bank Is to Own One: How Corporate Executives and Politicians Looted the S&L Industry* (Austin: University of Texas Press, 2005), 5–9, 19; Lawrence J. White, *The S&L Debacle: Public Policy Lessons for Bank and Thrift Regulation* (New York: Oxford University Press, 1991), 3–6, 72–76, 81.

9. Kitty Calavita, Henry N. Pontell, and Robert H. Tillman, *Big Money Crime: Fraud and Politics in the Savings and Loan Crisis* (Berkeley: University of California Press, 1997), 1, 10–15, 44–45, 57–58, 99–101; Black, *Best Way to Rob a Bank*, 11, 20–21, 45–46; Mason, *Buildings and Loans to Bail-Outs*, 218, 227, 275; White, *S&L Debacle*, 81; Richard W. Stevenson, "G.A.O. Puts Cost of S&L Bailout at Half a Trillion Dollars," *New York Times*, July 13, 1996; Robert A. Rosenblatt, "GAO Estimates Final Cost of S&L Bailout at $480.9

Billion," *Los Angeles Times*, July 13, 1996: estimate included direct spending, interest payments on bonds, tax breaks, and cleanup costs; Timothy Curry and Lynn Shibut, "The Cost of the Savings and Loan Crisis," *FDIC Banking Review* 13, no. 2 (December 2000): 33: estimating that as of 1999, the total cost was not $500 billion, but instead $153 billion with $124 billion of that amount borne by taxpayers, available at http://www.fdic.gov/bank/analytical/banking/2000dec/brv13n2_2.pdf.

10. Nobelman v. American Savings Bank, 508 U.S. 324 (1993); Anat Admati and Martin Hellwig, *The Bankers' New Clothes: What's Wrong with Banking and What to Do about It* (Princeton, NJ: Princeton University Press, 2013), 89: "This trend toward even larger banks was further reinforced in the financial crisis when some institutions were 'saved' from bankruptcy by having them acquired by other, usually larger, institutions." Mike Mayo, *Exile on Wall Street: One Analyst's Fight to Save the Big Banks from Themselves* (Hoboken, NJ: Wiley, 2012), 7: "The crisis didn't occur because of something that banks did. No, it was the natural consequence of the way banks *are*, even today" (emphasis in original).

Chapter 1. The Nobelmans

1. Graduated Payment Mortgage/Adjustable Rate Mortgage (GPM/ARM) Note, signed by borrower Leonard Nobelman and Harriet A. Nobelman, June 21, 1984, recorded on July 3, 1984, in Collin County, Texas (hereinafter, "Promissory Note"); Deed of Trust between borrower Leonard Nobelman and wife, Harriet A. Nobelman, trustees Guy R. Arrington, Roger C. Teufel, and Deborah O. Becker, and the beneficiary, Murray Investment Company, as of June 21, 1984, recorded on July 3, 1984, in Collin County, Texas (hereinafter, "Deed of Trust"); note that Michael J. Schroeder and two other individuals were named as substitute trustees pursuant to Appointment of Substitute Trustee, July 12, 1990, recorded on July 16, 1990; Warranty Deed from Miller Condominium Corporation to Leonard Nobelman and wife, Harriet Nobelman, signed June 21, 1984, and filed in Collin County, Texas, July 3, 1984. Assignment of Lien from Murray Investment Company to Murray Savings Association for Lot 507, signed June 25, 1984, and recorded in Collin County, Texas, July 3, 1984 (hereinafter, "Assignment to Murray S&L"); Assignment of Lien from Murray Savings Association to Murray Investment Company for Lot 507, signed July 26, 1984, and recorded in Collin County, Texas, July 30, 1984 (hereinafter, "Transfer Back"); Assignment of Lien from Murray Investment Company to American Savings and Loan Association for Lot 507, Blk. 5, Bk. 3, Pg. 527, signed July 27, 1984, and filed in Collin County, Texas, September 10, 1984 (hereinafter, "Assignment to American S&L").

2. In re Financial Corp. of America, 119 B.R. 728, 731 (Bkrtcy. C.D. Cal. 1990); Debora Vrana, "American Savings Has Regained Its Place as Financial Leader," *Los Angeles Times*, July 23, 1996, recalling 1988: "In what was the single largest rescue of a thrift, the government stepped in with a $5.4-billion bailout that included selling American to Robert M. Bass, a billionaire and corporate bailout specialist from Texas. Bass, who put up $350 million, received

a package of tax breaks as part of the deal." "Another 38 Savings Units Taken Over," Associated Press, April 7, 1989: "The largest of the 38 institutions taken over today was Murray Savings Association of Dallas, with assets of $1.44 billion at the end of 1988." United Press International, "Texas Thrift Placed in Receivership," May 5, 1989: Murray placed in conservatorship in April and in receivership in May 1989, had $1.4 billion in assets but $1.5 billion in liabilities, and became Murray Federal Savings Association. Steve Klinkerman, "Ranieri Unit Executes Deal for Failed Thrift in Dallas," *American Banker*, June 12, 1990: "The federal agency estimated that the transaction ultimately will cost taxpayers $504 million. . . . United, based in Houston, acquired about $1.15 billion of deposits, branches, and $809 million in assets from Murray. . . . United will have six months to evaluate the Murray assets it acquired and return undesirable loans and properties to the RTC." Bank United of Texas F.S.B, USAT Holdings, Inc., Hyperion Holdings, Inc., and Hyperion Partners, L.P. v. United States, U.S. Court of Federal Claims, No. 95-473, October 29, 2001, at 32: United Savings Association of the Southwest, which was created in May 1990 to bid on failed thrifts, in June 1990, purchased Murray Federal Savings Association (the entity that initially took over Murray). The purchase was funded through Hyperion Partners L.P., which was formed in 1988 by Lewis Ranieri; Sarah Bartlett, "A Job Easier Said Than Done for New Savings-Unit Owner," *New York Times*, February 20, 1989: Ranieri's investor group took over United Savings Association in late 1988; American Savings Bank v. United States, 519 F.3d 1316 (Fed. Cir. 2008), describing American Savings as the "largest failed thrift in the United States," and the government-guaranteed $8 billion note issued to American Savings Bank by the New West Federal Savings and Loan Association that took the bad assets; Charles Stein, "Robert Bass, the 'Shy' Billionaire," *Boston Globe*, February 1, 1989; Martin Mayer, *The Greatest-Ever Bank Robbery: The Collapse of the Savings and Loan Industry* (New York: Charles Scribner's Sons, 1990), 76, 310.

3. Transcript of Hearing before the Honorable R. C. McGuire, December 6, 1990, In re Leonard and Harriet Nobelman (hereinafter, "Bankruptcy Transcript"), p. 9: this and other documents from their bankruptcy filing cited herein are available from the National Archives and Records Administration, Southwest Region; In re Leonard and Harriet Nobelman, Notice of Modified Chapter 13 Plan and Motion for Valuation, and Right to Object to Confirmation and Valuation, October 25, 1990 (hereinafter "Modified Plan); Williams v. U.S. Fidelity & Guarantee Company, 236 U.S. 549, 554–55 (1915); one primary purpose of bankruptcy law includes to "relieve the honest debtor from the weight of oppressive indebtedness and permit him to start afresh free from obligations and responsibilities consequent upon business misfortunes"; In re Estel Ray Hougland and Ruth Evelyn Hoagland, 886 F.2d 1182, 1184 (9th Cir. 1989); Sapos v. Provident Institution of Savings, 967 F.2d 918 (3d Cir. 1992); Wilson v. Commonwealth Mortgage Bank, 895 F.2d 123 (3rd Cir. 1990); In re Danny L. Hart and Joanne E. Hart, 923 F.2d 1410 (10th Cir. 1991); In re Jimmie Bellamy and Cynthia Bellamy, 962 F.2d 176 (2d Cir. 1992).

4. Nobelman v. American Savings Bank, 508 U.S. 324 (1993); 129 B.R. 98 (N.D. Tex. 1991); In the Matter of Leonard and Harriet Nobelman [*sic*], 968 F.2d 483 (5th Cir. 1992): (the surname was misspelled in the docket as

acknowledged in the body of the opinion, and the court decided to maintain the error in the case title); Writ of certiorari was granted in 506 U.S. 1020 (1992); Jane Kaufman Winn, "Lien Stripping after Nobelman," *Loyola of Los Angeles Law Review* 27 (1994): 541, 542; Steve McGonigle, "Pair Lose Court Fight over Condo," *Dallas Morning News*, June 2, 1993.

5. Transcript of Oral Argument of Philip Palmer on Behalf of the Petitioners and Oral Argument of Michael J. Schroeder on Behalf of the Respondents in Nobelman v. American Savings Bank, April 19, 1993; Aaron Epstein, "Clarence Thomas Quiet but Still Controversial," *Miami Herald*, November 9, 1994: "All last term and so far this term he has asked no questions of any lawyers . . . in more than 100 cases"; Adam Liptak, "No Argument: Thomas Keeps 5-Year Silence," *New York Times*, February 12, 2011; author telephone interview with Rosemary Zyne, June 28, 2011.

6. Oral Argument of Philip Palmer on Behalf of the Petitioners.

7. For example, the first sentence of Part I, p. 326, of the majority opinion states: "In 1984, respondent American Savings Bank loaned petitioners Leonard and Harriet Nobelman $68,250 for the purchase of their principal residence, a condominium in Dallas, Texas." In addition, the second sentence of the second paragraph of the Fifth Circuit's opinion, 968 F.2d 483 (5th Cir. 1992), states: "The Nobelmans executed a note in the amount of $68,250.00, payable to American Savings Bank (American), and secured by a deed of trust on their principal residence—a condominium in a complex in Dallas, Texas." The federal district court also made a similar claim at the beginning of Part I of its opinion, 129 B.R. 98 (1991).

8. Bankruptcy Transcript; author interview with Marci Nobelman, Far North Dallas, September 11, 2011.

9. Affidavit of Leonard Nobelman, November 14, 1990, filed on November 15, 1990; In re Leonard and Harriet Nobelman, Case No. 390-35116-HCA-13, U.S. Bankruptcy Court for the Northern District of Texas, Dallas Division, p. 2; Affidavit of Debbie Putnam for Murray Mortgage Company, in Support of Motion for Relief from Stay and Demand for Adequate Protection, November 21, 1990; In re Leonard and Harriet Nobelman; Promissory Note; Bob Mahlburg, "High Court Rules against Homeowners in Bankruptcy," *Fort Worth Star-Telegram*, June 2, 1993; Partial Release of Lien, recorded on July 12, 1984, by RepublicBank; interview with Marci Nobelman, September 11, 2011; author site visit, September 2011.

10. Promissory Note and Rider to Deed of Trust: Graduated Payment/ Adjustable Rate Loan (which changed date of rate adjustment from August 1 to July 1).

11. Deed of Trust.

12. Assignment to Murray S&L; Transfer Back; Assignment to American S&L.

13. Bankruptcy Transcript, pp. 7, 9, 11; Trial Brief, p. 2; Leonard Nobelman, Owner, Texas Certificate of Title to a Motor Vehicle, February 3, 1986; Harriet A. Nobelman, Owner, Texas Certificate of Title to a Motor Vehicle, October 9, 1989; Mahlburg, "High Court Rules against Homeowners"; H. Jane Lehman, "Ruling Splits Courts on Issue of 'Cramdowns' As Lenders Gain 1st Victory,"

Chicago Tribune, September 6, 1992: Harriet's enjoyment of time by the pool was revealed in an acquaintance's comment written on a Web site where her obituary was posted.

14. Bankruptcy Transcript, pp. 9–10, 13.

15. Bankruptcy Petition 390-35116-HCA-13, filed August 6, 1990; Modified Plan.

16. Dean Baker, *False Profits: Recovering from the Bubble Economy* (Sausalito, CA: PoliPoint Press, 2010), 17; John Rebchook, "Denver Second Lowest for Housing Declines," *Inside Real Estate News*, May 31, 2011: "Only Dallas with an 11.2 percent decline from the peak to the bottom showed less of a drop than Denver"; Case-Shiller Home Price Index, Las Vegas, NV, as of May 31, 2011; S&P/Case-Shiller Condo Price Index (1995–2011); "Peaks and Troughs," *Housing Views*, August 28, 2012: showing chart using S&P/Case-Shiller Home Price Indices with peak dates and trough dates and then-current levels; S&P/Case-Shiller, Condo Price Index (1995–2012), *socketsite.com*, March 27, 2012.

17. In re Leonard and Harriet Nobelman, Trial Brief, December 4, 1990; author telephone interview with Michael J. Schroeder, June 30, 2011; Modified Plan.

18. Maggie Rivas, "Condo Prices Fall in Scandal-Tainted Market," *Dallas Morning News*, April 12, 1987; author telephone interview with Zyne; e-mail correspondence with Dallas resident Michael Ricker, September 24, 2011: an elderly acquaintance of his referred to the scandal as "Faulkner's Folly."

Chapter 2. The Condo King and His Empire

1. Associated Press, "Texas Stadium's Million Dollar Seats," *Victoria Advocate*, January 25, 1983; Eric Miller, "The Trouble in Dannyland," *D Magazine*, February 1984; "Condominiums Open," *Mid Cities Daily News*, May 3, 1981; Allen Pusey, "Faulkner Facing Up to His Fate," *Dallas Morning News*, November 17, 1991.

2. Simon William Straus, *History of the Thrift Movement in America* (Philadelphia: J. B. Lippincott, 1920), 17, 31–34; James L. Pledger, Commissioner, Texas Savings and Loan Department, "Self Evaluation Report to the Sunset Advisory Committee," August 1999, 7; David L. Mason, *From Buildings and Loans to Bail-Outs: A History of the American Savings and Loan Industry, 1831–1995* (New York: Cambridge University Press, 2004), 46; M. Manfred Fabritius and William Borges, *Saving the Savings and Loan: The U.S. Thrift Industry and the Texas Experience, 1950–1988* (New York: Praeger, 1989), 3, 43, 51, 69, 71–73; Richard Scott Carnell, Jonathan R. Macey, and Geoffrey P. Miller, *The Law of Banking Financial Institutions*, 4th ed. (New York: Aspen, 2009), 27–28.

3. "A Chronology of the I-30 Investigation," *Dallas Morning News*, October 8, 1987; Mason, *From Buildings and Loans to Bail-Outs*, 276–279.

4. Bobbi Miller, "Corridor Comeback," *Dallas Morning News*, December 11, 1989; Allen Pusey and Christi Harlan, "Empire Chief Reaped Millions," *Dallas*

Morning News, January 27, 1986: Empire made hundreds of millions of dollars in land transactions that helped Faulkner earn $70 million; Pusey, "Faulkner Facing Up to His Fate"; Mason, *From Buildings and Loans to Bail-Outs*, 278.

5. Mason, *From Buildings and Loans to Bail-Outs*, 278–279; Barry Bearak and Tom Furlong, "Where Did the $500 Billion Go?" *Buffalo News*, September 16, 1990: "An apostle of brokered deposits, Blain was transforming Empire Savings from a half-pint suburban thrift into a $330 million skyscraper."

6. James Russell, "If They Made a Movie of the S&L Fiasco, Ed Gray Would Be Cast as a Hero," *Miami Herald*, November 5, 1989: Merrill Lynch identified as active in brokered deposits; Robert A. Rankin, "Complex, Seamy Roots of the Thrift Crisis," *Philadelphia Inquirer*, February 12, 1989; Paul Muolo and Matthew Pedillo, *Chain of Blame: How Wall Street Caused the Mortgage and Credit Crisis* (New York: Wiley, 2010), 54–55.

7. Mason, *From Buildings and Loans to Bail-Outs*, 86, 150; The Federal Home Loan Bank Act of 1932, Pub. L. No. 72-304, 47 Stat. 725; Herbert Hoover, Statement about Signing the Federal Home Loan Bank Act, July 22, 1932: Hoover explained the law would "encourage homeownership" by permitting homeowners to "obtain long-term loans payable in installments."

8. Home Owner's Loan Act, Pub. L. No. 73-43, 48 Stat. 128; Mason, *Buildings and Loans to Bail-Outs*, 92, 95; The National Housing Act of 1934, Pub. L. No. 84-345, 48 Stat. 847.

9. Brokered Deposits Hearing before the Subcommittee on Financial Institutions and Consumer Affairs of the Committee on Banking, Housing and Urban Affairs, U.S. Senate, 99th Congress, June 5, 1985; Isaac Testimony, p. 3; Eric Lipton and Andrew Martin, "For Banks, Wads of Cash and Loads of Trouble," *New York Times*, July 3, 2009; Calavita, Pontell, and Tillman, *Big Money Crime*, 12; Mason, *From Buildings and Loans to Bail-Outs*, 152; "Liquidity Analysis: Decades of Change," *Supervisory Insights* 4, no. 2 (Winter 2007): 6: "In 1959 . . . the FHLB Bank Board limited brokered deposits to five percent of total deposits. In 1981, this limit was repealed, a decision that some observers subsequently viewed as an important contributor to the savings and loan crisis of the 1980s." Indeed, brokered deposits also played a key role in the failure of small and regional banks during the subprime meltdown and global financial crisis beginning in late 2007.

10. Federal Home Loan Bank Board Supervision of Empire Savings and Loan Association, Hearing before a Subcommittee of the Committee on Government Operations, House of Representatives, 98th Congress, Second Session, April 25, 1984 (hereinafter, "Empire Hearing").

11. Allen Pusey, "Fast Money and Fraud," *New York Times Magazine*, April 23, 1989; Mason, *From Buildings and Loans to Bail-Outs*, 279, 291.

12. Sherrill Shafer and Catherine Piche, "New Findings on Brokered Deposits," *Federal Reserve Bank of New York Quarterly Review*, Autumn 1984; United States v. Faulkner, Blain, Toler and Forman, 17 F.3d 745 (5th Cir. 1994) (hereinafter, U.S. v. Faulkner).

13. Martin Mayer, *The Greatest-Ever Bank Robbery: The Collapse of the Savings and Loan Industry* (New York: Charles Scribner's Sons, 1990), 65: net worth requirement lowered to 3 percent in 1982.

14. William K. Black, *The Best Way to Rob a Bank Is to Own One: How Corporate Executives and Politicians Looted the S&L Industry* (Austin: University of Texas Press, 2005), 19; Lawrence J. White, *The S&L Debacle: Public Policy Lessons for Bank and Thrift Regulation* (New York: Oxford University Press, 1991), 42–43: GAAP generally is based on historical book value, not current market value.

15. Paul M. Horvitz, "The Collapse of the Texas Thrift Industry: Causes of the Problem and Implications for Reform," in *Restructuring the American Financial System*, ed. George G. Kaufman (Boston: Kluwer, 1990), 61, 111; White, *S&L Debacle*, 89–90; David Moss, "An Ounce of Prevention: Financial Regulation, Moral Hazard, and the End of 'Too Big to Fail,'" *Harvard Magazine*, September–October, 2009: Glass-Steagall authorized deposit insurance "but also meaningful bank regulation, designed to ensure safety and soundness of insured banks."

16. Black, *Best Way to Rob a Bank*, 35; Tex. Const., art. XVI, § 16(a); George D. Braden et al., *The Constitution of the State of Texas: An Annotated and Comparative Analysis*, 170, digitized copy available at http://www.sll.texas.gov/library-resources/collections/bradens-annotated-texas-constitution/; Pledger, "Self Evaluation Report to the Sunset Advisory Committee," 7; Fabritius and Borges, *Saving the Savings and Loan*, 72–77; Mark A. Giltner, "Unlimited Branch Banking in Texas: The Next Step in Deregulation?" *Saint Mary's Law Journal* 19 (1988): 1034, fn. 84.

17. Martin E. Lowy, *High Rollers: Inside the Savings and Loan Debacle* (New York: Praeger, 1991), 52; Federal Deposit Insurance Corporation, "The S&L Crisis: A Chrono-Bibliography," 2002, available at http://www.fdic.gov/bank/historical/s&l/; Byron Harris, "The Party's Over," *Texas Monthly*, June 1987; Black, *Best Way to Rob a Bank*, 36; Lawrence J. White, "The S&L Debacle," *Fordham Law Review* 59, no. 6 (1991): S69; Tom S. King, *The Great Texas Savings & Loan Financial Debacle: An Insider's Perspective 1984–1992* (Bloomington, IN: Author House, 2006), 4.

18. The Depository Institutions Deregulation and Monetary Control Act of 1980, Pub. L. No. 96-221, 94 Stat. 132.

19. U.S. v. Faulkner: amount of land purchased less than $1 million, but resale either $14 million or $16 million, according to the court; Empire Hearing.

20. Mason, *From Buildings and Loans to Bail-Outs*, 280; "I-30 Figures Have Varied Backgrounds," *Dallas Morning News*, October 8, 1987; Mayer, *Greatest-Ever Bank Robbery*, 54; U.S. v. Faulkner.

21. Pusey, "Fast Money"; James O'Shea, *Daisy Chain: How Borrowed Billions Sank a Texas S&L* (New York: Pocket Books/Simon & Schuster, 1991), 34–36; U.S. v. Faulkner.

22. "Chronology of the I-30 Investigation"; Pusey, "Fast Money"; Kitty Calavita, Henry N. Pontell, and Robert H. Tillman, *Big Money Crime: Fraud and Politics in the Savings and Loan Crisis* (Los Angeles: University of California Press, 1997), 50–51; and Mason, *From Buildings and Loans to Bail-Outs*.

23. Pusey, "Fast Money"; Mason, *From Buildings and Loans to Bail-Outs*, 286; U.S. v. Faulkner.

24. Pusey, "Fast Money"; United States v. Paul Arlin Jensen, 41 F3d 946 (5th Cir. 1994); U.S. v. Faulkner; Associated Press, "Witness Given 13-Year Term," *The Victoria Advocate*, October 10, 1987; Allen Pusey and Christi Harlan, "I-30 Land Appraisers Reaped Gains; Faulkner Association Profitable for Two Men," *Dallas Morning News*, February 10, 1985; David Pasztor, "Crime Pays: How the Feds Let S&L Swindler Clifford Sinclair Get Away with Millions," *Dallas Observer*, November 24, 1994.

25. Albert and Ringer, "Questions Raised by 'Pen Square of Thrifts,' Get Scrutiny at Congressional Hearing," *American Banker*, April 25, 1984; U.S. v. Faulkner.

26. Pusey, "Fast Money"; Mason, *From Buildings and Loans to Bail-Outs*, 277; U.S. v. Faulkner.

27. Mason, *From Buildings and Loans to Bail-Outs*, 283.

28. Pusey, "Fast Money"; Mason, *From Buildings and Loans to Bail-Outs*, 279, table A1.1; Statement of John Bryant at Empire Hearings, April 25, 1984.

29. Pusey, "Fast Money"; Mayer, *Greatest-Ever Bank Robbery*, 131; Horvitz, "Collapse of the Texas Thrift Industry," 61, 111; White, *S&L Debacle*, 89–90; King, *Great Texas Savings & Loan Financial Debacle*, 26.

30. FDIC, "The Savings and Loan Crisis and Its Relationship to Banking," 171–172, in *An Examination of the Banking Crises of the 1980s and Early 1990s* (1997), available at http://www.fdic.gov/bank/historical/history/; Black, *Best Way to Rob a Bank*, 18–19.

31. Carl Felsenfeld, "Savings and Loan Crisis," *Fordham Law Review* 59, no. 6 (1991), citing Senate Report No. 1482, 89th Cong., 2d Sess., reprinted in 1966 U.S. Code Cong. and Admin. News.

32. Felsenfeld, "Savings and Loan Crisis"; Joseph M. Korff, "Banking," *Boston College Law Review* 8 (1967): 599–600, 603, 605, 616.

33. Empire Hearing; Mason, *From Buildings and Loans to Bail-Outs*, 281, 283–284; "Chronology of the I-30 Investigation."

34. Mason, *From Buildings and Loans to Bail-Outs*, 283–284.

35. O'Shea, *Daisy Chain*, 84–86; Lowy, *High Rollers*, 59–60; Black, *Best Way to Rob a Bank*, 45; Mayer, *Greatest-Ever Bank Robbery*, 128, 133; Mason, *From Buildings and Loans to Bail-Outs*, 284; "FHLBB Study Details Threat to FSLIC Fund," *Los Angeles Times*/Associated Press, July 26, 1985; Mayer, *Greatest-Ever Bank Robbery*, 35; Miller, "Trouble in Dannyland"; Pusey and Harlan, "I-30 Land Appraisers."

36. Empire Hearing; Albert and Ringer, "Questions Raised."

37. Bill Lodge, "I-30 Defendants Appeal Convictions," *Dallas Morning News*, December 2, 1993; Bill Lodge, "Faulkner Is Released from Prison," *Dallas Morning News*, December 19, 1998; Pusey, "Faulkner Facing Up to His Fate" Steve Blow, "Faulkner Seems to Have a New Lease on Life," *Dallas Morning News*, December 12, 1999; "4 Convicted of Fraud in Condo Case," *New York Times*, November 7, 1991.

38. Paul Zane Pilzer with Robert Deitz, *Other People's Money: The Inside Story of the S&L Mess* (New York: Simon & Schuster, 1989), 175–176; Pledger, "Self Evaluation Report to the Sunset Advisory Committee," 25–26; Gary S.

Becker, "Crime and Punishment: An Economic Approach," in *Essays in the Economics of Crime and Punishment* (New York: National Bureau of Economic Research, 1974), 9: the number of offenses committed declines as probability of apprehension and punishment increases.

39. Ed Housewright, "Condos Appraised Value Cut," *Dallas Morning News*, September 6, 1984; Harris, "Party's Over"; Calavita, Pontell, and Tillman, *Big Money Crime*, 51.

40. Housewright, "Condos Appraised Value Cut"; "I-30 Condos Up for Sale," Associated Press, March 3, 1988; Harris, "Party's Over," 112, 174; Financial Crisis Inquiry Commission, *The Financial Crisis Inquiry Report: Final Report of the National Commission on the Causes of the Financial and Economic Crisis in the United States*, authorized ed. (New York: Public Affairs, 2011), 35–36: the Texas housing bubble burst between 1985 and 1986.

41. Pusey, "Fast Money"; Miller, "Corridor Comeback."

Chapter 3. The Run on American Savings and Loan

1. Author's telephone interview with Bart Dzivi, September 19, 2011; The Committee of Bar Examiners of the State Bar of California, "General Bar Examination Pass Rate Summary," available at http://admissions.calbar.ca.gov/Portals/4/documents/Gen-Bar-Exam-Pass-Rate-Summary.pdf.

2. Michael A. Robinson, *Overdrawn: The Bailout of American Savings* (New York: Penguin Books, 1990), 3–4, 92, 123, 159: in July, institutions withdrew $1.4 billion and only $800 million was raised from retail depositors; Data Controls North, Inc. v. Financial Corporation of America (4th Cir. 1989): over six weeks from August into October, $6.8 billion was withdrawn; Dzivi interview; Martin Mayer, *The Greatest-Ever Bank Robbery: The Collapse of the Savings and Loan Industry* (New York: Charles Scribner's Sons, 1990), 104; Federal Deposit Insurance Corporation, "A Brief History of Deposit Insurance in the United States," paper prepared for the International Conference on Deposit Insurance, Washington, DC, September 1998, p. 39; Paul Zane Pilzer with Robert Deitz, *Other People's Money: The Inside Story of the S&L Mess* (New York: Simon & Schuster, 1989), 70; "Reserves Plummet for FSLIC," *Dow Jones*, July 4, 1986; "Thrift Industry Problems: Potential Demands on the FSLIC Insurance Fund," U.S. General Accounting Office Briefing Report, Washington, DC, February 1986; "Reserves Up at F.S.L.I.C.," *New York Times*, November 16, 1984: reserves were $6.43 billion on December 31, 1983.

3. Dzivi interview; Robinson, *Overdrawn*, 4.

4. Dzivi e-mail correspondence, June 27–28, 2013; Bartlett Naylor, "The Legend of Wild Bill and Black Bart," *Citizen Vox*, May 9, 2011; James S. Granelli, "Fugitive O. C. Banker Agrees to Return," *Los Angeles Times*, November 5, 1996.

5. Testimony of Paul Volcker at the Conduct of Monetary Policy Hearing Transcript, U.S. House of Representatives, Committee on Banking, Finance and Urban Affairs, July 14 and 21–23, 1981, p. 217: Volcker said that law permits S&Ls to come to the Fed for loans and "I would anticipate a good many of

these institutions coming to the Federal Reserve," available at http://fraser .stlouisfed.org/docs/historical/house/cmp/1980s/CMP_97HR_07141981.pdf.

6. Kenneth E. Scott, "Never Again: The S&L Bailout Bill," *Business Lawyer* 45 (June 1990): 1890.

7. David L. Mason, *From Buildings and Loans to Bail-Outs: A History of the American Savings and Loan Industry, 1831–1995* (Cambridge: Cambridge University Press, 2004), 71; First Charter Financial Corp. v. United States of America, 669 F.2nd 1342 (9th Cir. 1982); *It's a Wonderful Life* (1946, Liberty Films).

8. Seymour Dexter, *A Treatise on Co-Operative Savings and Loan Associations* (New York: Appelton, 1889), 75–76; Mason, *From Buildings and Loans to Bail-Outs*, 16–18, 107; Richard Green and Susan Wachter, "The American Mortgage in Historical and International Context," *Journal of Economic Perspectives* 19 (2005): 94.

9. Helen M. Burns, *The American Banking Community and New Deal Banking Reforms, 1933–1935* (Westport, CT: Greenwood Press, 1974), 3–4; National Currency Act of 1863 and National Bank Act of 1864; Adam J. Levitin and Susan M. Wachter, "The Public Option in Housing Finance," Georgetown Public Law Research Paper No. 1966550, November 28, 2012, p. 17.

10. Kenneth Snowden, "The Evolution of Interregional Mortgage Lending Channels, 1870–1940: The Life Insurance–Mortgage Company Connection," in *Coordination and Information: Historical Perspectives on the Organization of Enterprise* (Chicago: University of Chicago Press, 1995), 209; Martin Mayer, *The Bankers: The Next Generation* (New York: Plume, 1998), 6, 362; McFadden Act, Pub. L. No. 69-639, 44 Stat. 1224, 1232-33 (1927).

11. Mason, *From Buildings and Loans to Bail-Outs*, 17, 20, 59, 77; J. E. Morton, *Urban Mortgage Lending: Comparative Markets and Experience* (Princeton, NJ: Princeton University Press, 1956); Kenneth E. Scott, "The Dual Banking System: A Model of Competition in Regulation," 30 Stan. L. Rev. 1 (1977).

12. United States v. Winstar, 518 U.S. 838, 844 (1996): roughly 1,700 of a total of about 12,000 thrifts failed during the Great Depression; Carl Felsenfeld, "Savings and Loan Crisis," *Fordham Law Review* 59, no. 6 (1991): S10, citing 24 C.F.R. § 203.11 (1938) and 13 Fed. Reg. 6469 (1949).

13. The Banking Act of 1933, Pub. L. 73-66, 48 Stat. 162; R. Alton Gilbert, "Requiem for Regulation Q: What It Did and Why It Passed Away," *Federal Reserve Bank of St. Louis Review*, February 1986; William Birdthistle, "Breaking Bucks in Money Market Funds," *Wisconsin Law Review* 5 (2010): 1161.

14. Levitin and Wachter, "Public Option," 24; Green and Wachter, "American Mortgage," 95; Alex J. Pollock, "A 1930s Loan Rescue Lesson," *Washington Post*, March 14, 2008.

15. National Housing Act, Pub. L. No. 73-479, § 501, 48 Stat. 1246, 1261 (1934); Randall Dodd, "Subprime: Tentacles of a Crisis," *Finance and Development* 44, no. 4 (December 2007); William Poole, "Housing in the Macroeconomy," Federal Reserve Bank of St. Louis *Review*, May/June, 2003; Green and Wachter, "American Mortgage," 95–96; Levitin and Wachter, "Public Option," 26–27, 30.

16. HS-27, "Housing Units—Historical Trends for Selected Characteristics: 1940–2000": 15 million owner occupied in 1940 and 32 million in 1960,

available at http://www.census.gov/statab/hist/HS-27.pdf; Green and Wachter, "American Mortgage," 96; Mason, from *Buildings and Loans to Bail-Outs*, 106–107, 128–129; Bureau of the Census, table 2, "Population, Housing Units, Area Measurements, and Density: 1790 to 1990," available at http://www.census.gov/population/www/censusdata/files/table-2.pdf; Carlos Garriga, William T. Gavin, and Don Schlagenhauf, "Recent Trends in Homeownership," *Federal Reserve Bank of St. Louis Review* 88, no. 5 (September/October 2006), 398; Daniel K. Fetter, "The 20th Century Increase in U.S. Home Ownership: Facts and Hypotheses," NBER Chapter No. 12801 in *Housing and Mortgage Markets in Historical Perspective* (Cambridge, MA: National Bureau of Economic Research, 2013), 2, 22–23: "Broader changes in finance may explain about 40 percent of the overall increase in home ownership from 1940–1960. . . . Among the most remarkable changes in the 20th-century United States was the transformation in housing markets over the 1940's and 1950's."

17. Robinson, *Overdrawn*, 10–11, 14; "Merger with American Approved: State Savings Now Nation's Largest," *Lodi News-Sentinel*, August 5, 1983; Debora Vrana, "American Savings Has Regained Its Place as Financial Leader," *Los Angeles Times*, July 23, 1996.

18. Gilbert, "Requiem for Regulation Q," 26: interest rate caps of Reg Q applied to S&Ls and mutual savings banks; Arthur E. Wilmarth Jr., "The Expansion of State Powers, the Federal Response, and the Case for Preserving the Dual Banking System," *Fordham Law Review* 58, no. 6 (1990): 1139–1140.

19. U.S. Government Accountability Office, "Fannie Mae and Freddie Mac: Analysis of Options for Revising the Housing Enterprises' Long-Term Structures," GAO-09-782, September 2009; Robert Metz, "The Private Life of Fanny May," *New York Times*, August 21, 1968; Robert Metz, "Fanny May Nears Private Status and Investors Scent a Windfall," *New York Times*, September 1, 1968. Private investors already held some shares of Fannie Mae. This began after 1954. However, with the public offering of shares pursuant to the 1968 act, which took place in 1970, Fannie Mae no longer had government ownership; Andrew R. Mandala, "The Season's Leading Debutante—Fanny May on the Big Board," *New York Times*, September 5, 1970; Lawrence J. White, "Fannie Mae, Freddie Mac, and Housing Finance: Why True Privatization Is Good Public Policy," Cato Institute Policy Analysis, No. 528, October 7, 2004, pp. 5, 8.

20. Emergency Home Finance Act of 1970, Pub. L. No. 91-351, tit. III, 84 Stat. 450; Freddie Mac's shares were listed in 1984, but it was not until 1989 that the general public could own; Associated Press, "Mortgage Agency Enters New Field: It Will Finance Conventional Loans on Existing Homes," *New York Times*, December 16, 1971; Leland C. Brendsel, "Securitization's Role in Housing Finance: The Special Contributions of the Government-Sponsored Enterprises," *A Primer on Securitization*, ed. Leon T. Kendall and Michael J. Fishman (Cambridge, MA: MIT Press, 1996), 19–20; Marshall W. Dennis, *Residential Mortgage Lending*, 3d ed. (Upper Saddle River, NJ: Prentice Hall, 1992), 156.

21. Leon T. Kendall, "Securitization: A New Era in American Finance," in *A Primer on Securitization*, 1–2; Lewis S. Ranieri, "The Origins of Securitization, Sources of Its Growth, and Its Future Potential," in *A Primer on Securiti-*

zation, 32–33; John Tower, "Ginnie Mae Pool No. 1: A Revolution Is Paid Off," *Bloomberg News,* September 19, 1999; Division of Investment Management Report, U.S. Securities & Exchange Commission, "The Treatment of Structured Finance under the Investment Company Act," in *Protecting Investors: A Half Century of Investment Company Regulation,* May 1992, 5–8.

22. Division of Investment Management, "Treatment of Structured Finance," 7–9.

23. Brendsel, "Securitization's Role in Housing Finance," 18, 20.

24. U.S. Securities & Exchange Commission, Staff Report: Enhancing Disclosure in the Mortgage–Securities Markets, 2003; Bank of America National Trust and Savings Association, SEC Staff No-Action Letter, April 19, 1997; Ranieri, "Origins of Securitization," 32–33; Kendall and Fishman, "Securitization," 8.

25. Board of Governors of the Federal Reserve System, Table B-76, "Mortgage Debt Outstanding by Holder, 1950–2009," available at http://www.gpo.gov/fdsys/pkg/ERP-2010/pdf/ERP-2010-table76.pdf; Ranieri, "Origins of Securitization," 37; Division of Investment Management, "Treatment of Structured Finance," 8–9; Kendall, "Securitization," 15; Michael Lewis, *Liar's Poker* (New York: W. W. Norton, 1989), 83, 88–89.

26. Ranieri, "Origins of Securitization," 31–32; Bethany McLean and Joe Nocera, *All the Devils Are Here: The Hidden History of the Financial Crisis* (New York: Portfolio/Penguin, 2010), 5, 12; U.S. v. Winstar, 847.

Chapter 4. The Saturday Night Massacre

1. "Transcript of Press Conference with Paul A. Volcker, Chairman, Board of Governors of the Federal Reserve System," Washington, DC, October 6, 1979, available at http://fraser.stlouisfed.org/docs/historical/volcker/Volcker_19791006.pdf; David E. Lindsey, Athanasios Orphanides, and Robert H. Rasche, "The Reform of 1979: How It Happened and Why," *Federal Reserve Bank of St. Louis Review* 87, no. 2, part 2 (Special Issue, March/April 2005), see also p. 202, "Reflections on Monetary Policy 25 Years after October 1979 Proceedings of a Special Conference of the Federal Reserve Bank of St. Louis"; Alan S. Blinder, "The Anatomy of Double-Digit Inflation in the 1970s," in *Inflation: Causes and Effects,* ed. Robert E. Hall (Chicago: University of Chicago Press, 1982), 261–281; William L. Silber, "How Volcker Launched His Attack on Inflation," *Bloomberg.com,* August 20, 2012.

2. For inflation calculations, see the Bureau of Labor Statistics CPI Inflation Calculator, available at http://www.bls.gov/data/inflation_calculator.htm; Glenn H. Miller Jr., "Inflation and Recession, 1979–82: Supply Shocks and Economic Policy," *Federal Reserve Bank of Kansas City Economic Review* (June 1983): 11, 13, 18 (energy prices accounting for more than three-fourths of inflation increase), available at http://www.kc.frb.org/Publicat/econrev/EconRevArchive/1983/2q83mill.pdf; James D. Hamilton, "Historic Oil Shocks," in the *Routledge Handbook of Major Events in Economic History,* ed. Randall E. Parker and Robert Whaples (New York: Routledge, 2013); Alan S. Blinder, "Anatomy of Double-Digit Inflation," 271: "gasoline prices accounted for the

lion's share of the total contribution of energy"; Leonard Silk, "Crisis on Two Fronts," *New York Times*, October 24, 1973; Leonard Silk, "Economic Scene: An Opportunity for Reagan, *New York Times*, May 29, 1981; Joseph B. Treaster, *The Making of a Financial Legend* (Hoboken, NJ: Wiley, 2004), 160.

3. William Greider, *Secrets of the Temple: How the Federal Reserve Runs the Country* (New York: Simon & Schuster, 1987), 41: inflation was a "paradox of winners and losers."

4. Board of Governors of the Federal Reserve System, *The Federal Reserve System: Purposes & Functions*, 9th ed., June 2005, 3, 10–12, available at http://www.federalreserve.gov/pf/pdf/pf_complete.pdf; The twelve regional Fed banks were the model for the twelve Federal Home Loan Banks established twenty years later. The regional Fed banks provided liquidity support, supervision, and examination; DealBook, "Fed Tightens on Its Regional Directors," *New York Times*, November 30, 2009: "Fed's 12 regional banks are governed by boards that are almost by definition beholden to the banking industry."

5. Fred Hirsch, *Social Limits to Growth* (Cambridge: Harvard University Press, 1976), 175: inflation leads to collective bargaining for higher wages, which in turn leads to inflation, and then higher wages.

6. Greider, *Secrets of the Temple*, 41–43, 116, 118–119; Lindsey, Orphanides, and Rasche, "Reform of 1979," 199; Paul Lewis, "Europe Seeks Quick Slowdown of U.S. Economic Engine," *New York Times*, July 29, 1979.

7. Martin Mayer, *The Greatest-Ever Bank Robbery: The Collapse of the Savings and Loan Industry* (New York: Charles Scribner's Sons, 1990), 46: the ever-frugal Mark Taper of American Savings and Loan tried to keep this overhead at below 1 percent.

8. Pamela G. Hollie, "Inflation Driving Young Couples to Purchase More and Save Less," *New York Times*, April 22, 1979, A1; Peter T. Kilborn, "Consumer, Resigned to Inflation, Is Learning New Ways to Hedge," *New York Times*, April 23, 1979; Federal Reserve Releases, G19, consumer credit outstanding, seasonally adjusted, available at http://www.federalreserve.gov/releases/g19/hist/cc_hist_sa.html; Table B-76, "Mortgage Debt Outstanding by Holder, 1950–2009," available at gov/fdsys/pkg/ERP-2010/pdf/ERP-2010-table76.pdf.

9. John H. Allan, "The Lure of the Money Market Fund," *New York Times*, February 5, 1978; Kenneth T. Rosen and Larry Katz, "Money Market Mutual Funds: An Experiment in Ad Hoc Deregulation: A Note," *Journal of Finance* 38, no. 5 (June 1983): 1011, 1016; Jennifer S. Taub, "What We Don't Talk about When We Talk about Banking," in the *Oxford Handbook of the Political Economy of Financial Crises*, ed. Gerald Epstein and Martin Wolfson (New York: Oxford University Press, 2013), 455: for example, money market funds purchased short-term debt issued by the U.S. government. They also purchased short-term debt issued by businesses, known as commercial paper—an unsecured promissory note (an IOU) with a maturity of no more than 270 days, but often 30 days.

10. William A. Birdthistle, "Breaking Bucks in Money Market Funds," *Wisconsin Law Review* (2010): 1155, 1160, 1195; Jonathan Macey, "Reducing Sys-

temic Risk: The Role of Money Market Mutual Funds as Substitutes for Federal Insured Bank Deposits," Yale Law School Faculty Scholarship Series, 2011, p. 11; Jerry Markham, *A Financial History of the United States* (Armonk, NY: M. E. Sharpe, 2002), 6; Sylvia Porter, "Money Market Funds Are Blossoming," *Evening News*, September 3, 1974.

11. Greider, *Secrets of the Temple*, 395.

12. John A. Muth, "Rational Expectations and the Theory of Price Movements," *Econometrica* 29, no. 6 (1961): 315–335; William L. Silber, *Volcker: The Triumph of Persistence* (New York: Bloomsbury Press, 2012), 134–135; Transcript of Press Conference with Paul A. Volcker, pp. 8, 13; Treaster, *Making of a Financial Legend*, 159.

13. Board of Governors, *Federal Reserve System*, 42.

14. Ibid., 27–28.

15. Ibid., 16–17; M. A. Akhtar, *Understanding Open Market Operations* (Public Information Department, Federal Reserve Bank of New York, 1997), 2; R. W. Hafer, "The Prime Rate and the Cost of Funds: Is the Prime Rate Too High?" *Federal Reserve Bank of St. Louis Review* (May 1983): 17, 19.

16. Timothy A. Canova, "The Transformation of U.S. Banking and Finance: From Regulated Competition to Free-Market Receivership," *Brooklyn Law Review* 60, no. 4 (Winter 1995): 1311–1312; Akhtar, *Understanding Open Market Operations*, 7, 14; According to the Federal Reserve release dated October 11, 1979, the increase in reserve requirements was the imposition of a marginal reserve requirement on "managed liabilities." These included certain time deposits and repurchase agreements, for example, the part of the money supply the Fed was particularly focused on was known as M1. M1 was calculated by adding together the amount of paper and metal currency in circulation, the amount of money in all checking (and other transactional) accounts, and the nonborrowed amount banks kept on reserve at the Fed; Transcript of Press Conference with Paul A. Volcker, p. 10; Leonard Silk, "Fed Tries Way of Monetarists," *New York Times*, October 10, 1979; Stephen H. Axilrod, *Inside the Fed: Monetary Policy and Its Management, Martin through Greenspan to Bernanke* (Cambridge, MA: MIT Press, 2009), chap. 5.

17. Lindsey, Orphanides, and Rasche, "Reform of 1979"; Axilrod, *Inside the Fed.*

18. Treaster, *Making of a Financial Legend*, 159; Conduct of Monetary Policy Hearing Transcript, U.S. House of Representatives, Committee on Banking, Finance and Urban Affairs, July 14, 1981, p. 171; Silber, *Volcker: The Triumph of Persistence*, 111–112.

19. Axilrod, *Inside the Fed*, chap. 5; Federal Reserve, Selected Interest Rates–H.15; Bureau of Labor Statistics, Labor Force Statistics from Current Population Survey.

20. Freddie Mac, "30-Year-Fixed Rate Mortgages Since 1971": shown with 1.1 points in 1977 and 2.3 points in 1981, available at http://www.freddiemac.com/pmms/pmms30.htm.

21. Federal Reserve Act, 12 U.S.C. § 225a; Aaron Steelman, "The Federal Reserve's 'Dual Mandate': The Evolution of an Idea," Federal Reserve Bank of

Richmond, *Economic Brief*, December 2011, 3, available at http://www.richmondfed.org/publications/research/economic_brief/2011/pdf/eb_11-12.pdf; Bureau of Labor Statistics, Labor Force Statistics from Current Population Survey.

22. Christina Romer, "Dear Ben: It's Time for Your Volcker Moment," *New York Times*, October 29, 2011; "Statement by Paul A. Volcker, Chairman, Board of Governors of the Federal Reserve System before the Committee on Banking, Finance and Urban Affairs, House of Representatives, July 21, 1981, available at http://fraser.stlouisfed.org/docs/historical/volcker/Volcker_19810721.pdf; Judith Stein, *Pivotal Decade: How the United States Traded Factories for Finance in the Seventies* (New Haven, CT: Yale University Press, 2011), 231.

23. Conduct of Monetary Policy Hearing Transcript, p. 212: Representative Gonzales mentions that Chairman Volcker indicated that the standards of living of some Americans would have to be sacrificed; James M. Bickley, "Chrysler Corporation Loan Guarantee Act of 1979: Background, Provisions, and Cost," Congressional Research Service, 2008.

24. M. Manfred Fabritius and William Borges, *Saving the Savings and Loan: The U.S. Thrift Industry and the Texas Experience, 1950–1988* (New York: Praeger, 1989), 1; "Monetary Policy and Open Market Operations in 1979," *Federal Reserve Bank of New York Quarterly Review* 5 (Summer 1980), available at http://www.newyorkfed.org/research/quarterly_review/1980v5/v5n2article7.pdf; Mortgage-X Information Service, "Prime Rate: Historical Data," available at http://mortgage-x.com/general/indexes/prime.asp.

25. R. Dan Brumbaugh, *Thrifts under Siege: Restoring Order to American Banking* (Cambridge, MA: Ballinger, 1988), table 1-1; Birdthistle, "Breaking Bucks," 1170; Federal Reserve Bank of Richmond, *Instruments of the Money Market*, chap. 4: "Large Negotiable Certificates of Deposit," 1998; Bill Doyle, "Switch to Money Market Fund," *Miami News*, March 7, 1980; "Report of the Money Market Working Group: Submitted to the Board of Governors of the Investment Company Institute," March 17, 2009, 1, 18, available at http://www.ici.org/pdf/ppr_09_mmwg.pdf.

26. Carl Felsenfeld, "Savings and Loan Crisis," *Fordham Law Review* 59, no. 6 (1991): S15.

Chapter 5. Deregulation Inauguration

1. January 20, 1981, video available on C-SPAN archives, available at http://www.youtube.com/watch?v=hpPt7xGx4Xo.

2. Paul Muolo and Matthew Padilla, *Chain of Blame: How Wall Street Caused the Mortgage and Credit Crisis* (Hoboken, NJ: Wiley, 2010), 55; William K. Black, *The Best Way to Rob a Bank Is to Own One: How Corporate Executives and Politicians Looted the S&L Industry* (Austin: University of Texas Press, 2005), 43; Hearing before the Subcommittee on Financial Institutions and Consumer Affairs of the Committee on Banking, Housing, and Urban Affairs, U.S. Senate, on "The Brokered Deposits Market Concerning the

Benefits and Abuses to the Economy, the Consumer, and the Federal Insurance System," June 5, 1985, pp. 3–6, 48: $24 billion in brokered deposits with "bulk of funds" from Merrill Lynch and Dean Witter; Dan Skidmore, "Regan Says Reagan's Policies Delayed S&Ls' Worst Troubles," Associated Press, October 1, 1990.

3. Pub. L. No. 96-221, 94 stat. 132 (1980).

4. Federal Deposit Insurance Corporation, "Banking Legislation and Regulation," chapter 2 of *An Examination of the Banking Crisis of the 1980s and Early 1990s*, 93: The $100,000 limit was put into the bill "at a late-night House-Senate conference"; chapter available at http://www.fdic.gov/bank/historical/history/87_136.pdf and volume available at http://www.fdic.gov/bank/historical/history/; Carl Felsenfeld, "Savings and Loan Crisis," *Fordham Law Review* 59, no. 6 (1991): S14, S20, S23, S41, S51; David L. Mason, *From Buildings and Loans to Bail-Outs: A History of the American Savings and Loan Industry, 1883–1995* (New York: Cambridge University Press, 2004), 216; Lawrence J. White, *The S&L Debacle: Public Policy Lessons for Bank and Thrift Regulation* (New York: Oxford University Press, 1991), 72–73; Federal Deposit Insurance Corporation, "The Savings and Loan Crisis and Its Relationship to Banking," 175, available at http://www.fdic.gov/bank/historical/history/167_188.pdf; 45 Fed. Reg. 76,111 (1980).

5. Federal Deposit Insurance Corporation, "The Savings and Loan Crisis," 176, 180.

6. M. Manfred Fabritius and William Borges, *Saving the Savings and Loan: The U.S. Thrift Industry and the Texas Experience, 1950–1988* (New York: Praeger, 1989), 3, 95.

7. Marquette National Bank v. First of Omaha Service Corp., 439 U.S. 299 (1978); National Bank Act, Rev. Stat. § 5197, as amended, 12 U.S.C. § 5; Federal Deposit Insurance Corporation, "The S&L Crisis: A Chrono-Bibliography," 2002, available at http://www.fdic.gov/bank/historical/s&l/, citing Financial Institutions Regulatory and Interest Rate Control Act of 1978; Federal Deposit Insurance Corporation, "Savings and Loan Crisis," 179, figure 4.1; Joseph Sanchez, "The Death of Usury, the Democratization of Credit and the Financial Well Being of the American Consumer," March 27, 2011, 4–5.

8. Patricia A. McCoy and Elizabeth Renuart, "The Legal Infrastructure of Subprime and Nontraditional Home Mortgages," in *Borrowing to Live: Consumer and Mortgage Credit Revisited*, ed. Nicolas P. Retsinas and Eric S. Belsky (Joint Center for Housing Studies, Harvard University, James A. Johnson Metro Series, Brookings Institution Press, November 2008), 7, fn. 28; Donna Vandenbrink, "Usury Ceilings and DIDMCA," Chicago Federal Reserve Bank, 1985, pp. 25–26, available at https://chicagofed.org/digital_assets/publications/economic_perspectives/1985/ep_sep_oct1985_part4_vandenbrink.pdf; Robin Stein, "The Ascendency of the Credit Card Industry," *Frontline*, available at http://www.pbs.org/wgbh/pages/frontline/shows/credit/more/rise.html.

9. Stephen P. Pizzo, Mary Fricker, and Paul Muolo, *Inside Job: The Looting of America's Savings and Loans* (New York: McGraw-Hill, 1989), 19; Federal Deposit Insurance Corporation, "S&L Crisis"; Kitty Calavita, Henry N. Pontell, and Robert H. Tillman, *Big Money Crime: Fraud and*

Politics in the Savings and Loan Crisis (Berkeley: University of California Press, 1997), 12.

10. Federal Deposit Insurance Corporation, "The Savings and Loan Crisis," 173.

11. Black, *Best Way to Rob a Bank*, 5, 19; Carl Felsenfeld, "Savings and Loan Crisis," *Fordham Law Review* 59, no. 6 (1991): S20; Lawrence J. White, *The S&L Debacle: Public Policy Lessons for Bank and Thrift Regulation* (New York: Oxford University Press, 1991), 43, 77; Federal Deposit Insurance Corporation, "Savings and Loan Crisis"; Stanley M. Gorinson and Glenn B. Manishin, "Garn-St. Germain: A Harbinger of Change," *Washington and Lee Law Review* 40, no. 4 (1983); Kenneth E. Scott, "Never Again: The S&L Bailout Bill," *Business Lawyer* 45 (June 1990): 1883–1889: industry insolvent by $110 billion by end of 1981.

12. Martin Mayer, *The Greatest-Ever Bank Robbery: The Collapse of the Savings and Loan Industry* (New York: Charles Scribner's Sons, 1990), 23; Black, *Best Way to Rob a Bank*, 19; Skidmore, "Regan Says": "Pratt said he was rejected by Congress and the Reagan administration in his attempts to get money to pay for more S&L examiners. [Don] Regan, he said, would not take his calls."

13. Black, *Best Way to Rob a Bank*, 19; Bruce Bartlett, "Reagan's Tax Increases," *Capital Gains and Games*, April 6, 2010.

14. Joe Peek, "A Call to ARMs: Adjustable Rate Mortgages in the 1980s," *New England Economic Review* (March/April 1990): 4; Judith Miller, "Jay Janis and the 'Unshackling' of the Thrift Industry," *New York Times*, April 13, 1980; Adam J. Levitin and Susan M. Wachter, "The Public Option in Housing Finance," Georgetown Public Law Research Paper No. 1966550, November 28, 2012, pp. 40, 87; M. Manfred Fabritius and William Borges, *Saving the Savings and Loan: The U.S. Thrift Industry and the Texas Experience, 1950–1988* (New York: Praeger, 1989), 89; Testimony of Jay Janis before the Committee on Banking, Housing and Urban Affairs of the U.S. Senate, August 3, 1988, p. 5.

15. Richard D. Bingham, *Industrial Policy American Style: From Hamilton to HDTV* (Armonk, NY: M. E. Sharpe, 1998), 58; Mayer, *Greatest-Ever Bank Robbery*, 65; Federal Deposit Insurance Corporation, "Savings and Loan Crisis," 173.

16. Federal Deposit Insurance Corporation, "The Savings and Loan Crisis," 175.

17. Ibid., 173–174: RAP was permitted, but GAAP was used where it was more lenient; Steven F. Cahan and Eric N. Johnson, "Were S&L Financial Statements Misleading? Some Evidence and Policy Prescriptions," *Journal of Applied Business Research* 9, no. 1 (2011): 1–9; Michael A. Robinson, *Overdrawn: The Bailout of American* Savings (New York: Penguin Books, 1990), 40; Richard C. Breeden, "Thumbs on the Scale: The Role That Accounting Practices Played in the Savings and Loan Crisis," *Fordham Law Review* 59, no. 6 (1991): S77–S79; 47 Fed. Reg. 52,961, 52,962 (1982) and 47 Fed. Reg. 3543 (1982); Robert J. Laughlin, "Causes of the Savings and Loan Debacle," *Fordham Law Review* 59, no. 6 (1991): S13; Mayer, *Greatest-Ever Bank Robbery*, 67.

18. Mason, *From Buildings and Loans to Bail-Outs*, 222; Federal Deposit Insurance Corporation, "Savings and Loan Crisis," 174; Jerry Markham, *A Financial History of the United States* (Armonk, NY: M. E. Sharpe, 2002), 183; Laughlin, "Causes of the Savings and Loan Debacle," S312; Breeden, "Thumbs on the Scale," S78.

19. Michael Lewis, *Liar's Poker* (New York: W. W. Norton, 1989), 104–105.

20. Lewis S. Ranieri, "The Origins of Securitization, Sources of Its Growth, and Its Future Potential," in *A Primer on Securitization*, ed. Leon T. Kendall and Michael J. Fishman (Cambridge, MA: MIT Press, 1996), 33.

21. Fabritius and Borges, *Saving the Savings and Loan*, 4; Calavita, Pontell, and Tillman, *Big Money Crime*, 11–12; Michael M. Thomas, "The Greatest American Shambles," *New York Review of Books*, January 31, 1991.

22. 47 Fed. Reg. 58,220 (1982); Federal Deposit Insurance Corporation, "Savings and Loan Crisis," 175; Arthur E. Wilmarth Jr., "The Expansion of State Powers, the Federal Response, and the Case for Preserving the Dual Banking System," *Fordham Law Review* 58, no. 6 (1990): 1133, 1171, 1328; Laughlin, "Causes of the Savings and Loan Debacle," S314; Fabritius and Borges, *Saving the Savings and Loan*, 94; Jean Wells, "P.L. 97-320, Garn-St. Germain Depository Institutions Act of 1982: A Brief Explanation," Congressional Research Service, November 1982, CRS5–CRS7.

23. Patricia A. McCoy, Andrew D. Pavlov, and Susan M. Wachter, "Systemic Risk through Securitization: The Result of Deregulation and Regulatory Failure," *University of Connecticut Law Review* 41 (2009): 493, 499; Gorinson and Manishin, "Garn-St. Germain: A Harbinger of Change," 1313; Matthew Sherman, "A Short History of Financial Deregulation in the United States," Center for Economic and Policy Research, July 2009, p. 12.

24. Lei Ding, Carolina Katz Reid, Roberto G. Quercia, and Alan M. White, "The Impact of Federal Pre-emption of State Anti-Predatory Lending Laws on the Foreclosure Crisis," *Journal of Policy Analysis and Management* 31, no. 2 (Spring 2012): 367–387; Cathy Lesser Mansfield, "The Road to Subprime 'HEL' Was Paved with Good Congressional Intentions," *South Carolina Law Review* 51 (2000): 473.

25. Muolo and Pedillo, *Chain of Blame*, 53; Connie Bruck, *Predators' Ball: The Inside Story of Drexel Burnham and the Rise of the Junk Bond Raiders* (New York: Penguin, 1989); Kurt Eichenwald, "Milken Set to Pay a $600 Million Fine in Wall St. Fraud," *New York Times*, April 21, 1990.

26. James Bates, "Drexel's Junk Network: U.S. Says the Firm Had Some Local S&Ls on Very Sweet Strings," *Los Angeles Times*, November 16, 1990; Muolo and Pedillo, *Chain of Blame*, 54; Black, *Best Way to Rob a Bank*, 36.

27. SEC Commissioner James C. Treadway Jr., "The Integration of Securities and Banking Activities in the United States," July 29, 1984, available at http://www.sec.gov/news/speech/1984/072984treadway.pdf.

28. Black, *Best Way to Rob a Bank*, 32–33.

29. Ranieri, "Origins of Securitization," 32, 34–35.

30. Division of Investment Management Report, U.S. Securities & Exchange Commission, "The Treatment of Structured Finance under the Investment Company Act," in *Protecting Investors: A Half Century of Investment Company Regulation*, May 1992, 8; Lewis, *Liar's Poker*, 136; Ranieri, "Origins of Securitization," 37; Bethany McLean and Joe Nocera, *All the Devils Are Here: The Hidden History of the Financial Crisis* (New York: Portfolio/Penguin, 2010), 13; Mayer, *Greatest-Ever Bank Robbery*, 42.

31. David J. Bleckner, "Section 106 of the Secondary Mortgage Market Enhancement Act of 1984 and the Need for Overriding State Legislation," *Fordham Urban Law Journal* 13, no. 3 (1984): 681, 691–697.

32. McLean and Nocera, *All the Devils Are Here*, 13–14.

33. Marita Hernandez, "Veteran Convicted in Bank of America Scam," *Los Angeles Times*, June 9, 1990; John M. Broder, "Tangled Anatomy of Massive Fraud Case," *Los Angeles Times*, April 17, 1985; Thomas C. Hayes, "Fraud Is Denied in Mortgage Scheme," *New York Times*, February 5, 1985; Ranieri, "Origins of Securitization," 37; Laurence D. Fink, "The Role of Pension Funds and Other Investors in Securitized Debt Markets," in *A Primer on Securitization*, ed. Leon T. Kendall and Michael J. Fishman (Cambridge, MA: MIT Press, 1996), 117, 119; McLean and Nocera, *All the Devils Are Here*, 14; Bleckner, "Section 106," 699–701.

34. Ranieri, "Origins of Securitization," 37–38; McLean and Nocera, *All the Devils Are Here*, 15; Lewis, *Liar's Poker*, 100–101.

35. Fink, "Role of Pension Funds," 118; Robert A. Bennett, "Savings Institutions Are Healthier but Now Face Further Challenges," *New York Times*, December 30, 1982.

36. Nathaniel C. Nash, "Three Views: The Trouble Savings and Loan Associations," *New York Times*, September 25, 1988; Mayer, *Greatest-Ever Bank Robbery*, 61; William K. Black, "Why Was the S&L Crisis Not a Systemic Economic Crisis?" *Global Economic Intersection*, September 8, 2011, available at http://econintersect.com/wordpress/?p=12970; William K. Black, "If Obama Thinks the Response to the S&L Debacle Failed, Why Is He Adopting It?" *Huffington Post*, November 1, 2010; "How Pratt Has Helped Thrift Units," *New York Times*, Editorial, January 1, 1983.

Chapter 6. The Red Baron of Finance

1. Floyd Norris, "The Red Baron of Finance Is Going to Jail," *New York Times*, December 19, 1993; Michael A. Robinson, *Overdrawn: The Bailout of American Savings* (New York: Penguin Books, 1990), 17–20; John Brecher with Peter McAlevey, "Charles Knapp: The Real-Life Cash McCall," *Newsweek*, September 5, 1983, 58; Roger Gillott, "Charles Knapp: Former FCA Head in Merger Game," Associated Press, July 9, 1985; Fred R. Bleakley, "A Fast-Paced Chairman Comes to an Abrupt Halt," *New York Times*, August 29, 1984.

2. Robinson, *Overdrawn*, 19–20; Nick Vaccariello and Dave Smith, "Hollywood Executive Pretends to Be Dead, Thwarts Kidnapers," *Los Angeles Times*, August 11, 1971.

3. Vaccariello and Smith, "Hollywood Executive Pretends to Be Dead"; M. J. Stephey, "A Brief History of: Credit Cards," *Time*, April 23, 2009; *SEC News Digest*, June 19, 1973, available at http://www.sec.gov/news/digest/1973/dig061973.pdf; Securities & Exchange Commission *News Digest*, May 19, 1969, available at http://www.sec.gov/news/digest/1969/dig051969.pdf.

4. John Getze, "Traditional Rivals—Bank, S&L—Move Under 1 Roof," *Los Angeles Times*, August 19, 1976.

5. William Cary, "Federalism and Corporate Law: Reflections Upon Delaware," *Yale Law Journal* 83 (1974); The 39th Annual Report of the Securities & Exchange Commission for the Fiscal Year Ended June 30th 1973; Thomas L. Hazen, "A Look Beyond the Pruning of Rule 10b-5; Implied Remedies and Section 17(a) of the Securities Act of 1933," *Virginia Law Review* 64, no. 5 (June 1978): 645–646; Basic v. Levinson 485 U.S. 224 (1988).

6. Robinson, *Overdrawn*, 20; Martin E. Lowy, *High Rollers: Inside the Savings and Loan Debacle* (New York: Praeger, 1991), 95; Martin Mayer, *The Greatest-Ever Bank Robbery: The Collapse of the Savings and Loan Industry* (New York: Charles Scribner's Sons, 1990), 104.

7. Stephen P. Pizzo, Mary Fricker, and Paul Muolo, *Inside Job: The Looting of America's Savings and Loans* (New York: McGraw-Hill, 1989), 178; Mayer, *Greatest-Ever Bank Robbery*, 104–105; Robinson, *Overdrawn*, 20, 24–25; Thomka v. Financial Corp., 15 Cal. App. 4th 877 (1993): Thomka was hired in 1983 and said in 1987 he was fired after refusing to engage in misleading practices; Brecher with McAlevey, "Charles Knapp"; Pamela G. Hollie, "Thrift Unit Thrives as Maverick-Cost Savings Concern Leads U.S. in Growth," *New York Times*, November 3, 1980.

8. Robinson, *Overdrawn*, 24–25; Brecher with McAlevey, "Charles Knapp," 58; Mayer, *Greatest-Ever Bank Robbery*, 105–106.

9. Robinson, *Overdrawn*, 25–26.

10. Ibid., 21, 26–27.

11. Mayer, *Greatest-Ever Bank Robbery*, 106.

12. Robinson, *Overdrawn*, 27.

13. Ibid.; Bleakley, "A Fast-Paced Chairman."

14. Statement of Financial Accounting Standards No. 91, issued December 1986; Eric N. Berg, "Savings Industry Upset by Accounting Proposal," *New York Times*, July 17, 1986: FASB in 1986 proposed that thrifts should recognize origination fees over the life of the loans; Paul M. Clikerman, *Called to Account: Fourteen Financial Frauds That Shaped the Accounting Profession* (New York: Routledge, 2008); Robinson, *Overdrawn*, 30: This game would resemble one played with higher stakes by American International Group (AIG) some twenty years later, taking in premiums for credit "insurance" but not setting aside sufficient reserves should a loss event trigger an obligation to make payments. Congressional Oversight Panel, "June Oversight Report: The AIG Rescue, Its Impact on Markets, and the Government's Exit Strategy," June 10, 2010.

15. Mayer, *Greatest-Ever Bank Robbery*, 108.

16. Robinson, *Overdrawn*, 29–31, 71; Mayer, *Greatest-Ever Bank Robbery*, 108.

17. Robinson, *Overdrawn*, 30–32.

18. Ibid., 46–47; SEC Commissioner James C. Treadway Jr., Remarks to Sixteenth Annual Securities Regulation Seminar, "The Commissions Enforcement Program and the Integrity of Financial Statements," November 3, 1983, 4–5.

19. Robinson, *Overdrawn*, 22, 53; Mayer, *Greatest-Ever Bank Robbery*, 46, 109; Thomas C. Hayes, "Financial Seeks First Charter," *New York Times*, January 12, 1983.

20. Brecher with McAlevey, "Charles Knapp"; Robinson, *Overdrawn*, 54–55, 71–72, 82; Mayer, *Greatest-Ever Bank Robbery*, 104, 112.

21. Robinson, *Overdrawn*, 62–63.

22. Ibid., 68.

23. Ibid.

24. Ibid., 68–69; In re Financial Corporation of America, 796 F.2d 1126 (9th Cir. 1986): court detailed Andersen advice in light most favorable to nonmoving party, however as it was not in connection with the purchase or sale of a security, the 9th Circuit affirmed dismissal of the 10(b) claim.

25. Russ Roberts, host of *Econtalk*, "William Black on Financial Fraud," January 24, 2012.

26. Brecher, "Charles Knapp"; Susan Deutsch, "Once a White-Knuckled Flier, Brooke Knapp Has Conquered Her Fear—and a World Record," *People*, April 25, 1983.

27. Robinson, *Overdrawn*, 91.

28. Gary H. Stern and Ron J. Feldman, *Too Big to Fail: The Hazards of Bank Bailouts* (Washington, DC: Brookings, 2004), 13; GAO Staff Study, Financial Crisis Management: Four Financial Crises in the 1980s, May 1997; Federal Deposit Insurance Corporation, "Continental Illinois and 'Too Big to Fail,'" 236–237, available at http://www.fdic.gov/bank/historical/history/235_258.pdf; Richard J. Herring, "The Collapse of Continental Illinois National Bank and Trust Company: The Implications for Risk Management and Regulation," Case Study, Wharton Financial Institutions Center, available at http://fic.wharton.upenn.edu/fic/case%20studies/continental%20full.pdf.

29. Robinson, *Overdrawn*, 86; Herring, "Collapse of Continental Illinois"; William Greider, *Secrets of the Temple: How the Federal Reserve Runs the Country* (New York: Simon & Schuster, 1987), 525, 627, 629; William Isaac, *Senseless Panic: How Washington Failed America* (Hoboken, NJ: Wiley, 2010), 65–85; Nathaniel C. Nash, "Continental's $4.5 Billion Rescue," *New York Times*, July 29, 1984.

30. Federal Deposit Insurance Corporation, "Continental Illinois," 246; Greider, *Secrets of the Temple*, 524–525; U.S. Congress, House Committee on Banking, Finance, and Urban Affairs, Inquiry into Continental Illinois Corp. and Continental Illinois National Bank: Hearings before the Subcommittee on Financial Institutions Supervision, Regulation, and Insurance of the Committee on Banking, Finance, and Urban Affairs, House of Representatives, Ninety-eighth Congress, Second Session, September 18 and 19 and October 4,

1984, p. 212 (hereinafter "Continental Hearing Transcript"), available at http://fraser.stlouisfed.org/publication/?pid=745.

31. Continental Hearing Transcript, p. 300; Stern and Feldman, *Too Big to Fail*, 13.

32. William Safire, "Too Big to Fail or to Bailout," *New York Times*, April 6, 2008: The expression was also previously employed in 1975 both in connection with the 1971 bailout of Lockheed Martin and the expected financial rescue of New York City; Robinson, *Overdrawn*, 91, 93.

33. Robinson, *Overdrawn*, 91, 216; Mayer, *Greatest-Ever Bank Robbery*, 111.

34. Author's telephone interview with Bart Dzivi, September 19, 2011; Robinson, *Overdrawn*, 98; "A Red Face for the Red Baron," *Time*, August 27, 1984.

35. Robinson, *Overdrawn*, 86, 95–97; Vartanig G. Vartan, "A Rough Time at Thrift Units," *New York Times*, August 20, 1984; Martin H. Wolfson, *Financial Crises: Understanding the Postwar U.S. Experience* (Armonk, NY: M. E. Sharpe, 1994), 101.

36. Bleakley, "A Fast-Paced Chairman"; Robinson, *Overdrawn*, 99.

37. Robinson, *Overdrawn*, 107; Thomas C. Hayes, "Financial Corp.'s Climb Back," *New York Times*, October 9, 1985.

38. Ibid., 107, 110–111, 140; "FCA Deposits Up More Than $2 Billion in 4th Quarter," Associated Press, January 17, 1985.

39. Fed. Reg. 50,339 (November 1, 1983); Mayer, *Greatest-Ever Bank Robbery*, 119; James Bates and James S. Graneli, "Taggart Ties to Failed Texas S&L Questioned by House Committee," *Los Angeles Times*, November 8, 1989; Federal Deposit Insurance Corporation, "The S&L Crisis: A Chrono-Bibliography," 2002, available at http://www.fdic.gov/bank/historical/s&l/.

40. FAIC Securities, Inc. et al. v. United States, 768 F2d 252 (D.C. Cir. 1985); Isaac, *Senseless Panic*, 56–57, 60; Mayer, *Greatest-Ever Bank Robbery*, 119, 126; Wolfson, *Financial Crises*, 101; Robinson, *Overdrawn*, 185; Lawrence G. Baxter, "Judicial Responses to the Recent Enforcement Activities of the Federal Banking Regulators," *Fordham Law Review* 59, no. 6/8 (1991): S193; Lawrence J. White, *The S&L Debacle: Public Policy Lessons for Bank and Thrift Regulation* (New York: Oxford University Press, 1991), 137–139.

41. In July 2004, the Government Accounting Office was renamed the Government Accountability Office. White, *The S&L Debacle*, 135; "Bigger F.S.L.I.C. Loss Seen," *New York Times*, April 18, 1988: "doubling of the $6 billion deficit in 1986 to near $12 billion was a possibility"; William K. Black, *The Best Way to Rob a Bank Is to Own One: How Corporate Executives and Politicians Looted the S&L Industry* (Austin: University of Texas Press, 2005), 91, 94–95; Robinson, *Overdrawn*, 232–233; Mayer, *Greatest-Ever Bank Robbery*, 152, 158.

42. Mayer, *Greatest-Ever Bank Robbery*, 32.

43. Ibid., 112–113; White, *The S&L Debacle*, 140, 179; Black, *Best Way to Rob a Bank*, 169–173; Federal Deposit Insurance Corporation, "S&L Crisis"; Federal Deposit Insurance Corporation, "Savings and Loan Crisis and Its Relationship to Banking," 186, available at http://www.fdic.gov/bank

/historical/history/167_188.pdf; Nathaniel C. Nash, "Ex-Regulator Tells of Pressures by Senators," *New York Times*, November 8, 1989; T. Clark, Bryan M. Murtagh, and Carole Corcoran, "Regulation of Savings Associations under the Financial Institutions Reform, Recovery, and Enforcement Act of 1989," *Business Lawyer* 45 (1990): 1014: Additionally, under the CEBA, S&Ls were required to devote 60 percent of assets to housing-related investors; "FSLIC Bailout OK'd, Senate Approval Sends Bill to the President," United Press International, August 5, 1987.

44. Robinson, *Overdrawn*, 157, 217–220.

45. Ibid., 195–196, 204, 207, 214–215; Mayer, *The Greatest-Ever Bank Robbery*, 113–114, 240.

46. Ibid., 235–236; John Vaughan, "Federal Board Defends Exclusive Deal-Making," United Press International, September 6, 1988; Tom Furlong, "Despite Ongoing Woes, FCA's Chief Is Firmly in Charge," *Los Angeles Times*, February 8, 1988, available at http://articles.latimes.com/1988-02-08/business/fi-27905_1_american-savings/2; Mayer, *Greatest-Ever Bank Robbery*, 240; Black, *Best Way to Rob a Bank*, 183. The Chernobyl disaster was a catastrophic 1986 accident at a nuclear power plant in the Ukraine.

47. Furlong, "Despite Ongoing Woes."

48. Robinson, *Overdrawn*, 244, 246, 264–265; Associated Press, "Nation's Biggest S&L Asks $1.5 Billion Loan Bailout: American Losses Dive in Quarter," *Los Angeles Times*, January 27, 1988.

49. Nathaniel C. Nash, "2 Savings Bailouts Costing $7 Billion Confirmed by the U.S.," *New York Times*, December 29, 1988; Black, *Best Way to Rob a Bank*, 81–82, 181, 183.

50. David B. Hilder, "Financial Corporation of America Files for Chapter 11," *Wall Street Journal*, September 12, 1988; In re Financial Corporation of America, 119 B.R. 728 (Bkrtcy. C.D. Cal. 1990); Robinson, *Overdrawn*, 270–273; James S. Granelli, "Bankruptcy Court Approves Settlement with FCA Creditors," *Los Angeles Times*, October 27, 1994.

Chapter 7. The Bailout

1. "The Sale of American Savings: The Buyer, the Sellers . . . : Robert M. Bass—Texan with a Low Profile, *Los Angeles Times*, September 6, 1988; Peter Applebome, "Texas Deal Maker: Robert M. Bass; A Younger Brother Steps Out on His Own," *New York Times*, June 5, 1988.

2. Applebome, "Texas Deal Maker;" John Paul Newport Jr. and Reporter Associate Rosalind Klein Berlin, "Keeping Up with the Basses," *Fortune*, October 10, 1988.

3. Michael A. Robinson, *Overdrawn: The Bailout of American Savings* (New York: Penguin Books, 1990), 267; James S. Granelli, "New Figures Rank Collapse of American S&L as Costliest Ever," *Los Angeles Times*, May 20, 1994; Nathaniel C. Nash, "Talking Deals: The Bass Profits in Savings Bailouts," *New York Times*, March 1, 1990; S. C. Gwynne, "Help Your Country and Help Yourself," *Time*, February 20, 1989; Applebome, "Texas Deal Maker."

4. Nathaniel C. Nash, "Financiers Sense an Opportunity in the Savings Industry's Distress," *New York Times*, January 1, 1989; John Vaughan, "Federal Board Defends Exclusive Deal-Making," United Press International, September 6, 1988.

5. "Failed S&L Cost Disputed," Associated Press, September 14, 1990; American Savings Bank, F.A. v. United States, 98 Fed. Cl. 291 (2011), 295–296.

6. Susan Schmidt, "Cost Soars for Deals Made on S&Ls in '88; House Panel Told Deals Are a 'Disaster,'" *Washington Post*, September 15, 1990; Nathaniel C. Nash, "Bank Board's Wild Weekend of Round-the-Clock Deals," *New York Times*, January 3, 1989; Larry Reibstein, Carolyn Friday, and Nonny Abbott, "The Smart Money in S&Ls; Bailouts Offer Fat Tax Breaks for Fat-Cat Investors," *Newsweek*, January 9, 1989; "American Savings and Loan for Sale," *New York Times*, May 21, 1994; "Failed S&L Cost Disputed."

7. Robinson, *Overdrawn*, 294.

8. Nash, "Talking Deals."

9. "Failed S&L Cost Disputed"; Larry Light, Mike McNamee, and Wendy Zellner, "Were These Deals Too Sweet to Last?" *Businessweek*, February 11, 1991; Nathaniel C. Nash, "Race to S&L Finish Line 'Was Like a Sprint,'" *Palm Beach Post*, January 8, 1989; Nathaniel C. Nash, "Financiers."

10. Nathaniel C. Nash, "2 Savings Bailouts Costing $7 Billion Confirmed by US," *New York Times*, December 29, 1988.

11. Robert D. Hershey Jr., "Bush Signs Savings Legislation: Remaking of Industry Starts Fast," *New York Times*, August 10, 1989; T. Clark, Bryan M. Murtagh, and Carole Corcoran, "Regulation of Savings Associations under the Financial Institutions Reform, Recovery, and Enforcement Act of 1989," *Business Lawyer* 45 (1990): 1015; Pub. L. No. 101-73, 103 Stat. 183 (1989).

12. Timothy Curry and Lynn Shibut, "The Cost of the Savings and Loan Crisis: Truth and Consequences," *FDIC Banking Review* 13, no. 2 (December 2000): 28; available at http://www.fdic.gov/bank/analytical/banking/2000dec/brv13n2_2.pdf; Michael Jungman, "The Contributions of the Resolution Trust Corporation to the Securitization Process," in *A Primer on Securitization*, ed. Leon T. Kendall and Michael J. Fishman (Cambridge, MA: MIT Press, 1996), 69.

13. "Excerpts of Statement by the Senate Ethics Panel," *New York Times*, Febuary 28, 1991; Richard L. Burke, "Ethics Unit Singles Out Cranston, Chides Others in S&L Inquiry," *New York Times*, February 28, 1991; Nathaniel Nash, "Showdown Time for Danny Wall," *New York Times*, July 9, 1989.

14. E. Scott Reckard, "Federal Judge Overturns Charles Keating Conviction," Associated Press, April 3, 1996; E. Scott Reckard and David Rosenzweig, "Keating Pleads Guilty to Fraud: Legal Saga Ends," *Los Angeles Times*, April 17, 1999: "Keating pleaded guilty to four counts of bankruptcy and wire fraud, admitting that he siphoned $975,000 from his financial empire as it careened toward insolvency in 1989"; Jerry Knight, "Regulator's Role at SL under Fire," *Washington Post*, November 1, 1989; Patrick J. Sloyan, "Bank Board Probed: U.S. Investigating Reagan Aides on the Thrift Crackdown Delay," *Newsday*, June 15, 1990; Louise Story and Gretchen Morgenson,

"Financial Finger-Pointing Turns to Regulators," *New York Times*, November 22, 2011; Michael M. Phillips and Jessica Holzer, "Regulator Let IndyMac Backdate Infusion," *Wall Street Journal*, December 23, 2008; Ellen Nakashima and Binyamin Appelbaum, "Regulator Let IndyMac Bank Falsify Report, Agency Didn't Enforce Its Rules, Inquiry Finds," *Washington Post*, December 23, 2008; Nash, "Showdown Time for Danny Wall"; Christian Berthelsen, "Keating Pleads Guilty to 4 Counts of Fraud," *New York Times*, April 7, 1999; William K. Black, *The Best Way to Rob a Bank Is to Own One: How Corporate Executives and Politicians Looted the S&L Industry* (Austin: University of Texas Press, 2005), 81.

15. Bob Woodward, *Maestro: Greenspan's Fed and the American Boom* (New York: Simon & Schuster, 2000), 65–66; Martin Mayer, *The Greatest-Ever Bank Robbery: The Collapse of the Savings and Loan Industry* (New York: Charles Scribner's Sons, 1990), Appendix C, 324–326.

16. Kenneth E. Scott, "Never Again: The S&L Bailout Bill," *Business Lawyer* 45 (June 1990): 1884; Paul Muolo and Matthew Pedillo, *Chain of Blame: How Wall Street Caused the Mortgage and Credit Crisis* (New York: Wiley, 2010), 75.

17. Steve Stecklow, "S&L Defrauder Qualifies to Buy House from U.S. Bailout Agency," *Seattle Times*, November 27, 1992; "Another 38 Savings Units Taken Over," Associated Press, April 9, 1989; "United Savings Enters the Vital Dallas/Fort Worth Market with the Acquisition of Murray Federal Savings' Deposits and Locations," PR Newswire, June 11, 1990; David La Gesse, "Murray Savings Chairman Is Resigning," *Dallas Morning News*, July 12, 1989; In the Matter of Jack Crozier, a Former Officer and Director of Murray Savings and Loan Association of Dallas Stipulation and Consent to Issuance of Order of Prohibition, November 23, 1990.

18. American Savings Bank F.A. v. United States 519 F.3d 1316 (5th Cir. 2008); Nathaniel C. Nash, "Two Savings Bailouts Costing $7 Billion Confirmed by U.S.," *New York Times*, December 29, 1988; Thomas C. Hayes, "Fast Texas Profits Seen by NCNB," *New York Times*, August 1, 1988; "FDIC Expects Reviving S&Ls to Cost $50 Billion," Associated Press, August 4, 1988.

19. Michael W. Hudson, *The Monster: How a Gang of Predatory Lenders and Wall Street Bankers Fleeced America and Spawned a Global Crisis* (New York: Times Books, 2010), 40; Kitty Calavita, Henry N. Pontell, and Robert H. Tillman, *Big Money Crime: Fraud and Politics in the Savings and Loan Crisis* (Los Angeles: University of California Press, 1997), 144, 166–168; Stephen P. Pizzo, Mary Fricker, and Paul Muolo, *Inside Job: The Looting of America's Savings and Loans* (New York: McGraw-Hill, 1989), 329; Tom Furlong, "Charles Knapp: Once a Money King, Now a 'Business Leper,'" *Los Angeles Times*, June 9, 1990; Michael A. Hiltzik, "Boesky Begins His Life as a Prisoner in Lompoc, Calif.," *Los Angeles Times*, March 24, 1988; Mike Downey, "For Inmate 04302-112, Team Now Costs 2 Cups of Soup," *Los Angeles Times*, September 16, 1997; James B. Stewart, *Den of Thieves* (New York: Simon & Schuster, 1991), 67; "Boesky Secretly Taped Milken Talks: Discussions Held before Speculator Was Named as Informant," Associated Press, September 29, 1989; James F. Peltz, "Knapp Gets 6-1/2 Years for S&L Fraud," *Los Angeles Times*, December 15, 1993; Thomas S. Mulligan, "L.A. Financier is Resentenced in Arizona Fraud Case," *Los Angeles Times*, June 11, 1996.

20. Mayer, *Greatest-Ever Bank Robbery*, 61; Prepared statement of William K. Black before a hearing of the Senate Committee of the Judiciary, "Examining Lending Discrimination Practices and Foreclosure Abuses," March 7, 2012; Woodward, *Maestro*, 65.

21. Lawrence J. White, *The S&L Debacle: Public Policy Lessons for Bank and Thrift Regulation* (New York: Oxford University Press, 1991), 197; Timothy Curry and Lynn Shibut, "The Cost of the Savings and Loan Crisis," *FDIC Banking Review* 13, no. 2 (December 2000): 32–33.

22. Story and Morgenson, "Financial Finger-Pointing": "Mr. Dochow's conduct was referred to Justice for possible criminal charges in 2009, according to Eric Thorson, the inspector general of the Treasury Department. Mr. Thorson said Mr. Dochow's action 'was clearly improper and wrong.'"

Chapter 8. Friends of the Court

1. Bankruptcy Petition Cover Sheet, Case Number 390-35116-HCA-13, Received August 6, 1990, U.S. Bankruptcy Court, Northern District of Texas; The automatic stay is a feature of consumer and commercial bankruptcy alike. As a general rule, subject to several exceptions, once the automatic stay goes into effect, everything freezes. Creditors may not collect. Even checks that have been mailed by the debtor may not be cashed.

2. For exemptions, see 11 U.S.C. § 523(a).

3. In re Leonard and Harriet Nobelman, U.S. Bankruptcy Court Notice to Individual Consumer Debtor, signed August 1, 1990, filed August 6, 1990; In re Leonard and Harriet Nobelman, Notice of Modified Chapter 13 Plan and Motion for Valuation, and Right to Object to Confirmation and Valuation, October 25, 1990 (hereinafter "Modified Plan"); Transcript of Hearing before the Honorable R. C. McGuire, December 6, 1990; In re Leonard and Harriet Nobelman (hereinafter, "Bankruptcy Transcript"), p. 9.

4. American Bankruptcy Institute, "Annual Business and Non-Business Filings by Year (1980–2012)"; Katherine Porter, "Driven by Debt: Bankruptcy and Financial Failure in American Families," in *Broke: How Debt Bankrupts the Middle Class*, ed. Katherine Porter (Stanford, CA: Stanford University Press, 2012), 2: "Some will save their houses and see bankruptcy as a miraculous cure. Others will suffer continued hardships, skid farther down the economic ladder, and view bankruptcy as a plea for help that went unanswered."

5. Charles Warren, *Bankruptcy in United States History* (New Haven, CT: Yale University Press, 1935), 115; Ben S. Branch and Jennifer S. Taub, "Bankruptcy," in *Finance Ethics: Critical Issues in Theory and Practice*, ed. John R. Boatright (Hoboken, NJ: Wiley, 2010), 511–512, 518; U.S. Const. art. I, § 8, cl. 4: "The Congress shall have power . . . [t]o establish . . . uniform Laws on the subject of Bankruptcies throughout the United States"; Stephen J. Lubben, "The Bankruptcy Clause," *Case Western Law Review* 64, forthcoming.

6. Pub. L. 95-598, 92 Stat. 2549; Charles Jordan Tabb, "The History of Bankruptcy Laws in the United States," *American Bankruptcy Institute Law Review* 3 (1995): 32, 36.

7. George A. Akerlof and Paul Michael Romer, "Looting: The Economic Underworld of Bankruptcy for Profit," *Brookings Papers on Economic Activity* 24, no. 2 (1993): 2: businessmen in a lax regulatory environment have the incentive to loot the firms they manage through excessive compensation and high-risk projects, then default on their debt, thus externalizing the losses on society; Branch and Taub, "Bankruptcy," 513–515; Akerlof shared the 2001 Nobel Prize in economics with Michael Spence and Joseph E. Stiglitz.

8. Elizabeth Warren, "Sick and Broke," *Washington Post*, February 9, 2005; Stuart Vyse, *Going Broke: Why Americans Can't Hold on to Their Money* (New York: Oxford University Press, 2008), 10–11.

9. While after 2005, debtors may have fewer choices and be channeled into a Chapter 13, at the time, this was a choice they made.

10. The Nobelmans' Bankruptcy Petition, "Monthly Family Budget" chart, August 6, 1990; Amended Proof of Claim of American Savings, filed October 2, 1990; Proof of Claim, Community Credit Union, aka Richardson Credit Union.

11. Although they listed the Internal Revenue Service on their creditor matrix, dated August 6, 1990, they later revealed that this had been a mistake. Other mistakes included initially misspelling "Murray" as "Morran"; In re Leonard and Harriet Nobelman, Trial Brief, December 4, 1990, p. 2.

12. See 11 U.S.C. § 1322(b)(2).

13. 11 U.S.C. § 506(a)(1): "[It] is a secured claim to the extent of the value of such creditor's interest in the estate's interest in such property . . . and is an unsecured claim to the extent that the value of such creditor's interest is less than the amount of such allowed claim"; In 1991, STM took over portions of the Murray Mortgage Company's business, including its role in the Nobelmans' bankruptcy proceedings.

14. Trial Brief, 3–4; Deed of Trust between borrower Leonard Nobelman and wife, Harriet A. Nobelman, trustees Guy R. Arrington, Roger C. Teufel, and Deborah O. Becker, and the beneficiary, Murray Investment Company, as of June 21, 1984, recorded on July 3, 1984, in Collin County, Texas (hereinafter, "Deed of Trust"); Zyne also cited a case by the federal appeals court for the Third Circuit, which suggested that if rents, escrow accounts, and insurance proceeds are listed as collateral along with a home, the antimodification provision in Section 1322 is not triggered.

15. Trial Brief, p. 5.

16. In re Nobelman, Murray Mortgage Company Objection to Confirmation of the Chapter 13 Plan, filed November 5, 1990.

17. In re Nobelman, Trustee's Objection to Confirmation, filed November 14, 1990; In re Nobelman, Amended Trustee's Objection to Confirmation, November 27, 1990; In re Nobelman, Trail [*sic*] Brief in Support of Amended Trustee's Objection to Confirmation, filed December 5, 1990, pp. 5–6, 7.

18. In re Estel Ray Hougland and Ruth Evelyn Hoagland, 886 F.2d 1182, 1184 (9th Cir. 1989); Sapos v. Provident Institution of Savings, 967 F.2d 918 (3rd Cir. 1992); Wilson v. Commonwealth Mortgage Bank, 895 F.2d 123 (3rd Cir. 1990); In re Danny L. Hart and Joanne E. Hart, 923 F.2d 1410 (10th Cir. 1991); In re Jimmie Bellamy and Cynthia Bellamy, 962 F.2d 176 (2nd Cir.

1992); In re Steven H. L. Honnett, 116 B.R. 495 (Bkrtcy. E. D. Tex. 1990): On June 28, Judge Donald Sharp held that "11 U.S.C. § 506(a) may be utilized to bifurcate a secured mortgage lien into an allowed secured and an allowed unsecured claim." He also observed that "all relevant payment terms of the mortgage instrument [were] to remain intact save the necessary shortening of the maturity date." Thus, the plan did not constitute a modification. To reach his conclusion, Judge Sharp noted that "in reconciling the two statutes in the context of bifurcating a secured lender's lien the [Ninth Circuit in the *In re Hougland* decision, cited in this endnote above] found that § 1322(b)(2) served only to protect 'the truly secured portion of the residential real estate lender's claim.'"

19. In re Leonard and Harriet Nobelman, Debtors, Case No. 390-35116-HCA-13, in the U.S. Bankruptcy Court for the Northern District of Texas, Dallas Division, Findings of Fact and Conclusions of Law, filed February 14, 1991; In re Nobelman, 129 B.R. 98 (Bkrtcy. N. D. Tex. 1991), pp. 103–104; Order Denying Confirmation of Debtors' Modified Chapter 13 Plan, signed March 11, and entered March 12, 1991; In re Nobleman [*sic*], 986 F.2d 483 (5th Cir. 1992).

20. The U.S. Supreme Court, Frequently Asked Questions (FAQ), available at http://www.supremecourt.gov/faq.aspx#faqgi9; Nobelman Et. Ux. v. American Savings Bank, 506 U.S. 1020 (1992).

21. Telephone interviews with Rosemary Zyne, June 28, 2011, and with Michael Schroeder, June 30, 2011.

22. Brief of Amici Curiae, National Association of Realtors and the California Association of Realtors in Support of Respondent, p. 13.

23. Ibid., p. 12: "Lenders obviously would need to protect themselves . . . by increasing the amount of down payments they require"; Motion for Leave to File and Brief of Nationsbanc Mortgage Corporation as *Amicus Curiae* in Support of Respondent, p. 16; Brief of Federal National Mortgage Association as *Amicus Curiae* in Support of Respondent, In re Nobelman v. American Savings Bank, pp. 2–3; Brief of American Bankers Association, American Financial Services Association, and Credit Union National Association as *Amici Curiae* in Support of the Respondent, pp. 7–8.

24. Brief for *Amicus Curiae* Federal Home Loan Mortgage Corporation in Support of Respondent, In re Nobelman v. American Savings Bank.

25. Nobelman v. American Savings Bank, 508 U.S. 324 (1993), 328–330, 332.

26. Ibid., 332.

27. Jane Kaufman Winn, "Lien Stripping after Nobelman," *Loyola of Los Angeles Law Review* 27 (1994): 541, 543, 569: "Underlying the problems of statutory interpretation raised by *Nobelman* is the tension between two competing federal policies: the policy of promoting home ownership and the policy of granting debtors a fresh start in bankruptcy."

28. John Maynard Keynes, *The Collected Writings*, vol. 24 (Cambridge: Cambridge University Press for the Royal Economic Society, 2013), 258.

29. Jane Lehman, "Court Deals Setback to Bankrupt Homeowners," *Los Angeles Times*, June 13, 1993; Author interview with Marci Nobelman, Far

North Dallas, September 11, 2011; gravestone shows Leonard Nobelman's birth as March 22, 1936 and death January 3, 1994.

30. In re Nobelman, Motion for Relief from Stay or Act against Property, filed March 21, 1995; Corporation Assignment of Deed Trust, March 24, 1995, recorded on January 15, 1996: the sale was made to Alaska Seaboard Partners, Limited Partnership of Louisiana.

31. Substitute Trustee's Deed, Grantee Alaska Seaboard Partners; June 4, 1996, filed June 10, 1996: property "struck off" for $30,000 to Alaska Seaboard Partners, Limited Partnership of Nashua, New Hampshire.

32. According to records of the Delaware Secretary of State, Alaska Seaboard Partners Limited Partnership is a Delaware limited partnership formed May 17, 1995; according to the records of the Nevada Secretary of State, Alaska Seaboard Investments, Inc., is a Nevada-domiciled corporation, created May 18, 1995, with a president, secretary, and director identified as Robin P. Arkley II of 323 Fifth Street, Eureka, CA, and its treasurer's address is shown as 3050 Westfork Drive, Baton Rouge, LA, which is also the address for Security National Master Holding Company, LLC; according to the Security National Web site, in addition to being the president and CEO: "Mr. Arkley [was] the founder and owner of the highly successful real estate asset acquisition and management companies that collectively comprise Security National Holding Company, LLC"; according to the New Hampshire Secretary of State's Web site, Alaska Seaboard Partners Limited Partnership is a "foreign," meaning out-of-state, limited partnership created on May 30, 1995 with a principal office in Delaware, and the general partner is Alaska Seaboard Investments, Inc., a Nevada corporation; Oregon identifies the president and secretary as Robin P. Arkley II of 323 Fifth Street, Eureka, CA, also shown as the address for Alaska Seaboard Partners, Limited Partnership; according to records of the Louisiana Secretary of State, Alaska Seaboard Partners Limited Partnership was registered May 31, 1995, and it is identified as a non-Louisiana partnership with a Delaware domicile and a mailing address shown as 325 Fifth Street, Eureka, CA; the general partner of the limited partnership is identified as Alaska Seaboard Investments, Inc.; Special Warranty Deed for Unit 507 dated February 28, 1996, Grantor Alaska Seaboard Partners, LP Baton Rouge, LA, Grantee Richard L. Frey, to be effective June 16, 1996, filed for record in Collin County, June 27, 1996.

Chapter 9. Friend of the Family

1. Kirsten Grind, *The Lost Bank: The Story of Washington Mutual—The Biggest Bank Failure in American History* (New York: Simon & Schuster, 2012), 47, 67–68; "American Savings Sale Completed," *Los Angeles Times*, December 24, 1996: "Washington Mutual Inc. said Monday it has completed its $1.7-billion acquisition of Keystone Holdings Inc. and its subsidiary, Irvine thrift American Savings Bank, doubling its size and making it one of the largest thrifts on the West Coast;" American Savings Bank, F.A. v. United States, 98 Fed. Cl. 291, 296 (2011); Washington Mutual, Inc., *Annual Report* for Fiscal Year Ended December 31, 1996, filed with the Securities and Exchange Com-

mission (SEC) on Form 10-K, March 10, 1997 (hereinafter "Washington Mutual 1996 10-K"), pp. 1, 3, 5–6, 51; Washington Mutual, Inc., Proxy Statement filed November 12, 1996; American Savings Bank, F.A. v. United States, 98 Fed. Cl. 291, 295–296 (2011); Jacqueline S. Gold, "Homeboy: The Aggressive Kerry Killinger Wants Washington Mutual, the U.S.'s Biggest Thrift, to Get Even Bigger," *Institutional Investor* 36, no. 3 (March 2002); Patrice Apodaca, "220 to Be Laid Off at Irvine by New Parent; President Resigns," *Los Angeles Times*, January 7, 1997.

2. Grind, *Lost Bank*, 35–37; Gold, "Homeboy."

3. Wamu November 1996 Proxy, pp. 78–79; Federal Reserve Board, "Adoption of Revised Interagency Uniform Financial Institutions Rating System," press release, December 24, 1996, available at http://www.federalreserve.gov/boarddocs/press/general/1996/19961224/.

4. "Washington Mutual to Buy American Savings," *Deseret News*, July 22, 1996.

5. Marc J. Perry and Paul J. Mackun, "Population Change and Distribution: 1990–2000," U.S. Census Bureau, *Census 2000 Brief*, April 2001; Drew DeSilver, "Reckless Strategies Doomed WaMu," *Seattle Times*, October 25, 2009; Grind, *Lost Bank*, 111–112; Washington Mutual 1996 10-K, pp. 5–7, Washington Mutual, November 1996 Proxy, p. 4.

6. Joe Peek, "A Call to ARMs: Adjustable Rate Mortgages in the 1980s," *New England Economic Review* (March/April 1990): 47, 58; Patricia A. McCoy, Andrew D. Pavlov, and Susan M. Wachter, "Systemic Risk through Securitization: The Result of Deregulation and Regulatory Failure," *University of Connecticut Law Review* 41 (2009): 499, 502; Adam J. Levitin and Susan M. Wachter, "The Public Option in Housing Finance," Georgetown Public Law Research Paper No. 1966550, November 28, 2012, 40, note 187.

7. Martin H. Wolfson, *Financial Crises: Understanding the Postwar U.S. Experience* (Armonk, NY: M. E. Sharpe, 1994), 100; Cynthia Angell and Clare D. Rowley, "Breaking New Ground in U.S. Mortgage Lending," *FDIC Outlook*, last updated March 21, 2007, available at http://www.fdic.gov/bank/analytical/regional/ro20062q/na/2006_summer04.html.

8. "Interest-Only Mortgage Payments and Payment-Option-ARMs: Are They for You?" Booklet of the Board of Governors of the Federal Reserve System, Federal Deposit Insurance Corporation, National Credit Union Administration, Office of the Comptroller of the Currency and Office of Thrift Supervision, November 2006, 3; calculation based upon original loan amount of $300,000 for a term of thirty years.

9. Paul Jackson, "Fitch Mulls Downgrade of Wachovia over Option ARMs," *HousingWire*, June 28, 2008: Banks keep Option ARMs in their portfolios because they can book deferred interest income.

10. U.S. Senate Permanent Subcommittee on Investigations, Committee on Homeland Security and Government Affairs, Majority and Minority Staff Report: *Wall Street and the Financial Crisis: Anatomy of a Financial Collapse*, April 13, 2011 (hereinafter the "Levin-Coburn Final Report"), 3; Peter S. Goodman and Gretchen Morgenson, "Saying Yes, WaMu Built Empire on Shaky Loans," *New York Times*, December 27, 2008.

11. David Heath, "Wamu: Hometown Bank Turned Predatory," *Seattle Times*, October 26, 2009; Financial Crisis Inquiry Commission, *The Financial Crisis Inquiry Report: Final Report of the National Commission on the Causes of the Financial and Economic Crisis in the United States*, authorized ed. (New York: Public Affairs, 2011) (hereinafter *FCIC Report*), 105, 109; Testimony of Illinois Attorney General Lisa Madigan before the Financial Crisis Inquiry Commission, January 14, 2010, pp. 5–6, 12.

12. *FCIC Report*, 18; real estate appraisers' petition available at http://www.appraiserspetition.com/: petition addressed to the Executive Director of the Appraisal Subcommittee of the Federal Financial Institutions Examinations Council; interview with former independent appraiser from the Chicago area.

13. Press Release, "A. G. Schneiderman Secures $7.8 Million Settlement with First American Corporation and eAppraiseIT for Role in Housing Market Meltdown," September 28, 2012; Grind, *Lost Bank*, 178.

14. Angell and Rowley, "Breaking New Ground," chart 4; Joint Center for Housing Studies of Harvard University, *The State of the Nation's Housing, 2006* (Cambridge, MA: Harvard University Press, June 2006), 1, 17, 19: "[H]omebuyers scrambled to get in on still-hot markets last year. In stretching to afford ever more expensive homes, borrowers increasingly turned to mortgage products" including ARMS, IO loans and pay-option ARMs, available at http://www.jchs.harvard.edu/publications/markets/son2006/index.htm; Robert Pozen, *Too Big to Save? How to Fix the U.S. Financial System* (Hoboken, NJ: Wiley, 2010), 8, 13–14.

15. Angell and Rowley, "Breaking New Ground," note 13; Matt Taibbi, *Griftopia: Bubble Machines, Vampire Squids, and the Long Con That Is Breaking America* (New York: Spiegel & Grau–Random House, 2010), 88–89.

16. DeSilver, "Reckless Strategies"; Patricia A. McCoy, "Rethinking Disclosure in a World of Risk-Based Pricing," *Harvard Journal on Legislation* 44 (2007): 123, 153; Prepared Statement of Patricia A. McCoy, March 3, 2001, Hearing on "Consumer Protections in Financial Services: Past Problems, Future Solutions," before the U.S. Senate Committee on Banking, Housing, and Urban Affairs, March 3, 2009, pp. 8–9.

17. Mara Der Hovanesian, "Nightmare Mortgages," *Businessweek*, September 10, 2006; McCoy, Prepared Statement, 10; McCoy, "Rethinking Disclosure," 153.

18. Levin-Coburn Final Report, 59; *FCIC Report*, 14, citing Rob Barry, Matthew Haggman, and Jack Dolan, "Ex-Convicts Active in Mortgage Fraud," *Miami Herald*, January 29, 2009; Heath, "Hometown Bank."

19. Nick Timiraos, "Mortgage Increases Blunted," *Wall Street Journal*, March 29, 2010; Grind, *Lost Bank*, 116–117; Adam J. Levitin and Susan M. Wachter, "Explaining the Housing Bubble," *Georgetown Law Journal* 100 (2012): 1196, 1197, 1199.

20. Levin-Coburn Final Report, 24; Washington Mutual 1996 10-K, pp. 4–6: American Savings Bank's Option ARMs described: "In the event that a monthly payment is not sufficient to pay the interest accruing on the loan, the shortage is added to the principal balance and is repaid through future

monthly payments. This is referred to as negative amortization." The report noted that the delinquency rate at American Savings Bank was higher than that of the rest of WaMu.

21. Washington Mutual 1996 10-K, pp. 25–27; Debora Vrana, "American Savings Has Regained Its Place as Financial Leader," *Los Angeles Times*, July 23, 1996; Apodoca, "220 to Be Laid Off."

22. Gold, "Homeboy"; James S. Granelli, "U.S. Sells Stake in S&L Successor," *Los Angeles Times*, January 24, 1997; FDIC Press Release, "FDIC Sells Washington Mutual Stock," January 23, 2007; American Savings Bank, F.A. v. United States, 98 Fed. Cl. 291, 295–296 (2011); Greg Heberlein, "State Bank Goes Big Time—Washington Mutual to Acquire California Bank," *Seattle Times*, July 22, 1996; "Washington Mutual Names David Bonderman, J. Taylor Crandall to Board of Directors," *Business Wire*, January 13, 1997.

23. Bethany McLean, "Washington Mutual's Remarkable Rise: The Alexander the Great of the Thrift Industry," *Fortune*, December 9, 1997; Judith Schoolman, "Washington Mutual Takes Over an Institution of 142 Yrs.," *New York Daily News*, June 26, 2001; Grind, *Lost Bank*, 49, 54, 85, 99.

24. Grind, *Lost Bank*, 54; Gold, "Homeboy."

25. Pub. L. 103-328, 108 Stat. 2338; Pub. L. 106-102, 113 Stat. 1338; Arthur E. Wilmarth Jr., "The Dark Side of Universal Banking: Financial Conglomerates and the Origins of the Subprime Crisis," *Connecticut Law Review* 41, no. 4 (2009): 969, 975; Richard Scott Carnell, Jonathan R. Macey, and Geoffrey P. Miller, *The Law of Banking Financial Institutions*, 4th ed. (New York: Aspen, 2009), 26–27.

26. Mark C. Crowley, "How Washington Mutual Lost Its Heart," Guest Column, *Seattle Times*, September 23, 2011: former senior vice president recalled, "What really killed WaMu, however, was a change in the company's century-old culture and values—a misguided move that marginalized its historic regard and care for employees and customers in the interest of driving an ever-expanding bottom line for shareholders"; Heath, "Home Town Bank": "WaMu bore no resemblance to its homey image" as "Friend of the Family"; Gold, "Homeboy"; Dan Margolies, "US Senate Panel: High-Risk Loans Brought Down WaMu," *Reuters*, April 13, 2010: "The focus on high-risk loans eventually contributed to WaMu's failure in September 2008"; "Washington Mutual Launches National Advertising Campaign in Support of Its New WaMu Free Checking Account," *Business Wire*, March 31, 2006: In an ad campaign, WaMu ridiculed "stodgy bankers" who were portrayed as unfriendly to borrowers and other customers; "Whoohoo! WaMu Unveils New Ad Campaign Celebrating and Inspired by Their Customers," *Business Wire*, February 12, 2008: the 2008 campaign conveyed the messages: "we don't nickel and dime you," "we've got your back," and "we give you something back"; Robin Updike, "'Friend of the Family' Washington Mutual New TV Ads Focus on 'The Little Guy,'" *Seattle Times*, September 3, 1991; Erick Dash, "F.D.I.C. Sues Ex-Chief of Big Bank That Failed," *New York Times*, March 17, 2011: FDIC complaint alleged WaMu executives, including Killinger, "focused on short term gains to increase their own

compensation, with reckless disregard for WaMu's longer term safety and soundness."

27. Murray Morgan, *The Friend of the Family: 100 Years with Washington Mutual* (Seattle: Washington Mutual Financial Group, 1989), 2–3, 6–7, 11–13, 164.

28. Ibid., 79–81.

29. Ibid., 84–85.

30. Ibid., 85–86, 95, 102.

31. Ibid., 88, 90, 99–100; Helen M. Burns, *The American Banking Community and New Deal Banking Reforms 1933–1935* (Westport, CT: Greenwood Press, 1974), 68–69, 80–81.

32. Morgan, *Friend of the Family*, 140, 142; Grind, *Lost Bank*, 11–12; Michael Perino, *The Hellhound of Wall Street: How Ferdinand Pecora's Investigation of the Great Crash Forever Changed American Finance* (New York: Penguin, 2010), 291: "the most controversial provision of the Glass-Steagall bill was not the elimination of securities affiliates, but the creation of deposit insurance."

33. Morgan, *Friend of the Family*, 141; Grind, *Lost Bank*, 20.

34. Morgan, *Friend of the Family*, 144, Grind, *Lost Bank*, 10; Melissa Allison, "Wamu's Former CEO: Bank's Demise 'Abominable, to Put It Mildly,'" *Seattle Times*, September 26, 2008.

35. Morgan, *Friend of the Family*, 146–148.

36. Ibid., 148–149.

37. Ibid., 149–150; SEC Commissioner James C. Treadway Jr., Remarks to Sixteenth Annual Securities Regulation Seminar, "The Commissions Enforcement Program and the Integrity of Financial Statements," November 3, 1983, p. 2.

38. Morgan, *Friend of the Family*, 154–155; "New Money Market Product Hits Northwest: Washington Mutual's MegaFund Aims for High Yield; Rivals Fear Possible Price War," *American Banker*, March 6, 1984; Grind, *Lost Bank*, 16.

39. Gold, "Homeboy"; Grind, *Lost Bank*, 18–19, 29; Morgan, *Friend of the Family*, 149, 157–158; Washington Mutual, Inc., Proxy Statement, filed March 19, 1997.

40. Heberlein, "Washington Mutual to Buy Bank"; Grind, *Lost Bank*, 45.

41. Grind, *Lost Bank*, 36, 69, 89–90, 93–94; Kimberly L. Allers, "A New Banking Model—Washington Mutual Is Using a Creative Retail Approach to Turn the Banking World Upside Down," *Fortune*, March 31, 2003: In February 2003, Killinger attended an annual gathering of 3,500 senior executives where he "took the stage doing a rhythmically challenged two-step. The crowd cheered, clapped and pumped fists"; Jenny Mero, "People Are His Bottom Line," *Fortune*, April 16, 2007: in an interview Killinger said, "When I visit our financial centers, I'll have my wife with me, and often we'll have our eight-pound dog"; Crowley, "How Washington Mutual Lost Its Heart."

42. Grind, *Lost Bank*, 67–68; Kirsten Grind, "Insiders Detail Reasons for Wamu's Failure," *Puget Sound Business Journal*, January 25, 2009; Levin-Coburn Final Report, p. 51.

Chapter 10. The Factory Line

1. Kirsten Grind, *The Lost Bank: The Story of Washington Mutual—The Biggest Bank Failure in American History* (New York: Simon & Schuster, 2012), 68; Washington Mutual, Inc., Annual Report for Fiscal Year Ended December 31, 1996, filed with the Securities and Exchange Commission (SEC) on Form 10-K, March 10, 1997 (hereinafter, "WaMu 1996 10-K"), p. 25; Robert Stowe England, "WaMu—The Power of Yes," *Mortgage Banking* 61, no. 9 (June 30, 2001); U.S. Senate Permanent Subcommittee on Investigations, Committee on Homeland Security and Government Affairs, Majority and Minority Staff Report: *Wall Street and the Financial Crisis: Anatomy of a Financial Collapse*, April 13, 2011 (hereinafter the "Levin-Coburn Final Report"), 60.

2. Washington Mutual, Inc., Annual Report for Fiscal Year Ended December 31, 2002, filed with the Securities and Exchange Commission (SEC) on Form 10-K, March 17, 2003, pp. 2–3, 75–79: "In 2002 Washington Mutual was the largest servicer and second largest originator of mortgage loans in the nation. The Group's strategy is to remain a leading originator and servicer of home loans and to increase market share in both loan origination and loan servicing"; Washington Mutual, Inc., Annual Report for Fiscal Year Ended December 31, 2004, filed with the Securities and Exchange Commission (SEC) on Form 10-K, March 14, 2005 (hereinafter, "Washington Mutual 2004 10-K"): "substantial increase in loan volume for the Company's signature adjustable-rate home loan product, the Option ARM. The strong customer demand for this product during 2004 allowed the Company to direct over $31 billion of Option ARM volume for sale to the secondary market, while still retaining a majority of the volume for the loan portfolio."

3. Peter S. Goodman and Gretchen Morgenson, "Saying Yes, WaMu Built Empire on Shaky Loans," *New York Times*, December 27, 2008; Grind, *Lost Bank*, 68–69; Jacqueline S. Gold, "Homeboy: The Aggressive Kerry Killinger Wants Washington Mutual, the U.S.'s Biggest Thrift, to Get Even Bigger," *Institutional Investor* 36, no. 3 (March 2002); Craig Davis, "Today's Brand of Mortgage Company," *American Banker* 63, no. 1 (October 1, 2002): describing "The Power of Yes" brand as helping convey to customers WaMu will "ultimately say 'yes' to their mortgage application"; Federal Housing Finance Agency v. JPMorgan Chase & Co. et al., complaint Case 11 Civ. 6188, filed September 2, 2011; Tommy Fernandez, "As Refi Decline Looms, 2 Takes on Branding," *American Banker* 167, no. 202 (October 23, 2002): Craig Davis indicated Power of Yes campaign expected to boost sales; Gretchen Morgenson and Joshua Rosner, *Reckless Endangerment: How Outsized Ambition, Greed, and Corruption Led to Economic Armageddon* (New York: Henry Holt, 2011), 46, 194; *Frontline*, "The Untouchables," January 22, 2013.

4. Levin-Coburn Final Report, 50–51; Offices of Inspector General, Department of the Treasury Federal Deposit Insurance Corporation, Evaluation of Federal Regulatory Oversight of Washington Mutual Bank, Report No. EVAL-10-002, April 2010, p. 11 (hereinafter "OIG WaMu Report"): "In 2007, WaMu had only 144 employees overseeing more than 34,000 third-party brokers," available at http://www.fdicoig.gov/reports10/10-002EV.pdf.

5. Grind, *Lost Bank*, 139, 142; "Motivators of the Year," *Incentive* 177, no. 10 (October 2003): point person identified as Linda Lincoln, vice president of incentives and promotions for Washington Mutual; George Cunningham, "In Basket: Home Savings Honors," *Long Beach Press*, March 22, 1993; "Career Paths," *Long Beach Press*, May 22, 1995: American Savings Bank loan consultant named to President's Club for the fourth year.

6. England, "WaMu."

7. Grind, *Lost Bank*, 69; Washington Mutual, Inc., Annual Report for Fiscal Year Ended December 31, 2001, filed with the Securities and Exchange Commission (SEC) on Form 10-K, March 19, 2002, pp. 1, 36: showing mortgage originations by type, including single family residential (SFR) in 2000 and 2001; David Wessel, *In Fed We Trust: Ben Bernanke's War on the Great Panic* (New York: Crown Business, 2009), 55, 106; "Bernanke Defends Fed Record," *CNNMoney.com*, January 3, 2010.

8. Mortgage Bankers Association, "Mortgage Origination Estimates," May 14, 2008: table showing 1–4 family mortgage originations for purchases and for refinance from Q1990 through Q2008; Margaret M. McConnell, Richard W. Peach, and Alex Al-Haschimi, "After the Refinancing Boom: Will Consumers Scale Back Their Spending?" Federal Reserve Bank of New York, *Current Issues* 9, no. 12 (December 2003), available at http://www.newyorkfed.org/research/current_issues/ci9-12.pdf; U.S. Department of Housing and Urban Development, Office of Policy Development and Research, "An Analysis of Mortgage Refinancing, 2001–2003," November 2004, 1–3, 5: including estimates for 2003, available at http://www.huduser.org/Publications/pdf/MortgageRefinance03.pdf; Federal Reserve Selected Interest Rates, H.15 (monthly), available at http://www.federalreserve.gov/releases/h15/data.htm; Lawrence Mischel and Heidi Shierholz, "A Decade of Flat Wages: The Key Barrier to Shared Prosperity and a Rising Middle Class," Economic Policy Institute, Briefing Paper, August 21, 2013, p. 5; Art Pine, "U.S. Workers' Wages Lag in Recovery while Company Profits Soar," *Bloomberg*, May 10, 2004: "After inflation, real wage gains were 1.1 percent" between third quarter of 2001 and end of 2003.

9. HUD Analysis, p. 5.

10. Levin-Coburn Final Report, p. 48, citing Goodman and Morgenson, "Saying Yes."

11. OIG WaMu Report, p. 2.

12. Ibid., p. 8: WaMu management in 2005 decided to "shift its business strategy away from originating traditional fixed-rate and conforming single family residential loans, towards riskier nontraditional loan products and subprime loans . . . in anticipation of increased earnings and to compete with Countrywide Financial Corporation"; Michael W. Hudson, *The Monster: How a Gang of Predatory Lenders and Wall Street Bankers Fleeced America—and Spawned a Global Crisis* (New York: St. Martin's Press, 2010), 1–3.

13. Hudson, *Monster*, 211; Michael W. Hudson, "The Mortgage Salesman Who Wouldn't Sell," *Huffington Post*, December 22, 2011; Goodman and Morgenson, "Saying Yes."

14. Levin-Coburn, Final Report, pp. 2, 48, 58–69; OIG WaMu Report, p. 149.

15. The government agency Ginnie Mae securitized a little more than 5 percent, a number that would also fall by 2006; Financial Crisis Inquiry Commission, Preliminary Staff Report, "Securitization and the Financial Crisis," April 7, 2010, p. 3, available at http://fcic-static.law.stanford.edu/cdn_media/fcic-reports/2010-0407-Preliminary_Staff_Report_-_Securitization_and_the_Mortgage_Crisis.pdf; Financial Crisis Inquiry Commission, *The Financial Crisis Inquiry Report: Final Report of the National Commission on the Causes of the Financial and Economic Crisis in the United States,* authorized ed. (New York: Public Affairs, 2011) (hereinafter *FCIC Report*), 1.

16. Prepared Statement of Patricia A. McCoy, March 3, 2001, Hearing on "Consumer Protections in Financial Services: Past Problems, Future Solutions," before the U.S. Senate Committee on Banking, Housing, and Urban Affairs, March 3, 2009, p. 8.

17. *FCIC Report*, 102, 105; FCIC, "Securitization and the Financial Crisis," 10–11, fig. 4; Levin-Coburn Final Report, p. 116: "According to a 2007 presentation, by 2006, WaMu was the second largest nonagency issuer of mortgage backed securities in the United States behind Countrywide."

18. Hudson, *Monster*, 5; Grind, *Lost Bank*, 60–63; Paul Muolo and Matthew Padilla, *Chain of Blame: How Wall Street Caused the Mortgage and Credit Crisis* (Hoboken, NJ: Wiley, 2010), 75–76; *FCIC Report*, 70, fig. 5.2.

19. Testimony of Patricia Lindsay, The Financial Crisis Inquiry Commission, Commission Hearing, April 7, 2010, Official Transcript, pp. 123–124; *FCIC Report*, 67–68: for hard money lending to borrowers lacking strong credit histories "they would have to have a lot of equity . . . . We had three Cs that we looked at: we had the credit, collateral, and the capacity"; Margo Anderson, "From Subprime Mortgages to Subprime Credit Cards," Federal Reserve Bank of Boston, *Communities and Banking*, fall 2008: "A score of less than 660 is considered subprime," available at http://www.bostonfed.org/commdev/c&b/2008/fall/Anderson_subprime_credit_cards.pdf.

20. Bethany McLean and Joe Nocera, *All the Devils Are Here: The Hidden History of the Financial Crisis* (New York: Portfolio/Penguin, 2010), 30.

21. Grind, *Lost Bank*, 64; Muolo and Padilla, 79–80.

22. Levin-Coburn Transcript, April 13, 2010; Levin-Coburn Final Report, pp. 47, 55, 57, 76.

23. Drew DeSilver, "Reckless Strategies Doomed WaMu," *Seattle Times*, October 25, 2009.

24. Grind, *Lost Bank*, 62; Rami Grunbaum, "Ex-WaMu Insider Now an Angry Outsider," *Seattle Times*, April 13, 2008: "Lannoye, now 70, retired at the end of 1998 after a decade as chief credit officer and executive vice president of WaMu."

25. Grind, *Lost Bank*, 69; Kirsten Grind, "Insiders Detail Reasons for WaMu's Failure," *Puget Sound Business Journal*, January 16, 2009, available at http://www.bizjournals.com/seattle/stories/2009/01/26/story3.html?page=all.

26. John Cassidy, *How Markets Fail: The Logic of Economic Calamities* (New York: Farrar, Straus and Giroux, 2009), 257; "Long Beach Financial

Corporation Reports Record Quarterly Earnings," *Business Wire*, January 26, 1999: "Loan production for all of 1998 totaled $2.6 billion."

27. Grind, *Lost Bank*, 70; Levin-Coburn Final Report, p. 152; David Heath, "Policies at WaMu's Long Beach Mortgage Invited Fraud, *Seattle Times*, December 29, 2009: A former Long Beach underwriter recalled seeing forgeries by brokers, including "falsified pay stubs and tax returns." In order to get loans through, another Long Beach employee recalled that account executives would "offer kickbacks of money. . . . Or, 'I'll buy you a bottle of Dom Pérignon.' It was just crazy," available at http://seattletimes.com/html/businesstechnology/2010627929_longbeach30.html; "Ex-Long Beach Mortgage Executive Convicted of Fraud," *Businessweek*, September 25, 2012.

28. Laura Mandaro, "Exec Shake-Up at WaMu," *American Banker*, October 1, 2003; Grind, *Lost Bank*, 75–78; Levin-Coburn Final Report, pp. 75, 191: "Approximately 4,000 of the 13,000 loans in the warehouse had been reviewed . . . of these, approximately 950 were deemed saleable"; "Washington Mutual Overhauls Corporate Structure," Associated Press, October 1, 2003: WaMu "announced changes in its top management to try to prevent a repeat of the customer service problems that have marred the aggressive expansion of the nation's largest thrift . . . Craig S. Davis, 52, retired"; Bradley Meacham, "Veteran Retires, Leaving Two in Top Posts," *Seattle Times*, October 1, 2003; Mitchell Pacelle, "Banks Brace for a Fallout," *Asian Wall Street Journal*, September 11, 2003: announcement on September 9 by WaMu of expected third quarter loss on sale of mortgage loans, followed by stock price decline; Paul Muolo, "Will Killinger Survive? And How about WaMu?" *Mortgage Servicing News*, September 1, 2004.

29. Levin-Coburn Final Report, pp. 77–78.

30. Ibid., p. 79.

31. Paul Muolo, "Top Originator May Be Seeking National Executive," *Origination News* 14 (March 1, 2005); Levin-Coburn Hearing Transcript, p. 408, appendix exhibit 10.

32. Levin-Coburn Final Report, p. 52; Levin-Coburn Hearing Transcript.

33. Shawn Tully, "What Went Wrong at WaMu: Washington Mutual Built Itself into America's Biggest Mortgage Bank Almost Overnight. But This Year, POW! Profits Are Getting Hammered, and the CEO Is Apologizing to Wall Street," *Fortune*, August 9, 2004; Grind, *Lost Bank*, 102.

34. Tully, "What Went Wrong at WaMu."

35. Ibid.; "Double WaMu: Big Problems for a Big Mortgage Bank," *Economist*, August 19, 2004.

36. Tully, "What Went Wrong at WaMu"; Gold, "Homeboy"; Bethany McLean, "Washington Mutual's Remarkable Rise: The Alexander the Great of the Thrift Industry," *Fortune*, December 9, 1997.

37. Grind, *Lost Bank*, 102; Paul Muolo, "Will Killinger Survive? And How about WaMu?"; Levin-Coburn Final Report, p. 60; Washington Mutual, Inc., Annual Report for Fiscal Year Ended December 31, 2003, filed with the Securities and Exchange Commission (SEC) on Form 10-K, March 15, 2004, p. 24.

38. Grind, *Lost Bank*, 103–104; Levin-Coburn Final Report, pp. 60–61, 78, 103, 151: an employee "told the Subcommittee that the pressure to keep up

with the loan volume was enormous. Each month the LFC would set volume goals, measured in dollar value and the number of loans funded. At the end of each month the pressure to meet those goals intensified"; Washington Mutual Proxy Statement, filed March 23, 2005, p. 19.

39. Levin-Coburn Final Report, pp. 62–63; U.S. Senate Permanent Subcommittee on Investigation Exhibits: Hearing on "Wall Street and the Financial Crisis: The Role of High Risk Home Loans," April 13, 2010 (hereinafter "Levin-Coburn Hearing Exhibits"), exhibit #2b on p. 49: Washington Mutual, Asset Allocation Initiative: Higher Risk Lending Strategy and Increased Credit Risk Management, Board of Director Discussion, December 21, 2004.

40. Nomi Prins, *It Takes a Pillage: An Epic Tale of Power, Deceit, and Untold Trillions* (Hoboken, NJ: Wiley, 2009), 118; "Countrywide Dominates Adjustable Rate Mortgage Market," PR Newswire, June 2, 2004.

41. Remarks by Chairman Alan Greenspan, "Understanding Household Debt Obligations," at the Credit Union National Association 2004 Governmental Affairs Conference, Washington, DC, February 23, 2004.

42. Matt Taibbi, *Griftopia: Bubble Machines, Vampire Squids, and the Long Con That Is Breaking America* (New York: Spiegel & Grau–Random House, 2010), 72; Federal Reserve Selected Interest Rates, H.15; The Federal Reserve Board, Consumer Handbook on Adjustable Rate Mortgages, p. 78.

43. Washington Mutual 2004 10-K; Levin-Coburn Final Report, pp. 58, 61; Levin-Coburn Wall Street Hearing Exhibits, #2a, #2b, and #2c, pp. 30–78; Washington Mutual, Higher Risk Lending Strategy, "Asset Allocation Initiative," Board of Directors, Finance Committee Discussion, January 2005; Washington Mutual, Asset Allocation Initiative: Higher Risk Lending Strategy and Increased Credit Risk Management, Board of Director Discussion, December 21, 2004; Washington Mutual, Higher Risk Lending Strategy, and Increased Credit Risk Management, Board of Director Discussion, January 2005; DeSilver, "Reckless Strategies."

44. Levin-Coburn Final Report, p. 59; Jonathan Stempel, "Washington Mutual CEO Gets $18.09 Mln in Compensation for 2006," *Reuters*, March 19, 2007: "Compensation included a $1 million salary, $12.51 million of stock and option awards, $4,074,000 of incentive awards and $501,572 of other awards, according to the largest U.S. savings and loan's proxy filing with the U.S. Securities and Exchange Commission. The latter included the use of a corporate aircraft and retirement plan contributions." Bruce Feirstein, "100 to Blame: Infectious Greed, the International Monetary Fund, and More," *Vanity Fair*, September 18, 2009; Gretchen Morgenson, "Slapped Wrists at WaMu," *New York Times*, December 17, 2011.

45. Diana McCabe and Hang Nguyen, "Creative New Financing Mortgages Are No Longer Set in Stone," *Pittsburgh Post-Gazette*, October 27, 2002: WaMu executive describes ability to switch between payment options as a consumer benefit.

46. Levin-Coburn Final Report, pp. 64–65, 116.

47. *FCIC Report*, 104, 116–117; John C. Coffee Jr., *Gatekeepers: The Role of the Professions and Corporate Governance* (New York: Oxford University Press, 2006), 23.

48. *FCIC Report*, 117, 127–130; Gary B. Gorton and Nicholas S. Souleles, "Special Purpose Vehicles and Securitization," in *The Risks of Financial Institutions* (Chicago: University of Chicago Press, 2007), 550.

49. *FCIC Report*, 129, 131–132, 203.

50. Ibid., 131; Vikas Bajaj and Julie Creswell, "Bear Stearns Staves Off Collapse of 2 Hedge Funds," *New York Times*, June 21, 2007: the $316 billion in mortgage-related CDOs was only part of the total $520 billion in CDOs, which including those backed by other bonds.

51. *FCIC Report*, 102–103.

52. Muolo and Padilla, *Chain of Blame*, 186; Shawn Tully, "Wall Street's Money Machine Breaks Down," *Fortune*, November 12, 2007; Steven Pearlstein, "So You Just Squandered Billions . . . Take Another Whack at It," *Washington Post*, September 2, 2009.

53. Claire A. Hill, "Why Did Rating Agencies Do Such a Bad Job Rating Subprime Securities?" *University of Pittsburgh Law Review* 71 (2011): 585, 588, 596: acknowledging, but also challenging the conventional wisdom regarding conflicts of interest.

54. William K. Black, "The Two Documents Everyone Should Read to Better Understand the Crisis," *Huffington Post*, February 25, 2009.

55. Matt Taibbi, "The Last Mystery of the Financial Crisis," *Rolling Stone*, June 19, 2013.

56. Black, "Two Documents Everyone Should Read."

57. *FCIC Report*, 49, 86, 96–97.

58. Levin-Coburn Final Report, pp. 95–98, and Levin-Coburn Exhibits, 22a and 23b; Grind, *Lost Bank*, 142–143, 145.

59. Levin Coburn Final Report, pp. 489, 501, exhibit 63a: Script of the 2005 President's Club Awards event held in 2006.

60. Marcy Gordon, "Risk Officers Say They Tried to Warn WaMu of Risky Mortgages," *USA Today*, April 13, 2010.

61. Dean Baker, *False Profits: Recovering from the Bubble Economy* (Sausalito, CA: PoliPoint Press, 2010), 31, 34.

Chapter 11. The Bubble

1. James K. Galbraith, "Who Are These Economists, Anyway?" *Thought & Action*, Fall 2009, 85–97, available at http://www.nea.org/assets/docs/HE/TA09EconomistGalbraith.pdf.

2. U.S. Senate Permanent Subcommittee on Investigations, Committee on Homeland Security and Governmental Affairs, Exhibits, Hearing on "Wall Street and the Financial Crisis: The Role of High Risk Home Loans," April 13, 2010 (hereinafter "Levin-Coburn High Risk Hearing Exhibits"), 551, exhibit 78, e-mail from Washington Mutual chairman and CEO Kerry Killinger to James Vanasek, March 10, 2005, 10:03 a.m; U.S. Senate Permanent Subcommittee on Investigations, Committee on Homeland Security and Government Affairs, Majority and Minority Staff Report: *Wall Street and the Financial*

Crisis: Anatomy of a Financial Collapse, April 13, 2011 (hereinafter the "Levin-Coburn Final Report"), 67–68.

3. Levin-Coburn High Risk Hearing Exhibits, p. 551.

4. Levin-Coburn High Risk Hearing Exhibits, #2a, #2b, and #2c, pp. 30–78: Washington Mutual, Higher Risk Lending Strategy, "Asset Allocation Initiative," Board of Directors, Finance Committee Discussion, January 2005; Washington Mutual, Asset Allocation Initiative: Higher Risk Lending Strategy and Increased Credit Risk Management, Board of Director Discussion, December 21, 2004; Washington Mutual, Higher Risk Lending Strategy, and Increased Credit Risk Management, Board of Director Discussion, January 2005; Levin-Coburn Final Report, pp. 65–70: "Despite Mr. Killinger's awareness that housing prices were unsustainable, could drop suddenly, and could make it difficult for borrowers to refinance or sell their homes, Mr. Killinger continued to push forward with WaMu's High Risk Lending Strategy," and in June 2005, in a strategic direction memo to the board, Killinger wrote: "In order to reduce the impact of interest rate changes on our business, we have accelerated development of Alt-A, government and sub-prime loan products, as well as hybrid ARMs and other prime products." Gretchen Morgenson and Joshua Rosner, *Reckless Endangerment: How Outsized Ambition, Greed, and Corruption Led to Economic Armageddon* (New York: Henry Holt, 2011): In September 2004, Countrywide officials "advised top management that risky lending practices were imperiling the company," 193; Kirsten Grind, *The Lost Bank: The Story of Washington Mutual—The Biggest Bank Failure in American History* (New York: Simon & Schuster, 2012), 135, 162; Adam Davidson, "Washington Mutual Executive Predicted Collapse," NPR, October 3, 2008.

5. Levin-Coburn Final Report, pp. 42, 58, 66; Levin-Coburn High Risk Hearing Exhibits, p. 30, exhibit 2a, p. 49, exhibit 2b, p. 63, exhibit 2c; John Cassidy, *How Markets Fail: The Logic of Economic Calamities* (New York: Farrar, Straus and Giroux, 2009), 246.

6. Levin-Coburn Final Report, p. 154: In February 2008, the human resources committee of the board of directors "approved a bonus plan for executive officers that tried to shield the executive bonuses from any impact caused by WaMu's mounting mortgage losses"; and also citing Valerie Bauerlein and Ruth Simon, "WaMu Board Shields Executives Bonuses," *Wall Street Journal*, March 5, 2008: "The board of Washington Mutual Inc. has set compensation targets for top executives that will exclude some costs tied to mortgage losses and foreclosures when cash bonuses are calculated this year."

7. Levin-Coburn Final Report, p. 95: referencing Vanasek testimony from April 13, 2010.

8. Ibid., pp. 110–111; Melissa Allison, "WaMu's Former CEO: Bank's Demise 'Abominable to Put It Mildly,'" *Seattle Times*, September 26, 2008.

9. Dean Baker, "The Run-Up in Home Prices: Is It Real or Is It Another Bubble?" Center For Economic and Policy Research, August 2002, pp. 2–5, available at http://www.cepr.net/documents/publications/housing_2002_08.pdf.

10. Baker, "Run-Up"; James Crotty and Gerald Epstein, "Crisis and Regulation: Avoiding Another Meltdown," *Challenge* 52 (January/February 2009): 7,

citing John Gapper, "The Fatal Banker's Fall," *Financial Times*, October 1, 2008.

11. Robert J. Shiller, *Irrational Exuberance* (Princeton, NJ: Princeton University Press, 2000): Shiller shared the 2012 Nobel Prize in Economics with Eugene F. Fama and Lars Peter Hansen; David Leonhardt, "Be Warned: Mr. Bubble's Worried Again," *New York Times*, August 21, 2005; Jonathan R. Laing, "The Bubble's New Home," *Barron's*, June 20, 2005.

12. Financial Crisis Inquiry Commission, *The Financial Crisis Inquiry Report: Final Report of the National Commission on the Causes of the Financial and Economic Crisis in the United States*, authorized ed. (New York: Public Affairs, 2011) (hereinafter *FCIC Report*), 4, 17.

13. Hyman P. Minsky, *Stabilizing an Unstable Economy* (New Haven, CT: Yale University Press, 1986), 230; Hyman P. Minsky, "The Financial Instability Hypothesis," Levy Economics Institute of Bard College, Working Paper No. 74 (May 1992), 6–8; Paul McCulley, "The Shadow Banking System and Hyman Minsky's Economic Journey," *Research Foundation Publications* 2009, no. 5: 267.

14. Minsky, *Stabilizing an Unstable Economy*; Minsky, "Financial Instability Hypothesis," 8; McCulley, "Shadow Banking System," 261.

15. Martin H. Wolfson, *Financial Crises: Understanding the Postwar U.S. Experience* (Armonk, NY: M. E. Sharpe, 1994), 10–11, 17; John Geanakoplos, "The Leverage Cycle," Cowles Foundation Discussion Paper No. 1715R, July 2009, 2, revised January 2010.

16. McCulley, "Shadow Banking;" Address of William McChesney Martin Jr., Chairman, Board of Governors of the Federal Reserve System before the New York Group of the Investment Bankers Association of America, Waldorf Astoria Hotel, October 19, 1955, 12, available at http://fraser.stlouisfed.org/docs/historical/martin/martin55_1019.pdf.

17. *FCIC Report*, 4; Remarks by Chairman Alan Greenspan to the American Bankers Association Annual Convention, Palm Desert, California (via satellite), September 26, 2005.

18. Remarks by Greenspan, Palm Desert; David Leonhardt and Motoko Rich, "The Trillion-Dollar Bet," *New York Times*, June 16, 2005: "Even if home prices rise a little, borrowers who have taken out option ARMs and made only minimum payments for five years could find themselves in a hole. . . . In the first quarter of 2005, 70 percent of option ARM borrowers made the minimum payment, according to UBS. In the first quarter of 2005, 70 percent of Option ARM borrowers made the minimum payment, according to UBS."

19. *FCIC Report*, 17, 20.

20. Dean Baker, *False Profits: Recovering from the Bubble Economy* (Sausalito, CA: PoliPoint Press, 2010), 31: by early 2007, the vacancy rate would grow 50 percent higher above the peak; Remarks by Chairman Alan Greenspan at the Annual Conference of the Association of Private Enterprise Education, Arlington, Virginia, April 12, 1997: "the market-stabilizing private regulatory forces should gradually displace many cumbersome, increasingly ineffective government structures," available at http://www.federalreserve.gov/boarddocs/speeches/1997/19970412.htm.

21. Testimony of Dr. Alan Greenspan, "The Financial Crisis and the Role of Federal Regulators," Hearing before the Committee on Oversight and Government Reform, House of Representatives, October 23, 2008, pp. 11–13.

22. Remarks of Chairman Alan Greenspan, "Technology and Financial Services," before the Journal of Financial Services Research and the American Enterprise Institute Conference, in Honor of Anna Schwartz, Washington, DC, April 14, 2000, available at http://www.federalreserve.gov/boarddocs/speeches/2000/20000414.htm.

23. Speculators can also sell put options on shares they do not yet own; James Saft, "Black Monday and the Greenspan Put," Opinion, *Reuters*, October 19, 2012: the Fed used open market operations to drive down interest rates by 50 basis points when the market crashed in October 1987; Mark Carlson, "A Brief History of the 1987 Stock Market Crash with a Discussion of the Federal Reserve Response," Finance and Economic Discussion Series, Divisions of Research & Statistics and Monetary Affairs, Federal Reserve Board, November 2006, p. 21; Paul Krugman, "Dubya's Double Dip?" *New York Times*, August 2, 2002.

24. Remarks by Chairman Alan Greenspan, "Risk and Uncertainty in Monetary Policy," at the Meeting of the American Economic Association, San Diego, California, January 3, 2004, available at http://www.federalreserve.gov/boarddocs/speeches/2004/20040103/default.htm.

25. *FCIC Report*, 10, 22, 76–77; Patricia A. McCoy, Andrew D. Pavlov, and Susan M. Wachter, "Systemic Risk through Securitization: The Result of Deregulation and Regulatory Failure," *University of Connecticut Law Review* 41 (2009): 500, 512–513.

26. *FCIC Report*, 11, 79, 94; Joe Nocera, "Sheila Bair's Bank Shot," *New York Times*, July 9, 2011; Prepared Statement of Patricia A. McCoy, March 3, 2001, Hearing on "Consumer Protections in Financial Services: Past Problems, Future Solutions," before the U.S. Senate Committee on Banking, Housing, and Urban Affairs, March 3, 2009, pp. 12–13.

27. *FCIC Report*, 21; Levin-Coburn Final Report, p. 24.

28. Office of the Comptroller of the Currency, Board of Governors of the Federal Reserve System, Federal Deposit Insurance Corporation, Office of Thrift Supervision, and National Credit Union Administration, "Interagency Guidance on Nontraditional Mortgage Products Risks," September 29, 2006, 3, available at http://www.federalreserve.gov/boarddocs/srletters/2006/SR0615a2.pdf.

29. Ibid., 4.

30. Ibid., 9.

31. Levin-Coburn Final Report, pp. 93–95; High Risk Hearing Exhibits, exhibit #77, p. 548.

32. Greenspan remarks at the Annual Conference of the Association of Private Enterprise Education, 1997.

33. Greenspan, "Financial Crisis," 12.

34. Dr. Alan Greenspan, Testimony before the Financial Crisis Inquiry Commission Hearing, "Subprime Lending and Securitization and

Government-Sponsored Enterprises," April 7, 2010, p. 27, official transcript available at http://fcic-static.law.stanford.edu/cdn_media/fcic-testimony/2010-0407-Transcript.pdf.

35. DealBook, "Lippmann, Deutsche Trader, Steps Down," *New York Times*, April 21, 2010; Levin-Coburn Final Report, pp. 336–338.

36. Levin-Coburn Final Report, p. 359.

37. Ibid., p. 339; Gretchen Morgenson and Louise Story, "Banks Bundled Bad Debt, Bet against It and Won," *New York Times*, December 23, 2009; Michael Lewis, *The Big Short: Inside the Doomsday Machine* (New York: W. W. Norton, 2010), 65; Patrick Fitzgerald, "Emails Show Ex-Deutsche Trader Lippman Wanted Lehman Derivatives," *Wall Street Journal*, March 29, 2013.

38. Cassidy, *How Markets Fail*, 246; Gretchen Morgenson, "Lending Magnate Settles Fraud Case," *New York Times*, October 15, 2010; Excerpts of e-mails from Angelo Mozilo, "Sept. 26, 2006-following up a meeting with Sambol the previous day about the Pay-Option ARM loan portfoio," available at http://www.sec.gov/news/press/2009/2009-129-email.htm.

39. Testimony of Kerry Killinger, U.S. Senate Permanent Subcommittee on Investigations, Committee on Homeland Security and Governmental Affairs, Hearing on "Wall Street and the Financial Crisis: The Role of High Risk Home Loans," April 13, 2010, official transcript: In response to a question from Senator Carl Levin, Killinger said, "We had that long-term strategy, but . . . we put most of those strategies on hold." Written Statement of Kerry K. Killinger Submitted to the U.S. Senate Permanent Subcommittee on Investigations, April 13, 2010, pp. 2, 13: "Beginning in 2005, two years before the financial crisis hit, I was publicly and repeatedly warning of the risks of a housing downturn." He also stated that between 2003–2007: "Washington Mutual's market share for most higher risk residential loan products also declined dramatically." He noted that WaMu originated $63.3 billion of Option ARMs in 2005 and $42.6 billion in 2006. To decrease WaMu's exposure to the housing market, he said it took steps beginning in 2005, including that it "sold the majority of new Option ARM originations." Levin-Coburn Final Report, pp. 59, 67, 68–72, 104: "Over a five-year period from 2003 to 2008, Washington Mutual Bank shifted its loan originations from primarily traditional 30-year fixed and government backed loans to primarily higher risk home loans. . . . Mr. Killinger's claim that the High Risk Lending Strategy was put 'on hold' is contradicted, however, by WaMu's SEC filings, its internal documents, and the testimony of other WaMu executives. Washington Mutual's SEC filings contain loan origination and acquisition data showing that the bank did implement its High Risk Lending Strategy. Although rising defaults and the 2007 collapse of the subprime secondary market prevented WaMu from fully executing its plans, WaMu dramatically shifted the composition of the loans it originated and purchased, nearly doubling the percentage of higher risk home loans from 36% to 67%. . . . In late 2003, WaMu conducted two focus group studies to 'explore ways to increase sales of Option ARMs, Washington Mutual's most profitable mortgage loan products.'"

40. "The Top 25 Subprime Lenders," *Businessweek*, May 6, 2009: listing top 25 subprime issuers from 2005–2007, citing the Center for Public Integrity.

41. Jeff Madrick and Frank Partnoy, "Why Fannie and Freddie Are Not to Blame for the Crisis," *New York Review of Books Blog*: "The market for home loans shifted away from the traditional, conservative, fixed-rate mortgages backed by Fannie Mae to riskier, subprime, adjustable-rate mortgages sold by private firms such as Countrywide and New Century," available at http://www.nybooks.com/blogs/nyrblog/2011/jul/13/why-fannie-and-freddie-are-not-blame-crisis/.

42. Charles Duhigg, "Pressured to Take More Risk, Fannie Reached Tipping Point," *New York Times*, October 4, 2008; Gretchen Morgenson, "Housing Policy's Third Rail," *New York Times*, August 7, 2010; U.S. House of Representatives Committee on Oversight and Government Reform, Staff Report, "How Countrywide Used Its VIP Loan Program to Influence Washington Policymakers," July 5, 2012, pp. 7, 84–85.

43. Levin-Coburn Final Report, pp. 139–142; *FCIC Report*, 122.

44. W. Scott Frame and Lawrence J. White, "Fussing and Fuming over Fannie and Freddie: How Much Smoke, How Much Fire," Federal Reserve Bank of Atlanta, Working Paper 2004-26, October 2004; Raj Date, "The Giants Fall: Eliminating Fannie Mae and Freddie Mac," in *Make Markets Be Markets*, Roosevelt Institute, March 2010, p. 28.

45. Date, "Giants Fall," 28, Frame and White, "Fussing and Fuming," 3–4; Madrick and Partnoy, "Why Fannie and Freddie Are Not to Blame;" Jason Thomas, "Housing Policy, Subprime Markets and Fannie Mae and Freddie Mac: What We Know, What We Think We Know and What We Don't Know," November 2010, p. 7: "Neither GSE acquired junior pieces of securitizations or had any exposure to CDOs," available at http://research.stlouisfed.org/conferences/gse/Van_Order.pdf.

46. *FCIC Report*, 39; Date, "Giants Fall," 24.

47. Duhigg, "Pressured to Take More Risk."

48. Ibid.; *FCIC Report*, 179.

49. Duhigg, "Pressured to Take More Risk"; *FCIC Report*, 178–179, 181–183: Fannie's regulator the Office of Federal Housing Enterprise Oversight wrote, "During 2006 and 2007, modeled loan fees were higher than actual fees charged due to an emphasis on growing market share and competing with Wall Street and the other GSEs"; Max Abelson, "Daniel Mudd, Fannie Mae's Former CEO, Is Doing Awesome," *BloombergBusinessweek*, May 30, 2013.

50. Levin-Coburn Final Report, pp. 88, 216; Dina ElBoghady, "Senate Panel: Lax Oversight Contributed to Washington Mutual Collapse," *Washington Post*, April 16, 2010; Grind, *Lost Bank*, 224.

51. Chairman Ben S. Bernanke, "The Economic Outlook," before the Joint Economic Committee, March 28, 2007; Dean Baker, *False Profits*, 31–32; Grind, *Lost Bank*, 151; Ruth Simon and James R. Hagerty, "More Borrowers with Risky Loans Are Falling Behind," *Wall Street Journal*, December 5,

2006: there were about $625 billion subprime mortgages originated in 2005 alone, part of the overall $10 trillion in mortgages outstanding.

52. Transcript of the Federal Open Market Committee Meeting, June 28–29, 2006, pp. 155–156, available at http://www.federalreserve.gov/monetarypolicy/fomchistorical2006.htm; Binyamin Appelbaum, "Inside the Fed in 2006: A Coming Crisis, and Banter," *New York Times*, January 12, 2012.

53. Transcript of the Federal Open Market Committee June 2006 Meeting, p. 12.

54. Transcript of the Federal Open Market Committee Meeting, September 20, 2006, pp. 41–42: the Twelfth District also includes the Northern Mariana Islands, American Samoa, and Guam.

55. Andrew Ross Sorkin, *Too Big to Fail: The Inside Story of How Wall Street and Washington Fought to Save the Financial System—and Themselves* (New York: Viking, 2009), 188; Interview with Alan Greenspan, *CNBC*, October 7, 2011, available at http://video.cnbc.com/gallery/?video=3000050025.

56. Federal Reserve Bank of St. Louis, "The Financial Crisis: A Timeline of Events and Policy Actions," available at http://timeline.stlouisfed.org/index.cfm?p=timeline; "Freddie Mac Announces Tougher Subprime Lending Standards to Help Reduce the Risk of Future Borrower Default: Company Also to Develop Model Subprime Mortgages," press release, February 27, 2007.

57. Kirstin Downey, "Ameriquest Settlement Is Due Next Week," *Washington Post*, January 21, 2006; "Roland E. Arnall, 68, Founded High-Risk Lender Ameriquest," *Washington Post*, March 20, 2008.

58. Grind, *Lost Bank*, 153–154; *FCIC Report*.

59. Levin-Coburn Final Report, pp. 125–130, 135–136: "The Subcommittee investigation determined that . . . of these loans, about 1,900 with a total value of a little over $1 billion were assembled into a pool and used in the WMALT 2007-OA3 securitization in March 2007. . . . None of the materials associated with the sale of the WMALT 2007-OA3 securities informed investors of the process used to select the delinquency-prone Option ARMs from WaMu's investment portfolio and include them in the securitization. . . . Predictably, the securitization performed badly. Approximately 87% of the securities received AAA ratings. Within 9 months, by January 2008, those ratings began to be downgraded. As of February 2010, more than half of the loans in WMALT Series 2007-OA3 were delinquent, and more than a quarter were in foreclosure. All of the investment grade ratings have been downgraded to junk status, and the investors have incurred substantial losses"; High Risk Hearing Exhibits, exhibit #40b on pp. 393–394: e-mail February 20, 2007 from Cheryl A. Feltgen with "gain on sale is attractive." In same exhibit is e-mail from Feltgen to recipients including Home Loans Group president David Schneider dated February 18, 2007, stating that: "This seems to me to be a great time to sell as many Option ARMs as we possibly can. Kerry Killinger was certainly encouraging us to think seriously about it at the MBR last week. What can I do to help?" MBR meant monthly business review.

60. Bernanke, "Economic Outlook"; Federal Reserve Bank of St. Louis, "Financial Crisis"; Prepared Statement of Vickie A. Tillman, Executive Vice President, Standard & Poor's Credit Market, Services before the U.S. House of

Representatives, Subcommittee on Capital Markets, Insurance and Government Sponsored Enterprises, September 27, 2007, p. 22: "In an April 27, 2007, article entitled *Special Report: Subprime Lending: Measuring the Impact*, we stated: 'The consequences of the U.S. housing market's excesses, a topic of speculation for the past couple of years, finally have begun to surface. . . . Recent-vintage loans continue to pay the price for loosened underwriting standards and risk-layering in a declining home price appreciation market, as shown by early payment defaults and rising delinquencies"; Keith Harney, "Numbers Don't Lie, but They Do Confuse," *Washington Post*, March 10, 2007: In 2006, median prices on existing homes fell by 3.1 percent.

61. Nocera, "Sheila Bair's Bank Shot"; Grind, *Lost Bank*, 161, 166.

62. Levin-Coburn Final Report, p. 57.

63. Levin-Coburn Final Report, pp. 393–394, 554, 555: "Goldman rushed Timberwolf to market, and it closed on March 27, 2007, approximately six weeks ahead of schedule" and "Despite Mr. Montag's assessment of Timberwolf, he continued to press for the sale of Timberwolf securities to Goldman clients"; U.S. Senate Permanent Subcommittee on Investigations, Committee on Homeland Security and Governmental Affairs, Hearing on "Wall Street and the Financial Crisis: The Role of Investment Banks," April 17, 2010, official transcript: Levin said, "Timberwolf references a variety of assets, including $15 million from an Abacus CDO and more from a Washington Mutual Option ARM." When questioned about this e-mail, Dan Sparks at Goldman, who received the e-mail, said they would "know what type of investors wanted Long Beach or Washington Mutual loans to invest in, in securitized format"; Henry Sender, Francesco Guerrera and Stephanie Kirchgaessner, "Goldman 'Criticised $1Bn Loan Product,'" *Financial Times*, April 27, 2010: Bear hedge fund owned $300 billion of the $1 billion deal.

64. Levin-Coburn Final Report; *FCIC Report*, 8, 239–240.

65. Levin-Coburn High Risk Hearing Exhibits, #2a, p. 42: "Lags in Effects of Expansion" slide in Washington Mutual, Higher Risk Lending Strategy, "Asset Allocation Initiative," Board of Directors, Finance Committee Discussion, January 2005; Levin-Coburn Final Report, p. 10: "Timberwolf securities lost 80% of their value within five months of being issued and today are worthless," and pp. 431–432, note 1770; Bethany McLean and Joe Nocera, *All the Devils Are Here: The Hidden History of the Financial Crisis* (New York: Portfolio/Penguin, 2010), 217; Levin-Coburn Final Report, p. 197.

Chapter 12. First to Fall

1. William D. Cohan, *House of Cards: A Tale of Hubris and Wretched Excess on Wall Street* (New York: Doubleday, 2009), 167–172, 203, 220, 265–266, 371; Kate Kelly, "Bear CEO's Handling of Crisis Raises Issues," *Wall Street Journal*, November 1, 2007.

2. Given the Jump Start Our Business Startups Act of 2012, these private funds can now be offered through general solicitations to the public, but if so,

they must still be sold only to accredited investors; Gretchen Morgenson, "Bear Stearns Says Battered Hedge Funds Are Worth Little," *New York Times*, July 18, 2007; Cohan, *House of Cards*, 371; Kelly, "Bear CEO's Handling"; "James Cayne Lashes Back at WSJ Report," *CNNMoney.com*, November 1, 2007; the North American Bridge Championship in Nashville ran from July 19–29, 2007.

3. Jennifer Taub, "The Sophisticated Investor and the Global Financial Crisis," in *Corporate Governance Failures: The Role of Institutional Investors in the Global Financial Crisis*, ed. James Hawley, Shyam Kamath, and Andrew Williams (Philadelphia: University of Pennsylvania Press, 2010), 199.

4. Cohan, *House of Cards*, 282–283, 306–307, 341; Financial Crisis Inquiry Commission, *The Financial Crisis Inquiry Report: Final Report of the National Commission on the Causes of the Financial and Economic Crisis in the United States*, authorized ed. (New York: Public Affairs, 2011) (hereinafter *FCIC Report*), 238; Julie Creswell and Vikas Bajaj, "$3.2 Billion Move by Bear Stearns to Rescue Fund," *New York Times*, June 23, 2007: the funds were called the High-Grade Structured Credit Fund and the High-Grade Structured Credit Strategies Enhanced Leverage Fund.

5. Cohan, *House of Cards*, 283, 312, 329.

6. Ibid., 283–284, 345–347, 349, 353; Matthew Goldstein, "Bear Stearns Subprime Bath," *Bloomberg*, June 12, 2007; Creswell and Bajaj, "$3.2 Billion"; Vikas Bajaj and Julie Creswell, "Bear Stearns Staves Off Collapse of 2 Hedge Funds," *New York Times*, June 21, 2007; Landon Thomas Jr., "Prosecutors Build Bear Stearns Case on Emails," *New York Times*, June 20, 2008.

7. Jody Shenn, "Merrill Sells Portion of $850 Million Bear Funds," *Bloomberg*, June 21, 2007; David Thomas, "The Collapse of Bear Stearns: Five Years On," *Financial News*, March 19, 2013; Cohan, "Rise and Fall"; Scott Patterson, *The Quants: How a New Breed of Math Whizzes Conquered Wall Street and Nearly Destroyed It* (New York: Crown Business, 2010), 206; Yalman Onaran and Jody Shenn, "Cioffi's Hero-to-Villain Hedge Funds Masked Bear Peril in CDOs," *Bloomberg*, July 3, 2007.

8. U.S. Senate Permanent Subcommittee on Investigations, Committee on Homeland Security and Government Affairs, Majority and Minority Staff Report: *Wall Street and the Financial Crisis: Anatomy of a Financial Collapse*, April 13, 2011 (hereinafter the "Levin-Coburn Final Report"), pp. 32, 47, 124; *FCIC Report*, 213, 240: Merrill could only sell $181 million of the collateral; Kelly, "Bear CEO's Handling"; Cohan, *House of Cards*, 371, 374–377.

9. William D. Cohan, "The Rise and Fall of Jimmy Cayne," *Fortune*, updated August 25, 2008; "James Cayne Lashes Back"; *FCIC Report*, 241.

10. Levin-Coburn Final Report, pp. 98–99.

11. Ibid.; Kirsten Grind, *The Lost Bank: The Story of Washington Mutual—The Biggest Bank Failure in American History* (New York: Simon & Schuster, 2012), 166.

12. U.S. v. Milken, 759 F. Supp. 109 (S.D.N.Y, 1990): "Milken pled guilty to a six-count felony information charging him with conspiracy, securities fraud, market manipulation and tax fraud"; In re The Drexel Burnham Lambert

Group, Inc., 995 F.2d 1138 (2nd Cir. 1993), pp. 1141–1142; Kurt Eichenwald, "Milken Set to Pay a $600 Million Fine in Wall St. Fraud," *New York Times*, April 21, 1990; Stefan Fatsis, "Milken Pleads Guilty to Six Charges," Associated Press, April 24, 1990; Michael Lewis, "The Man Who Crashed the World," *Vanity Fair*, August 2009; Scot J. Paltrow, "Sobbing, Michael Milken Pleads Guilty to Six Felonies," *Los Angeles Times*, April 25, 1990; William W. Bratton and Adam J. Levitin, "A Transactional Genealogy of Scandal: From Michael Milken to Enron to Goldman Sachs," *Southern California Law Review* 86 (2013): 783–868.

13. Richard R. Zabel, "Credit Default Swaps: From Protection to Speculation," *Pratt's Journal of Bankruptcy Law*, September 2008; Gillian Tett, *Fool's Gold: The Inside Story of J.P. Morgan and How Wall St. Greed Corrupted Its Bold Dream and Created a Financial Catastrophe* (New York: Free Press, 2009), 21, 47–48; Simon Johnson and James Kwak, *13 Bankers: The Wall Street Takeover and the Next Financial Meltdown* (New York: Pantheon, 2010), 82; Bethany McLean and Joe Nocera, *All the Devils Are Here: The Hidden History of the Financial Crisis* (New York: Portfolio/Penguin, 2010), 62; David Teather, "The Woman Who Built Financial 'Weapon of Mass Destruction,'" *Guardian*, September 19, 2008, as amended on September 29, 2008; Matthew Philips, "The Monster That Ate Wall Street," *Newsweek*, September 26, 2008.

14. Tett, *Fool's Gold*, 67–68; Johnson and Kwak, *13 Bankers*, 81.

15. Congressional Oversight Panel, "June Oversight Report: The AIG Rescue, Its Impact on Markets, and the Government's Exit Strategy," June 10, 2010 ("COP AIG Report"), 21, available at http://www.gpo.gov/fdsys/pkg/CPRT-111JPRT56698/pdf/CPRT-111JPRT56698.pdf; Tett, *Fool's Gold*, 62–63; Financial Crisis Inquiry Commission (FCIC) Official Transcript, Hearing on "The Role of Derivatives in the Financial Crisis," June 30, 2010 (hereinafter "FCIC Derivatives Hearing"), p. 5: statement of chairman Phil Angelides that notional value of "credit derivatives grew from less than a trillion dollars at the beginning of this decade to a peak of $58 trillion by 2007"; Others note that the notional (or face value) of credit default swap (CDS) contracts in the early 2000s was $900 billion. By 2002, the notional value of CDS contracts grew to $2.19 trillion. By the 2007 peak, it was somewhere around $60 trillion. See, for example, Houman B. Shadab, "Guilty by Association? Regulating Credit-Default Swaps," *Entrepreneurial Business Law Journal* 4, no. 2 (2010): 433, available at http://ssrn.com/abstract=1368026, citing Bank for International Settlements, OTC Derivatives Statistics; Testimony of Joseph Cassano at the FCIC Derivatives Hearing, pp. 147–148.

16. Andrew Ross Sorkin, *Too Big to Fail: The Inside Story of How Wall Street and Washington Fought to Save the Financial System—and Themselves* (New York: Viking, 2009), 157; Gretchen Morgenson, "How Countrywide Covered the Cracks: Angelo Mozilo's Public Bravado and Private Doubts," *New York Times*, October 16, 2010.

17. David Wessel, *In Fed We Trust: Ben Bernanke's War on the Great Panic* (New York: Crown Business, 2009), 194; Maurice R. Greenberg and Lawrence A. Cunningham, *The AIG Story* (Hoboken, NJ: Wiley, 2013), 230–231: while traditionally AIG wrote CDS protection against the most creditworthy entities

like "blue-chip American corporations" or Triple-A rated European banks, in 2005, with a new "corporate culture" AIG began writing protection against risky mortgage-linked securities; Testimony of Scott Polakoff, "American International Group: Examining What Went Wrong, Government Intervention, and Implications for Future Regulation," Hearing before the Committee on Banking, Housing, and Urban Affairs of the U.S. Senate, March 5, 2009; Robert O'Harrow Jr. and Brady Dennis, "Credit Rating Downgrade, Real Estate Collapse Crippled AIG: AIG's Financial Products Unit Fell into a Spiral It Didn't Foresee and Couldn't Escape," *Los Angeles Times*, January 2, 2009: Apparently, AIG wrote more CDSs for mortgage-related securities in the last three quarters of 2005 than it did in the previous seven years.

18. Nomi Prins, *Other People's Money: The Corporate Mugging of America* (New York: New Press, 2004), 108–109.

19. Robert Pozen, *Too Big to Save? How to Fix the U.S. Financial System* (Hoboken, NJ: Wiley, 2010), 77; Lewis, "Man Who Crashed the World," 71.

20. "American International Group Q2 2007 Earnings Call Transcript," August 9, 2007; *FCIC Report*, 268.

21. Sorkin, *Too Big to Fail*, 158; Brady Dennis, "Former AIG Financial Products Leader Joe Cassano to Testify on Capitol Hill," *Washington Post*, June 30, 2010; Financial Crisis Inquiry Commission Hearing, June 30, 2010, official transcript, pp. 145, 151: Cassano testimony.

22. Pozen, *Too Big to Save?* 78; William D. Cohan, "How Goldman Killed A.I.G.," Opinionator, *New York Times*, February 16, 2011; FCIC official transcript, p. 154: apparently even AIG's chief financial officer was unaware of these "collateral call" provisions until late 2007.

23. Sorkin, *Too Big to Fail*, 159; Pozen, *Too Big to Save?* 78; *FCIC Report* 268–269.

24. *FCIC Report*, 144, fig. 8.2; McLean and Nocera, *All the Devils Are Here*, 277.

25. "Factbox: How Goldman's ABACUS Deal Worked," *Reuters*, April 16, 2010.

26. McLean and Nocera, *All the Devils Are Here*, 227.

27. Securities and Exchange Commission, "Goldman Sachs to Pay Record $550 Million to Settle SEC Charges Related to Subprime Mortgage CDO: Firm Acknowledges CDO Marketing Materials Were Incomplete and Should Have Revealed Paulson's Role," press release, July 15, 2010.

28. Joe Nocera, "Sheila Bair's Bank Shot," *New York Times*, July 9, 2011; Sheila Bair, *Bull by the Horns: Fighting to Save Main Street from Wall Street and Wall Street from Itself* (New York: Simon & Schuster, 2012), 143: This was a charge that followed Bair. For example, Treasury Secretary Geithner in a leaked story said "Bair isn't a team player."

29. Levin-Coburn Final Report, pp. 58, 59, 74; Rami Grunbaum, "Top WaMu Lawyer Out as Its Legal Issues Grow," *Seattle Times*, December 16, 2007; Grind, *Lost Bank*, 173, 175.

30. Washington Mutual, Inc., 2007 Annual Report, on Form 10-K, filed on February 29, 2008, pp. 24, 39, 103–104: Five-Year Summary of Selected

Financial Data, and Consolidated Statements of Income, Deposits, and Consolidated Statements of Financial Condition.

31. Ibid., 39, 103.

32. Ibid., 103; Ari Levy, "WaMu Slumps as Gimme Credit Cites Liquidity Concern," *Bloomberg*, July 24, 2008.

33. Washington Mutual 2007 10-K.

34. Kirsten Grind, "Insiders Detail Reasons for WaMu's Failure," *Puget Sound Business Journal*, January 25, 2009.

35. Charles Duhigg, "Pressured to Take More Risk, Fannie Reached Tipping Point," *New York Times*, October 4, 2008.

36. Grind, *Lost Bank*, 176.

37. Levin-Coburn Final Report, p. 47: "Financial Crisis Time Line": "January 30, 2008: S&P downgrades or places on credit watch over 8,000 RMBS and CDO securities"; John Gillespie and David Zweig, *Money for Nothing: How the Failure of Corporate Boards Is Ruining American Business and Costing Us Trillions* (New York: Free Press, 2010), 237–238; Grind, *Lost Bank*, 103–104; Robin Sidel and Peter Lattman, "WaMu CEO Loses Chairman Title," *Wall Street Journal*, June 3, 2008.

38. Marcy Gordon, "Risk Officers Say They Tried to Warn WaMu of Risky Mortgages," *USA Today*, April 13, 2010; Levin-Coburn Final Report, p. 115: "According to Mr. Cathcart, he attended all of the Board meetings until the end of 2007 or the beginning of 2008, at which time he was no longer invited. Mr. Cathcart felt he was excluded from Board meetings and calls with investment bankers because he was forthright about WaMu's mortgage loss rates, whereas senior management used older, more favorable numbers."

39. Levin-Coburn Final Report, pp. 214–215.

40. Kirsten Grind, "A Bank on the Run: How WaMu's Demise Hit Home," *Wall Street Journal*, June 8, 2012.

41. Daily Intelligencer, "Jimmy Cayne Closes on Sweet Plaza Pad," *New York Magazine*, March 12, 2008; James B. Stewart, "The Real Cost of Bailing Out Bear Stearns," *Wall Street Journal*, March 26, 2008; Kate Kelly, "Where in the World Is Bear's Jimmy Cayne? Playing Bridge," *Wall Street Journal*, Deal Blog, March 14, 2008; "James Cayne Lashes Back"; Aronson v. Lewis, 473 A.2d 805 (Del. 1984), Smith v. Van Gorkom, 488 A.2d 858 (Del. 1985).

42. Kelly, "Where in the World"; Stewart, "Real Cost"; Barry Ritholtz, *Bailout Nation* (Hoboken, NJ: Wiley, 2009), 177.

43. Andrew Ross Sorkin and Landon Thomas Jr., "JP Morgan Acts to Buy Ailing Bear Stearns at Huge Discount," *New York Times*, March 16, 2008; Dealbook, "JPMorgan Raises Bear Bid to $10 Per Share," *New York Times*, March 24, 2008; "JPMorgan to Buy Bear Stearns at Fraction of Value," *Reuters*, March 16, 2008; Stephen Labaton, "Testimony Offers Details of Bear Stearns Deal," *New York Times*, April 4, 2008; Roddy Boyd, "Bear Stearns Second Brush with Bankruptcy," *CNNMoney*, updated May 2, 2008; Gretchen Morgenson and Joshua Rosner, *Reckless Endangerment: How Outsized Ambition, Greed, and Corruption Led to Economic Armageddon* (New York: Henry Holt, 2011), 302; Cohan, "Rise and Fall."

44. Labaton, "Testimony Offers"; Henry M. Paulson, *On the Brink: Inside the Race to Stop the Collapse of the Global Financial System* (New York: Business Plus, 2010), 100–101, 110, 112; Cohan, *House of Cards*, 94; Sorkin, *Too Big to Fail*, 59, 68; Kate Kelly, "Bear Stearns Neared Collapse Twice in Frenzied Last Days," *Wall Street Journal*, May 29, 2008; Jonathan Macey, "Brave New Fed," Opinion, *Wall Street Journal*, March 31, 2008.

45. Scott Lanman, "Fed Releases Details on Bear Stearns Portfolios," *Bloomberg*, March 31, 2010; Craig Torres, Bob Ivry, and Scott Lanman, "Fed Reveals Bear Stearns Assets Swallowed to Get JPMorgan to Rescue Firm," *Bloomberg*, April 1, 2010; "Maiden Lane LLC Holdings as of 1/29/2010," 86, available at http://www.newyorkfed.org/markets/ML_Holdings.pdf: showing holding valued at $280,783,00 (rounded to thousands).

46. Labaton, "Testimony Offers"; Greg Farrell, "Bear Stearns, JPMorgan CEOs Outline Details of Rescue," *USA Today*, April 5, 2008; Sorkin, *Too Big to Fail*, 71; Barrie McKenna, "Bear Rescue Halted Financial Implosion, U.S. Senate Told," *Globe and Mail*, April 4, 2008.

47. Eric Dash, "Measuring Wall Street Apologetics," *New York Times*, August 17, 2010; Cohan, "Rise and Fall"; William Cohan, "The Trials of Jimmy Cayne," *Fortune*, August 4, 2008.

48. Cohan, "The Rise and Fall"; Report of Anton R. Valukas, Examiner In re Lehman Brothers Holdings, Inc., Chapter 11 Case No. 08-13555 (Bankr. S.D.N.Y., March 11, 2010); Andrew Ross Sorkin, *Too Big to Fail*; Jennifer Taub "A Whiff of Repo 105," The Baseline Scenario, March 16, 2010, http://baselinescenario.com/2010/03/16/a-whiff-of-repo-105/; Annie Lowrey, "When Are Repo Transactions Fraud?" *Washington Independent*, April 12, 2010, http://washingtonindependent.com/82016/when-are-repo-transactions-fraud.

49. Nocera, "Sheila Bair's Bank Shot."

50. Federal Reserve Bank of St. Louis, "The Financial Crisis: A Timeline of Events and Policy Actions," available at http://timeline.stlouisfed.org/pdf/CrisisTimeline.pdf.

51. Gretchen Morgenson, "Approve This Deal; or Else," *New York Times*, June 15, 2008; Geraldine Fabrikant, "WaMu Tarnishes Star Equity Firm," *New York Times*, September 26, 2008; Washington Mutual, Inc., "Quarterly Report on Form 10-Q, for the Quarter Ended June 30, 2008," 77: In April 2008, the Parent completed a significant recapitalization which resulted in the receipt of approximately $7.2 billion, $5.0 billion of which has been contributed to its principal banking subsidiary, Washington Mutual Bank"; Dealbook, "TPG Leads $7 Billion WaMu Investment," *New York Times*, April 9, 2008; Grind, *Lost Bank*, 189.

52. For sources on Blain, Knapp, and Popejoy, see part I of this book.

Chapter 13. Surf and Turf

1. U.S. Senate Permanent Subcommittee on Investigations, Committee on Homeland Security and Governmental Affairs, Exhibits, Hearing on "Wall Street and the Financial Crisis: The Role of Bank Regulators," April 13, 2010

(hereinafter "Levin-Coburn Bank Regulators Hearing Exhibits), exhibit #66, pp. 262–263; Zachery Kouwe, "Sheila Bair Is One Tough Cookie," *DealBreaker*, April 16, 2010; Kirsten Grind, *The Lost Bank: The Story of Washington Mutual—The Biggest Bank Failure in American History* (New York: Simon & Schuster, 2012), 250–251.

2. Federal Reserve Bank of St. Louis, "A Timeline of Events and Policy Actions," available at http://timeline.stlouisfed.org/pdf/CrisisTimeline.pdf; Graham Bowley and Gretchen Morgenson, "Bank Agrees to Buy Troubled Loan Giant for $4 Billion," *New York Times*, January 11, 2008.

3. Federal Deposit Insurance Corporation, Failed Bank List, available at http://www.fdic.gov/bank/individual/failed/banklist.html; Karey Wutkowski, "FDIC Says IndyMac Failure Costlier Than Expected," *Reuters*, August 26, 2008; Memorandum from Arthur J. Murton to the Board of Directors of the FDIC, "Restoration Plan, Notice of Proposed Rulemaking on Risk-Based Assessments, and the Designated Reserve Ratio for 2009"; Information for IndyMac Bank, FSB, and IndyMac Federal Bank, FSB, available at http://www.fdic.gov/bank/individual/failed/IndyMac.html.

4. Financial Crisis Inquiry Commission, *The Financial Crisis Inquiry Report: Final Report of the National Commission on the Causes of the Financial and Economic Crisis in the United States*, authorized ed. (New York: Public Affairs, 2011) (hereinafter *FCIC Report*), 268–269; Statement of Scott M. Polakoff, Acting Director of the Office of Thrift Supervision, Hearing before the Committee on Banking, Housing, and Urban Affairs, U.S. Senate, "American International Group: Examining What Went Wrong, Government Intervention, and Implications for Future Regulation," March 5, 2009, pp. 3, 5–7; Congressional Oversight Panel, "June Oversight Report: The AIG Rescue, Its Impact on Markets, and the Government's Exit Strategy," June 10, 2010 ("COP AIG Report"), 19–21, available at http://www.gpo.gov/fdsys/pkg/CPRT-111JPRT56698/pdf/CPRT-111JPRT56698.pdf; "American International Group Q2 2007 Earnings Call Transcript," August 9, 2007.

5. Financial Crisis Inquiry Commission, Preliminary Staff Report, "Governmental Rescues of 'Too Big to Fail' Financial Institutions," August 31, 2010, 25–26, available at http://fcic-static.law.stanford.edu/cdn_media/fcic-reports/2010-0831-Governmental-Rescues.pdf; COP, "June Oversight Report," 33–35.

6. *FCIC Report*, 350; COP, "June Oversight Report," 17–18: "Although AIG's insurance subsidiaries were subject to the oversight of state and foreign regulators, OTS was the firm's consolidated supervisor, responsible for coordinating overall supervision"; Polakoff, "American International Group," 8–9; Jeff Gerth, "Was AIG Watchdog Not Up to the Job?" *ProPublica*, November 10, 2008; Robert Colby, Deputy Director, Division of Market Regulation, U.S. Securities & Exchange Commission, Testimony Concerning the Consolidated Supervision of U.S. Securities Firms and Affiliated Industrial Loan Corporations before the U.S. House of Representatives Financial Services Committee, April 25, 2007, pp. 153–154; Michael Gruson, "Supervision of Financial Conglomerates in the European Union," June 23, 2004: need for the directive stemmed from the recognition that, "[t]he scope for potential supervisory problems increases if a financial conglomerate spans a number of financial

markets due to the web of financial interrelationships characteristic of financial conglomerates."

7. *FCIC Report*, 350–351; Dealbook, "As Regulator Watched, A.I.G. Unit Piled on Risk," *New York Times*, March 5, 2009.

8. Levin-Coburn Bank Regulators Hearing Exhibits, exhibit #66, pp. 262–263; Grind, *Lost Bank*, 244, 248; Levin-Coburn Final Report, pp. 167, 175; Kirstin Grind, "The Downfall of Washington Mutual," *Puget Sound Business Journal*, September 28, 2009; Office of Thrift Supervision (OTS), "Fact Sheet on Washington Mutual Bank," September 25, 2008: "Since July 2008, the pressure on WMB increased as market conditions continued to worsen. Significant deposit outflows began on September 15, 2008," available at http://files.ots.treas.gov/730021.pdf.

9. U.S. Senate Permanent Subcommittee on Investigations, Committee on Homeland Security and Government Affairs, Majority and Minority Staff Report: *Wall Street and the Financial Crisis: Anatomy of a Financial Collapse*, April 13, 2011 (hereinafter the "Levin-Coburn Final Report"), p. 201; Sheila Bair, *Bull by the Horns: Fighting to Save Main Street from Wall Street and Wall Street from Itself* (New York: Simon & Schuster, 2012), 75; Henry M. Paulson, *On the Brink: Inside the Race to Stop the Collapse of the Global Financial System* (New York: Business Plus, 2011), 316; Federal Deposit Insurance Corporation, "The FDIC's Role as Receiver," 213, available at http://www.fdic.gov/bank/historical/managing/history1-08.pdf; Grind, "Downfall of Washington Mutual"; *FCIC Report*, 37, 365–366; Remarks of Martin J. Gruenberg, Vice Chairman, FDIC at the Symposium on Deposit Insurance Cross Border Issues; International Association of Deposit Insurers, "The FDIC's Approach to Large Bank Resolution Implementation Issues," Basel, Switzerland, May 3, 2007.

10. Levin-Coburn Bank Regulators Hearing Exhibits, exhibit #66, pp. 262–263; Wutkowski, "FDIC Says."

11. Historical information, including mergers and acquisitions, available on the FDIC Web site through "Bank Find" function, available at http://research.fdic.gov/bankfind/: The certificate number is a unique identifier assigned to banking institutions for the issuance of insurance certificates.

12. FDIC, "Bank Find."

13. "American Savings and Loan for Sale," *New York Times*, May 21, 1994.

14. Simon Johnson and James Kwak, *13 Bankers: The Wall Street Takeover and the Next Financial Meltdown* (New York: Pantheon, 2010), 190, citing "The Watchmen," *This American Life*, broadcast June 5, 2009, program #382.

15. Nathaniel C. Nash, "Talking Deals: The Bass Profits in Savings Bailouts," *New York Times*, March 1, 1990; OTS, "Fact Sheet on Washington Mutual Bank"; Washington Mutual, Inc., Quarterly Report on Form 10-Q, for the Quarter Ended June 30, 2008, pp. 2, 54; Krishna Guha and Joanna Chung, "Deposit Insurance System May Face WaMu Test," *Financial Times*, September 15, 2008: "Washington Mutual had $143bn in insured deposits on June 30—about three times the size of the deposit insurance fund."

16. Levin-Coburn Bank Regulators Hearing Exhibits, exhibit #66, pp. 262–263.

17. Levin-Coburn Final Report, 201–202: An FDIC assistant regional director wrote in an e-mail: "On 9/15 I met with Dochow and he agreed to space and information sharing. . . . I am prepared for more of Dochow's stalling tactics and misrepresentations," and he later explained to a Senate committee: "I personally think they didn't want us there. I mean, we were denied physical access and the access to this examiner library . . . of electronic materials that WaMu puts together for the regulators. . . . [Y]ou shouldn't have to go 4 months without having to have that"; Levin-Coburn Bank Regulators Hearing Exhibits, exhibit #53, p. 238.

18. Office of Thrift Supervision (OTS), *Annual Report, 2007*, 22, available at http://www.ots.treas.gov/_files/481047.pdf; Office of Thrift Supervision, biography, "Darrel Dochow," available at http://www.ots.treas.gov/_files /240006.pdf.

19. Office of Thrift Supervision, *Annual Report, 2007*, 24; Washington Mutual, Inc., 2007 Annual Report, on Form 10-K, filed on February 29, 2008, p. 19.

20. OTS, biography "Darrel Dochow"; Jerry Knight, "Regulator's Role at SL under Fire," *Washington Post*, November 1, 1989; Patrick J. Sloyan, "Bank Board Probed: U.S. Investigating Reagan Aides on the Thrift Crackdown Delay," *Newsday*, June 15, 1990; Louise Story and Gretchen Morgenson, "Financial Finger-Pointing Turns to Regulators," *New York Times*, November 22, 2011; Michael M. Phillips and Jessica Holzer, "Regulator Let IndyMac Backdate Infusion," *Wall Street Journal*, December 23, 2008; Ellen Nakashima and Binyamin Appelbaum, "Regulator Let IndyMac Bank Falsify Report, Agency Didn't Enforce Its Rules, Inquiry Finds," *Washington Post*, December 23, 2008: "In September 1987 Dochow halted an examination of Lincoln, which was meant to determine whether the bank had an adequate capital cushion, at the request of his then-boss, Federal Home Loan Bank Board Chairman M. Danny Wall, according to a congressional investigation"; Mike Mayo, *Exile on Wall Street: One Analyst's Fight to Save the Big Banks from Themselves* (Hoboken, NJ: Wiley, 2012), 108–109.

21. "OTS Appoints Michael E. Finn Northeast Regional Director, June 27, 2007"; Levin-Coburn Bank Regulators Hearing Exhibits, exhibit #49, p. 215.

22. Levin-Coburn Bank Regulators Hearing Exhibits, exhibit #59, p. 246.

23. Christine E. Blair and Rose M. Kushmeider, "Challenges to the Dual Banking System: The Funding of Bank Supervision," *FDIC Banking Review*, March 2006: "In addition, the Federal Reserve supervises the holding companies of commercial banks, and the FDIC has backup supervisory authority over all insured depository institutions."

24. OTS, "Fact Sheet on Washington Mutual Bank"; Levin-Coburn Bank Regulators Hearing Exhibits, exhibit #78, p. 304, #44, p. 192; Levin-Coburn Final Report, pp. 210–211; Bethany McLean and Joe Nocera, *All the Devils Are Here: The Hidden History of the Financial Crisis* (New York: Portfolio/Penguin, 2010), 215.

25. *FCIC Report*, 173–174; McLean and Nocera, *All the Devils Are Here*, 303; Kathleen C. Engel and Patricia A. McCoy, *The Subprime Virus: Reckless Credit, Regulatory Failure, and Next Steps* (New York: Oxford University Press, 2011), 160; Mayo, *Exile on Wall Street*, 108–109.

26. Henry M. Paulson Jr., Robert K. Skeel, and David G. Nason, "The Department of the Treasury Blueprint for a Modernized Financial Regulatory Structure," March 2008: this document also recommended that the President's Working Group become an ongoing body focused on matters including systemic risk, notably this and other recommendations were implemented through the creation by Dodd-Frank Act of the Financial Stability Oversight Board (FSOC); Remarks by Secretary Henry M. Paulson Jr. on Blueprint for Regulatory Reform, March 31, 2008; David J. Lynch, Sue Kirchhoff, and Adam Shell, "Paulson's Financial Reform Plan Gets Mixed Response," *USA Today*, March 28, 2008, updated April 1, 2008; Group of Thirty, "The Structure of Financial Supervision: Approaches and Challenges in a Global Marketplace," 2008; Daniel Hemel, "Regulatory Consolidation and Cross-Border Coordination: Challenging the Conventional Wisdom," *Yale Journal on Regulation* 28, no. 1 (2011): noting that in 2009, a bipartisan group, the Committee on Capital Markets Regulation, called for merger and consolidation of the same regulators as well as the FDIC; Lawrence A. Cunningham and David Zaring, "The Three or Four Approaches to Financial Regulation: A Cautionary Analysis against Exuberance in Crisis Response," *George Washington Law Review* 78 (2009): 39: describing Paulson's and similar plans as "bewildering."

27. *FCIC Report*, 54, citing Fed chairman Alan Greenspan's statement before the Senate Committee on Banking, Housing and Urban Affairs, 103rd Cong., 2d Sess., March 2, 1994, reprinted in the *Federal Reserve Bulletin*, May 1, 1994.

28. Paul Kiel, "Banks' Favorite (Toothless) Regulator," *ProPublica*, November 25, 2008; Binyamin Appelbaum and Ellen Nakashima, "Banking Regulator Played Advocate over Enforcer," *Washington Post*, November 23, 2008: "In 2004, the year that risky loans called option adjustable-rate mortgages took off, then-OTS director James Gilleran lauded the banks for their role in providing home loans. 'Our goal is to allow thrifts to operate with a wide breadth of freedom from regulatory intrusion,' he said in a speech"; *FDIC 2003 Annual Report*, available at http://www.fdic.gov/about/strategic/report/2003annualreport/intro_insurance.html.

29. Levin-Coburn Final Report, p. 197; Levin-Coburn Bank Regulators Hearing Exhibits, exhibit # 51a, pp. 218–222; Joe Nocera, "Sheila Bair's Bank Shot," *New York Times*, July 9, 2011.

30. *FCIC Report*, xvi.

Chapter 14. Legal Enablers of the Toxic Chain

1. *The Lost Bank: The Story of Washington Mutual—The Biggest Bank Failure in American History* (New York: Simon & Schuster, 2012), 252–253.

2. Ibid., 239–240; Ari Levy and Linda Shen, "Washington Mutual Falls on $22 Billion Loss Estimate," *Bloomberg*, June 9, 2013; DealBook, "TPG Leads $7 Billion WaMu Investment," *New York Times*, April 9, 2008; Ari Levy, "Washington Mutual Drop Wipes Out Most of TPG Holding," *Bloomberg*, July 15, 2008.

3. Louise Story, "Ex-Bank Executives Settle F.D.I.C. Lawsuit," *New York Times*, December 13, 2011: FDIC entered into a $65 million settlement with

senior WaMu executives including Killinger, though they did not admit or deny wrongdoing; Lawrence G. Baxter, "'Capture' in Financial Regulation: Can We Channel It Toward the Common Good?" *Cornell Journal of Law and Public Policy* 21 (2011): 175, 176: article "regards regulatory capture to be present *whenever a particular sector of the industry, subject to the regulatory regime, has acquired persistent influence disproportionate to the balance of interests envisaged when the regulatory system was established*" (emphasis in original).

4. See part I of this book for details and sources regarding Blain, Faulkner, and Knapp.

5. Congressional Oversight Panel, Special Report on Regulatory Reform, January 2009: This report was submitted under § 125(b)(2) of Title I of the Emergency Economic Stabilization Act of 2008, Pub. L. No. 110-343, 2, 62–63, available at http://www.un.org/ga/president/63/commission/regulatoryre form.pdf; Jennifer S. Taub, "What We Don't Talk about When We Talk about Banking," in *The Handbook of the Political Economy of Financial Crises*, ed. Gerald Epstein and Martin H. Wolfson (New York: Oxford University Press, 2013), 449–450; Jane D'Arista and Tom Schlesinger, "The Parallel Banking System," in *Transforming the U.S. Financial System: Equity and Efficiency for the 21st Century* (Armonk, NY: M. E. Sharpe, 1993): "Over the last two decades, the U.S. system has been reshaped by the spread of multifunctional financial conglomerates and the emergence of an unregulated parallel banking system. Along with other powerful trends like securitization, these events have broken down the carefully compartmentalized credit and capital marketplace established in New Deal legislation"; David Moss, "An Ounce of Prevention: Financial Regulation, Moral Hazard, and the End of 'Too Big to Fail,'" *Harvard Magazine*, September–October, 2009.

6. Nadezhda Malysheva and John R. Walter, "How Large Has the Federal Financial Safety Net Become?" Federal Reserve Bank of Richmond Working Paper, WP 10-03R, March 2010, revised February 2010, pp. 1–2, 4: comparing the size of the federal safety net in 1999 to 2008, with 45 percent of financial firms in the safety net in 1999 and 57.5 percent protected by end of 2008.

7. Patricia A. McCoy and Elizabeth Renuart, "The Legal Infrastructure of Subprime and Nontraditional Home Mortgages," in *Borrowing to Live: Consumer and Mortgage Credit Revisited*, ed. Nicolas P. Retsinas, Eric S. Belsky Joint Center for Housing Studies, Harvard University, James A. Johnson Metro Series, Brookings Institution Press, November 2008, p. 7, fn. 28; Donna Vandenbrink, "Usury Ceilings and DIDMCA," Chicago Federal Reserve Bank, 1985, 25–26; Stephen P. Pizzo, Mary Fricker, and Paul Muolo, *Inside Job: The Looting of America's Savings and Loans* (New York: McGraw-Hill, 1989).

8. Joe Peek, "A Call to ARMs: Adjustable Rate Mortgages in the 1980s," *New England Economic Review* (March/April 1990): 47, 58; Patricia A. McCoy, Andrew D. Pavlov, and Susan M. Wachter, "Systemic Risk through Securitization: The Result of Deregulation and Regulatory Failure," *University of Connecticut Law Review* 41 (2009): 493, 499; Stanley M. Gorinson and Glenn B. Manishin, "Garn-St. Germain: A Harbinger of Change," *Washington and Lee Law Review* 40, no. 4 (1983): 1313; Matthew Sherman, "A Short History of Financial Deregulation in the United States," Center for Economic Policy Research, July 2009, 12; Lei Ding, Carolina Katz Reid,

Roberto G. Quercia, and Alan M. White, "The Impact of Federal Pre-emption of State Anti-Predatory Lending Laws on the Foreclosure Crisis," *Journal of Policy Analysis and Management* 31, no. 2 (Spring 2012): 367–387; Cathy Lesser Mansfield, "The Road to Subprime 'HEL' Was Paved with Good Congressional Intentions," *South Carolina Law Review* 51 (2000): 473; Nathaniel C. Nash, "Three Views: The Trouble with Savings and Loan Associations," *New York Times*, September 25, 1988: Pratt said, "The development of mortgage-backed securities and other asset-backed securities, plus commercial paper, threatens both thrifts and banks, but it threatens thrifts first."

9. Nobelman v. American Savings Bank, 508 U.S. 324 (1993); In re Estel Ray Hougland and Ruth Evelyn Hoagland, 886 F.2d 1182, 1184 (9th Cir. 1989); Sapos v. Provident Institution of Savings, 967 F.2d 918 (3d Cir. 1992); Wilson v. Commonwealth Mortgage Bank, 895 F.2d 123 (3rd Cir. 1990); In re Danny L. Hart and Joanne E. Hart, 923 F.2d 1410 (10th Cir. 1991); In re Jimmie Bellamy and Cynthia Bellamy, 962 F.2d 176 (2d Cir. 1992).

10. *FCIC Report*, 41, 122, 124, 179; Gretchen Morgenson and Joshua Rosner, *Reckless Endangerment: How Outsized Ambition, Greed, and Corruption Led to Economic Armageddon* (New York: Henry Holt, 2011), 52; Bethany McLean and Joe Nocera, *All the Devils Are Here: The Hidden History of the Financial Crisis* (New York: Portfolio/Penguin, 2010), 49; Charles Duhigg, "Pressured to Take More Risk, Fannie Reached Tipping Point," *New York Times*, October 4, 2008; Alan Zibel, "'Liar's Loans Threaten to Prolong Mortgage Crisis," *Huffington Post*, August 18, 2008: "Fannie Mae and Freddie Mac . . . lost a combined $3.1 billion between April and June. Half of their credit losses came from sour liar loans, which are officially called Alternative-A loans (Alt-A for short) because they are seen as a step below A-credit, or prime, borrowers"; "Freddie Mac Announces Tougher Subprime Lending Standards to Help Reduce the Risk of Future Borrower Default," PR Newswire, February 27, 2007: "the company will no longer purchase 'No Income, No Asset' documentation loans and will limit 'Stated Income, Stated Assets' products to borrowers whose incomes derive from hard-to-verify sources, such as the self-employed and those in the 'cash economy'"; Statement of Richard F. Syron before the Committee on Oversight and Government Reform U.S. House of Representatives, December 9, 2008, available at http://oversight-archive.waxman.house.gov/documents/20081209103407.pdf.

11. 15 U.S.C. § 1639(*l*)(2); Kathleen C. Engel and Patricia A. McCoy, *The Subprime Virus: Reckless Credit, Regulatory Failure, and Next Steps* (New York: Oxford University Press, 2011), 194–195: "There was a lot riding on his decision to stay his hand, because the Fed was the only federal agency with the statutory power to crack down on lax mortgages by originators of every stripe"; *FCIC Report*, 10–11.

12. *FCIC Report*, 10, 15–16; Gretchen Morgenson and Joshua Rosner, *Reckless Endangerment: How Outsized Ambition, Greed, and Corruption Led to Economic Armageddon* (New York: Henry Holt, 2011), 194.

13. *FCIC Report*, 10–11.

14. Morgenson and Rosner, *Reckless Endangerment*, 114; McCoy, Pavlov, and Wachter, "Systemic Risk through Securitization," 514–515.

15. *FCIC Report*, 13.

16. Watters v. Wachovia Bank, 550 U.S. 1 (2007): In his dissent, Stevens wrote, "Almost invariably the finding of preemption has been based on this Court's interpretation of statutory language or of regulations plainly authorized by Congress. Never before have we endorsed administrative action whose sole purpose was to preempt state law rather than to implement a statutory command"; Kathleen Gray, "Gov. Rick Snyder Signs Executive Order to Create Insurance, Financial Services Department," *Detroit Free Press*, January 18, 2013: in 2013, the Michigan Department of Insurance and Financial Services has now taken over the responsibilities of the former Office of Financial and Insurance Regulation; *FCIC Report*, 13; Tony Mauro, "Thomas Recusal Mystery Solved," *Legal Times*, April 24, 2007; Linda Greenhouse, "Ruling Limits State Control of Big Banks," *New York Times*, April 18, 2007.

17. *FCIC Report*, 119; McLean and Nocera, *All the Devils Are Here*, 13–14; David J. Bleckner, "Section 106 of the Secondary Mortgage Market Enhancement Act of 1984 and the Need for Overriding State Legislation," *Fordham Urban Law Journal* 13, no. 3 (1984): 681, 691–697; Michael Lewis, *Liar's Poker* (New York: W. W. Norton, 1989); 104–104; Secondary Mortgage Market Enhancement Act of 1984, Pub. L. No. 98-440, 98 Stat. 1689 (1984).

18. Ginnie Mae pooled home loans, including Veterans Administration (VA) and Federal Housing Administration (FHA) mortgages; Lewis S. Ranieri, "The Origins of Securitization, Sources of Its Growth, and Its Future Potential," in *A Primer on Securitization*, ed. Leon T. Kendall and Michael J. Fishman (Cambridge, MA: MIT Press, 1996), 37–38; McLean and Nocera, *All the Devils Are Here*, 15; Lewis, *Liar's Poker*, 100–101.

19. Alan S. Blinder, "Six Errors on the Path to the Financial Crisis," *New York Times*, January 24, 2009.

20. *FCIC Report*, 89; "Lewis S. Ranieri: Your Mortgage Was His Bond," *Business Week*, November 28, 2004; Shawn Tully, "Lewie Ranieri Wants to Fix the Mortgage Mess," *Fortune*, December 9, 2009.

21. The Banking Act of 1933, Pub. L. 73-66, 48 Stat. 162; Helen M. Burns, *The American Banking Community and New Deal Banking Reforms 1933–1935* (Westport, CT: Greenwood Press, 1974), 78, 81; Arthur E. Wilmarth Jr., "Did Universal Banks Play a Significant Role in the U.S. Economy's Boom-and-Bust Cycle of 1921–33? A Preliminary Assessment," *Current Developments in Monetary and Financial Law* 4 (2005): 559–645; J. Robert Brown Jr., "The 'Great Fall': The Consequences of Repealing the Glass-Steagall Act," *Stanford Journal of Law, Business, & Finance* 2, no. 1 (1995): 129–130: warning "the repeal of Glass-Steagall will provide, at best, marginal benefits while causing considerable damage to the securities markets"; Michael Perino, *The Hellhound of Wall Street: How Ferdinand Pecora's Investigation of the Great Crash Forever Changed American Finance* (New York: Penguin, 2010), 289: national banks had one year to sell their securities, and affiliates and investment banks were banned from taking deposits; Vincent P. Carosso, *Investment Banking in America: A History* (Cambridge, MA: Harvard University Press, 1970), 353: "The electorate was in an angry mood. It had decided that the bankers were responsible for its losses, and the conviction that thousands of innocent investors had be mulcted by self-serving financiers."

22. Arthur E. Wilmarth Jr., "Conflicts of Interest and Corporate Governance Failures at Universal Banks during the Stock Market Boom of the 1990s: The Cases of Enron and WorldCom," in *Corporate Governance in Banking: A Global Perspective*, ed. Benton E. Gup (Northampton, MA: Elgar, 2007), 97; Wilmarth, "Did Universal Banks," 561.

23. Wilmarth, "Did Universal Banks," 1–2; Pub. L. No. 106-102, 113 Stat. 1338.

24. Robert Pozen, *Too Big to Save? How to Fix the U.S. Financial System* (Hoboken, NJ: Wiley, 2010), 143.

25. Ibid., 144: "Thus a prime mortgage with a 30 percent downpayment and a subprime mortgage with a minimal downpayment would have the same 4 percent capital requirement"; Morgenson and Rosner, *Reckless Endangerment*, 134–136; *Federal Register* 66, no. 230 (November 29, 2001): 59,625, available at http://www.gpo.gov/fdsys/pkg/FR-2001-11-29/pdf/01-29179.pdf; *FCIC Report*, 476: "Beginning in 2002, for example, the Basel regulations provided that mortgages held in the form of MBS—presumably because of their superior liquidity compared to whole mortgages—required a bank to hold only 1.6 percent risk-based capital, while whole mortgages required risk-based capital backing of four percent."

26. *FCIC Report*.

27. 17 CFR 270.3a-7; U.S. Securities and Exchange Commission, *Exclusion from the Definition of Investment Company for Structured Financings*, Investment Company Act Release No. 19105 (Nov. 19, 1992), 57 FR 56248 (Nov. 27, 1992); 15 U.S.C. §§ 3(c)(1) and 3(c)(5); Division of Investment Management Report, U.S. Securities and Exchange Commission, "The Treatment of Structured Finance under the Investment Company Act," in *Protecting Investors: A Half Century of Investment Company Regulation*, May 1992, pp. 3–4.

28. Division of Investment Management, *Protecting Investors*, 4–5, 19–20.

29. Frank Partnoy and Lynn E. Turner, "Bring Transparency to Off-Balance Sheet Accounting," in *Make Markets Be Markets* (Roosevelt Institute, March 2010), 85, 87; Morgenson and Rosner, *Reckless Endangerment*, 235–236, citing Joseph Mason.

30. "Citigroup's 'Last Roman CDO' Shows Enron Accounting," *Bloomberg*, May 12, 2008.

31. "Jennifer Taub Interview on Off-Balance Sheet Reform," *Rortybomb*, April 30, 2010; Partnoy and Turner, "Bring Transparency," 86; Bethany McLean and Peter Elkind, *The Smartest Guys in the Room: The Amazing Rise and Scandalous Fall of Enron* (New York: Penguin, 2003); Bethany McLean, "Uh-oh. It's Enron All Over Again," *Fortune*, November 14, 2007: "Like Enron's off-balance-sheet vehicles, SIVs were invisible to those on the outside—and to many on the inside—until they weren't. When times were good, these creations made money for their sponsors, but when times changed, they became a problem for the rest of us."

32. *FCIC Report*, 137–139; Bradley Keoun, Jesse Westbrook, and Ian Katz, "Citigroup 'Liquidity Puts' Draw Scrutiny from Crisis Inquiry," *Bloomberg*, April 13, 2010: "Chief Executive Officer Charles O. 'Chuck' Prince, Executive Committee Chairman Robert Rubin and regulators testified before the com-

mission last week they didn't know about risks posed by the instruments. The bank's annual report for 2003—signed by Prince and posted on the Securities and Exchange Commission's Web site in early 2004—disclosed the risk of 'contingent liquidity facilities' tied to CDOs."

33. U.S. Senate Permanent Subcommittee on Investigations, Committee on Homeland Security and Government Affairs, Majority and Minority Staff Report: *Wall Street and the Financial Crisis: Anatomy of a Financial Collapse*, April 13, 2011 (hereinafter the "Levin-Coburn Final Report"), pp. 359, 393–394, 554, 555; Henry Sender, Francesco Guerrera, and Stephanie Kirchgaessner, "Goldman Criticised $1Bn Loan Product," *Financial Times*, April 27, 2010.

34. See discussion in chapter 12, including referencing these sources: Richard R. Zabel, "Credit Default Swaps: From Protection to Speculation," *Pratt's Journal of Bankruptcy Law*, September 2008; Gillian Tett, *Fool's Gold: The Inside Story of J.P. Morgan and How Wall St. Greed Corrupted Its Bold Dream and Created a Financial Catastrophe* (New York: Free Press, 2009), 21, 47–48, 67–68; Simon Johnson and James Kwak, *13 Bankers: The Wall Street Takeover and the Next Financial Meltdown* (New York: Pantheon, 2010), 81–82; Bethany McLean and Joe Nocera, *All the Devils Are Here: The Hidden History of the Financial Crisis* (New York: Portfolio/Penguin, 2010), 62; David Teather, "The Woman Who Built Financial 'Weapon of Mass Destruction,'" *The Guardian*, September 19, 2008, as amended on September 29, 2008; Matthew Philips, "The Monster That Ate Wall Street," *Newsweek*, September 26, 2008.

35. Commodity Futures Modernization Act, H.R. 5660 (CFMA), including § 117; "The Bet That Blew Up Wall Street," *60 Minutes*, October 26, 2008.

36. Lynn A. Stout, "How Deregulating Derivatives Led to a Disaster, and Why Re-Regulating Them Can Prevent Another," *Lombard Street* 1, no. 7 (2009); Lynn A. Stout, "Why the Law Hates Speculators: Regulation and Private Ordering in the Market for OTC *Derivatives*," *Duke Law Journal* 48 (1999): 701, 769–771: arguing that deregulating financial derivatives might increase market risk, erode returns, and lead to price distortions and market bubbles.

37. *FCIC Report*, 299; Nelson D. Schwartz and Eric Dash, "Where Was the Wise Man?" *New York Times*, April 27, 2008; Jake Tapper, "I Was Wrong to Listen to Wrong Advice Against Regulating Derivatives," *ABC News*, April 17, 2010.

38. Simon Johnson and James Kwak, *13 Bankers: The Wall Street Takeover and the Next Financial Meltdown* (New York: Pantheon, 2010), 9; Manuel Roig-Franzia, "Brooksley Born, the Cassandra of the Derivatives Crisis," *Washington Post*, May 26, 2009; Over-the-Counter Derivatives, 63 Fed. Reg. 26,114 (May 12, 1998); *FCIC Report*, 299.

39. Executive Order 12631, Working Group on Financial Markets, Mar. 18, 1988, 53 FR 9421; Report of the President's Working Group on Financial Markets, "Over-the-Counter Derivatives Markets and the Commodity Exchange Act," November 1999, 12, 15–17; Alan Greenspan, chairman, "Regulation, Innovation, and Wealth Creation," presented to the Society of Business Economists, London, September 25, 2002: After the CFMA, in 2002, when the topic

of regulation arose, Alan Greenspan objected, "This market, presumed to involve dealings among sophisticated professionals, has been largely exempt from government regulation. In part, this exemption reflects the view that professionals do not require the investor protections commonly afforded to markets in which retail investors participate. But regulation is not only unnecessary in these markets, it is potentially damaging, because regulation presupposes disclosure and forced disclosure of proprietary information can undercut innovations in financial markets"; available at http://www.federalreserve.gov/boarddocs/speeches/2002/200209252/default.htm.

40. Review & Outlook, "'No Line Responsibilities': What Robert Rubin Did for His $115 Million," *Wall Street Journal*, December 3, 2008; Jonathan Stempel and Dan Wilchins, "Robert Rubin Quits Citgroup amid Criticism," *Reuters*, January 9, 2009; Schwartz and Dash, "Where Was the Wise Man?"; Carol Loomis, "Robert Rubin on the Job He Never Wanted," *Fortune*, November 26, 2007; *FCIC Report*, 19.

41. Erik R. Sirri, Remarks at the National Economists Club: Securities Markets and Regulatory Reform, April 9, 2009, http://www.sec.gov/news/speech/2009/spch040909ers.htm; Julie Satow, "Ex-SEC Official Blames Agency for Blow-Up of Broker-Dealers," *New York Sun*, September 18, 2008; Lee A. Pickard, "SEC's Old Capital Approach Was Tried—and True," *American Banker*, August 8, 2008.

42. Robert Colby, Deputy Director, Division of Market Regulation, U.S. Securities & Exchange Commission, Testimony concerning the Consolidated Supervision of U.S. Securities Firms and Affiliated Industrial Loan Corporations, before the U.S. House of Representatives Financial Services Committee, April 25, 2007, pp. 153–154: "European Union's Financial Conglomerates Directive . . . essentially requires non-EU financial institutions doing business in Europe to be supervised on a consolidated basis," available at http://www.sec.gov/news/testimony/2007/ts042507rc.htmFCIC; *FCIC Report*, 154; Robert L. D. Colby, acting director, Division of Market Regulation, U.S. Securities and Exchange Commission, testimony before the U.S. House Subcommittee on Financial Institutions and Consumer Credit hearing, "Prudential Supervision of U.S. Securities Firms": "Building upon those initiatives, in 2004 the Commission amended its net capital rule to establish a voluntary, alternative method of computing net capital for well capitalized broker-dealers that have adopted strong risk management practices. This alternative method permits a broker-dealer to use mathematical models to calculate net capital requirements for market and derivatives-related credit risk. As a condition to that exemption, the broker-dealer's ultimate holding company must consent to group-wide Commission supervision, thus becoming consolidated supervised entities, or CSEs," September 14, 2006, http://www.sec.gov/news/testimony/2006/ts091406rldc.htm.

43. Andrew W. Lo, "Reading about the Financial Crisis: A 21 Book Review," *Journal of Economic Literature* 50, no. 1: 151–178; Bethany McLean, "The Meltdown Explanation That Melts Away," Opinion, *Reuters*, March 12, 2012; William D. Cohan, "How We Got the Crash Wrong," *Atlantic*, June 2012: "Clearly, the SEC did a poor job of monitoring Wall Street once it obtained this

increased regulatory authority. But the rule change *increased* rather than *decreased* the SEC's oversight of the financial sector, and did not suddenly permit a dramatic increase in leverage"; Erik R. Sirri, Remarks at the National Economists Club.

44. Pickard, "SEC's Old Capital Approach"; John Carney, "The SEC Rule That Broke Wall Street," *CNBC*, March 21, 2012: "What the 2004 amendments accomplished, then, was not a dramatic unleashing of leverage but a re-orientation of the balance sheets of the Wall Street investment banks toward mortgage-backed securities. Instead of 'originating to distribute,' the investment banks now had a regulatory incentive to hold mortgage-securities instead of other assets"; James Kwak, "What Did the SEC Really Do in 2004?" *Baseline Scenario*, January 30, 2012: "Lo is correct that the allowable leverage ratio did not change. He is also correct that the real issue for broker-dealer firms is not a traditional leverage ratio (assets to equity), but net capital (a measure of financial position). But the rule did change the way that broker-dealers were allowed to calculate their net capital; in other words, it changed the way you calculate the denominator"; Robert Pozen, *Too Big to Save? How to Fix the U.S. Financial System* (Hoboken, NJ: Wiley, 2010), 131; John Plender, "Financial Crisis Served Up with Relish," *Financial Times*, February 1, 2010.

45. McLean, "The Meltdown"; Cohan, "How We Got the Crash Wrong"; SEC Chair Mary Schapiro, testimony during the question-and-answer session after prepared remarks before the House Committee on Financial Services hearing, "Public Policy Issues Raised by the Report of the Lehman Bankruptcy Examiner," April 20, 2010, archived Webcast, http://www.house.gov/apps/list/hearing/financialsvcs_dem/hrfc_04202010.shtml.

46. William D. Cohan, "The Rise and Fall of Jimmy Cayne," *Fortune*, updated August 25, 2008.

47. Cohan, "The Rise and Fall of Jimmy Cayne"; Adam Copeland, Antoine Martin, and Michael Walker, "The Tri-Party Repo Market before the 2010 Reforms," Federal Reserve Bank of New York, Staff Report No. 477, November 2010, 1; Michael J. Fleming, Warren B. Hrung, and Frank M. Keane, "Repo Market Effects of the Term Securities Lending Facility," December 16, 2008, available at http://newyorkfed.org/research/conference/2009/cblt/Fleming_Hrung_Keane_2008.pdf: indicating the total the repo market was sized at $4.5 trillion; In 2010, Paul McCulley told the FCIC that the crisis within the shadow banking system became "a crisis of the shadow banking system" on September 15, 2008, when Lehman Brothers filed for bankruptcy protection. This transformed the run into a chaotic process, leading to the run on the money market mutual funds and a variety of U.S. and other government interventions to end the run.

48. Sarah N. Lynch, "U.S. SEC Urges Money Funds to Be Prepared for Tri-Party Repo Defaults," *Reuters*, July 22, 2013; "Repo Runs: Evidence from the Tri-Party Repo Market," Federal Reserve Bank of New York, Staff Report no. 506, July 2011, revised March 2012, 5, available at http://www.newyorkfed.org/research/staff_reports/sr506.pdf: "Money market mutual funds represent between a quarter and a third of the cash invested in the tri-party repo market."

49. Philip E. Strahan, "Liquidity Risk and Credit in the Financial Crisis," Federal Reserve Bank of San Francisco Economic Letter, May 14, 2012, available at http://www.frbsf.org/economic-research/publications/economic-letter/2012/may/liquidity-risk-credit-financial-crisis/: "When the overall supply of liquidity falls, borrowers draw on funds from existing credit lines en masse. Thus, in the 2007–08 financial crisis, nonfinancial firms lost access to short-term funds when the commercial paper market dried up . . . Many businesses drew funds from existing credit lines simply because they feared continued disturbances in the credit markets."

50. 11 U.S.C. § 101(47) used to define repurchase agreement (and reverse repurchase agreement) to encompass those with terms of no more than one year that are backed by certificates of deposit, bankers acceptances or securities that are direct obligations of, or that are fully guaranteed as to principal and interest by, the United States or any agency of the United States. The change with BAPCPA expanded the definition to also include agreements backed by collateral types: mortgage-related securities, mortgage loans, interests in mortgage-related securities or mortgage loans, and qualified foreign government securities.

51. These lenders depended upon another safe harbor provided for securities contracts, but it was not sufficiently clear that it would protect them; Burroughs and Tross, "The Treatment": BAPCPA "expanded the definition of both a 'repurchase agreement' and a 'securities contract,' and exempted repurchase agreements from the obligations and restrictions imposed by . . . the automatic stay under Section 362(a) . . . the opportunity for the debtor to assume or reject repurchase agreements under Section 365 . . . the avoidance of pre-petition payments or transfers by the debtor as 'preferences' under Sections 547 and 550" and "the prohibition against ipso facto clauses under Section 365(e)(1)"; Philip Anker, Andrew N. Goldman, and James Millar, "Safe Harbor or Adrift in Bankruptcy: Treatment of Mortgage 'Repurchase Agreements' and Servicing Rights in Bankruptcy Court," Wilmer Hale, February 22, 2008, analyzing Calyon New York Branch v. Am. Home Mortgage Corp. (In re Am. Home Mortgage, Inc.), 379 B.R. 503 (Bankr. D. Del. 2008): the special treatment of mortgage-related collateral was affirmed in this Delaware bankruptcy court decision in early 2008 in the wake of the subprime crisis.

52. 11 U.S.C. § 559: "[t]he exercise of a contractual right of a repo participant . . . to cause the liquidation, termination, or acceleration of a repurchase agreement . . . shall not be stayed, avoided, or otherwise limited"; 11 U.S.C. § 362(b)(7): excludes from the automatic stay found in Section 362(a) cash lenders in repos backed by protected collateral; Stephen J. Lubben, "The Bankruptcy Code without Safe Harbors," *American Bankruptcy Law Journal* 84 (2010): 123; Thomas M. Hoenig and Charles S. Morris, "Restructuring the Banking System to Improve Safety and Soundness," Federal Reserve Bank of Kansas City, May 2011, p. 3, available at http://www.kansascityfed.org/publicat/speeches/Restructuring-the-Banking-System-05-24-11.pdf: "bankruptcy law for repurchase agreement collateral should be rolled back to the pre-2005 rules, which would eliminate mortgage-related assets from being exempt from the automatic stay in bankruptcy when the borrower defaults on its repurchase obligation"; Mary Fricker, "Consider This," available on repowatch blog

home page, last checked October 20, 2013: "The financial crisis was not caused by homeowners borrowing too much money. It was caused by giant financial institutions borrowing too much money, much of it from each other on the repurchase (repo) market. This matters, because we can't prevent the next crisis by fixing mortgages. We have to fix repos."

53. See part I of this book.

54. U.S. Senate Permanent Subcommittee on Investigations, Committee on Homeland Security and Governmental Affairs, Exhibits, Hearing on "Wall Street and the Financial Crisis: The Role of Bank Regulators," April 13, 2010, exhibit #68, p. 266.

Chapter 15. The Great Betrayal

1. Naomi Zeveloff, "Liveblog: Barack Obama Rally in Golden," *Colorado Independent*, September 16, 2008; Jeff Zeleny, "Candidates on Wall Street Turmoil," *New York Times*, September 15, 2008; Russ Britt, "Did McCain Economy Gaffe Prompt a Correction?" *MarketWatch*, September 15, 2008.

2. "Lehman Files for Bankruptcy Protection: Wall Street Titan Goes Under after Frenzied Search for Buyer Falls Short," *MarketWatch*, September 15, 2008; Linda Sandler, "Lehman Had $200 Billion Overnight Repos before Failure," *Bloomberg*, January 28, 2011; Vincent P. Carosso, *Investment Banking in America: A History* (Cambridge, MA: Harvard University Press, 1970), 20, 82–83; "History of Lehman Brothers," Lehman Brothers Collection—Contemporary Business Archives, Harvard, available at http://www.library.hbs.edu/hc/lehman/history.html; Michael J. de la Merced, Vikas Bajaj, and Andrew Ross Sorkin, "As Morgan and Goldman Shift, a Wall St. Era Ends," *New York Times*, Dealbook, September 21, 2008; Federal Reserve Bank of St. Louis, "A Timeline of Events and Policy Actions," available at http://timeline.stlouisfed.org/pdf/CrisisTimeline.pdf.

3. Karen Dolan, "A Large Money Market Fund Breaks the Buck," *Morningstar*, September 17, 2008; Jonathan Stempel, "Reserve Primary Fund Founder Fails to End SEC Fraud Case: SEC Said Defendants Fraudulently Blocked Redemptions," *Reuters*, May 29, 2012; SEC v. Reserve Management Company, Inc., RESRV Partners, Inc., Bruce Bent Sr., and Bruce Bent II (Defendants) and the Reserve Primary Fund (Relief Defendant), Complaint filed May 5, 2009; Aaron Elstein, "Inside the Panic at Reserve Fund," *Crain's New York Business*, May 10, 2009; Chris Cumming, "Reserve's Former CIO Takes the Stand in Bent's Trial," *Mutual Fund Wire*, October 23, 2012.

4. Chairman Mary L. Schapiro, U.S. Securities and Exchange Commission Testimony on "Perspectives on Money Market Mutual Fund Reforms" before the Committee on Banking, Housing, and Urban Affairs of the U.S. Senate, June 21, 2012; Geoffrey Colvin and Katie Benner, "GE under Siege," *Fortune*, October 15, 2008: "Lots of firms use commercial paper, frequently just for paying day-to-day bills, but no company uses it anything like GE. GE Capital alone has about $74 billion of commercial paper outstanding; the next largest player, J.P. Morgan, has about $47 billion"; Philip E. Strahan,

"Liquidity Risk and Credit in the Financial Crisis," Federal Reserve Bank of San Francisco Economic Letter, May 14, 2012, p. 1, citing Victoria Ivashina and David Scharfstein, "Bank Lending during the Financial Crisis of 2008," *Journal of Financial Economics* 97, no. 3 (2010): 319–338; David M. Katz, "CFOs React: AEP's Holly Koeppel," Banking & Capital Markets, *CFO.com*, December 16, 2008, available at http://www.frbsf.org/economic-research/publications/economic-letter/2012/may/liquidity-risk-credit-financial-crisis/el2012-15.pdf.

5. Schapiro, "Perspectives"; Diana B. Henriques, "Treasury to Guarantee Money Market Funds," *New York Times*, September 19, 2008; U.S. Securities and Exchange Commission, "Statement of SEC Chairman Mary Schapiro on Money Market Fund Reform," August 22, 2012, available at http://www.sec.gov/news/press/2012/2012-166.htm; Federal Reserve Bank of St. Louis, "A Timeline of Events": regarding the commercial paper funding facility.

6. Kirsten Grind, *The Lost Bank: The Story of Washington Mutual—The Biggest Bank Failure in American History* (New York: Simon & Schuster, 2012), 304; Christopher Palmeri, "JPMorgan Chase to Buy Washington Mutual," *Bloomberg*, September 26, 2008; In re: Washington Mutual, Inc., U.S. Bankruptcy Court, District of Delaware, No. 08-12229; Dawn Kopecki, "Dimon Beset by Bad Loans as JP Morgan Pushes Overseas," *Bloomberg*, November 2, 2010: "Jamie Dimon wanted Washington Mutual Inc. and he wanted it bad."

7. Congressional Oversight Panel, "June Oversight Report: The AIG Rescue, Its Impact on Markets, and the Government's Exit Strategy," June 10, 2010, pp. 2, 54–57; Robert Pozen, *Too Big to Save? How to Fix the U.S. Financial System* (Hoboken, NJ: Wiley, 2010), 78–79: "these exchanges constituted unjustified gifts by the U.S. government to the most sophisticated investors in the world, who had made bad judgments about whether this AIG subsidiary could deliver on its promised credit protection"; Mary Williams Walsh, "Audit Faults New York Fed in A.I.G. Bailout," *New York Times*, November 16, 2009; Office of the Special Inspector General of the Troubled Asset Relief Program, "Factors Affecting Efforts to Limit Payments to AIG Counterparties," November 17, 2009, pp. 10, 13: AIG had $20 billion in commercial paper outstanding compared to Lehman's $8 billion, insured $38 billion in retirement funds, and was otherwise entwined with an array of commercial enterprises; David Ellis, "U.S. Seizes Fannie and Freddie: Treasury Chief Paulson Unveils Historic Government Takeover of Twin Mortgage Buyers. Top Executives Are Out," *CNNMoney*, September 7, 2008; ProPublica, "Preferred Stock Investments: Fannie and Freddie Bailout," Bailout Tracker, as of October 23, 2013.

8. *Lou Dobbs Tonight* transcript, *CNN*, December 16, 2008: "BUSH: I've abandoned free market principles to save the free market system. I think when people review what has taken place in the last six months and put it all in one package, they'll realize how significantly we have moved."

9. Susan Davis, "Obama's Remarks on Economic Crisis," *Wall Street Journal*, Washington Wire, September 28, 2008; Center for Responsible Lending, "Solution to Housing Crisis Requires Adjusting Loans to Fair Market Value through Court-Supervised Modifications," Issue Brief, April 1, 2008.

10. David M. Herszenhorn, "Administration Is Seeking $700 Billion for Wall Street," *New York Times*, September 20, 2008; Mark Landler and Steven Lee Myers, "Buyout Plan for Wall Street Is a Hard Sell on Capitol Hill," *New York Times*, September 23, 2008; *The Situation Room*, "Selling the Bailout to Congress," *CNN*, September 23, 2008.

11. Landler and Myers, "Bailout Plan"; Chris Isadore, "Bailout Plan under Fire," *CNNMoney.com*, September 23, 2008; Adam Davidson, "Bailout Seeks Broad New Powers for Treasury Chief," *N.P.R. Morning Edition*, September 23, 2008; U.S. Treasury, "Legislative Proposal for Treasury Authority to Purchase Mortgage-Related Assets," available at http://money.cnn.com/2008/09/20/news/economy/treasury_proposal/: mortgage-related assets were defined as "residential or commercial mortgages and any securities, obligations, or other instruments that are based on or related to such mortgages, that in each case was originated or issued on or before September 17, 2008."

12. Thomas B. Edsall, "Obama Says Bailout Bill Should Not Include Bankruptcy Reform," *Huffington Post*, September 26, 2008, updated October 26, 2008; Obama's Statement on Economy, Divide, Clearwater, Florida," *Real Clear Politics*, September 24, 2008, available at http://www.realclearpolitics.com/articles/2008/09/obamas_statement_on_eco.html.

13. Paul Kiel and Olga Pierce, "Dems: Obama Broke Pledge to Force Banks to Help Homeowners," *ProPublica*, February 4, 2011; author telephone interview with Julia Gordon.

14. Lewis Ranieri speaking at the Milken Institute Conference on Financial Innovation, cited by Mike Konczal in "The Financial Innovation That Wasn't," *RortyBomb*, July 31, 2009.

15. Pub. L. No. 110-343, 122 Stat. 3765; Matt Taibbi, "Secrets and Lies of the Bailout," *Rolling Stone*, January 4, 2013: "Treasury would buy $700 billion of troubled mortgages from the banks and then modify them to help struggling homeowners. Section 109 of the act, in fact, specifically empowered the Treasury secretary to 'facilitate loan modifications to prevent avoidable foreclosures.' With that promise on the table, wary Democrats finally approved the bailout on October 3rd, 2008. 'That provision,' says [Neil] Barofsky, 'is what got the bill passed'"; Paul Keil, "Gov't Has Spent Small Fraction of $50 Billion Pledged for Loan Mods," *ProPublica*, November 11, 2010; Joe Nocera, "Sheila Bair's Bank Shot," *New York Times*, July 9, 2011: Nocera wrote: "Without question, it is difficult to get mortgage modifications right. But many Democrats originally voted for TARP because it contained a provision mandating that $50 billion of the $700 billion in bailout money go to mortgage modification. The Paulson Treasury ignored that part of the law—and the Geithner Treasury has barely touched that $50 billion."

16. Vikas Bajaj, "Economic Crisis a Study in the Power of Fear," *New York Times*, October 8, 2008: "Fear can be seen at every turn: in headlines raising questions about another 1930s-style Depression and in the crowds gathered around office televisions to track stocks or to parse the latest pronouncements from the Federal Reserve chairman, Ben Bernanke, or Treasury Secretary Henry Paulson Jr."; Alan M. Winkler, Testimony before the U.S. Senate Committee on Banking, Housing, and Urban Affairs, "The New Deal: Accomplishments and Failures," March 31, 2009; Adam Cohen, *Nothing to Fear: FDR's*

Inner Circle and the Hundred Days That Created Modern America (New York: Penguin, 2009), 1; David Leonhardt, "Lesson from a Crisis: When Trust Vanishes, Worry," *New York Times*, September 30, 2008; Paul Krugman, "Moment of Truth," *New York Times*, op-ed, October 9, 2008: "They'd better do something soon—in fact, they'd better announce a coordinated rescue plan this weekend—or the world economy may well experience its worst slump since the Great Depression."

17. Sheila Bair, *Bull by the Horns: Fighting to Save Main Street from Wall Street and Wall Street from Itself* (New York: Simon & Schuster, 2012), 6, 115, 119; Barry Ritholtz, "Was the TARP a Ruse?" *Big Picture*, June 9, 2009.

18. Ben S. Bernanke, *Essays on the Great Depression* (Princeton, NJ: Princeton University Press, 2004); Roger Lowenstein, "The Education of Ben Bernanke," *New York Times*, January 20, 2008; Paul Krugman, "Fighting Off Depression," *New York Times*, op-ed, January 4, 2009: "Milton Friedman, in particular, persuaded many economists that the Federal Reserve could have stopped the Depression in its tracks simply by providing banks with more liquidity, which would have prevented a sharp fall in the money supply. Ben Bernanke, the Federal Reserve chairman, famously apologized to Friedman on his institution's behalf: 'You're right. We did it. We're very sorry. But thanks to you, we won't do it again.'"

19. *PBS NewsHour* forum in Kansas City, MO, July 26, 2009, transcript available at http://www.pbs.org/newshour/bb/business/july-dec09/bernanke_07-27.html.

20. Thomas L. Hogan, Linh Le, and Alexander William Salter, "Ben Bernanke and Bagehot's Rules," August 2013: "the Fed appears to have violated the Bagehot doctrine by lending to potentially insolvent institutions, not charging a high penalty rate of interest, and not requiring sound collateral for its last-resort loans," available at http://ssrn.com/abstract=2316832 or http://dx.doi.org/10.2139/ssrn.2316832.

21. Paul Krugman, "The Mellon Doctrine," *New York Times*, March 31, 2011.

22. U.S. Senate Democrats, Legislative Bulletin, S. 896 the Helping Families Save Their Homes Act of 2009, April 30, 2009, available at http://democrats.senate.gov/2009/04/30/s-896-the-helping-families-save-their-homes-act-of-2009/; Video of Senate session April 30, 2009, beginning at 10:52 a.m. shown at the 1:21:30 mark, available at http://c-spanvideo.org/program/SenateSession4363.

23. The Durbin Amendment (S.A. 1014), available at http://thomas.loc.gov/cgi-bin/query/C?r111:./temp/~r111ztgwfx; The Helping Families Save Their Homes Act of 2009, H.R. 1106; Dawn Kopecki, "Mortgage 'Cram-Down' Bankruptcy Bill May Aid 1 Million in U.S.," *Bloomberg*, March 6, 2009.

24. Letter to Hon. John M. Spratt Jr., chairman, Committee on the Budget, from Douglas W. Elmendorf, director, Congressional Budget Office, February 25, 2009; Renae Merle, "Bankruptcy Filings Would Rise under Mortgage Bill, CBO Says," *Washington Post*, February 25, 2009; Michele J. White and Ning Zhu, "Saving Your Home in Chapter 13 Bankruptcy": presenting "new evidence that nearly all debtors who use Chapter 13 are homeowners who wish to save

their homes"; Alex Ulum, "Why a Mortgage Cramdown Bill Is Still the Best Bet to Save the Economy," *Nation*, October 20, 2011: In fact the CBO estimated the government would come out slightly ahead, due to increased bankruptcy fees.

25. Stephen Labaton, "Senate Refuses to Let Judges Fix Mortgages in Bankruptcy," *New York Times*, May 1, 2009: "The House bill contains the bankruptcy provision. But the Senate's defeat of the so-called bankruptcy cramdown measure all but makes certain it will disappear from the final bill"; Jane Hamsher, "Over $42 Million Paid to Lobbyists to Defeat 'Cramdown' in 1Q 2009": lobbying reports identify issues lobbied but do not break down the dollars issue-by-issue, thus the totals reflect spending by each firm for the quarter during which this and other consumer-related financial matters were hot button issues; David Lereah, *Why the Real Estate Boom Will Not Bust—And How You Can Profit from It: How to Build Wealth in Today's Expanding Real Estate Market* (New York: Random House, 2005).

26. Adam J. Levitin and Joshua Goodman, "The Effect of Bankruptcy Strip-Down on Mortgage Markets," Georgetown Law and Economics, Research Paper No. 1087816, February 6, 2008; Adam J. Levitin, "Resolving the Foreclosure Crisis: Modification of Mortgages in Bankruptcy," *Wisconsin Law Review* (2009): 565, 577: "permitting modification would have little or no impact on mortgage credit cost or availability. Because lenders face smaller losses from bankruptcy modification than from foreclosure, the market is unlikely to price against bankruptcy modification. . . . Permitting modification of all mortgages in bankruptcy would thus create a low-cost, effective, fair, and immediately available method for resolving much of the current foreclosure crisis without imposing costs on the public fisc or creating a moral hazard for borrowers or lenders."

27. U.S. Government Accounting Office, "Farm Finance: Participants' Views on Issues Surrounding Chapter 12 Bankruptcy," Briefing Report to Congressional Requesters, GAO/RCED-89-142BR, 18: cost of credit issue; Robert N. Collender, "Bankruptcy Costs under Chapter 12," U.S. Department of Agriculture, Economic Research Service, September 1992, pp. 15, 16: "impact of the increased bankruptcy costs imposed by Chapter 12 can be expected to fall disproportionately on financially weak or beginning farmers. . . . To offset the costs . . . interest rates to farm borrowers will have to be between 0.25 and 1.0 percent higher on average"; James T. Massey, "Farmers Home Administration and Farm Credit System Update," *Nebraska Law Review* 73 (1994): 187, 194.

28. GAO, "Farm Finance"; Thomas J. Fitzpatrick IV and James B. Thomson, "Stripdowns and Bankruptcy: Lessons from Agricultural Bankruptcy Reform, Economic Commentary," Federal Reserve Bank of Cleveland, August 3, 2010; Letter from John Blanchfield and Ryan Zagone of the American Bankers Association to Thomas Fitzpatrick and James Thomson, August 26, 2010; Letter from Fitzpatrick and Thomson in response to Letter from Blanchfield and Zagone, September 8, 2010.

29. Lawrence A. Cunningham, *Contracts in the Real World: Stories of Popular Contracts and Why They Matter* (New York: Cambridge University Press, 2012), 2, 82, 213.

30. See parts I and II of this book; Bair, *Bull by the Horns*, 28: "The moral hazard problem is worse for very large institutions that the market perceives as too big to fail. With the very largest financial institutions, the markets assume that the government will protect everyone, not just insured depositors, if they get in trouble"; Mark Zandi, *Financial Shock: A 360° Look at the Subprime Mortgage Implosion, and How to Avoid the Next Financial Crisis* (Upper Saddle River, NJ: Pearson Education, 2009), 111–112, 114; Antje Berndt and Anurag Gupta, "Moral Hazard and Adverse Selection: Originate-to-Distribute Model of Bank Credit," March 2009, available at http://www.frbatlanta.org/filelegacydocs/seminars/seminar_berndt_041609.pdf: the authors studied the originate-to-distribute model as applied to commercial loans that were sold into the secondary market either whole or securitized: "The highly deregulated nature of the secondary loan market is perhaps one of the reasons for the moral hazard and adverse selection problems that we detect."

31. John D. Geanakoplos and Susan P. Koniak, "Matters of Principal," *New York Times*, op-ed, March 4, 2009: "It is not just your home values and your neighborhoods that will deteriorate if you insist that your underwater neighbors not get relief; it is your tax dollars . . . It is your job that will be at stake when your neighbors can no longer afford to buy goods and services, causing more companies to cut jobs."

32. U.S. Senate Roll Call Votes, 111th Congress on Senate Amendment 1014 to S. 896, the Helping Families Save their Homes Act of 2009, April 30, 2009 (on a vote of 45–51), available at http://www.senate.gov/legislative/LIS/roll_call_lists/roll_call_vote_cfm.cfm?congress=111&session=1&vote=00174: note that Senator Sanders, an independent, voted with the Democrats; Author's in-person conversation with Barney Frank, Northampton, MA, October 14, 2012; Ryan Grim, "Dick Durbin: Banks 'Frankly Own the Place,'" *Huffington Post*, May 30, 2009.

33. Mary Orndorff, "Spencer Bachus Finally Gets His Chairmanship," *Birmingham News*, December 9, 2010; The Helping Families Save Their Homes Act of 2009, H.R. 1106 roll call (234-191), with Spencer Bacus a "nay."

34. Editorial, "As Foreclosures Surge . . . ," *New York Times*, May 3, 2009: "The Obama administration sat by last week as 12 Senate Democrats joined 39 Senate Republicans to block a vote on an amendment that would have allowed bankruptcy judges to modify troubled mortgage"; Michael Barr's response to a question posed by author after his luncheon remarks at the Association of American Law Schools Conference, New Orleans, January 5, 2013.

35. Pub.L. 111–22; Alan Zibel, "Numbers Up, but Mortgage-Relief Effort Still Falters," *Wall Street Journal*, October 6, 2011: "the numbers are well below the initial goal trumpeted by President Barack Obama in February 2009 of helping 3 million to 4 million borrowers"; Special Inspector General for the Troubled Asset Relief Program, "Rising Redefaults of HAMP Mortgage Modifications Hurt Homeowners, Communities, and Taxpayers," July 24, 2013, p. 1, available at http://www.sigtarp.gov/Audit

%20Reports/Rising_Redefaults_of_HAMP_Mortgage_Modifications.pdf; Barofsky, *Bailout*, 19; The Congressional Oversight Panel, The Final Report of the Congressional Oversight Panel, Section IV, Foreclosure Mitigation, March 16, 2011, pp. 68–73, available at http://www.gpo.gov/fdsys/pkg/CHRG-112shrg64832/pdf/CHRG-112shrg64832.pdf: "In a December 2010 report, the Panel estimated that HAMP would prevent only 700,000 to 800,000 foreclosures if it continues on its current trajectory—far fewer than the three to four million foreclosures that Treasury initially aimed to prevent, and vastly fewer than the eight to 13 million foreclosures expected by 2012."

36. Alejandro Lazo, "Banks are Foreclosing while Homeowners Pursue Loan Modifications," *Los Angeles Times*, April 14, 2011; Paul Kiel, "Bank of America Lied to Homeowners and Rewarded Foreclosures, Former Employees Say," *ProPublica*, June 14, 2013: "The employee statements were filed late last week in federal court in Boston as part of a multi-state class action suit brought on behalf of homeowners who sought to avoid foreclosure through the government's Home Affordable Modification Program (HAMP) but say they had their cases botched by Bank of America."

37. Neil Barofsky, *Bailout: An Inside Account of How Washington Abandoned Main Street while Rescuing Wall Street* (New York: Simon & Schuster, 2012), 125–126; White and Zhu, "Saving Your Home," 3: "all mortgages have a servicer who acts on owners' behalf, but mortgage servicing contracts compensate servicers only for the costs of foreclosing, not for the costs of renegotiating. These contracts also limit or prohibit servicers from changing the terms of the underlying mortgages . . . many homes in default have second mortgages . . . because many second mortgages are now worthless, lenders' best strategy is block modifications and refinancings unless they are paid for giving up their claims."

38. Barofsky, *Bailout*, 193, 196–198; COP Final Report: "The Panel articulated three major concerns with HAMP in the April 2010 report: (1) its failure to deal with the foreclosure crisis in a timely way; (2) the unsustainable nature of many HAMP modifications, given the large debt burdens and negative equity that many participating homeowners continued to carry; and (3) the need for greater accountability in HAMP, particularly with regard to the activities of participating servicers."

39. Barry Ritholtz, "Rick Santelli's Planted Rant?" *Big Picture*, February 28, 2009: "But his rant somehow felt *wrong*. After we've pissed through over $7 trillion dollars in Federal bailouts to banks, brokers, automakers, insurers, etc., this was a pittance, the least offensive of all the vast sums of wasted money spent on 'losers' to use Santelli's phrase. It seemed like a whole lot of noise over 'just' $75 billion, or 1% of the rest of the total ne'er-do-well bailout monies"; Matt Taibbi, "Secrets and Lies of the Bailout," *Rolling Stone*, January 4, 2013; Eric Etheridge, "Rick Santelli: Tea Party Time," *New York Times*, Opinionator, February 20, 2009.

40. Geanakoplos and Koniak, "Matters of Principal."

41. Barofsky, *Bailout*, 199; author's telephone interview with Senator Ted Kaufman, June 18, 2012.

Chapter 16. Dispelling Myths about the Crisis

1. Financial Crisis Inquiry Commission, Hearing on Subprime Lending and Securitization and Government Sponsored Enterprises, Session 1, April 7, 2010, televised as "Causes of 2008 Financial Collapse, Financial Institution Representatives," CSPAN, available at http://c-spanvideo.org/program/Causesof: the power failed about 11:44 a.m.; "History of the Commission: About the FCIC at Stanford Law School," available at http://fcic.law.stanford.edu/about: the FCIC was established under the Fraud Enforcement and Recovery Act of 2009.

2. FCIC Official Transcript, Testimony of Alan Greenspan before the Financial Crisis Inquiry Commission, Hearing on Subprime Lending and Securitization and Government Sponsored Enterprises, Session 1, Federal Reserve, April 7, 2010 ("FCIC April Transcript"), pp. 29, 113–114, available at http://fcic-static.law.stanford.edu/cdn_media/fcic-testimony/2010-0407-Transcript.pdf.

3. Testimony of Dr. Alan Greenspan, U.S. House of Representatives, Committee on Oversight and Government Reform, October 23, 2008; Edmund L. Andrews, "Greenspan Concedes Error on Regulation, *New York Times,* October 24, 2008: "Yes, I've found a flaw. I don't know how significant or permanent it is. But I've been very distressed by that fact."

4. FCIC April Transcript, pp. 64–65, 94; Alan Greenspan, "Regulators Must Risk More, and Intervene Less," *Financial Times,* July 26, 2011.

5. FCIC April Transcript, pp. 108–109; Gary S. Becker, "Crime and Punishment: An Economic Approach," in *Essays in the Economics of Crime and Punishment* (New York: National Bureau of Economic Research, 1974), 9; Robert H. Lande and Joshua P. Davis, "Comparative Deterrence from Private Enforcement and Criminal Enforcement of the U.S. Antitrust Laws," *Brigham Young University Law Review* (2011): 315: "Perhaps more surprisingly, there is evidence that private antitrust enforcement does more than DOJ criminal enforcement to deter anticompetitive behavior"; Samuel W. Buell, "Liability and Admissions of Wrongdoing in Public Enforcement of Law," *University of Cincinnati Law Review* 81 (2013): "analysis of the deterrent effects of the three main components of settlements in public enforcement of law: liability, admission, and remedy" concluding that "[a]ll three components have beneficial deterrent effects. . . . Virtually every day one can find a corporate manager somewhere declaring that criminal liability of her firm is her greatest fear, or a person under investigation vociferously maintaining in the press that he is not a criminal and has done nothing wrong."

6. Manuel Roig-Franzia, "Brooksley Born: The Cassandra of the Derivatives Crisis," *Washington Post,* May 26, 2009.

7. Ibid.

8. FCIC April Transcript, pp. 87–88.

9. Ibid., p. 93.

10. Ibid., pp. 94–95.

11. Gertrude Stein, *Everybody's Autobiography* (New York: Random House, 1937), 298: "what was the use of my having come from Oakland it was not

natural to have come from there yes write about it if I like or anything if I like but not there, there is no there there."

12. This section identifying the top ten myths about the financial crisis is drawn from my previous three-part series, "Mythbusters: Telling the Truth about the Financial Crisis," *Pareto Commons*, January 31, 2011, February 6, 2011, and February 10, 2011.

13. U.S. Senate Permanent Subcommittee on Investigations, Committee on Homeland Security and Government Affairs, Majority and Minority Staff Report: *Wall Street and the Financial Crisis: Anatomy of a Financial Collapse*, April 13, 2011 (hereinafter the "Levin-Coburn Final Report"), p. 1; Jennifer Taub, "Bipartisan Senate Panel Report Slams Banks and Bureaucrats: 'Please Sir, I Want Some More,'" *Pareto Commons*, April 15, 2013.

14. Sewell Chan and Eric Dash, "Staff Losses and Dissent May Hurt Crisis Panel," *New York Times*, August 31, 2010; Financial Crisis Inquiry Commission, *The Financial Crisis Inquiry Report: Final Report of the National Commission on the Causes of the Financial and Economic Crisis in the United States*, authorized ed. (New York: Public Affairs, 2011) (hereinafter *FCIC Report*): commissioners who voted to adopt the majority report were: Phil Angelides, Brooksley Born, Byron Georgiou, Bob Graham, Heather H. Murren, and John W. Thompson; commissioners who signed the Primary Dissent were Keith Hennessey, Douglas Holtz-Eakin, and Bill Thomas; the Solo Dissent was signed by Peter Wallison; the Primary Dissent begins on p. 413 and the Solo Dissent on pp. 443–450 in the hard copy of the book, and to p. 538 in the electronic version available on the FCIC Web site, making the electronic version of the report a total of 633 pages.

15. *FCIC Report*, xvi, xx, 414, 428, 464; Ben W. Heineman Jr., "FCIC: The Private Sector Failed," *Atlantic*, January 31, 2011: "The bipartisan commissioners emphatically concluded that one of the primary causes of the meltdown was massive failure of private sector decision-making, especially in major financial institutions"; Barbara Roper, "Non-Partisan FCIC Report Draws Partisan Dissent," *Huffington Post*, February 1, 2011: "I doubt the Democratic members of the Commission would find much if anything to disagree with in this account"; Lawrence Baxter, "What Caused the Financial Crisis? The FCIC Report," *Pareto Commons*, January 27, 2011.

16. Levin-Coburn Final Report, p. 1; *FCIC Report*, xvii, 417–419, 443; James R. Barth, Gerard Caprio Jr., and Ross Levine, *Guardians of Finance: Making Regulators Work for Us* (Cambridge, MA: MIT Press, 2012), 1: "challenging the repeated false narrative that, [i]t was a terrible accident precipitated by an unforeseeable confluence of events. . . . The story is told and retold by a chorus of luminaries who include Treasury Secretary Timothy Geithner and his predecessors in the position, Henry Paulson and Robert Rubin. Ben Bernanke and Alan Greenspan are in the choir."

17. *FCIC Report*, xxvii.

18. Ibid., 414; Raymond H. Brescia, " Part of the Disease or Part of the Cure: The Financial Crisis and the Community Reinvestment Act," *University of South Carolina Law Review* 60 (2009): 617; WSJ Staff, "Don't Blame CRA

(the Sequel)," *Wall Street Journal*, Real Time Economics, December 4, 2008: "Loans originated by lenders regulated under CRA in general were 'significantly less likely to be in foreclosure' than those originated by independent mortgage companies that weren't covered by CRA"; "Fed's Krozner: Don't Blame the CRA," *Wall Street Journal*, Real Time Economics, December 3, 2008; Remington Shepard, "Still Wrong: Crowley Revives Myth That Community Reinvestment Act Caused Financial Crisis," Media Matters for America," October 11, 2011.

19. *FCIC Report*, 123, 125–126: "The nonprime mortgage securitization process created a pipeline through which risky mortgages were conveyed and sold throughout the financial system. This pipeline was essential to the origination of the burgeoning numbers of high-risk mortgages. The originate-to-distribute model undermined responsibility and accountability for the long-term viability of mortgages and mortgage-related securities and contributed to the poor quality of mortgage loans"; Primary Dissent, 437: "There is vigorous debate about how big a role these two firms played in securitization relative to 'private label' securitizers. There is also vigorous debate about why these two firms got involved in this problem. We think both questions are less important than the multiple points of contact Fannie Mae and Freddie Mac had with the financial system."

20. *FCIC Report*, xxvi, 323.

21. Ibid., 424, 437, 444.

22. Ibid., 15.

23. Ibid., 418, 424, 447.

24. Ibid., xviii.

25. Ibid., 424: nonbank mortgage lenders identified included New Century and Ameriquest.

26. Ibid., 470.

27. Ibid., 37, 366; Larry Wall, "Too Big to Fail after FDICIA," Federal Reserve Bank of Atlanta, *Economic Review* 95, no. 1 (2010): 1: "The exception may be invoked if failure to do so would 'have serious adverse effects on economic conditions or financial stability' and providing additional FDIC coverage 'would avoid or mitigate such adverse effects.' FDICIA allows the exception only with the agreement of a two-thirds majority of the Board of Directors of the Federal Deposit Insurance Corporation, a two-thirds majority of the Board of Governors of the Federal Reserve System, and the Secretary of the Treasury ('in consultation with the President')."

28. James K. Galbraith, "Who Are These Economists, Anyway?" *Thought & Action*, Fall 2009, pp. 85–97; Mike Mayo, *Exile on Wall Street: One Analyst's Fight to Save the Big Banks from Themselves* (Hoboken, NJ: Wiley, 2012), 2–3.

29. *FCIC Report*, 429.

30. Ibid., 470.

31. Ibid., xvii.

32. Hyman P. Minsky, *Stabilizing an Unstable Economy* (New Haven, CT: Yale University Press, 1986), 230; Hyman P. Minsky, "The Financial Instability Hypothesis," Levy Economics Institute of Bard College, Working Paper No.

74 (May 1992), 6–8; Paul McCulley, "The Shadow Banking System and Hyman Minsky's Economic Journey," *Research Foundation Publications* 2009, no. 5: 267; Charles J. Whalen, "Hyman Minsky's Theory of Capitalist Development," Institute for Industry Studies, Cornell University, Working Paper no. 277, August 1999: "Counter-cyclical fiscal policy . . . and lender-of-last-resort monetary initiatives have been among the most potent stabilizers employed in the past half century"; Stephany Griffith-Jones and José Antonio Ocampo, with Ariane Ortiz, "Building on the Counter-Cyclical Consensus: A Policy Agenda," October 2009, pp. 1, 9: "The pro-cyclical nature of finance calls for regulation that leans against the wind."

33. *PBS NewsHour* forum in Kansas City, MO, July 26, 2009; Simon Johnson, "Tunnel Vision or Worse from Banking Regulators," *New York Times*, Economix, January 20, 2011; Top 50 Holding Companies Summary Page, National Information Center, as of September 1, 2013, available at http://www.ffiec.gov/nicpubweb/nicweb/Top50Form.aspx; Bureau of Economic Analysis, Press Release, "National Income and Product Accounts, Gross Domestic Product, 2nd quarter 2013 (second estimate); Corporate Profits, 2nd quarter 2013 (preliminary estimate)," as of September 1, 2003, available at http://www.bea.gov/newsreleases/national/gdp/gdpnewsrelease.htm.

34. Anat R. Admati, Peter M. DeMarzo, Martin F. Hellwig, and Paul Pfleiderer, "Fallacies, Irrelevant Facts, and Myths in the Discussion of Capital Regulation: Why Bank Equity is *Not* Expensive," Working Paper 86, Rock Center for Corporate Governance at Stanford University (2011), 8; The Editors, "Why Should Taxpayers Give Big Banks $83 Billion a Year?" *Bloomberg*, February 20, 2013: "So what if we told you that, by our calculations, the largest U.S. banks aren't really profitable at all? What if the billions of dollars they allegedly earn for their shareholders were almost entirely a gift from U.S. taxpayers?"

35. Jennifer S. Taub, "It's Not a Bailout—It's a Funeral," *Baseline Scenario*, June 17, 2010: "As Paul Krugman noted, politicians continue to repeat these twisted talking points because they hope that if they slap the "bailout" label on any provision of the bill that gets tough on big banks, we will be fooled into backing down"; Paul Krugman, "Punks and Plutocrats," *New York Times*, op-ed, March 29, 2010: "Frank Luntz, the G.O.P. strategist, circulated a memo on how to oppose financial reform. His key idea was that Republicans should claim that up is down—that reform legislation is a 'big bank bailout bill,' rather than a set of restrictions on the banks."

36. Remarks of Senator Ted Kaufman at "Five Years On, Learning Lehman's Lessons from the Panic of 2008: Are We Better Prepared for the Next Financial Crisis?" Better Markets and George Washington University Law School, Center for Law, Economics & Finance, September 12, 2013; Senator Jeff Merkley and Senator Carl Levin, Policy Essay, "The Dodd-Frank Act Restrictions on Proprietary Trading and Conflicts of Interest: New Tools to Address Evolving Threats," *Harvard Journal on Legislation* 48, no. 2 (2011): 515; Scott Patterson, "Q&A: The Volcker Rule," *Wall Street Journal*, June 13, 2012.

37. Testimony of Jamie Dimon, The Official Transcript of the First Public Hearing of the Financial Crisis Inquiry Commission Hearing, January 13, 2010 ("FCIC January Transcript"), p. 60, available at http://fcic-static.law.stanford.edu

/cdn_media/fcic-testimony/2010-0113-Transcript.pdf; RealtyTrac Staff, "1.8 Million U.S. Properties with Foreclosure Filings in 2012," January 4, 2013: "In January 2013, 10.9 million homeowners nationwide—representing 26 percent of all outstanding homes with a mortgage—were seriously underwater"; RealtyTrac Staff, "Judicial Foreclosure Actions Hit 30-Month High in April, Overall U.S. Foreclosure Activity Drops to 6-Year Low," May 7, 2013: "11.3 million mortgages nationwide were seriously underwater"; Kathleen M. Howley, "Subprime Borrowers with Best Credit Score Denied Help," *Bloomberg*, July 16, 2013: nearly 10 million still underwater; Jeffrey P. Cohen, Cletus C. Coughlin, and David A. Lopez, "The Boom and Bust of U.S. Housing Prices from Various Geographic Perspectives," *Federal Reserve Bank of St. Louis Review* 95 (September/October 2012): 341; Richard Fry and Paul Taylor, "An Uneven Recovery, 2009–2011: A Rise in Wealth for the Wealthy; Declines for the Lower 93%," Pew Research Center Report, April 23, 2013.

38. Nomi Prins, *It Takes a Pillage: An Epic Tale of Power, Deceit, and Untold Trillions* (Hoboken, NJ: Wiley, 2009), 43; *New York Times*, "Adding Up the Government's Total Bailout Tab," *New York Times*, July 24, 2011; David Wessel, "Separating Fact From Fiction on the Fed's Loans," *Wall Street Journal*, October 7, 2011.

39. Steve Eder, "Wall Street Lawyer: Don't Blame Pay," *Wall Street Journal*, February 5, 2011.

40. FCIC January Transcript, pp. 20, 78.

Epilogue

1. Press Pass, "JPMorgan Chase CEO Jamie Dimon," NBC News *Meet the Press* with David Gregory, May 13, 2012.

2. C-SPAN Archives of Senate Banking Committee Hearing, June 13, 2012; JP Morgan Chase & Co., Form 10Q for the quarterly period ended March 31, 2012, 47, 87: note that of this $180 billion in equity capital, only $120 billion was "tangible common equity," meaning some of it included items like $48 billion "good will."

3. The prohibition on proprietary trading by bank holding companies, savings and loan holding companies, FDIC-insured depository institutions, and other banking entities went into effect July 21, 2012; Erik Schatzker, Christine Harper, and Mary Childs, "JP Morgan Shifts CIO to Prop Trading," *Bloomberg*, April 13, 2012; U.S. Senate Permanent Subcommittee on Investigations Committee on Homeland Security and Governmental Affairs, Majority and Minority Staff Report, "JPMorgan Chase Whale Trades: A Case History of Derivatives Risk and Abuses," March 15, 2013 (the "Whale Report"), 3: "[I]n early 2012, the bank's Chief Investment Office (CIO), which is charged with managing $350 billion in excess deposits, placed a massive bet on a complex set of synthetic credit derivatives that, in 2012, lost at least $6.2 billion. . . . In 2008, the CIO began calling its credit trading activity the Synthetic Credit Portfolio. Three years later, in 2011, the SCP's net notional size jumped from $4 billion to $51 billion."

4. Nelson D. Schwartz and Jessica Silver-Greenberg, "JPMorgan Chase Executive Resigns in Trading Debacle," *New York Times*, May 13, 2012: With Dimon at the helm, the CIO "was retooled to make larger bets with the bank's money, a former employee said. Bank executives said the chief investment office expanded after JPMorgan Chase's 2008 acquisition of Washington Mutual, which added riskier securities to the company's portfolio. The idea behind the strategy was to offset that risk"; Dawn Kopecki, "JPMorgan's Drew Forfeits 2 Years' Pay as Managers Ousted," *Bloomberg.com*, July 13, 2012; David Benoit, "Whale of a Call," *Wall Street Journal*, May 10, 2012; Maureen Farrell, "JPMorgan's Trading Loss: $5.8 Billion," *CNNMoney*, July 13, 2012; Jonathan Weil, "Regulators Snooze while JPMorgan Lights the Fuse," Editorial, *Investors Business Daily*, May 16, 2012.

5. Nelson D. Schwartz and Jessica Silver-Greenberg, "Loss Stains JPMorgan's Chief, One of Banking's Top Risk Managers," *New York Times*, May 11, 2012; part II in this book.

6. Michael Hudson, "Ex-WaMu Worker Claims He Was Shunned for Refusing to Push Toxic Loans on Borrowers: The Mortgage Salesman Who Wouldn't Sell," *PublicIntegrity.org*, December 22, 2011: "Saffer says he thought Option ARMs were dangerous for most customers. That's because once negative amortization pushed loan balances too high, the loans would automatically readjust and monthly payments would soar"; Dawn Kopecki, "Dimon Beset by Bad Loans as JP Morgan Pushes Overseas," *Bloomberg*, November 2, 2010.

7. Tom Braithwaite and Kara Scannell, "JP Morgan's Legal Burden Sends Shivers through the industry," *Financial Times*, October 13, 2013.

8. Federal Housing Finance Agency (FHFA) v. JPMorgan Chase & Co., complaint, September 2011, available at http://www.fhfa.gov/webfiles/22597/FHFA%20v%20JP%20Morgan.pdf; Federal Housing Finance Agency, News Release, "FHFA Sues 17 Firms to Recover Losses to Fannie Mae and Freddie Mac," September 2, 2011, available at http://www.fhfa.gov/webfiles/22599/PLSLitigation_final_090211.pdf: included on the list of defendants were: "1. Ally Financial Inc. f/k/a GMAC, LLC, 2. Bank of America Corporation, 3. Barclays Bank PLC, 4. Citigroup, Inc., 5. Countrywide Financial Corporation, 6. Credit Suisse Holdings (USA), Inc., 7. Deutsche Bank AG, 8. First Horizon National Corporation, 9. General Electric Company, 10. Goldman Sachs & Co., 11. HSBC North America Holdings, Inc., 12. JPMorgan Chase & Co., 13. Merrill Lynch & Co. / First Franklin Financial Corp., 14. Morgan Stanley, 15. Nomura Holding America Inc., 16. The Royal Bank of Scotland Group PLC, and 17. Société Générale."

9. Ibid.; U.S. Senate Permanent Subcommittee on Investigations, Committee on Homeland Security and Government Affairs, Majority and Minority Staff Report: *Wall Street and the Financial Crisis: Anatomy of a Financial Collapse*, April 13, 2011, 125–130, 135–136.

10. Harriet Nobelman's obituary, available at http://www.legacy.com/obituaries/dallasmorningnews/obituary.aspx?n=Harriet-Nobelman&pid=151976706; author interview with Marci Nobelman, Far North Dallas, September 11, 2011.

11. "Disgraced Texas I-30 Condo Developer Dies," Associated Press, June 1, 2012; Joe Simnacher, "James L. Toler, Former Garland Mayor Was a Central Figure in S&L Scandal," *Dallas Morning News*, March 1, 2012; Jeff Mosier, "Convicted I-30 Condo Fraudster D. L. 'Danny' Faulkner Dies," *Dallas Morning News*, May 31, 2012.

12. FDIC Press Release, "Home Bank, Lafayette, Louisiana, Assumes All of the Deposits of Statewide Bank, Covington, Louisiana," March 12, 2010; Greg LaRose, "FDIC Closes Statewide Bank in Covington, Home Bank to Acquire Assets," *New Orleans City Business*, March 12, 2010: "Originally chartered in 1926 as Algiers Homestead, it was renamed Statewide Bank in 2003 when board member Robin Arkley II, a Eureka, Calif., lawyer and investor, purchased the institution"; Thadeus Greenson, "Bank of America Sues Arkley for $50 Million," *Humboldt Herald*, April 26, 2010; Thadeus Greenson, "Bank of America Sues Rob Arkley for $50 million; Eureka Businessman Reportedly Caught Up in Mortgage Crisis," *Times-Standard*, May 2, 2010; "Land Barons at It Again," *Northcoast Environmental Law Center* 35, no. 6 (July 1, 2005); Greg LaRose, "FDIC Inspector General to Probe Statewide Failure," *New Orleans City Business*, March 23, 2010; "So Who Is Rob Arkley?" *Arkley Watch*, March 15, 2006.

13. Diana Marcum, "Stockton Bankruptcy Will Make History; Residents Reeling," *Los Angeles Times*, June 27, 2012; Jim Christie, "Stockton California Files for Bankruptcy," *Reuters*, June 28, 2012; Ryan Wood, "City of Stockton Bankruptcy: Opposition to the Chapter 9 Bankruptcy Filing," *Bay Area Bankruptcy Buzz*, August 30, 2012; Ron French, "Sense of Surrender Permeates Bankrupt Stockton, California; Is That What's in Store for Detroit?" *Bridge Magazine*, July 19, 2013.

14. In re City of Stockton, California, Opinion Regarding Chapter 9 Order for Relief, June 12, 2013.

15. Hudson, "Ex-WaMu Worker" Louise Story, "Ex-Bank Executives Settle F.D.I.C. Lawsuit," *New York Times*, December 13, 2011; "FDIC Announces Settlement with Washington Mutual Directors and Officers: The Settlement Totals $64.7 Million from Cash, Insurance, and the Turn Over of Proceeds from Bankruptcy Claims," press release, December 15, 2011; Gretchen Morgenson, "Slapped Wrists at WaMu," *New York Times*, December 17, 2011.

16. Jonathan Stempel, " Ex-Goldman VP Tourre Seeks to Toss Fraud Verdict in SEC case," *Reuters*, October 1, 2013; Bob Van Voris, "Tourre Juror Says Panel Found Goldman Banker Shady," *Bloomberg*, August 3, 2013.

17. Statement of Manhattan U.S. Attorney Preet Bharara on the Countrywide, Bank of America and Rebecca Mairone Verdict, press release, October 23, 2013; Landon Thomas Jr., "Jury Finds Bank of America Liable in Mortgage Case," *New York Times*, Dealbook, October 23, 2013; Patricia Hurtado, "BofA's Countrywide Found Liable for Defrauding Fannie Mae," *Bloomberg*, October 24, 2011.

18. Former FDIC Chair to Lead Systemic Risk Council, Monitor Financial Regulation, press release, June 6, 2012.

19. Louise Story and Gretchen Morgenson, "Financial Finger-Pointing Turns to Regulators," *New York Times*, November 22, 2011; Binyamin Appel-

baum and Ellen Nakashima, "Regulator Let IndyMac Fail, Falsify Report," *Washington Post*, December 23, 2008; Edmund L. Andrews, "Irregularity Uncovered at IndyMac," *New York Times*, December 22, 2008: "Two months before IndyMac Bancorp collapsed in July, at a cost of $8.9 billion to taxpayers, a top federal banking regulator allowed the bank to backdate a capital infusion and gloss over its deepening problems, the Treasury Department's independent investigator said Monday."

20. Liaquat Ahamed, "Timothy Geithner on Populism, Paul Ryan, and His Legacy," *New Republic*, January 24, 2013; Henry Sender, "Geithner Joins Top Table of Public Speakers with Lucrative Appearances," *Financial Times*, July 7, 2013.

21. U.S. Senate Committee on Banking, Housing, and Urban Affairs Hearing, Financial Stability Oversight Council Annual Report to Congress, May 21, 2013; video available at http://www.c-spanvideo.org/clip/4452583; Simon Johnson, "Can Jack Lew Save Financial Reform?" *Bloomberg*, July 23, 2013; Remarks of Secretary Lew at the 2013 Delivering Alpha Conference hosted by CNBC and Institutional Investor, July 17, 2013, available at http://www.treasury.gov/press-center/press-releases/Pages/jl2016.aspx.

22. Interview with Jon Stewart on *The Daily Show*, October 21, 2013; Interview with Renee Montagne on NPR's *Morning Edition*, October 18, 2013.

23. Zachary A. Goldfarb, "Former Bear Stearns Executives Acquitted of Lying to Investors," *Washington Post*, November 11, 2009; John Bougearel, "Bear Stearns Tannin and Cioffi Found Not Guilty of Misleading Investors," *StockAnalyst.com*, November 10, 2009: "The defense witnesses called Glenn Hubbard from Columbia University of Business. In Tannin and Cioffi's defense, he told jurors that the funds failed because lenders stopped extending credit."

24. SEC v. Reserve Management Company, Inc., RESRV Partners, Inc., Bruce Bent Sr., and Bruce Bent II (Defendants) and the Reserve Primary Fund (Relief Defendant), Complaint, May 5, 2009; Grant McCool, "Fund Pioneer Bent, Testifying at Trial, Tries to Shift Blame," *Reuters*, October 12, 2012; Kirsten Grind and Julie Steinberg, "Reserve Primary's Managers Cleared in SEC Fraud Case," *Wall Street Journal*, November 12, 2012; Nathaniel Popper and Jessica Silver-Greenberg, "Money-Market Pioneer and Son Cleared of Fraud," *New York Times*, November 12, 2012.

25. Letter from Edward J. DeMarco, acting director, Federal Housing Finance Agency, to Senators Tim Johnson and Richard C. Shelby, July 31, 2012; Paul Krugman, "More DeMarco," *New York Times*, August 1, 2012; Paul Krugman, "Debt, Depression, DeMarco," *New York Times*, August 2, 2012; Robin Harding, "Regulator Blocks U.S. Mortgage Relief Plan," *Financial Times*, July 31, 2012; Kathleen Pender, "Good News for Principal Reduction Backers," SFGate, May 1, 2013; Jim Morrill, "Confirmation Delay Leaves Mel Watt—and His Potential Successors—in Limbo," *Charlotte Observer*, August 7, 2013; George Zornick, "Huge Victory on Filibuster Will Be Tested Soon," *Nation*, July 16, 2013.

26. Special Inspector General for the Troubled Asset Relief Program, "Rising Redefaults of HAMP Mortgage Modifications Hurt Homeowners, Communities, and Taxpayers," July 24, 2013, pp. 1, 4, 23: "Principal reduction is

not mandatory. . . . 87% did not see their unpaid mortgage balance decrease or saw it increase; between 26% and 35% of these homeowners redefaulted"; Diana Olick, "The Government's Mortgage Fix Is Failing," *CNBC*, April 25, 2013: of the 862,000 homeowners with permanent modifications, only about 83,000 had any principal reduced.

27. Les Christie, "Richmond, Calif., Inches Closer to Eminent Domain Plan," *CNNMoney*, September 20, 2013; Nick Timiraos, "Investor Group Calls Richmond, Calif., Eminent Domain Plan Unconstitutional," *Wall Street Journal*, August 7, 2013; Les Christie, "California City's Drastic Foreclosure Remedy: Seizure," July 30, 2013; Robert Rogers, "Judge: Wall Street Suit against Richmond's Eminent Domain Plan Is Premature," *Contra Costa Times*, September 12, 2013.

28. Peter Goonan, "Springfield Set to Require $10,000 Bonds and Registration of Vacant and Roreclosed Properties," *MassLive.com*, October 21, 2013; HousingWire Staff, "Illinois City Aims to Keep Vacant Property Ordinance Alive," *HousingWire*, September 18, 2013.

29. Louise Armistead, "Banks 'Ports in the Storm' during Crisis Says JP Morgan's Dimon," *Telegraph*, January 23, 2013; Julia LaRoche, "We Did the U.S. Government a Favor by Buying Bear Stearns," *Business Insider*, October 10, 2012; Peter Eavis, "Despite Cries of Unfair Treatment, JPMorgan Is No Victim," *New York Times*, News Analysis, September 30, 2013.

30. Dan Fitzpatrick, "Dimon Takes a 'Whale' of a Pay Cut," *Wall Street Journal*, January 16, 2013; Joe Adler and Rachel Witkowski, "Are Regulatory Orders against JPM Just a 'Slap on the Wrist'?" *American Banker*, January 14, 2013.

31. Jessica Silver-Greenberg and Ben Protess, "JP Morgan Chase Faces Full Court Press of Federal Investigations," *New York Times*, March 26, 2013; Josh Rosner, "JP Morgan Chase: Out of Control," *Big Picture*, March 12, 2013; U.S. Attorney's Office, Southern District of New York, "United States v. Bernard L. Madoff and Related Cases," available at http://www.justice.gov/usao/nys/vw_cases/madoff.html.

32. Jamie Dimon, "Letter to Shareholders," April 11, 2013, pp. 10, 12.

33. The Whale Report, pp. 2, 190.

34. Ibid., pp. 224–225: "According to the OCC, when it requested resumption of the daily Investment Bank P&L reports, Douglas Braunstein, JPMorgan Chase's Chief Financial Officer, agreed to the request but had apparently not informed Mr. Dimon. At a meeting shortly thereafter in which both Mr. Braunstein and Mr. Dimon were present, according to the OCC, when Mr. Braunstein stated that he had ordered resumption of the reports, Mr. Dimon reportedly raised his voice in anger at Mr. Braunstein. The OCC said that Mr. Dimon then disclosed that he was the one who had ordered a halt to the reports and expressed the opinion that the OCC did not need the daily P&L figures for the Investment Bank"; Testimony of Ina Drew, at Senate Permanent Subcommittee on Investigations, Committee on Homeland Security and Government Affairs, Hearing, "JPMorgan Chase Whale Trades: A Case History of Derivatives Risks and Abuse," March 15, 2013, video available at http://www.hsgac.senate.gov/subcommittees/investigations/hearings/chase-whale-trades

-a-case-history-of-derivatives-risks-and-abuses; Dawn Kopecki, Clea Benson, and Hugh Son, "JPMorgan Report Piles Pressure on Dimon in Too-Big Debate," *Bloomberg*, March 15, 2013; Gretchen Morgenson, "JP Morgan's Follies for All to See," *New York Times*, March 15, 2013.

35. Testimony of Scott Waterhouse, Whale Hearing, March 15, 2013; Jennifer Taub, "Thirteen Ways of Looking at a Whale," *Pareto Commons*, March 16, 2013.

36. Karl Plume and Gunna Dickson, "Dimon Might Leave JPMorgan if Stripped of Chairmanship—WSJ," *Reuters*, May 11, 2013; JPMorgan Chase & Company, 8-K, May 23, 2013, Item 5.07: 84.21 percent of outstanding shares were present, proposal 6 regarding the requirement to separate the Chairman and CEO received 32.23 percent support.

37. Paul Toscano, "Dimon: I Wouldn't Have Left if I Lost the Leadership Vote," *CNBC.com* video: "They do a better job in the mortgage business than us . . . but we had the old Bear Stearns, WaMu"; Fitzpatrick, "Dimon Takes."

38. Eleazar David Melendez, "Julien Grout, Former JPMorgan Junior Trader, Challenged the London Whale," *Huffington Post*, March 15, 2013; author's notes taken while watching the press conference live on August 14, 2013.

39. Dan Fitzpatrick and Saabira Chaudhuri, "Buffer for Legal Tab Batters J.P. Morgan," *Wall Street Journal*, October 11, 2011; Dawn Kopecki, "JPMorgan Pays $920 Million to Settle London Whale Probes," *Bloomberg*, September 20, 2013.

40. Neil Irwin, "Everything You Need to Know about JPMorgan's $13 Billion Settlement," *Washington Post, Wonkblog*, October 21, 2013; Nick Summers, "JPMorgan's $13 Billion Settlement: Jamie Dimon Is a Colossus No More," *BloombergBusinessweek*, October 24, 2013.

41. Ben Protess and Jessica Silver-Greenberg, " U.S. Deal With JPMorgan Followed a Crucial Call," *New York Times*, October 20, 2013.

42. Christine Harper, "Breaking Up Banks Hard to Do as Market Forces Fail," *Bloomberg*, June 27, 2012.

43. Federal News Service, Transcripts, Hearing of the Senate Banking Committee, "A Breakdown in Risk Management: What Went Wrong at JPMorgan Chase," June 13, 2012.

Acknowledgments

"It should be a narrative," my new editor, William Frucht, calmly asserted. His suggestion silenced me. I had been talking on and on, without pause, nervously jabbing a fork into my Caesar salad, trying to explain my approach to a book on the financial crisis. By the time of that lunch meeting on June 16, 2011, I had already written several academic papers and blog entries about the legal acts and omissions that enabled the 2008 meltdown. I planned to structure the book similarly—a chapter on excessive bank leverage, one on predatory home loans, another on fragile short-term funding, and so on. But he looked skeptical, so I kept talking until he interrupted—"It should be a narrative"—and I knew he was right.

Driving home to Northampton, Massachusetts, from New Haven, Connecticut, I tried to recall what inspired me to take on the topic of the financial crisis in the first place. My thoughts returned to September 2008, during the panic that ensued with the failure of Lehman Brothers. At the time, I wrote an op-ed for my local newspaper about the Bush administration's proposal to use $700 billion to buy up toxic mortgage-linked securities from the sinking banks. In that piece, I fretted that the result would be a disparity between bailed-out banks and foreclosed-upon families. I supported the government intervention but also recommended that homeowners be permitted to use the bankruptcy courts to modify their mortgages—to reduce interest rates and lower the outstanding balances on underwater loans. I knew that the legal obstacle was a 1993 Supreme Court decision called *Nobelman v. American Savings Bank* that interpreted the Bankruptcy Code to forbid courts from helping homeowners in this way. So Congress would need to amend the law. I remembered first learning about the *Nobelman* case in 1992 (just before the Supreme Court agreed to hear it) as a student at Harvard Law School in Professor Elizabeth Warren's course on bankruptcy.

After my op-ed was published in 2008, I e-mailed a copy to a broad list, including my former professor. In her reply e-mail, Warren was encouraging: "Terrific piece—and exactly right on every point. Please keep writing. There is so much that needs changing. Unless many voices demand it, we're doomed to repeat this terrible sequence of events." As I drove home—now nearly three years later—I began wondering about Leonard and Harriet Nobelman, the homeowners who brought their case to the Supreme Court. I wanted to know where they were now. Perhaps they could be part of the narrative.

When I arrived home, I opened my laptop and began searching the Web for their whereabouts. I discovered that Leonard, who suffered from severe diabetes, had died in early 1994. Then I searched for his wife, Harriet. According to the *Dallas Morning News*, Harriet had passed away on June 12, 2011. This was four days earlier. I kept reading—her funeral service was scheduled for June 16, 2011, at 11:00 a.m. central time. In other words, it had taken place while my editor and I were meeting that day. This sad and uncanny coincidence compelled me to dig into their case, to contact the attorneys involved, to obtain their bankruptcy file from the National Archives, and to meet with their daughter. This inquiry and similar ones, driven by an abiding sense of injustice regarding the more than five million families who have lost their homes to foreclosure, pushed me to research and write this book.

I have Executive Editor William Frucht to thank for inspiring this journey and, along the way, for his honest feedback, skillful line edits, and thoughtful consultations. This book would not have been possible without the dedication of his colleagues at Yale University

Press, including my former editor, Michael O'Malley, who initially accepted this book project, Assistant Editor Jaya Chatterjee, and Assistant Managing Editor Mary Pasti, as well as the hard work of Michael Haggett and Debbie Masi at Westchester Publishing Services and their team, including Fran Lyon.

Well before *Other People's Houses* was conceived, I had the great fortune to meet Jane D'Arista of the Political Economy Research Institute (PERI) and Gerald Epstein of the University of Massachusetts Amherst Economics Department and PERI. Without their guidance and friendship, this project could not have flourished. In September 2009, after reading a paper of mine on the financial crisis, Epstein and D'Arista kindly invited me to the launch of SAFER—a committee of economists and other experts for Stable, Accountable, Fair, and Efficient Financial Reform. It was through this association that I gained exposure to many brilliant academics, authors, activists, and policy makers whose work expanded my own views on political economy and financial market regulation. Through SAFER, I am also thankful to have met and received guidance and generous support from Lance Lindblom, former president and CEO of the Nathan Cummings Foundation.

SAFER also led to an affiliation with Americans for Financial Reform (AFR)—a coalition of more than 250 consumer, civil rights, investor, retiree, community, labor, faith-based, and business groups—which has worked tirelessly in the public interest during the Dodd-Frank legislative process and beyond. It was through AFR that I closely followed the reform legislation and rulemaking process in Washington, including through meetings and conference calls with Senate staffers and staff at various regulatory agencies and through work on policy briefs and comment letters. I am grateful for the collegiality of those at AFR, including Executive Director Lisa Donner, Policy Director Marcus Stanley, former legislative and policy liaison Dana Chasin, and also others who worked with AFR on systemic risk issues, including Mary Bottari (Center for Media and Democracy), Jane D'Arista (PERI), Jerry Epstein (UMass Amherst, PERI), Micah Hauptman (Public Citizen), Dennis Kelleher (Better Markets), Heather McGhee (Demos), Bart Naylor (Public Citizen), Heather Slavkin

(AFL-CIO), Zephyr Teachout (Fordham Law School), and Wallace Turbeville (Demos).

Along the way, I have formulated concepts that are included in *Other People's Houses* and shared them at conferences, colloquiums, and lectures. I would like to thank those who invited me to such forums (in reverse chronological order, including the sponsoring entities): Dennis Kelleher and Art Wilmarth (Better Markets and George Washington University Law School, Center for Law, Economics & Finance); David Donald (Chinese University of Hong Kong, Centre for Financial Regulation and Economic Development); James Hawley (the Harvard Kennedy School); Thomas Palley, Pia Bungarten, and Gustav Horn (AFL-CIO, Friedrich Ebert Stiftung, and Macroeconomic Policy Institute); Andrew Samwick and Charlie Wheelan (Rockefeller Center for Public Policy at Dartmouth College); David Tatman (North American Securities Administrators Association); William Birdthistle and Tamar Frankel (Boston University School of Law); Barbara Black (Corporate Law Center at the University of Cincinnati Law School); Renee Jones (Boston College Law School); Eric Robins (National Association for Business Economics); Mike Konczal (Roosevelt Institute); Zephyr Teachout (Fordham Law School); Angela Harris, Martha McCluskey, and Athena Mutua (University at Buffalo Law School); Gerald Epstein (Political Economy Workshop, UMass Amherst); James Hawley, Shyam Kamath, and Andrew Williams (the Elfenworks Center for Fiduciary Capitalism at St. Mary's College); and Larry Beeferman (The Labor and Worklife Program at Harvard Law School).

I am grateful to the many individuals with whom I spoke (on and off the record) who helped enrich this book—including Bart Dzivi, Julia Gordon, Senator Ted Kaufman, Marci Nobelman, Michael Ricker, Michael Schroeder, and Rosemary Zyne—as well as the numerous authors and other sources identified in the endnotes. I am appreciative of the encouragement and support of colleagues at the Vermont Law School; and former colleagues from the UMass Amherst, Isenberg School of Management, in particular, Ben Branch, Tom O'Brien, Mila Sherman, and Larry Zacharias. I am also deeply indebted to many excellent teachers and mentors, especially from my early years at Brookside, Kingswood, and Cranbrook schools, including Elizabeth Clark, Deborah Rutzen, and John Shilts.

Additionally, I would like to thank those who read various portions or iterations of the manuscript and shared helpful comments, including Ginnie Burnham, Timothy Canova, Christine Cimini, Lawrence Cunningham, Jane D'Arista, Mary Fricker, Gerald Friedman, Jon Friedman, Julia Gordon, Michael Kuch, James Kwak, Bart Naylor, Sean Nolon, Frank Pasquale, Jonah Richmond, Jessica West, Alan White, and Martin Wolfson, as well as those whose input was passed along through the anonymous review process. In addition, I benefited from assistance from our law librarians, including Michele LaRose and Jane Woldow, and help with books at home from Emily Barnes-Taub, and help from those who read and provided useful feedback on earlier financial crisis work, including Lawrence Baxter, J. Robert Brown, Lynne Dallas, Stephen Davis, Mike Konczal, James Kwak, Jon Lukomnik, Nell Minow, Marcy Murninghan, Narissa Nields, Christopher Rogers, Ed Waitzer, and Art Wilmarth. They have all helped make this book clearer and hopefully more enjoyable to read. All errors and oversights are, of course, my own.

I am also thankful for support and inspiration from my friends and family over the years, including Karen Barnes, Hosie Baskin, Lisa Baskin, Karima Bennoune, Jennie Breitmeyer, Sarah Buttenwieser, Deborah Cahillane, Susan Cain, Michael Cohen, Chia Collins, Carolyn Edgar, Jen Fulcher, Rob Green, Jill Greenberg, Amy Gutman, Cheryl Hanna, Richard Hardie, Lisa Melendy, Sabine Merz, Barbara Parlin, Jody Riseman, Liv Rockefeller, Liesl Schillinger, Ken Shure, Felicia Sloin, Mikal Weiss, and Mark Wineburg; my parents, Shelley Goodman Taub and Steve Taub; my brothers and my sisters-in-law, Adam Taub and Tracy Kruzic Taub, and Drew and Diana Taub; and my daughters, Emily Barnes-Taub and Arella Taub. I am especially grateful for the perpetual encouragement, creative guidance, and editorial comments provided by my husband, Michael Kuch, to whom this book is dedicated.

INDEX